# THE ULTIMATE
# SPORTS
## FACT AND QUIZ BOOK

# THE ULTIMATE SPORTS
## FACT AND QUIZ BOOK

### RUSSELL DEMPSEY

Cartoons by
**PETER COUPE**

STOPWATCH

Published by
Stopwatch Publishing Limited
1-7 Shand Street
London SE1 2ES

For Bookmart Limited
Desford Road
Enderby
Leicester LE9 5AD

This edition published 1998

ISBN 1 - 900032 - 28 - 7

Printed in Finland

# FOREWORD

The Ultimate Sports Fact and Quiz Book was conceived as a celebration of all sport, as well as being a wide-ranging test of sporting knowledge. The book has something for everyone, from the pub quizzer to the serious fan, and for all sports lovers from ages 8 to 80! Dip into the book at any point and you will find facts, brain-teasers, amusing quotes, even strange nicknames, to do with all your favourite sports.

Whether you want to impress your friends and family with your sudden and intimate knowledge of the Olympic Games, or even test how much you really do know about football, the Ultimate Sports Fact and Quiz Book has all the answers – and most of the questions!

Enjoy your ringside seat to the wonderful world of sport.

Russell Dempsey

# CONTENTS

## Quiz  9
## Facts  261

# THE ULTIMATE SPORTS QUIZ BOOK

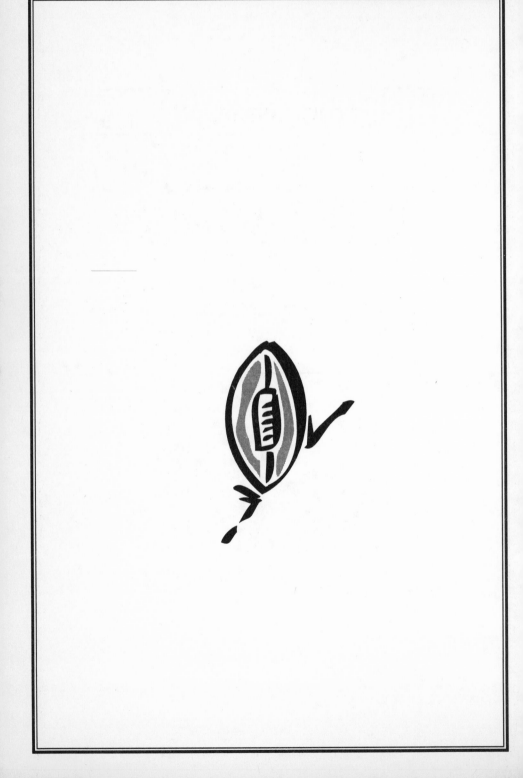

# QUIZ CONTENTS

FOOTBALL CRAZY!                     13

THE WORLD CUP 1930-1998             21

TRUE OR FALSE?                      47

MOTOR SPORTS                        55

HORSE RACING                        69

GOLF                               81

FIRST NAMES, NICKNAMES             89

TENNIS                            101

SNOOKER                           113

BRITISH FOOTBALL                  119

FOOTBALL AROUND THE WORLD         137

CRICKET                           145

WHO SAID THAT?                    163

BOXING                            173

OLYMPIC GAMES                     185

RUGBY UNION AND LEAGUE            219

ATHLETICS                         229

MIXED BAG                         237

# THE ULTIMATE SPORTS FACT AND QUIZ BOOK

# FOOTBALL CRAZY!

# Quiz 01 FOOTBALL CRAZY!

1. Who managed Arsenal before Arsene Wenger?

2. **How many times have Arsenal done the League-Cup double?**

3. How many times have Manchester United also done the double?

4. **Which other English club achieved a major trophy-winning double in 1998?**

5. What was that double?

6. **Who won the Scottish Premier League in 1998?**

7. Who won the Scottish Cup in the same year?

8. **Who were the Scottish FA Cup sponsors from 1989 to 1998?**

9. Who has scored the most goals in the English Premiership since it began?

10. **Who is the oldest player to have appeared in the English Premiership?**

11. Which club was fined by the FA in 1994 because of 'financial irregularities'?

12. **How many Premiership points were finally deducted from the club?**

13. Who was fined £1,000 for giving a 'Hitler salute' to the crowd at Tottenham in 1996?

14. **Who scored 30 goals for England in his 33 appearances?**

15. Who played for Hungary 84 times and for Spain four times?

ANSWERS 1. Bruce Rioch  2. **Twice**  3. Twice  4. **Chelsea**  5. Coca-Cola Cup and European Cup-Winners Cup  6. **Celtic**  7. Hearts  8. **Tennents**  9. Alan Shearer  10. **John Burridge**  11. Tottenham Hotspur  12. **Six**  13. Mark Bosnich (Aston Villa)  14. **Nat Lofthouse**  15. Ferenc Puskas

# *Quiz* 02 FOOTBALL CRAZY!

1. Who won the 1997 FA Cup?

2. **Which team did they beat?**

3. Who won the 1997 Coca-Cola Cup?

4. **Which team lost in this final?**

5. Who finished second in the English First Division in 1998?

6. **Who forced Newcastle United to a replay in the fourth round of the 1998 FA Cup?**

7. Which Scottish club plays at Pittodrie Stadium?

8. **Who was the first professional footballer to receive a knighthood?**

9. Who has made the most first-class appearances in the history of British football?

10. **Who was the first English manager to receive a knighthood?**

11. Who holds the record for the fastest goal in an FA Cup Final at Wembley?

12. **What was the timing of that goal?**

13. Who previously held the record?

14. **What was the timing of that goal?**

15. Who is the first player this century to win four FA Cup winners medals?

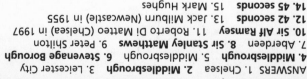

ANSWERS 1. Chelsea **2. Middlesbrough** 3. Leicester City
**4. Middlesbrough** 5. Middlesbrough **6. Stevenage Borough**
7. Aberdeen **8. Sir Stanley Matthews** 9. Peter Shilton
**10. Sir Alf Ramsey** 11. Roberto Di Matteo (Chelsea) in 1997
**12. 42 seconds** 13. Jack Milburn (Newcastle) in 1955
**14. 45 seconds** 15. Mark Hughes

# *Quiz* 03 FOOTBALL CRAZY!

1. What was the name of the trophy that Brazil won outright in 1970?

2. **Which former League referee became a government minister?**

3. What was his title when he died in 1998?

4. **Who won the Tournoi de France in 1997?**

5. Who did England beat in that tournament?

6. **Who beat England in their final match of that tournament?**

7. Who scored the only goal in that match?

8. **Name the clever dog who found a stolen World Cup in a garden.**

9. Who was the Player of the Year in the English Press vote for the 1997-98 season?

10. **Who got the vote from the Professional Footballers' Association?**

11. Who beat Fulham in the Division Two promotion play-off semi-finals?

12. **Who beat Bolton Wanderers in their last Premiership match of the 1997-98 season, resulting in their relegation?**

13. Who was unable to captain Scotland in the 1998 World Cup because of injury?

14. **Which club plays at Griffin Park?**

15. Whose home is Spotland?

# *Quiz* 04 FOOTBALL CRAZY!

1. Who became the chief executive of the English Premier League in 1997?

2. **Whom did he replace in that role?**

3. With which club did John Lukic play his first League game?

4. **Whose Arsenal club scoring record did Ian Wright beat?**

5. Which England defender was said to 'Bite Yer Legs'?

6. **Which League team did he play for?**

7. What is Ronaldo's nationality?

8. **Which club did Kenny Dalglish manage after leaving Liverpool?**

9. Was he their manager when they won the Premiership title?

10. **Who is the multi-millionaire owner of Blackburn Rovers?**

11. Who knocked England out of the European Championship in 1996?

12. **In which round did that happen?**

13. Where was that match played?

14. **Which club holds the record for the most FA Cup wins?**

15. In 1997, which club reached the FA Cup Final and was relegated in the same season?

# THE ULTIMATE SPORTS FACT AND QUIZ BOOK

# *Quiz* 05 FOOTBALL CRAZY!

1. How many times did Manchester United win the Championship in the first six Premiership years?

2. **Which other clubs were champions during the first six years of the Premiership?**

3. Who said that there were only two teams on Merseyside – Liverpool and Liverpool Reserves?

4. **Who scored 60 goals for Everton in only 39 League matches in the 1927-28 season?**

5. Were Everton champions that season?

6. **Who was Joe Mercer's coach when he managed Manchester City?**

7. Which club did Mercer captain when they won the League's First Division title?

8. **Which Spanish club did Terry Venables manage?**

9. Who won the European Champions Cup five years running?

10. **Who won it three times between 1989 and 1994?**

11. How many times have Liverpool won the UEFA Cup?

12. **In which Italian city does Juventus play?**

13. The Wee Blue Devils were a famous forward line of which country?

14. **In which country do Boca Juniors play?**

15. Who is Edson Arantes do Nascimento?

# *Quiz* 06  FOOTBALL CRAZY!

1. Who was manager of Chelsea when they won the Coca-Cola Cup in 1998?

2. **Who was Chelsea's previous manager?**

3. When did Derby County move to their new ground?

4. **What was the name of their old ground?**

5. Who tops the list of England international goalscorers with 49?

6. **Who comes second on that list with 48?**

7. Who was the first player to score 200 goals in the Scottish Premier League?

8. **Who holds the record as Scotland's youngest cap?**

9. Who holds the same record for Northern Ireland?

10. **What are the first-choice colours of Plymouth Argyle shirts?**

11. What is the club's nickname?

12. **What Test cricketer made his League soccer debut for Scunthorpe?**

13. Which country does Bruce Grobbelaar play for?

14. **Which whom does Dwight Yorke play international football?**

15. In how many FA Cup Finals have Manchester United appeared?

ANSWERS 1. Gianluca Vialli 2. **Ruud Gullit** 3. 1997 4. **Baseball Ground** 5. Bobby Charlton 6. **Gary Lineker** 7. Ally McCoist 8. **Denis Law** 9. Norman Whiteside 10. **Green and white** 11. The Pilgrims 12. **Ian Botham** 13. Zimbabwe 14. **Trinidad & Tobago** 15. Fourteen

# Quiz 07 FOOTBALL CRAZY!

1. Who hosted the 1966 World Cup?

2. **Who was the commentator who delivered the immortal words at a World Cup final: "They think it's all over..."?**

3. What was the scoreline in that match?

4. **What was Geoff Hurst's claim to fame in that match?**

5. With whom did Bobby Charlton play his last League match?

6. **Which country won the 1996 European Championship?**

7. Which club won the 1998 European Champions Cup?

8. **Who were the beaten finalists in that match?**

9. Who was manager of Leicester City when they won the Coca-Cola Cup in 1997?

10. **Who play at Saltergate?**

11. Which League club did Jimmy Hill play for at inside-forward?

12. **Which of his teammates became the first £100-a-week player in Britain?**

13. Who finished runners-up to Brazil in the 1994 World Cup?

14. **Who was Celtic's manager when they won nine consecutive Scottish League Championships between 1966 and 1974?**

15. How many FA Cup winners' medals did George Best win?

ANSWERS 1. England 2. Kenneth Wolstenholme 3. England 4, West Germany 2 4. He scored a hat-trick 5. Preston 6. Germany 7. Real Madrid 8. Juventus 9. Martin O'Neill 10. Chesterfield 11. Fulham 12. Johnny Haynes 13. Italy 14. Jock Stein 15. None

# THE WORLD CUP
## 1930–1998

# *Quiz 01*   THE WORLD CUP 1930-1998

1. Which was the last host nation before France to win the World Cup?

2. **What was the half-time score in the 1998 Final in Paris?**

3. Who was the scorer?

4. **Who deputised as captain of France for the suspended Laurent Blanc in the Final?**

5. Who was sent off after two yellow cards in the Final?

6. **Name the French coach who announced his retirement after leading his team to their Paris triumph.**

7. Who scored France's winning goal?

8. **How many Carling Premiership club players were in the triumphant French side?**

9. Can you name three of them?

10. **Which English national league had the most players taking part in the 1998 finals matches?**

11. Which Carling Premiership club had most players in the 1998 finals?

12. **What was the score in the third-place play-off?**

13. Who was the leading scorer in the 1998 finals and what was his total?

14. **How many red cards were shown in the tournament?**

15. How many different nations have won the World Cup?

# *Quiz* 02    THE WORLD CUP<br>1930-1998

1. How many matches did England play in the 1998 World Cup, including the qualifying rounds?

2. **How many times were they beaten?**

3. Who beat them?

4. **How many points did Scotland win in their group finals matches?**

5. Which two teams beat them?

6. **Who scored Scotland's two goals in the finals?**

7. Only two teams had 100% records in the group matches. Can you remember them?

8. **Only two teams failed to win a point in their three group games. Who were they?**

9. How many of England's chosen 22 finals players had previous World Cup finals experience?

10. **Who scored England's single goal against Romania?**

11. Who was the goalkeeper called up at short notice by Scotland when Andy Goram made his shock withdrawal?

12. **Who was the oldest player in the 1998 finals?**

13. Who was the only hat-trick scorer in the eight groups matches?

14. **Five teams each scored just a single goal in their three group games. Name three of them.**

15. Who was the first player to be shown the red card in the finals?

ANSWERS 1. Twelve **2. Three** 3. Italy, Romania, Argentina **4. One** 5. Brazil and Morocco **6. Collins (pen) and Burley** 7. France and Argentina **8. USA and Japan** 9. None **10. Michael Owen** 11. Jonathan Gould (Celtic) **12. Jim Leighton (Scotland)** 13. Gabriel Batistuta **14. Bulgaria, USA, Colombia, Tunisia, Japan** 15. Anatoli Nankov (Bulgaria)

# *Quiz* 03     THE WORLD CUP
### 1930-1998

1. Who was presented with 264 bottles of wine for scoring Italy's opening goal of the finals?

2. **That match resulted in a 2-2 draw. Who did Italy play?**

3. Who scored the penalty for Italy to equalise five minutes from the end?

4. **Which was the only team not to concede a goal in their three group matches?**

5. They then conceded two goals in each of their remaining two matches in the tournament. England was one of the opponents, who was the other?

6. **Who scored England's two goals in that match?**

7. The Argentinians went out 2-1 in the quarter-finals to Holland. Who scored the goal that put them out in the last minute of normal time?

8. **Who recorded the highest win in the group matches?**

9. Who did they beat?

10. **South Korea and Jamaica each suffered 5-0 defeats in the group games. Who were their conquerors?**

11. Why was Japan striker Wagner Lopes so desperate to play against Argentina in their group tie?

12. **Who scored the first goal of the 1998 finals?**

13. Who scored Brazil's second goal of the finals?

14. **Who was shown the first yellow card of the tournament?**

15. Who was the Dutchman who was sent off in Holland's match with Belgium?

ANSWERS **1.** Christian Vieri **2. Chile 3.** Roberto Baggio
**4. Argentina 5.** England and Holland **6. Shearer (pen) and Owen**
**7.** Dennis Bergkamp **8. Spain (6-1) 9.** Bulgaria **10. Holland and
Argentina, respectively 11.** He was born in Brazil **12. Cesar Sampaio**
**13.** Tommy Boyd (own goal) **14. Cesar Sampaio 15.** Patrick Kluivert

# *Quiz* 04 — THE WORLD CUP 1930-1998

1. Clashing in midfield in the Romania v Colombia group match were two players with more than 200 caps between them. Who were they?

2. **Who scored for England in their 2-0 opening win over Tunisia?**

3. Youssef al-Thyniyan helped himself to a goal for which team?

4. **For which team did Ivica Vastic score a vital last-minute goal?**

5. For which team did Anton Polster do the same?

6. **Both those goals earned 1-1 draws. Who were the two opponents?**

7. Against which team did Ronaldo score his first 1998 finals goal?

8. **Scotland played ten matches to qualify for the finals and were beaten only once. Who did that?**

9. Which Brazilian player said: "Art for art's sake is bunk. We were lucky the way we won against the Scots, so let's just be thankful"?

10. **Which World Cup goalkeeper takes all his team's penalties and free kicks?**

11. The American coach resigned following defeats in all three group matches. What was his name?

12. **David Beckham was only the second England player ever to be sent off in a World Cup match. Who was the first?**

13. Who scored the three penalty goals for England in their shoot-out with Argentina?

14. **Name the two players who missed Argentina's second penalty and England's second?**

15. When South Africa and Saudi Arabia drew 2-2, how many of those goals were penalties?

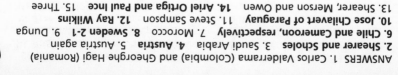

13. Shearer, Merson and Owen  14. Ariel Ortiga and Paul Ince  15. Three
10. Jose Chilavert of Paraguay  11. Steve Sampson  12. Ray Wilkins
6. Chile and Cameroon, respectively  7. Morocco  8. Sweden 2-1  9. Dunga
2. Shearer and Scholes  4. Austria  5. Austria again
ANSWERS 1. Carlos Valderrama (Colombia) and Gheorghe Hagi (Romania)  3. Saudi Arabia

# *Quiz* 05

## THE WORLD CUP 1930-1998

1. An entire team bleached its hair white to celebrate reaching the second round. Name the country.

2. **The same team were then eliminated in that round. By whom?**

3. Who scored the only goal in that match from the penalty spot?

4. **Which match was decided on the golden-goal rule?**

5. Who scored the golden goal in that match?

6. **Who scored Germany's two goals in their 2-1 defeat of Mexico?**

7. What was the colour of England's strip in their match with Argentina?

8. **Who scored the first goal against England for Argentina?**

9. Which member of the Holland squad in France had been sent home from Euro 96 after accusing the coach of favouritism?

10. **The same Dutch player scored the winning goal in the 90th minute against which second-round opponents?**

11. Who scored twice for Brazil in their 3-2 defeat of Denmark?

12. **What was the 'score' in the penalty shoot-out between Italy and France in the quarter-finals?**

13. Who came on as a substitute for England in the sixth minute of extra time against Argentina?

14. **Two other substitutes were introduced by England during the normal second half of that match. Who were they?**

15. Which Argentinian player was involved when David Beckham was shown the red card?

# *Quiz* 06 THE WORLD CUP 1930-1998

1. What was FIFA's decision after Beckham's sending-off?

2. **What nationality is Kim Milton Nielsen, the referee who sent off Beckham?**

3. Which Brazilian won his 111th cap in the 1998 Final?

4. **In the Final who was playing in his 18th World Cup tie?**

5. Which coach at the finals said of Argentina: "They are very good at inciting irritation"?

6. **Who scored the first goal in the 1998 semi-final match between France and Croatia?**

7. Who scored the two goals that put France in the Final for the first time?

8. **Who missed the vital penalty for Italy when the shoot-out score with France stood at 4-3 in the quarter-finals?**

9. Who claimed that he had been struck by Laurent Blanc when the French captain was sent off in the semi-finals?

10. **What was the score when that happened?**

11. Name the Englishman who was one of the linesmen in the 1998 Final.

12. **He was also a linesman in one of the quarter-finals. Which one?**

13. What nationality is Said Belqola, the referee of the Final?

14. **What was the outcome of the penalty shoot-out in the Brazil-Holland semi-final?**

15. Who missed the fourth spot kick for Holland?

ANSWERS **1.** He was banned from England's next two competitive matches and fined £2,000 **2. Danish** **3.** Claudio Taffarel **4. Taffarel** **5.** Guus Hiddink (Holland) **6. Davor Suker** **7.** Lilian Thuram **8. Luigi Di Biagio** **9.** Slaven Bilic (Croatia) **10. France 2 Croatia 1** **11.** Mark Warren **12. Italy v France** **13.** Morocco **14. Brazil won 4-2** **15.** Frank De Boer

# Quiz 07 THE WORLD CUP 1930-1998

1. Where was England's first 1998 World Cup qualifying game played?

2. **Who scored the first goal in that match?**

3. What was the result?

4. **Who did Scotland face in their first qualifying game for 1998?**

5. There were two new caps in England's first qualifying game for 1998. Andy Hinchcliffe was one, who was the other?

6. **How many captains had England had before Alan Shearer?**

7. When was Shearer appointed?

8. **In what year was the first World Cup played?**

9. When did England first compete in the World Cup finals?

10. **Who did England meet in their first match in the 1966 finals?**

11. Where was the 1934 World Cup played?

12. **Austria withdrew from the 1938 World Cup. Why?**

13. Who won the 1950 World Cup – Mexico, Uruguay or Brazil?

14. **Who was England's right-back in the 1950 World Cup team?**

15. Two British teams qualified for the 1954 finals. Who were they?

ANSWERS **1.** Moldova **2. Nick Barmby 3.** England won 3-0 **4. Austria 5.** David Beckham **6. He was the 100th 7.** For the first match with Moldova **8. 1930 9.** 1950 **10. Uruguay 11.** Italy **12. Austria was invaded by Germany 13.** Uruguay **14.** Alf Ramsey **15.** England and Scotland

# Quiz 08

## THE WORLD CUP 1930-1998

1. Which two teams played in the first game of the first World Cup?

2. **What was the score?**

3. How many British teams qualified for the 1958 World Cup?

4. **Northern Ireland got through to the quarter-finals. Name the other British team that did the same.**

5. Who beat Ireland 4-0 in the quarter-finals?

6. **Who did Brazil beat 1-0 in the quarter-finals?**

7. What happened to England in 1958?

8. **Who played in the Final that year?**

9. What was the result?

10. **How many goals did Pele score in that Final?**

11. Where was the 1950 World Cup held?

12. **England's opening match was against Chile. What was the result?**

13. Who scored for England?

14. **England lost 0-1 to the group winners. Who were they?**

15. Who also beat England 1-0 in that group?

ANSWERS 1. France and Mexico  2. **France won 4-1**  3. All four
4. **Wales**  5. France  6. **Wales**  7. Lost 0-1 to Russia in a group play-off
8. **Brazil and Sweden**  9. Brazil won 5-2  10. **Two**  11. Brazil  12. **England won 2-0**  13. Mortensen and Mannion  14. **Spain**  15. USA

# *Quiz* 09    THE WORLD CUP 1930-1998

1. How many nations competed in the very first World Cup finals?

2. **How many nations qualified for the finals in Spain in 1982?**

3. In 1982, did England progress to the quarter-finals?

4. **Who were the two other teams with Spain in the second round?**

5. What was the result of the England v West Germany match?

6. **And the score in the match with Spain?**

7. Who went through to the semi-finals from that group?

8. **Did they reach the Final?**

9. Who beat them 3-1 in the Final?

10. **Where was the 1954 World Cup held?**

11. Where did England finish in Group 4?

12. **Who did they meet in the quarter-finals?**

13. What was the score?

14. **Who won the World Cup in that year?**

15. Who were the beaten finalists?

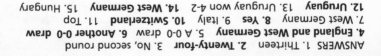

ANSWERS **1.** Thirteen **2. Twenty-four 3.** No, second round **4. England and West Germany 5.** A 0-0 draw **6. Another 0-0 draw 7.** West Germany **8. Yes 9.** Italy **10. Switzerland 11.** Top **12. Uruguay 13.** Uruguay won 4-2 **14. West Germany 15.** Hungary

# *Quiz* 10 — THE WORLD CUP 1930-1998

1. In Mexico in 1970, why did the World Cup Committee agree to play Sunday matches at midday in temperatures of 98°F?

2. **Which three countries were in Group 3 with England in 1970?**

3. England won two of those games. But who beat them?

4. **What was the score?**

5. Who did England meet in the quarter-finals?

6. **What was the result?**

7. Who scored England's goals?

8. **Who knocked out West Germany in the semi-finals?**

9. Who won the Final?

10. **Who is the only man to have scored three goals in a World Cup Final?**

11. How many goals were scored by England in the 1966 World Cup finals?

12. **How many of those were scored by Bobby Charlton?**

13. Where was the 1938 World Cup staged?

14. **How many years elapsed before the next tournament?**

15. Why could all four British countries play in the World Cup for the first time in 1950?

ANSWERS 1. To keep international television happy  2. **Brazil, Romania and Czechoslovakia**  3. Brazil  4. **Brazil 1 England 0**  5. West Germany  6. **West Germany won 3-2**  7. Peters and Mullery  8. **Italy**  9. Brazil  10. **Geoff Hurst**  11. Eleven  12. **Three**  13. France  14. **Twelve years**  15. Because they had rejoined FIFA

# Quiz 11 THE WORLD CUP 1930-1998

1. Which is the only country to have taken part in every World Cup finals stage?

2. **In 1978 hosts Argentina met Peru in a quarter-final match. What was the score?**

3. Peru's goalkeeper that day was Quiroga. Where was he born?

4. **Who won the World Cup in 1978?**

5. What was the score?

6. **What happened in Uruguay when that nation won the first World Cup?**

7. What happened in Argentina after their team lost in the Final to Uruguay?

8. **Which German won the World Cup both as a player and manager?**

9. Who signed the Romanian World Cup star Dan Petrescu for Chelsea?

10. **How many times has Italy been in the World Cup finals?**

11. Two countries have won successive World Cups. Brazil was one, which was the other?

12. **In which successive years did that team win the trophy?**

13. In which successive years did Brazil perform the same feat?

14. **How many countries contested the 1998 World Cup finals?**

15. What was the previous highest number?

ANSWERS 1. Brazil 2. **Argentina 6 Peru 0** 3. Argentina 4. **Argentina** 5. Argentina 3 Holland 1 (after extra time) 6. **A national holiday was declared** 7. The Uruguayan Consulate in Buenos Aires was stoned by an angry mob 8. **Franz Beckenbauer** 9. Glenn Hoddle 10. **Fourteen** 11. Italy 13. 1934 and 1938 12. 1958 and 1962 14. **Thirty-two** 15. Twenty-four

# *Quiz* 12    THE WORLD CUP 1930-1998

1. Canada has only ever qualified once for the World Cup. In what year?

2. **How many first-round matches did they win?**

3. How many goals did they score altogether?

4. **How many were scored against them?**

5. Which other country had a similar experience in 1974?

6. **Which other three teams were in their first-round group?**

7. Who won the cup in 1974?

8. **Who was beaten 2-1 in the Final?**

9. How many teams competed in the 1998 World Cup qualifying rounds?

10. **Which country in the Asian section of the qualifiers won by a World Cup record score?**

11. Which country were they playing?

12. **What was the score?**

13. What was the score in the Europe v Rest of the World match played on the occasion of the draw for the 1998 World Cup?

14. **How many times did Brazilian player Ronaldo score for the Rest of the World?**

15. Which player represented England in that match?

ANSWERS 1. 1986 2. None 3. None 4. Five 5. Australia 6. East Germany, West Germany and Chile 7. West Germany 8. Holland 9. 171 10. Iran 11. The Maldives 12. 17-0 13. Rest of the World 5 Europe 2 14. Twice 15. Paul Ince

# *Quiz* 13    THE WORLD CUP 1930-1998

1. Which country hosted the 1994 World Cup?

2. **How many British countries qualified?**

3. How far did the Republic of Ireland progress in the finals?

4. **Who won the Ireland v Italy match in Group E?**

5. Who scored the winning goal?

6. **Who did the Irish meet in the second round?**

7. What was the score?

8. **How far did Italy go?**

9. What was the score in the Final?

10. **Who won the 1994 Final?**

11. In Italy in 1990, which stage did England reach in the finals?

12. **Who did they meet then?**

13. What was the score after extra time?

14. **What was the score in the penalty shoot-out?**

15. What was the result of the penalty shoot-out between Argentina and Italy in the semi-finals?

15. Argentina 4, Italy 3
11. Semi-finals  **12. West Germany**  13. 1-1  **14. West Germany 4, England 3**
9. Brazil 0, Italy 0 after extra time  **10. Brazil won 3-2 on penalties**
5. Ray Houghton  **6. Holland**  7. Holland won 2-0  **8. All the way to the Final**
ANSWERS **1.** USA  **2. None**  3. To the second round  **4. The Republic won 1-0**

# *Quiz 14* THE WORLD CUP 1930-1998

1. Bolivia had a man sent off in the third minute against Germany in the USA 1994 finals. What was his name?

2. **What happened in his next two games in the tournament?**

3. How many times did Bolivia play in World Cup finals?

4. **Who scored the first ever goal in World Cup history?**

5. Who was the first player to be sent off in a World Cup final match?

6. **That match was against Romania in Uruguay. What was the gate to the nearest thousand?**

7. What was the biggest win in a finals series?

8. **In what year did that happen?**

9. Who scored three for Hungary in that match?

10. **South Korea were victims of the next highest win in a finals match, beaten 9-0 by which country?**

11. Who got a hat-trick that day?

12. **What year was that?**

13. What other team recorded a 9-0 win in a 1974 finals match?

14. **Who were the victims in that match?**

15. Who scored a hat-trick in that match?

11. Kocsis  12. 1954  13. Yugoslavia  14. Zaire  15. Bajevic
7. Hungary beat El Salvador 10-1  8. 1982  9. Kiss  10. Hungary
4. Lucien Laurent (France)  5. Mario De Las Casas (Peru)  6. Just 300!
ANSWERS 1. Marco Etcheverry  2. He didn't play again  3. Three

# *Quiz* 15   THE WORLD CUP 1930-1998

1. Who captained West Germany when they lost in two consecutive World Cup Finals?

2. **In what years were those finals?**

3. Who captained West Germany in the 1990 Final?

4. **Who skippered Argentina in that Final?**

5. How many players were sent off in that match?

6. **Name those two players.**

7. West Germany won that 1990 Final by the only goal from the penalty spot. Who was the scorer?

8. **That goal was scored in which minute – 35th, 65th or 85th?**

9. Who scored the very first World Cup penalty in a finals series?

10. What year was that?

11. Who was the Spanish striker known as 'El Buitre' (The Vulture)?

12. **He scored four goals in a second-round match in 1986 against whom?**

13. Spain were knocked out in their next match, a quarter-final, on a penalty shoot-out. Who beat them?

14. **What was the penalty 'score'?**

15. Who was top scorer in the 1986 finals with six goals altogether?

ANSWERS 1. Karl-Heinz Rummenigge  2. 1982 and 1986  3. Lothar Matthaus
4. Diego Maradona  5. Two  6. Monson and Dezotti, both of Argentina
7. Andy Brehme  8. 85th  9. Manuel Rosas (Mexico)  10. 1930
11. Emilio Butragueno  12. Denmark  13. Belgium  14. 5-4
15. Gary Lineker

# *Quiz* 16    THE WORLD CUP 1930-1998

1. England's shock defeat by USA in 1950 was inflicted by the single goalscorer of the match. Who was he?

2. **What was his country of origin?**

3. Who holds the record for the highest individual scoring aggregate in a World Cup finals?

4. **How many did he score?**

5. In what year?

6. **Who was the second highest individual goalscorer with ten in one tournament in finals history?**

7. When did he achieve that total?

8. **Which British player was sent home after being found guilty of taking illegal substances?**

9. Where and when did that happen?

10. **How long did FIFA suspend him from international football?**

11. Who in 1982 became the youngest player to participate in the finals?

12. **What age was he when he played for Northern Ireland against Yugoslavia in their first match of that series?**

13. Which English clubs did he play for during his international career?

14. **The Irish played five matches during the 1982 finals. How many did they lose?**

15. Who beat them?

ANSWERS 1. Larry Gaetjens 2. Haiti 3. Just Fontaine 4. Thirteen 5. 1958 6. Gerd Muller 7. 1970 8. Willie Johnston 9. Argentina 1978 10. One year 11. Norman Whiteside 12. 17 years 41 days 13. Manchester United and Everton 14. One 15. France 4-1

# *Quiz* 17    THE WORLD CUP 1930-1998

1. New Zealand had their World Cup moment of glory with one finals appearance. What year was that?

2. **Scotland played them in the first of their three matches. What was the score?**

3. Which South American team beat the New Zealanders 4-0?

4. **Tunisia, England's group rivals in 1998, appeared once previously in the finals. In what year?**

5. Tunisia won one, lost one and finally drew with former champions. Who were they?

6. **What was the score in that match?**

7. Turkey had their moment of glory, in 1954. Who did they beat 7-0 in those finals?

8. **Who then beat the Turks 7-2 in the next match?**

9. When did East and West Germany compete as a unified Germany and where?

10. **Who beat them in the quarter-finals of that tournament?**

11. When did Holland beat East Germany in a quarter-final match?

12. **When did Holland draw 2-2 with West Germany in a quarter-final match?**

13. When did Holland lose 2-1 to West Germany in a second-round match?

14. **When did Holland lose 2-1 to West Germany in a World Cup Final?**

15. Who was the English referee in that Final?

# *Quiz* 18

## THE WORLD CUP 1930-1998

1. Which Italian goalkeeper went a record 517 minutes without conceding a goal in a World Cup series?

2. **What year was that?**

3. Whose headed goal finally broke the spell?

4. **Who beat the Italians on a penalty shoot-out in that match to go through to the Final?**

5. Who did Italy beat that year in the third-place play-off?

6. **What was the final score?**

7. Who scored for the losing side in that match?

8. **Who is the only player to have scored five in one World Cup finals match?**

9. What was the final score in that match in the 1994 series?

10. **What was Roger Milla's dubious claim to fame in that game?**

11. Russia still went out at the first-round stage in 1994, having been beaten by Sweden and who else?

12. **Sweden's 3-1 win included a penalty. Who scored it?**

13. Who is the only manager to lead a team to two World Cup Final triumphs prior to 1998?

14. **Which was that team and in which years?**

15. Whose did Geoff Hurst replace in England's 1966 World Cup side?

# Quiz 19
## THE WORLD CUP
## 1930-1998

1. Who is the oldest player to have taken part in World Cup finals?

2. **How old was he when the Russians beat his team in 1994?**

3. In how many World Cup finals matches did Diego Maradona play?

4. **How many finals matches did Uwe Seeler of West Germany have?**

5. Austria qualified twice for the semi-finals of the World Cup. Who beat them in 1934?

6. **Who beat them in the semi-finals in 1954?**

7. In which year did they win the play-off for third place?

8. **Who did they beat 3-1 in that play-off?**

9. What football song was top of the charts in England in April 1970?

10. **Who performed that hit?**

11. How many teams did England beat in the 1970 finals?

12. **Can you name the team or teams?**

13. Which British countries took part in the 1974 finals?

14. **Twelve goals were scored in a quarter-final match in Switzerland in 1954. Who were the teams?**

15. What was the final score?

---

15. Austria won 7-5
14. Switzerland and Austria
13. Scotland only
12. Romania and Czechoslovakia
11. Two
10. England's World Cup Squad
9. Back Home
8. Uruguay
7. 1954
6. West Germany
5. Italy
4. Twenty-one also
3. Twenty-one
2. 42 years 39 days
ANSWERS 1. Roger Milla (Cameroon)

# *Quiz* 20 — THE WORLD CUP 1930-1998

1. Who scored the first World Cup finals hat-trick in 1930?

2. **What was the result in that match?**

3. Argentina also hit another team for six in those 1930 finals. Name the losing team?

4. **How many times did that same prolific player score in this 6-1 win?**

5. What position did Harald Schumacher play for Germany?

6. **How many times did he appear in a World Cup Final?**

7. In what year or years.

8. **How many winners' medals did he collect?**

9. Who succeeded him in the same position at the next World Cups?

10. **Did he get a winners' medal?**

11. Schumacher gave a French striker the elbow – literally! – in a memorable semi-final in 1982. Who was the Frenchman with a headache?

12. **What was the score after extra time in that semi-final clash?**

13. What was the penalty shoot-out 'score'?

14. **Despite their on-field rivalry, Schumacher and Battiston became close friends. To what extent?**

15. Czechoslovakia have been the losers in how many Cup Finals? In what years?

15. Two – in 1934 and 1962
13. West Germany 5, France 4    14. Harald was best man at Patrick's wedding
8. None    9. Illgner    10. Yes – in 1990    11. Patrick Battiston    12. 3-3
3. USA    4. Two    5. Goalkeeper    6. Two    7. 1982 and 1986
ANSWERS 1. Guillermo Stabile (Argentina)    2. Argentina 6, Mexico 3

# *Quiz* 21  THE WORLD CUP 1930-1998

1. How many times have Bulgaria qualified for World Cup finals, including France 1998?

2. **How many times have they progressed beyond the group stages?**

3. They reached the semi-finals once. When and where was that?

4. **They were beaten 2-1 by Italy in that semi-final. Who got both Italian goals?**

5. Who beat Bulgaria 4-0 in the play-off for third place?

6. **In that 1994 Final, whose was the vital penalty shot that sailed over the Brazil crossbar, leaving Italy with losers' medals?**

7. Who was the Brazilian captain in that match?

8. **And Italy's captain?**

9. Kuwait have made only one appearance in a World Cup finals stage. When was that?

10. **They played three matches in those finals without winning. Who beat them 1-0 in their last match?**

11. Who was the solitary goalscorer?

12. **Name the England manager in that series.**

13. How many hat-tricks had been scored in all World Cup finals before the 1998 matches – more or less than 30?

14. **Only three players have scored two hat-tricks each in all finals. Can you name them?**

15. Only one World Cup Final has ended 0-0 even after extra time. Which was that?

# *Quiz* 22    THE WORLD CUP 1930-1998

1. How many matches did England play in the World Cup finals of 1966?

2. **How many of these games did they lose?**

3. Which was the only team to deny England victory in the 1966 finals?

4. **How many of the England squad appeared in every match in the 1966 finals?**

5. How many games did Jimmy Greaves play?

6. **How many games did Geoff Hurst play?**

7. Three of the England 1966 squad played only once each in the finals. Who were they?

8. **Can you name all the ever-present players in every England game in the 1966 finals?**

9. Who was England's top scorer in those matches?

10. **How many did he score?**

11. The highest attendance for a World Cup match was 205,000. Where was that?

12. **When was it and who were the contestants?**

13. What was the match result?

14. **Who is the only player to have scored in successive World Cup Final matches?**

15. Only one player has scored in every match of a World Cup finals. Who was he?

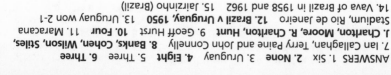

ANSWERS 1. Six 2. **None** 3. Uruguay 4. **Eight** 5. Three 6. **Three**
7. Ian Callaghan, Terry Paine and John Connelly 8. **Banks, Cohen, Wilson, Stiles,**
J. Charlton, Moore, R. Charlton, Hunt 9. Geoff Hurst 10. **Four** 11. Maracana
Stadium, Rio de Janeiro 12. **Brazil v Uruguay, 1950** 13. Uruguay won 2-1
14. Vava of Brazil in 1958 and 1962 15. Jairzinho (Brazil)

# *Quiz* 23    THE WORLD CUP 1930-1998

1. Who was the oldest player to get a World Cup winners' medal?

2. **How old was he?**

3. Who was the oldest player to captain a World Cup winners' side?

4. **According to FIFA who scored the fastest goal in a World Cup final?**

5. What was the recorded time?

6. **Who did England play in that match and in what year?**

7. Who scored the 1,000th goal in World Cup finals in 1978?

8. **Who were the opponents in that match?**

9. Who was the first substitute used in a World Cup finals match?

10. **In what year was that?**

11. Up to the 1998 finals, who were the only country to have won the World Cup outside their continent?

12. **Which three countries have hosted the World Cup twice?**

13. Who has appeared in four World Cup Finals, twice as a player and twice as a manager?

14. **Which Scotland manager resigned after the team's defeat in their first match of the 1954 finals?**

15. What happened in their next match?

ANSWERS **1.** Dino Zoff (Italy) in 1982 **2.** 40 **3.** Dino Zoff in that same match **4. Bryan Robson 5.** 27 seconds **6. France in 1982 7.** Rob Rensenbrink (Holland) **8. Scotland 9.** Anatoly Puzach (USSR) **10. 1970 11.** Brazil **12. Italy, Mexico and France 13.** Franz Beckenbauer **14. Andy Beattie 15.** Uruguay beat them 7-0

# *Quiz* 24    THE WORLD CUP 1930-1998

1. Which was the first black African country to reach the finals?

2. **What year was that?**

3. Before the 1998 finals, what was the highest number of red cards to be shown in one finals?

4. **What year was that?**

5. Who scored the first penalty in a World Cup Final match?

6. **What year was that Final?**

7. Who also scored from the penalty spot later in that match for the eventual winners?

8. **Who was the first player in 1974 to be banned from FIFA for drug-taking during a finals?**

9. Which country did he play for?

10. **Which was the only World Cup finals to be held outside Europe and South America?**

11. Who captained a team in the Final of the World Cup and played for another country in the finals eight years later?

12. **What were those countries?**

13. Did he score in any of those games?

14. **How many goals did he score in the 1954 finals altogether?**

15. Hungary scored 17 goals in their first two matches in the 1954 finals. Who were the opposition and what were the scores?

---

ANSWERS 1. Zaïre 2. 1974 3. Sixteen 4. 1990 5. Johan Neeskens of Holland 6. 1974 7. Paul Breitner (West Germany) 8. Ernest Jean-Joseph 9. Haiti 10. USA 1994 11. Ferenc Puskas 12. Hungary (1954) and Spain (1962) 13. Yes, for Hungary in the Final 14. Five 15. South Korea (9-0) and West Germany (8-3)

# *Quiz* 25    THE WORLD CUP 1930-1998

1. Two past winners failed to qualify for the 1994 World Cup finals. Who were they?

2. **Who was fined £10,000 and received a one-match touchline ban for arguing with a referee in the 1994 finals?**

3. How many times have Scotland failed to get past the first round having qualified for the finals?

4. **Who were banned from a World Cup finals by FIFA after using over-age players in a World under-20 tournament?**

5. Which finals were those?

6. **Which was the first black African country to reach the quarter-finals?**

7. What year was that?

8. **Fifteen penalties were awarded in normal time in the finals of 1994. How many were goals?**

9. Which country first appeared in the World Cup in Italy in 1990 and beat Scotland in their first match?

10. **They also beat another country 2-1 in their third match. Who was the losing side?**

11. Who eventually knocked them out in the second round?

12. **The Republic of Ireland have played nine games in the finals. How many of these have they won?**

13. Who eliminated the Republic in the Italy 1990 finals?

14. **Who scored the only goal of that game?**

15. Who had the Irish beaten in the previous second-round match on a penalty shoot-out?

# TRUE OR FALSE?

# *Quiz 01*    TRUE OR FALSE?

1. Football:  The 1991 FA Cup Final was won by Tottenham Hotspur against Nottingham Forest.

2. **Football:  The score in that match was 2-1 after extra time.**

3. Cricket:  West Indies won the First Test of the 1998 series against England.

4. **Tennis:  Virginia Wade won the Wimbledon women's singles in 1977.**

5. Tennis:  The losing finalist in that 1977 final was Chris Evert.

6. **Cycling:  Tom Simpson of Great Britain died in 1967 during the Tour of Britain.**

7. Cycling:  Jacques Anquetil of France won the Tour de France five times.

8. **Golf:  The Ryder Cup was named after an American.**

9. Football:  Brazil won the Jules Rimet Trophy outright in 1970.

10. **Boxing:  Muhammad Ali beat George Foreman on points in Zaire in 1974.**

11. Boxing:  That contest was postponed for a week because Foreman sustained an injury during training.

12. **Horse Racing:  Lester Piggott rode his first Derby winner in 1954 at the age of 19.**

13. Horse Racing:  Piggott's first Derby winner was Never Say Die.

14. **Football:  England's first defeat at Wembley was against Hungary in 1953.**

15. Boxing:  Henry Cooper won the British heavyweight title for the first time by beating Joe Erskine.

Brian London

ANSWERS 1. True  2. **True**  3. False – Second Test  4. **True**  5. False – it was Betty Stove  6. **False**  7. True  8. **True – Samuel Ryder**  9. True  10. **False – he won in the eighth round**  11. False – it was 30 days  12. **False – he was 18**  13. True  14. **True – beaten 6-3**  15. False – it was

# Quiz 02    TRUE OR FALSE?

1. Cricket: Sunil Gavaskar has twice scored two separate hundreds in a Test match.

2. **Cricket: Graham Gooch is the only man to have scored a triple-hundred and a hundred in the same Test.**

3. Horse Racing: Steve Donoghue rode six Derby winners.

4. **Football: Bobby Charlton scored 48 goals for England.**

5. Football: Gary Lineker scored 48 goals for England.

6. **Show Jumping: Harvey Smith made his famous 'V' sign at Wembley in 1971.**

7. Athletics: Eric Liddell refused to run on a Sunday in the 100 metres Olympics of 1924 on religious grounds.

8. **Athletics: Liddell competed instead in the 400 metres and won a silver medal.**

9. Horse Racing: Sea Bird II won the English Derby and the Arc de Triomphe.

10. **Football: Peter Shilton was the last goalkeeper to captain England.**

11. Football: Malcolm Macdonald scored four England goals against Cyprus in 1975.

12. **Motor Racing: The first British Grand Prix was at Brooklands in 1926.**

13. Motor Racing: Juan Manuel Fangio was World Champion driver four times.

14. **Motor Racing: Fangio was Argentinian.**

15. Rugby League: St. Helens beat Batley in the first Challenge Cup final in 1897.

ANSWERS 1. False 2. **True** – three times 3. True 4. **False** – 49 5. True 6. **False – it was Hickstead** 7. True 8. **False** – he won gold 9. True 10. **False – David Seaman** 11. False – all five 12. **True** 13. False – it was five times 14. **True** 15. False – Batley won

# Quiz 03    TRUE OR FALSE?

1. Boxing: Alan Minter won the world middleweight title from Vito Antuofermo.

2. **Boxing: Minter was a southpaw.**

3. Boxing: Minter lost his world title to Sugar Ray Leonard.

4. **Cricket: Wilfred Rhodes took 100 wickets in a season more than any other cricketer.**

5. Horse Racing: Sir Gordon Richards was champion jockey 26 times.

6. **Horse Racing: He rode only one Derby winner.**

7. Horse Racing: The French Derby is run at Longchamp.

8. **Horse Racing: Red Rum won the Grand National twice.**

9. Squash: Sue Wright won the British national championship in February 1998.

10. **Squash: Sue Wright regained the title European Champion of Champions in February 1998.**

11. Snooker: Terry Griffiths won the World Championship in 1989.

12. **Tennis: Martina Hingis became the French Open champion in 1997.**

13. Snooker: Stephen Hendry beat Mark Williams in the 1998 B & H Masters Final.

14. **Athletics: The fastest-ever London Marathon men's race was won in 1997 by Portugal's Antonio Pinto.**

15. Football: Bobby Charlton was the first to make 100 appearances in full international matches.

ANSWERS 1. True  2. **True**  3. False – Marvin Hagler  4. **True – 23 times**
5. True  6. **True – Pinza in 1953.**  7. False – Chantilly  8. **False – three times**
9. True  10. **True**  11. False – it was 1979  12. **False – Eva Majoli**
13. False – Mark Williams won  14. **True**  15. False – Billy Wright

# Quiz 04  TRUE OR FALSE?

1. Football: John Charles signed for Leeds United as an amateur at the age of 16.

2. **Football: Charles also played for Juventus and Roma.**

3. Rugby League: St. Helens won the Silk Cut Challenge Cup in 1997 by beating Bradford Bulls.

4. **Swimming: Olympic champion David Willkie was born in Malta.**

5. Rugby Union: Jason Leonard was banned for one international match for punching the All Blacks' captain at Old Trafford.

6. **Rugby Union: Leonard is England's most capped prop.**

7. Boxing: Randolph Turpin held the world middleweight title for two months and two days.

8. **Boxing: Jack 'Kid' Berg's real name was Gershon Mendeloff.**

9. Golf: Gary Player has won the South African Open 11 times.

10. **Hockey: Chris Spice, England's first director of performance, and England coach Barry Dancer are both Australians.**

11. Darts: The line from which a player throws is called a hockey.

12. **Cycling: Reg Harris was the first Englishman to wear the yellow jersey in the Tour de France.**

13. Cycling: The first British cyclo-cross championship was held in 1955.

14. **Cricket: Brian Lara scored 350 in one day for Warwickshire against Durham in 1994.**

15. Cricket: Ian Botham holds the record for scoring most sixes in a season.

# Quiz 05    TRUE OR FALSE?

1. Athletics:  Brendan Foster became Tory Leader William Hague's personal fitness coach in 1998.

2. **Boxing:  Barry McGuigan coached actor Daniel Day Lewis for his lead role in the film 'The Boxer'.**

3. Rugby Union:  Gareth Edwards first played for Wales at the age of 19.

4. **Speedway:  England team manager Dave Jessup won 111 international caps.**

5. Table Tennis:  The first championships were organised by the Ping Pong Association.

6. **Football:  Diego Maradona played for Napoli for seven years.**

7. Football:  Maradona did not play for Argentina in the 1990 World Cup Final against West Germany.

8. **Skating:  Torvill and Dean won gold in the figure skating at the Winter Olympics in Sarajevo.**

9. Skating:  The couple won only silver at the Winter Games in Lillehammer.

10. **Athletics:  There are nine hurdles in a 110 metres hurdle race.**

11. Golf:  Bobby Jones and Walter Hagen met once, over 72 holes in 1926.  Jones won 12 and 11.

12. **Golf:  The first Ryder Cup match in 1927 was won by USA against Great Britain 91/2-21/2.**

13. Cricket:  The highest individual Test innings by an Englishman is 365 by Len Hutton.

14. **Cricket:  Don Bradman had a Test career average of 99.94.**

15. Football:  The Colman's Football Food Guide of English league grounds, published in 1998, rated Huddersfield Town at No. 1.

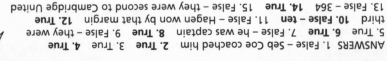

ANSWERS 1. False – Seb Coe coached him  2. True  3. True  4. True  5. True  6. True  7. False – he was captain  8. True  9. False – they were third  10. False – ten  11. False – Hagen won by that margin  12. True  13. False – 364  14. True  15. False – they were second to Cambridge United

# Quiz 06    TRUE OR FALSE?

1. Tennis: Fred Perry won his third successive Wimbledon singles title in 1936.

2. **Tennis: Billie Jean King was the youngest winner of a Grand Slam tournament this century.**

3. Snooker: Ken Doherty is the only player to be World champion at junior, amateur and professional levels.

4. **Boxing: Oscar De La Hoya was the only USA champion in the Olympic Games boxing in 1992.**

5. Boxing: Rocky Marciano won every one of his 49 professional bouts.

6. **Boxing: Marciano won every one of his 12 amateur contests.**

7. Rugby Union: William Webb Ellis started it all by picking up a football on the playing-fields of Eton in 1823.

8. **Rugby Union: John Dawes captained Wales and the British Lions and became the Welsh national coach.**

9. Football: Dixie Dean scored 60 goals in 42 League games in 1927-28.

10. **Football: David Jack of Bolton scored the first FA Cup Final goal at Wembley.**

11. Horse Racing: The Derby is the oldest of the five Classic races.

12. **Bowls: Paul Foster won the World Indoor Championship in 1998 at the age of 26.**

13. Tennis: Petr Korda won his first Grand Slam title, the Australian Open, at the age of 30.

14. **Rugby Union: Jeremy Guscott scored two tries on his debut for England against Romania in 1989.**

15. Skating: Katarina Witt was 18 when she won her first Olympic figure skating title at Sarajevo in 1984.

ANSWERS 1. True 2. **False– Martina Hingis** 3. True 4. **True** 5. True 6. **False – he lost four** 7. False – it was Rugby School 8. **True** 9. False – 39 games 10. **True** 11. False – St. Leger 12. False – only 24 13. True 14. **False – he got three** 15. True

# *Quiz* 07   TRUE OR FALSE?

1. Football: Each of the England players in the World Cup winning team of 1966 received a bonus of £2,000.

2. **Football: Sir Matt Busby was manager of the Manchester United teams which won five First Division titles.**

3. Athletics: Jeffrey Archer ran the 100 yards in 9.6 sec to set an Oxford University record.

4. **Boxing: Jackie Paterson became world flyweight champion in 1943 by knocking out Peter Kane in the tenth round in Glasgow.**

5. Boxing: Muhammad Ali fought once for the world heavyweight title as Cassius Clay.

6. **Boxing: He won that bout in 1964 by beating Floyd Patterson.**

7. Horse Racing: Dick Francis was the National Hunt champion jockey in 1953-54 with 76 winners.

8. **Rugby Union: Jon Callard scored all the points for Bath in their 19-18 defeat of Brive in the 1998 Heineken Cup.**

9. Tennis: Boris Becker was the youngest Grand Slam tournament winner at Wimbledon in 1985.

10. **Tennis: Michael Chang was 17 years 4 months in 1989 when he won the French Open.**

11. Football: Youri Djorkaeff of France was the first goal scorer at the new Stade de France on January 28, 1998.

12. **Football: Ally McCoist was the first player to complete 200 goals in the Scottish Premier Division.**

13. Golf: Tom Weiskopf was runner-up four times in the US Masters.

14. **Cricket: Graham Gooch was the leading run-scorer in an English season four times.**

15. General: There have been more False answers than True in these seven pages!

# MOTOR SPORTS

# *Quiz* 01    MOTOR SPORTS *MOTORBIKES*

1. Who was the 1997 World 500cc champion?

2. **How many times had he previously held the title?**

3. What is his nationality?

4. **What happened in 1997 during the final round of the 500cc competition?**

5. How many laps remained when that happened?

6. **What was he riding?**

7. Who won that final round?

8. **When was the first 500cc World Championship held?**

9. Who was the first champion?

10. **What was his machine?**

11. Whose hopes of taking the 500cc crown were dashed after a crash at Assen in 1997?

12. **What is his nationality?**

13. Which two Japanese brothers finished third and fifth in the 1997 500cc Championship?

14. **Nobuatsu Aoki planned to leave the Honda team in 1998 for which outfit?**

15. Where did the youngest of the three Aoki brothers, Haruchika, finish in 1997 and in which class?

15. Eighth in the 250cc class

12. **Spanish**   13. Nobuatsu and Takuma Aoki   14. Suzuki

8. **1949**   9. Britain's Leslie Graham   10. An AJS   11. Alex Criville

5. Eleven   6. **Repsol Honda**   7. Doohan's teammate Tadayuki Okada

ANSWERS 1. Mike Doohan   2. **Three times**   3. Australian   4. He crashed out

# Quiz 02

## MOTOR SPORTS
### MOTORBIKES

1. How many world motorcycling titles had John Surtees won when he switched to racing cars in 1961?

2. **Who successfully combined motorcycle racing and Formula One cars in the 1960s?**

3. How many times was he World motorcycling champion?

4. **How old was he when he won his first World championship on a 250cc Honda?**

5. In 1967, his Isle of Man TT victory gave him how many consecutive wins?

6. **Who was his great Italian rival who won seven successive World 500cc Championships when he tried his luck on four wheels?**

7. Which Italian teenager won the 125cc Championship in 1997?

8. **Another Italian claimed the 250cc crown for the fourth successive time that year. Who is he?**

9. At which stage was the 250cc Championship finally decided?

10. **Which team was Max Biaggi riding for in 1997?**

11. In the late 1960s, a confident young British teenager started to make his mark on the home circuits. Can you name him?

12. **He had his first win at Brands Hatch in 1968, but when did he win his first Grand Prix?**

13. Where was it?

14. **His first ex-works 125cc Suzuki twin was six years old. How much did it cost?**

15. How old was he when he won his first British 125cc Championship – 21, 20 or 19?

ANSWERS 1. Seven 2. **Mike Hailwood** 3. Ten 4. 21 5. Five 6. **Giacomo Agostini** 7. Valentino Rossi 8. **Max Biaggi** 9. In the final round in Australia 10. **Eru Kanemoto Honda** 11. Barry Sheene 12. 1971 13. Belgium 14. **£2,000** 15. 20

# Quiz 03 — MOTOR SPORTS *MOTORBIKES*

1. What was Barry Sheene's average speed in the 1977 Belgian Grand Prix – 131.86mph, 134.98mph or 139.68mph?

2. **Where did he almost lose his life in a horrific crash?**

3. How long after the crash did he win his first World 500cc Championship?

4. **How many World 500cc Championships did he win?**

5. One of Sheene's greatest rivals was a Venezuelan who won the 350cc World Championship in 1975. Who was he?

6. **Who was the British rider in the 1950s, noted for his impeccable style, who won four World 500cc Championships?**

7. Carl Fogarty lost his World Superbike Championship to an American in 1997. Can you name him?

8. **How long had the new champion been competing in Superbike racing?**

9. What nationality is John Kocinski?

10. **Niall Mackenzie, twice winner of the MCN British Superbike title in 1996 and 1997, rides for which team?**

11. Australian Peter Goddard won the 1997 World Endurance Championship for which team?

12. **On what machine?**

13. Which team did Biaggi desert to join Honda in 1997?

14. **Which three-times World champion has designed a two-stroke machine for his son?**

15. How many of the first five in the 125cc World Championship of 1997 were Japanese?

11. Suzuki  12. 75cc four-stroke  13. Aprilia  14. Kenny Roberts  15. Four
6. Geoff Duke  7. John Kocinski  8. Two years  9. American  10. Yamaha
3. The following year – 1976  4. Two – 1976 and 1977  5. Johnny Cecotto
ANSWERS 1. 134.98mph, a record at the time  2. Daytona, 1975

# *Quiz* 04  MOTOR SPORTS RACING CARS

1. Who was US Sprint car champion and twice Indy car champion before winning the 1978 Grand Prix Championship?

2. **Which team was he with in 1978?**

3. Who was the youngest-ever winner of the 1995 BTCC?

4. **Was he 18, 19, or 21?**

5. Who was too broad to fit in his 1995 McLaren?

6. **What was done about it?**

7. When did Nigel Mansell win the World Championship?

8. **In which car?**

9. He won another title in 1993. What was it?

10. **When did he first retire?**

11. Why was David Mann two hours late starting in the 1997 Pirelli International Rally Championships?

12. **Who took Ayrton Senna's place at Williams after Senna was tragically killed at Imola in 1994?**

13. What was Senna's successor's position at Williams before Imola?

14. **Where and when was his first Grand Prix win?**

15. Who was the medical student who won the 1981 British Formula 3 Championship?

14. Portugal 1995  15. Jonathon Palmer
11. His car was stolen  12. David Coulthard  13. Williams' test driver
7. 1992  8. Williams  9. The Indy Car Championship  10. 1995
21 days  5. Nigel Mansell  6. McLaren built a car with a larger chassis
ANSWERS 1. Mario Andretti  2. Lotus  3. James Thompson  4. 21 years

# *Quiz* 05    MOTOR SPORTS *RACING CARS*

1. When was the first post-war British Grand Prix held?

2. **Where was it held?**

3. When did Jacques Villeneuve win the F1 World Championship?

4. **When and where was his first Grand Prix race?**

5. Who is considered to be one of the best-ever British drivers not to have won a World Championship?

6. **How many times was he runner-up?**

7. When and where was his last Grand Prix win?

8. **Who was the 500cc World motorbike champion who made his debut in the 1992 Indy Lights?**

9. Which country banned motor racing in 1955 when 80 people were killed?

10. **In which European city was a street race run as part of the 1997 FIA GT Championship?**

11. In how many Grands Prix did Emerson Fittipaldi compete?

12. **How many times was he World champion?**

13. When?

14. **Who was the first British Grand Prix driver to win the World Championship?**

15. When was that?

# Quiz 06  MOTOR SPORTS RACING CARS

1. Who was the first driver to win a World Championship in a car named after him?

2. **What nationality was he?**

3. How many times was he World champion?

4. **In which years?**

5. Who was known as 'The Shunt'?

6. **How did he get his nickname?**

7. With whom was he driving when he won the 1976 World Championship?

8. **Argentinian Juan Manuel Fangio won five World Championships in a single decade. Was it in the 1950s, 1960s or 1970s?**

9. How many of the World titles were won driving a Maserati?

10. **Who was the first driver to win World Championships on motorbikes and cars?**

11. Who was South American karting champion before joining the motor-racing circuit?

12. **Which Formula One circuit is on an island in the middle of a river?**

13. Nigel Mansell looked certain to win on that track in 1991 – but what happened?

14. **Who in 1968 won the German Grand Prix with a margin of four minutes?**

15. Who won a Grand Prix at his 96th attempt?

ANSWERS 1. **Jack Brabham** 2. **Australian** 3. Three 4. **1959, 1960 and 1966** 5. James Hunt 6. **He was involved in several crashes** 7. McLaren 8. **1950s** (151-54-55-56-57) 9. Three 10. **John Surtees** 11. Ayrton Senna 12. **Montreal** 13. Mansell stalled just before the finish and Nelson Piquet swept to victory 14. **Jackie Stewart** 15. Finland's Mika Hakkinen

## *Quiz* 07    MOTOR SPORTS RACING CARS

1. Which father and son have both won the World Championship?

2. **When was that?**

3. Who became 1963 World Champion by winning seven out of ten Grands Prix?

4. **When did he win his second World Championship and the Indy 500 in the same year?**

5. On which circuit would you find Pouhon Corner?

6. **Who won his first Grand Prix at Spa in 1992?**

7. Is Curva Grande on the Monaco, Monza or Montreal track?

8. **Which manufacturer has scored the most victories at Le Mans?**

9. How many?

10. **In 1981, who collapsed at Le Mans on the winner's rostrum?**

11. Who gave Ligier their first Grand Prix win for 15 years at Monaco in 1996?

12. **Who won the first Formula One World Championship in 1950?**

13. What car was he driving?

14. **Why was Michael Schumacher given a two-race ban at Silverstone in 1994?**

15. Which French car won the Le Mans 24-hours in 1972, 1973 and 1974?

ANSWERS 1. Graham and Damon Hill 2. **Graham in 1962 and 1968 and Damon in 1996** 3. Jim Clark 4. **1965** 5. Spa-Francorchamps 6. **Michael Schumacher** 7. Monza 8. Porsche 9. Fifteen 10. **Derek Bell** 11. Olivier Panis 12. **Guiseppe Farina** 13. An Alfa-Romeo 14. He ignored a black flag 15. The Matra

# *Quiz* 08    MOTOR SPORTS RACING CARS

1. Who played Michael Delaney in the film 'Le Mans'?

2. **Who won the British Touring Car Championship in 1980-81-82?**

3. Name the ex-Formula One driver who won just one BTCC race?

4. **He achieved that 1993 victory at which circuit?**

5. Who had three consecutive RAC Rally successes in 1960-61-62?

6. **Who was his wife's famous racing brother?**

7. In what two-stroke car did he perform that hat-trick?

8. **Who won the 1964 Monte Carlo Rally in a Mini Cooper?**

9. Who was Roger Clark's co-driver in winning the 1972 RAC Rally?

10. **Which two current F1 drivers collided at the first corner in the Monaco Grand Prix of 1994?**

11. Who was the first Englishman to be named Indycars Rookie of the Year?

12. **Who was the first woman to qualify for the Indy 500?**

13. Who on the 1987 RAC Rally won the World Championship for the second year in succession?

14. **What was his car?**

15. In what year did Williams start using Renault engines?

ANSWERS 1. Steve McQueen  2. **Win Percy**  3. Julian Bailey  4. **Knockhill**
5. Eric Carlsson  6. **Stirling Moss**  7. Saab 96  8. **Paddy Hopkirk**
9. Tony Mason  10. **Mika Hakkinen and Damon Hill**  11. Nigel Mansell
12. **Janet Guthrie**  13. Juha Kankkunen  14. **Lancia Delta**  15. 1989

# *Quiz* 09    MOTOR SPORTS<br>RACING CARS

1. Who was Richie Ginther runner-up to for the 1963 World Championship?

2. **With whom did Ginther finish equal on points that year?**

3. In 1965, racing for Honda, where was Ginther's only Grand Prix win?

4. **In what year did British Karting Champion, Johnny Herbert, win the British Formula Three title?**

5. With whom had Herbert just signed a contract when he suffered foot injuries in an accident at Brands Hatch?

6. **When did Herbert make his debut in Formula One?**

7. Where was that and what was the result?

8. **What happened next when Herbert failed to recover quickly from his foot injuries?**

9. Who became 1967 World Champion for Brabham-Repco after winning Grands Prix at Monaco and Germany?

10. **What nationality was he?**

11. In which year did he pull out of Formula One after winning the Argentinian Grand Prix?

12. **Who died in a crash at Monza in 1961 when he had the World Championship in his sights?**

13. Who went on to win the Championship that year?

14. **Who was named runner-up?**

15. How many of the McRae family finished in the 1991 Scottish Rally top ten?

# Quiz 10 — MOTOR SPORTS RACING CARS

1. At which track is the statue of Ayrton Senna, in memory of his fatal crash in 1994?

2. **By what time margin did Scot Colin McRae won the 1998 Portuguese 1,000-mile rally: 1.1, 2.1, or 3.1 seconds?**

3. Who is the only competitor ever to have won both Formula One and BTCC titles?

4. **Where and when was his fatal crash?**

5. Where is the Adelaide hairpin?

6. **Who collided there with Ayrton Senna's McLaren on the first lap, knocking him out of the 1993 race?**

7. Who won his third World Championship in 1984 by just half a point?

8. **Who was his McLaren teammate and runner-up?**

9. Who beat three former World Champions to win the Kenya Safari Rally in March 1998?

10. **How many other British drivers have won a round in the Rally World Championship?**

11. Max Mosley, unpaid president of FIA, has a famous father. Who was he?

12. **Who was awarded the 1970 Formula One World Championship posthumously?**

13. Who finished second?

14. **Who won the Riverside NASCAR stock-car race three times from 1964-66 while still competing in Formula One?**

15. Who won nine out of sixteen Formula One races in 1992 to win the World Championship?

ANSWERS **1.** Imola **2. 2.1 seconds** **3.** Jim Clark **4. Hockenheim on April 7, 1968** **5.** Magny-Cours, France **6. Michael Schumacher** **7.** Niki Lauda **8. Alain Prost** **9.** Richard Burns **10. Two** **11.** Sir Oswald Mosley, leader of the British Fascists **12. Jochen Rindt** **13.** Jacky Ickx **14. Dan Gurney** **15.** Nigel Mansell

# THE ULTIMATE SPORTS FACT AND QUIZ BOOK

## *Quiz* 11 — MOTOR SPORTS RACING CARS

1. After whom is the Villeneuve Chicane named at San Marino?

2. **Why?**

3. Which Grand Prix is raced through narrow French streets?

4. **Which two drivers have somersaulted through the chicane and landed in the harbour at this track?**

5. How old were Graham Hill and Nigel Mansell when they became World Champions in 1968 and 1992, respectively?

6. **Who won the British Formula Ford Junior title in 1997?**

7. Which National Hunt jockey competed in Formula First in 1997?

8. **On which Grand Prix track did Ayrton Senna beat Nigel Mansell by one-thousandth of a second in 1986?**

9. Who did David Coulthard appoint as his manager at the start of the 1998 Formula One series?

10. **Who is Williams' technical director?**

11. Who was the first winner on the new Gilles Villeneuve circuit in Montreal in 1978?

12. **Who headed the Rally World Championship table in May 1998 after his second consecutive win in Corsica?**

13. On which track is the Abbey Curve?

14. **The son of a former Formula One World Champion took part in the 1997 Formula Vauxhall Junior. Who is he?**

15. When was his father Formula One Champion?

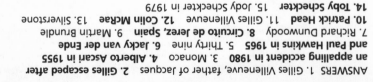

ANSWERS 1. Gilles Villeneuve, father of Jacques  2. **Gilles escaped after an appalling accident in 1980**  3. Monaco  **4. Alberto Ascari in 1955 and Paul Hawkins in 1965**  5. Thirty nine  6. **Jacky van der Ende**  7. Richard Dunwoody  **8. Circuito de Jerez, Spain**  9. Martin Brundle  **10. Patrick Head**  11. Gilles Villeneuve  **12. Colin McRae**  13. Silverstone  **14. Toby Scheckter**  15. Jody Scheckter in 1979

# *Quiz* 12  MOTOR SPORTS RACING CARS

1. Who won the 1997 Euro Kart Championship?

2. **Who drove for Benetton in 1989 and then rejoined them in 1995?**

3. Which former international motorcyclist came second in the 1972 Italian Formula One Grand Prix?

4. **What was the Silverstone circuit built on?**

5. Who were the 1997 Ladies' Rally champions?

6. **Who notched up his only Grand Prix win in Canada in 1995 and quit the Benetton team at the end of 1997?**

7. Who finished second to Villeneuve in 1997 having scored just one win at San Marino?

8. **What does a striped yellow and red flag indicate when waved?**

9. Who partnered Damon Hill in the 1998 Jordon team?

10. **Who was priced as 6-4 favourite at the start of the 1998 Formula One World Championship?**

11. Who was Johnny Herbert's new teammate for the start of the 1998 series?

12. **Two Japanese drivers joined Tyrrell Ford and Minardi Ford teams for the 1998 Formula One campaign. Name them.**

13. Who designed the new McLaren Mercedes?

14. **Which rival team did he help to victory with his designs before joining McLaren?**

15. In the single-seater Formula 3000 series of 1990, who had a clean sweep of street circuit wins?

# Quiz 13   MOTOR SPORTS RACING CARS

1. Which World Championship winner of the 1960s and 1970s was a member of the British clay-pigeon shooting team?

2. **How many times was he Formula One champion?**

3. Which team did he drive for?

4. **How many times did he also win The Race of Champions?**

5. When did he form his Stewart Grand Prix Formula One Team?

6. **Which Grand Prix did Damon Hill win on October 13, 1996 to secure the World Championship?**

7. Who was his teammate who would have overtaken Hill on points had he won?

8. **What happened to his teammate in that race?**

9. When did Damon stop racing with the Williams team?

10. **Which team did he then join?**

11. How many sets of tyres are allowed for each car during a Grand Prix?

12. **Why was the FIA GT race at Silverstone in 1997 brought to an early close?**

13. Which British Formula One driver finished 6th, 7th and 7th again in consecutive years of the Drivers' World Championship?

14. **In which consecutive years?**

15. In what way was he connected with Grand Prix racing after retiring as a driver?

ANSWERS 1. Jackie Stewart 2. **Three** 3. Tyrrell 4. **Two** 5. 1997 6. **Japanese Grand Prix** 7. Jacques Villeneuve 8. **He lost a right rear wheel** 9. 1996 10. **TWR Arrows** 11. Seven 12. **Torrential rain** 13. Martin Brundle 14. **1992, 1993 and 1994** 15. Television commentator

# HORSE RACING

# *Quiz* 01    HORSE RACING

1. Where was the first recorded horse race?

2. **Did it take place in 1440, 1540 or 1640?**

3. To whom was Lester Piggott apprenticed at the age of twelve?

4. **How old was he when he rode his first winner?**

5. What happened on Lester's first Derby ride in 1951?

6. **Name Lester's first Derby winner.**

7. What was the starting price 2-1, 12-1 or 33-1?

8. **The legendary jockey Fred Archer was apprenticed at Newmarket in 1868. At what age?**

9. How many winners did he ride in his career – 1,260, 2,430 or 2,746 ?

10. **How many Derby winners did Archer ride?**

11. How old was he when he died?

12. **Who trains at Jackdaws Castle Stable?**

13. Steve Donoghue rode a former hurdler and famous champion on the Flat. What was the name of the horse?

14. **Who said of that jockey: "He helped the least, the last and the poorest of us"?**

15. How old was Steve Donoghue when he retired?

# *Quiz* 02   HORSE RACING

1. In what year did National Hunt racing begin at Aintree?

2. **Who rode five Grand National winners between 1856 and 1870?**

3. The same jockey rode 15 times in the National. How many times did he have a fall?

4. **How many times did Golden Miller win the Gold Cup?**

5. What were Bryan Marshall's two Grand National winners?

6. **Why was his first winning ride in England on an outsider so unique?**

7. Who was riding Devon Loch in the 1956 Grand National when the horse collapsed 40 yards from the finish?

8. **What was the winner of that race?**

9. Who owned Devon Loch?

10. **Who training Aldaniti, the 1981 National winner?**

11. Who was the jockey?

12. **What was so remarkable about that 1981 triumph?**

13. Who rode Red Rum to his third and final victory at the 1977 National?

14. **Who won a gold medal in the European Junior Showjumping Championships before riding for Fred Winter?**

15. On what landmark date was Arkle's last race?

overcome injury   13. Tommy Stack   14. John Francome   15. Boxing Day 1967
11. Bob Champion   12. Bob had conquered cancer and the horse had
7. Dick Francis   8. ESB   9. The Queen Mother   10. Josh Gifford
and Royal Tan (1954)   6. In a three horse race the other two fell
ANSWERS 1. 1829   2. **George Stevens**   3. Never   4. Five   5. Early Mist (1953)

# *Quiz* 03  HORSE RACING

1. Name the colourful racing tipster whose famous cry was "I gotta horse"?

2. **What was Jason Titley's winning Grand National mount in 1995?**

3. Who was the first US-based jockey to win at Royal Ascot?

4. **In what year?**

5. Which jockey did American racing fans call 'The Six Million Dollar Kid'?

6. **Which father and son have both finished second in the Grand National?**

7. What were their mounts?

8. **Which famous horse pipped the father's mount at the winning post?**

9. Who trains and is also a commentator on the Irish racing circuit?

10. **Name the American female jockey who rode a winning double on her first visit to Britain.**

11. On which racecourse was that?

12. **Who was the last mare to win the Grand National?**

13. What year was it – 1930, 1951 or 1969?

14. **Which owner in 1998 switched 120 two year olds from Britain to France to be trained?**

15. Which jockey accused of "not trying" after finishing 64 lengths behind the winner in a 1998 selling hurdle, announced his retirement?

ANSWERS 1. Prince Monolulu  2. **Royal Athlete**  3. Gary Stevens  4. **1997**
5. Steve Cauthen  6. **Richard and Mark Pitman**  7. Crisp and Garrison
Savannah  8. **Red Rum**  9. Ted Walsh  10. **Julie Krone**  11. Redcar
12. **Nickel Coin**  13. 1951  14. **Sheik Mohammed**  15. Richard Guest

# Quiz 04    HORSE RACING

1. How many Epsom Derby winners did Lester Piggott ride?

2. **How old was he when he rode the first of those winners?**

3. How many times was he champion jockey?

4. **Which Derby winner did he consider the best horse he had ever ridden?**

5. Who was its trainer?

6. **On which horse did Piggott win the Triple Crown in 1970?**

7. Who replaced him as jockey to Robert Sangster and Vincent O'Brien?

8. **Name the jumps jockey who set a record for the fastest 100 winners in 1978.**

9. Whose record did he beat?

10. **What was the first horse to win the Champion Hurdle and Gold Cup?**

11. Who was the jockey?

12. **Who broke Jonjo O'Neill's record of 149 winners in a season?**

13. Which horse performed a hat-trick of Cheltenham Gold Cup wins in 1964, 1965 and 1966?

14. **Who was the jockey?**

15. Which two Classics are restricted to fillies?

ANSWERS 1. Nine 2. **Eighteen** 3. Eleven 4. **Sir Ivor** 5. Vincent O'Brien 6. **Nijinsky** 7. Pat Eddery 8. **Jonjo O'Neill** 9. Fred Winter (1953) 10. **Dawn Run** 11. Jonjo O'Neill 12. **Peter Scudamore** 13. Arkle 14. **Pat Taaffe** 15. One Thousand Guineas and The Oaks

# THE ULTIMATE SPORTS FACT AND QUIZ BOOK

## *Quiz* 05    HORSE RACING

1. In what year was the first Epsom Derby held – 1720, 1780 or 1820?

2. **Who beat Steve Donoghue's record of 264 winning rides in a season?**

3. The new record holder was rewarded with a silver cigarette case and a pair of racing pigeons. Who was the donor?

4. **How old was Gordon Richards when he rode his first Derby winner?**

5. Name the horse.

6. **Who said of Richards: "He was absolutely straight and always did his best to win"?**

7. Who rode three winners within seven days of getting his jockey's licence?

8. **Where was he born?**

9. How old was he when he came to England to ride for Robert Sangster?

10. **What was his first winning Classic ride?**

11. Which filly did he ride to win the St. Leger in 1985?

12. **Who was the Texan jockey who weighed 40 ounces at birth?**

13. How old was he when he won his first race?

14. **What age was he when he rode his last race?**

15. How many wins did he record in his career – 2,420 or 5,630 or 8,833?

15. 8,833
11. Oh So Sharp    12. Willie Shoemaker    13. Seventeen    14. Sixty
9. Eighteen    10. Tap On Wood in the 1979 Two Thousand Guineas
5. Pinza    6. King George V    7. Steve Cauthen    8. Kentucky, USA
ANSWERS 1. 1780    2. Gordon Richards    3. King George V    4. Fifty

# Quiz 06   HORSE RACING

1. Who rode the Whitbread Gold Cup winner in 1967 and trained the winner in 1998?

2. **Who won the Champion Hurdle at the 1998 Cheltenham Festival?**

3. What was special about the Irish celebration of this triumph?

4. **Martin Pipe's assistant was once a table tennis champion. What is his name?**

5. What was Adrian Maguire's spectacular big race win in Scotland in 1998?

6. **Name the horse.**

7. What happened days later on his 27th birthday?

8. **Who set a record price for a foal in 1997?**

9. Name of the foal?

10. **What did it cost?**

11. The foal is a full brother to what Classic winner?

12. **How many times has Pat Eddery been champion jockey?**

13. Who in 1998 broke Peter Scudamore's record of 200 winners in a season?

14. **What was the new record holder's 200th winner?**

15. Who was its trainer?

# *Quiz* 07    HORSE RACING

1. Who was champion National Hunt jockey in 1997?

2. **Who did Richard Dunwoody ride to victory in the 1994 Grand National?**

3. How many obstacles have to be jumped in the Grand National?

4. **How many times did Red Rum win the National at Aintree?**

5. Who was his trainer?

6. **Where was Red Rum buried?**

7. When was that and at what age?

8. **Which Epsom Derby winner shared the same name as a famous Italian opera singer?**

9. Name the first jockey to ride 1,000 winners under National Hunt rules?

10. **What was the name of Lester Piggott's final Classic winner?**

11. When was that?

12. **Who trained that winner?**

13. What award was taken from Piggott when he was imprisoned for tax irregularities?

14. **Who trained a hat-trick of Grand National winners in 1953, 1954 and 1955?**

15. Can you name one of those horses.

Royal Tan, Quare Times
13. His OBE for 'services to racing' **14. Vincent O'Brien** 15. Early Mist,
**8. Pinza** 9. Stan Mellor 10. Shadeed 11. 1985 **12. Michael Stoute**
5. Ginger McCain **6. By the winning post at Aintree** 7. In 1995 aged 30
ANSWERS 1. Tony McCoy **2. Miinnehoma** 3. Thirty **4. Three times**

# *Quiz* 08  HORSE RACING

1. In what year was the Grand National run at Gatwick?

2. **Who rode the first two Schweppes Gold Trophy winners in 1963 and 1964 on the same horse?**

3. Name the horse.

4. **When was the last time a grey won the Grand National?**

5. What was its name?

6. **How many of the English Classics did Steve Cauthen win?**

7. Over how many years did he achieve this feat?

8. **A filly won the Eclipse Stakes for the first time in 1985. What was its name?**

9. Who rode nine French Derby winners?

10. **Who rode four winners of the Prix de l'Arc de Triomphe?**

11. Name the broadcaster whose mount twice won the King George VI Chase.

12. **What was that horse?**

13. Who rode all seven winners at an afternoon meeting in 1997?

14. **Where was that course?**

15. How many Epsom Derby winners did Gordon Richards ride?

ANSWERS 1. 1915  2. **Josh Gifford**  3. Rosyth  4. **1961**  5. Nicolaus Silver
6. **All five**  7. Seven  8. **Pebbles**  9. Yves St. Martin  10. **Yves St. Martin**
11. Richard Pitman  12. **Pendil**  13. Frankie Dettori  14. Ascot  15. One

# Quiz 09    HORSE RACING

1. Who won the 200th Derby in 1979?

2. **The race was won by the greatest margin since 1925. Was it in four, six or seven lengths?**

3. Who was the jockey?

4. **Which horse won the Derby the following year?**

5. Name the jockey

6. **On which course is the Rowley Mile?**

7. What is the name of the racecourse at Esher, Surrey?

8. **Who said of Desert Orchid: "If you employed him, you'd give him a gold watch"?**

9. Who also said of Dessie: "There is no mystery. My horse just runs faster than the others"?

10. **Who said: "I have ridden some brilliant horses – West Tip, Charter Party and Kribensis. Desert Orchid is on top of the lot"?**

11. Where was the London track known as 'Ally Pally'?

12. **What did jockeys Bill Williamson and Scobie Breasley have in common?**

13. What have racecourses Lingfield and Southwell in common?

14. **How many Derby winners did Steve Donoghue ride?**

15. How many times did Brown Jack win the Queen Alexandra Stakes?

15. Six in succession, 1929-34
12. **Both Australians**  13. Both have all-weather tracks  **14. Six**
Elsworth  9. Elsworth again  **10. Richard Dunwoody**  11. Alexandra Park
5. Willie Carson  **6. Newmarket**  7. Sandown Park  **8. His trainer David**
ANSWERS 1. Troy  **2. Seven lengths**  3. Willie Carson  **4. Henbit**

# Quiz 10 HORSE RACING

1. Which is the oldest of the five Classics?

2. **Why was the race so called?**

3. Lester Piggott's father Keith trained a Grand National winner. Who was it?

4. **What kind of bet is a 'pony'?**

5. And how much would you invest for an each way 'monkey'?

6. **How did Formosa in 1868 and Sceptre in 1902 create racing history?**

7. Which of the Classics did each of these fillies fail to win?

8. **Which two races make up the Autumn Double?**

9. For which newspaper is Robin Goodfellow the racing correspondent?

10. **Whose newspaper's correspondent is known as The Scout?**

11. Who was the champion jockey who, unlike his father, failed to win the Grand National?

12. **What was his father's winning mount?**

13. In what year did he win it?

14. **Where is the Whitbread Gold Cup run?**

15. Who trained Garrison Savannah?

ANSWERS 1. St. Leger 2. It was named after Colonel Anthony St. Leger
3. Ayala 4. £25 5. £1,000 6. Each won four Classics 7. The Derby
8. Cambridgeshire and Cesarewitch Stakes 9. Daily Mail 10. The Express
11. Peter Scudamore 12. Oxo 13. 1959 14. Sandown 15. Jenny Pitman

# Quiz 11 HORSE RACING

1. Walter Swinburn was out of action for six months after a serious fall. In which country?

2. **How many Epsom Derby winners has Swinburn ridden?**

3. He rode the winner of the 1996 Breeders' Cup Turf. What was it?

4. **What have former England footballers Francis Lee and Mick Channon got in common?**

5. Which football club manager started the 1998 Flat season with a two year old winner?

6. **What was its name?**

7. Who is the trainer?

8. **Which former Portsmouth, Newcastle and Coventry player trained his first winner in January 1998?**

9. Which National Hunt jockey holds the record for nine successive centuries of winners?

10. **Whose record did he break in 1998?**

11. What is Rule 151 about?

12. **Name the jockey who rode winners Bosra Sham (1,000 Guineas) and Lady Carla (The Oaks) in the 1996 Classics.**

13. Which horse won the 1997 Prix de l'Arc de Triomphe by five lengths?

14. **Who was his jockey?**

15. And who was his trainer?

ANSWERS **1.** Hong Kong **2. Three 3.** Pilsudski **4. Both became trainers 5.** Alex Ferguson of Manchester United **6. Queensland Star 7.** Jack Berry **8. Mick Quinn 9.** Richard Dunwoody **10.** Peter Scudamore **11.** It governs 'non triers' **12. Pat Eddery 13.** Peintre Celebre **14.** Olivier Peslier **15.** Andre Fabre

# GOLF

# *Quiz* 01 GOLF

1. Where was the first British Open played?

2. **In what year?**

3. The Green Jacket is presented to the winner of which competition?

4. **Who presents the Green Jacket each year?**

5. Which 18 hole course was used first for British Open tournaments and when?

6. **Name four members of the successful 1985 European Ryder Cup team**

7. Who in the 1920s and 1930s was known as golf's first glamour boy?

8. **Which British golfer won the US Masters in 1991 and was named World No. 1?**

9. Who was the first golfer to achieve a round of 63 in the Open?

10. **Who won the tournament that year?**

11. How many times did Ben Hogan (USA) play in the Open – and how many times did he win?

12. **Who was the first golfer to win the Grand Slam – US Masters, US Open and British Open – in one year?**

13. What year was it?

14. **When was the Walker Cup first played?**

15. What is the women's equivalent of the Walker Cup?

ANSWERS 1. Prestwick 2. 1860 3. US Masters 4. **The previous year's winner** 5. St. Andrews in 1873 6. **Seve Ballesteros, Jose-Maria Canizares, Manuel Pinero, Jose Rivero, Bernhard Langer, Ken Brown, Howard Clark, Nick Faldo, Sandy Lyle, Sam Torrance, Paul Way and Ian Woosnam** 7. Walter Hagen 8. **Ian Woosnam** 9. Mark Hayes at Turnberry in 1977 10. **Tom Watson (USA)** 11. He played and won only once in 1953 12. **Ben Hogan** 13. 1953 14. 1922 15. Curtis Cup

# *Quiz* 02     GOLF

1. How old was Tony Jacklin when he won the British Open?

2. **Where was it played and in which year?**

3. Who was the next British player to win that title?

4. **How many times did Jacklin captain the European team in the Ryder Cup?**

5. What was the last year of his captaincy?

6. **How many times did Europe win the Ryder Cup under his captaincy?**

7. Who was the last amateur to win the British Open?

8. **When did he win it?**

9. Who, playing in Hawaii in 1993, picked up his ball and left the course after missing a short putt at the 11th?

10. **What happened next?**

11. Who became the US Masters first million dollar earner in 1998?

12. **Who won the title in 1998?**

13. How many US Masters titles has Nick Faldo won?

14. **In the 1996 US Masters who led by six strokes before the final day but failed to win?**

15. Who won the title that year to complete a US Masters hat-trick?

ANSWERS 1. Twenty five 2. **Royal Lytham in 1969** 3. Sandy Lyle 4. **Four**
5. 1989 6. **Twice and one draw** 7. Bobby Jones (USA) 8. **1930**
9. John Daly 10. **He was suspended from the US tour** 11. Nick Faldo
12. **Mark O'Meara** 13. Three 14. **Greg Norman** 15. Nick Faldo

# THE ULTIMATE SPORTS FACT AND QUIZ BOOK

## *Quiz* 03     GOLF

1. How many times has the US Open been won by a qualifier – two, three or four times?

2. **Can you name one of the players?**

3. Who was chosen to play in the Ryder Cup before he had won a 72 hole tournament?

4. **Who won the US Masters with a record total and by a record margin?**

5. What was his total score?

6. **What was the winning margin?**

7. Who captained the 1995 European Ryder Cup team for the third time?

8. **Where was it played?**

9. What was the result?

10. **Which two players decided to share the title when bad light stopped play in the play-off for the 1986 Lancombe Trophy.**

11. Who won a fully furnished house at Gleneagles after achieving a hole in one?

12. **When was the treasured Claret Cup first contested at the British Open?**

13. Who won it that year?

14. **Who scored the lowest ever final round in the US Masters?**

15. What was it and in what year?

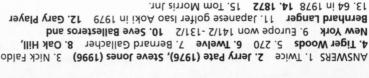

ANSWERS **1.** Twice **2. Jerry Pate (1976), Steve Jones (1996)** **3.** Nick Faldo **4. Tiger Woods** **5.** 270 **6. Twelve** **7.** Bernard Gallacher **8.** Oak Hill, **New York** **9.** Europe won 14 1/2 - 13 1/2 **10.** Seve Ballesteros and **Bernhard Langer** **11.** Japanese golfer Isao Aoki in 1979 **12.** Gary Player **13.** 64 in 1978 **14.** 1872 **15.** Tom Morris Jnr.

# *Quiz* 04

## GOLF

1. Who said: "Playing golf is better than working for a living"?

2. **Where did Jack Nicklaus finish in the 1998 US Masters?**

3. How did 'Fuzzy' Zoeller get his nickname?

4. **Who won three major championships in five weeks in 1971?**

5. Can you name two of them?

6. **Who was called up to serve in the US Navy the day after winning the USPGA in 1942?**

7. Who drove eight hours from Memphis to Indianapolis to play in the USPGA when Nick Price withdrew in 1991?

8. **Who won the championship that year?**

9. Where is the Postage Stamp hole?

10. **How many major titles has Jack Nicklaus won?**

11. How many times has he won the British Open?

12. **In what years?**

13. **How many times has a British golfer won the Open at Royal Birkdale?**

14. Who donated £2,000 of his £5,500 first prize to an orphanage after winning the Open?

15. Who was the 18 year old who beat Colin Montgomerie 5 and 4 to win the British Amateur Championship in 1984?

*The Club Secretary*

# Quiz 05     GOLF

1. Who has won the British Open six times?

2. **How many times did Tom Watson take the title?**

3. In which country is the Million Dollar Classic played?

4. **On which course are rattlesnakes among the challengers faced by golfers?**

5. Where was the 1997 Ryder Cup played?

6. **Who captained the European team?**

7. Which golfer was top of the bill at the London Palladium telling golfing stories and doing trick shots?

8. **Who was the first American golfer to reach one million dollars in prize money?**

9. In what year?

10. **Which South African golfer always dresses in black?**

11. Why?

12. **On which course were ten emergency telephones installed?**

13. Why?

14. **Who is known as 'The Peacock'?**

15. What do the brilliant colours he wears represent?

ANSWERS 1. Harry Vardon  2. **Five times**  3. Sun City, South Africa
4. **Arizona**  5. Valderrama, Spain  6. **Seve Ballesteros**  7. Henry Cotton
8. **Arnold Palmer**  9. 1968  10. **Gary Player**  11. He believes that black
absorbs more of the sun's rays to give him extra strength  12. **Mojave,
California**  13. Because a number of people have fainted in the heat
14. **Payne Stewart**  15. Colours of the National Football League teams

# *Quiz* 06

## GOLF

1. Who won the US Open in 1988 by beating Nick Faldo in a play-off?

2. **How many times did Curtis Strange win the US Open?**

3. When was Faldo ranked No. 1 in the world?

4. **What was his ranking in April 1998?**

5. How many times did Henry Cotton win the British Open?

6. **Who was the youngest US Open champion?**

7. Who was the oldest?

8. **Who won the US Open in 1964 accompanied by a doctor carrying ice packs over the last 18 holes?**

9. Why was he under doctor's orders?

10. **Who was the ultimate winner?**

11. An 'unknown' golfer won the 1998 Cannes Open. Who was he?

12. **How much was his prize?**

13. Which master golfer played in his youth with pebbles for balls and clubs made from wooden sticks?

14. **What was his first real club?**

15. Who finished the 1998 MCI Heritage Classic with a 12 over par 83, his worst ever round in America?

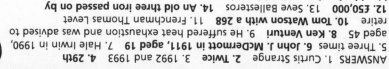

ANSWERS 1. Curtis Strange 2. **Twice** 3. 1992 and 1993 4. **29th** 5. Three times 6. **John J. McDermott in 1911, aged 19** 7. Hale Irwin in 1990, aged 45 8. **Ken Venturi** 9. He suffered heat exhaustion and was advised to retire 10. **Tom Watson with a 268** 11. Frenchman Thomas Levet 12. **£50,000** 13. Seve Ballesteros 14. **An old three iron passed on by his older brother** 15. Nick Faldo

# Quiz 07

## GOLF

1. Who described his green play thus: "I play like a motorbike – all putt-putt-putt"?

2. **Where is the Road Hole?**

3. Argentinian Roberto de Vicenzo tried for 19 years to win the Open. When did he finally triumph?

4. **How old was he?**

5. Who was runner-up?

6. **Who was the oldest player at 62 to complete four rounds at the 1998 Augusta National?**

7. Whose first job in the local steelworks paid £3 a week?

8. **Where is Bruce's Castle?**

9. Why were Tom Watson and Jack Nicklaus stranded on the beach during the nailbiting 1977 Turnberry Open?

10. **Which player described the Hazeltine National Course at Chaska, Minnesota, chosen for the 1970 US Open, as: "Needing 80 acres of corn plus a few cows. They ruined a good farm when they built this course"?**

11. Who won that year?

12. **What happened to the Hazeltine National Course?**

13. What happened to that outspoken player?

14. **Gary Player won how many major titles over three decades?**

15. Where and when were his first and last major tournament wins?

ANSWERS **1.** Roberto de Vicenzo (Argentina) **2. The 17th at St. Andrews 3.** In 1967 at Hoylake **4. Forty four 5.** Jack Nicklaus **6. Gary Player 7.** Tony Jacklin **8. The ninth at Turnberry 9.** Extra marshals were called for to clear the ninth tee of spectators **10. Dave Hill 11.** Tony Jacklin, with Hill runner-up **12. There were improvements and the layout was changed 13.** He was fined $150 for speaking out **14. Nine 15.** The Open at Muirfield in 1959 and the US Masters in 1978

# FIRST NAMES, NICKNAMES

# *Quiz* 01    FIRST NAMES, NICKNAMES

1. Who was Golden Boy, the youngest of two boxing brothers?

2. **A former England cricket captain was often referred to as Johnny Won't Hit Today after his initials. His name?**

3. Who was the Arsenal footballer with the initials D.C.S?

4. **Who was the original Brylcreem Boy of Test cricket?**

5. Who was the British middle distance runner of the 1950s and 1960s known as Puff Puff because of his breathing style?

6. **Who was the football legend with the Christian names Robert Frederick?**

7. Bobby Jones, golf immortal, had an endearing name for his trusty putter. What was it?

8. **Still on golf, who is known as The Golden Bear?**

9. And The Great White Shark?

10. **Who was the boxing champion known as Smokin' Joe?**

11. Who is Boyks?

12. **Who is footballer Stan the Man**

13. Whose initials P.B.H. are familiar to every cricket statistician?

14. **Who was the jockey known as The Head Waiter because of his spectacular late finishing technique?**

15. And who is the National Hunt jockey better known as Stormin' Norman?

# THE ULTIMATE SPORTS FACT AND QUIZ BOOK

## *Quiz* 02 — FIRST NAMES, NICKNAMES

1. Who was Gorgeous Gussie with the frilly knickers?

2. **H.W. Austin's name is in the tennis record books. What did the fans call him?**

3. Who was the world heavyweight champion known as The Manassa Mauler?

4. **And the giant man of the ring nicknamed The Ambling Alp?**

5. The Stroller played 12 times for Scotland before becoming a top line football club manager. Who is he?

6. **Which famous racehorse trainer is known as The Duke?**

7. Snooker's high-speed potter Alex Higgins had an apt nickname. What was it?

8. **Gilbert Jessop, regarded as England's fastest scoring batsman, was known by what nickname?**

9. Edson Arantes do Nascimento had a four-letter nickname from his schooldays. What was it?

10. **Name the cricketer whose dour batting and 'stickability' in a crisis earned him the nickname Barnacle?**

11. Jess Willard knocked out Jack Johnson in the 26th round of a scheduled 45 rounder. His nickname?

12. **William Ralph Dean was the idol of Goodison Park fans. What did they call him?**

13. Who was the brilliant Brazilian they called Little Bird?

14. **Who was the legendary world champion boxer nicknamed Homicide Hank?**

15. Who was the world light heavyweight champion from France known as Orchid Man?

# *Quiz* 03

## FIRST NAMES, NICKNAMES

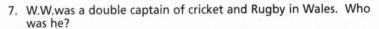

1. Centre forwards really earned their nicknames. What did they call Malcolm Macdonald?

2. **And who was the Lion of Vienna?**

3. P.F. Warner, later Sir Pelham, played 15 times for England and became President of the MCC. What was his nickname?

4. **What do the initials FIFA stand for?**

5. Who were the two forwards known as the SAS at Blackburn?

6. **The sayings of Shanks are written in soccer's history books. Who was he?**

7. W.W. was a double captain of cricket and Rugby in Wales. Who was he?

8. **Some say he was the greatest heavyweight of all, The Brown Bomber. What was his name?**

9. This sportsman must have been great with a nickname Peerless. What was his name?

10. **This man acclaimed 'I am the greatest'. Modesty was not his other name. Who was he?**

11. Rod Laver's nickname was an apt description of the way he played. What was it?

12. **Who was The Black Bradman?**

13. What do the initials of cricket's rule-makers MCC stand for?

14. **Who were The Busby Babes?**

15. Who was the Wimbledon champion known as Little Mo?

ANSWERS 1. Supermac  2. **Nat Lofthouse**  3. Plum  4. **Federation International de Football Association**  5. Sutton and Shearer  6. **Bill Shankly**  7. Wilfred Wooller  8. **Joe Louis**  9. Jim Driscoll  10. **Muhammad Ali**  11. Rocket  12. **George Headley (West Indies)**  13. Marylebone Cricket Club  14. **The young Manchester United side of the 1950s**  15. Maureen Connolly

# *Quiz* 04

## FIRST NAMES, NICKNAMES

1. What was the Rumble in the Jungle and where was it?

2. **What do football commentator John Motson's friends call him?**

3. Who was the famous sports commentator known as The Man They Can't Gag?

4. **Which of England's hard-working bowlers has the initials A.R.C?**

5. Who were the legendary Three W's of West Indies cricket?

6. **The Lion and The Tiger met twice in featherweight bouts in the early 1960s. Who were they?**

7. Which England batsman was known as Mr. Elegance?

8. **A. Breasley, the Australian jockey, believed in Santa Claus. He rode him to victory in the 1964 Derby. The Aussie was better known as what?**

9. Big Jack and his younger brother – he called him Our Kid – made World Cup history in 1966. Who are they?

10. **Who were known in cricket as the Middlesex Twins?**

11. He was Ancient Archie, a senior citizen among world boxing champions. Name him.

12. **G.S., I.M. and T.M. collected 165 caps altogether with Australia. What is the surname of these cricketers from the same cradle?**

13. Who is known as Queen of the Channel, the Surrey long distance swimmer who is still breaking records around the world?

14. **Deadly was the nickname of the bowler who took 297 Test wickets. What was his name?**

15. Which great Australian cricket all rounder is nicknamed Nugget.

# *Quiz* 05    FIRST NAMES, NICKNAMES

1. Scotland's footballers beat England 5-1 at Wembley on March 31, 1928, and were henceforth known as what?

2. **What were Scotland's forward line dubbed that day?**

3. Who was the Welsh flyweight known as The Ghost with the Hammer in his Hand?

4. **A football club manager known as The Doc once claimed that he'd had 'more clubs than Jack Nicklaus'. What's his name?**

5. Who is known as Beefy?

6. **B.J.T.B. are the initials of the cricketer who invented the googly, the off-break bowled with a leg break action. What was his name?**

7. What name did the Australians give to the googly?

8. **Who is the Flat race jockey described as The Choirboy?**

9. Which national side in Rugby Union is known as The Wallabies?

10. **Who in Rugby are called the Ba-Bas?**

11. The nom de plume Hotspur is used by a racing writer in which British daily newspaper?

12. **What was the nickname of James J. Braddock, who lost his world heavyweight title to Joe Louis?**

13. A cricketer with the first names of I.V.A. played 121 times for his country. Who is he?

14. **Who is El Tel?**

15. Who was known as The Wizard of Dribble?

# *Quiz* 06  FIRST NAMES, NICKNAMES

1. Which footballer was known as The Doog?

2. **Which football club has the nickname The Red Imps.**

3. And who are The Owls and The Blades?

4. **They were called The Dream Team at the Olympic Games in Barcelona. Who were they?**

5. These two Surrey cricketers with the initials E.A. and A.V. are lifelong associates! Their name?

6. **Who was the tennis player known as the Bounding Basque who was still appearing in the Wimbledon Championships in his seventies?**

7. Who played 761 League games for Port Vale and was called Mr. Loyalty by the club's fans?

8. **Who was the world middleweight boxing champion known in the United States as Man of Steel?**

9. Was Mysterious Billy Smith a champion of his sport in the 1890s as a boxer, jockey or discus thrower?

10. **What was the nickname of the French tennis star Rene Lacoste?**

11. Who was described as 'the Kevin Keegan of Rugby Union' by the Newcastle United chairman Sir John Hall?

12. **Who were the Rugby League team known as The Wires?**

13. What sport would you be playing in order to win a Brownlow Medal?

14. **What was snooker star Cliff Thorburn's nickname?**

15. Spell out the name of golfer J.M.O.

ANSWERS **1.** Derek Dougan **2. Lincoln City 3.** Sheffield Wednesday and Sheffield United **4. USA Basketball team 5.** Bedser twins **6. Jean Borotra 7.** Roy Sproson **8. Tony Zale 9.** World welterweight boxing champion **10. The Crocodile 11.** Rob Andrew **12. Warrington 13.** Australian Rules football **14. The Grinder 15.** Jose-Maria Olazabal

# *Quiz* 07

## FIRST NAMES, NICKNAMES

1. His initials are J.P.R. and for years he was the scourge of England's Rugby defences. What was his name?

2. **Which Colombian goalkeeper is known as El Loco?**

3. Who were the two West Indies players referred to in a song as 'those two little friends of mine'?

4. **Which US tennis player was known as Big Bill?**

5. Which over-blown American heavyweight, known as Two Ton was said to have 'trained' for a title fight on beer and cigars?

6. **Who was the tough little Scottish centre forward labelled Wee Hughie?**

7. Who was the British boxing promoter known as Harry the Hoarse?

8. **Name the England cricket captain with the full initials of A.P.F.C.**

9. Who was the often truculent tennis star known as Nasty?

10. **Who was the Winter Games gold medallist of 1998 better known to his fans as The Hermannator?**

11. The cry 'Come on Steve!' was heard for many years across the Epsom Downs on Derby Day. Who was it for?

12. **Who is known as The Prince of Trinidad by his island admirers?**

13. Who are the Pumas of Rugby Union?

14. **Name the American baseball ace with the nickname Yankee Clipper.**

15. Which British boxer was called The Dark Destroyer?

# Quiz 08

## FIRST NAMES, NICKNAMES

1. London football fans called him The Cat. His real name?

2. **Who was the England cricketer they called Gnome?**

3. The Peacock cuts a dashing figure on golf courses. Who is he?

4. **Equally popular on the world golf stage is Lee Trevino. What is his nickname?**

5. Name the famous English Rugby Union club known as The Tigers.

6. **Which Rugby Union international team are the All Blacks?**

7. Who was the great England batsman known as The Master?

8. **What was his second Christian name?**

9. Which Surrey and England cricketer was nicknamed The Colonel?

10. **What was Ricardo Gonzales nickname in tennis circles?**

11. What is the British skier E. Edwards better known as?

12. **Tabloid racing readers know him as Punters' Pal. Who is he?**

13. Which former England football skipper was called Captain Marvel?

14. **Which cricketer was called The Noob?**

15. Which of his title opponents did Muhammad Ali call The Rabbit?

# *Quiz* 09    FIRST NAMES, NICKNAMES

1. Z.Z. are the lazy initials of this international footballer. Who is he?

2. **They made a film about the famous world champion boxer Jake La Motta. How else was he known?**

3. Muhammad Ali was formerly Cassius M. Clay. What was his middle name?

4. **Carl Olson beat Randolph Turpin in a world middleweight title fight in New York in 1953. What was Olson's nickname?**

5. One of La Motta's world title victims was Pernell Whitaker. What was his nickname?

6. **What famous European soccer club is known as The Old Lady?**

7. Who is known as Mad Dog on the Grand Prix motor racing circuit?

8. **Who is the cricket commentator with the initials P.A?**

9. Who is the TV personality of the golf world with the same initials?

10. **The Bearded Wonder is just one statistic about this cricket broadcaster. He is?**

11. Who was the dreaded footballer with the nickname Chopper?

12. **Who was known in his pomp as Fiery Fred?**

13. And what was the nickname of the Australian leg-break bowler Bill O'Reilly?

14. **Who was the Louisville Lip?**

15. Many argue that The Black Pearl was the greatest footballer of all time. His name?

# Quiz 10     FIRST NAMES, NICKNAMES

1. Who was the old-time champion boxer known as Gentleman Jim?

2. **Who was the world heavyweight champion known as The Black Uhlan?**

3. Which tennis star was known as Superbrat?

4. **Curtly Ambrose has been called a few names in his time by battered English batsmen, but what is his nickname among Caribbean fans?**

5. What were the Christian names of Dr. W.G. Grace?

6. **Which Sussex and England wicketkeeper has the initials L.E.G?**

7. And what were the initials of the old England captain Wyatt of Warwickshire?

8. **Who is the flat racing jockey they call The Shoe?**

9. Who is the American jockey nicknamed The Kid who rode two Epsom Derby winners?

10. **Where would you go to find the Fremantle Doctor of cricket fame?**

11. Who is the former England batsman known as Lulu?

12. **Who is the Test cricketer with the illustrious Christian names of Nixon Alexei McNamara?**

13. Who is the football club chairman sometimes described unflatteringly as Deadly Doug?

14. **Rugby supporters in Scotland know the big international forward George Weir by what nickname?**

15. What is the slang term for an amateur jockey in horse racing?

ANSWERS 1. James J. Corbett **2. Max Schmeling** 3. John McEnroe **4. The Mighty Ambi** 5. William Gilbert **6. Leslie Ames** 7. R.E.S. **8. Willie Shoemaker** 9. Steve Cauthen **10. WACA ground at Perth, Australia – the wind that blows in from the sea** 11. David Gower **12. N.A.M. McLean of the West Indies** 13. Doug Ellis of Aston Villa **14. Doddie** 15. Pork Butcher

# *Quiz* 11

## FIRST NAMES, NICKNAMES

1. Who is the record breaking American sprinter of the 1990s with the nickname The Kansas Cannonball?

2. **Which organisation has the initials B.H.B?**

3. What was the Derby winner named after an Italian singer?

4. **What national football team is known as The Reggae Boyz?**

5. Which England footballer has the Christian name Sulzeer?

6. **Everyone knows that Peter B. Schmeichel is Manchester United's goalkeeper. But what does the B stand for?**

7. The great cricket writer and broadcaster E.W. Swanton is more familiarly known by what first name?

8. **The late lamented broadcasting personality Brian Johnston was better recognised by what nickname?**

9. Johnston had pet names for all his pressbox colleagues. So who is Blowers?

10. **Three darts scoring twenty, five and one is known as what?**

11. And at what point are you said to be in darts when needing one and double one to win?

12. **Which F1 champion was called The Professor?**

13. Which former county cricket captain has the Christian name initials A.C.D?

14. **Who was the cricketer P.G.H?**

15. Which darts player is known as The Cheeky Cockney?

# TENNIS

# *Quiz* 01

## TENNIS

1. Which two players competed in a 1969 Wimbledon match that went to 112 games and lasted five hours 12 minutes?

2. **Who was the winner?**

3. Who became the youngest men's Wimbledon singles champion in 1985?

4. **How old was he?**

5. Who did he beat in the final?

6. **Who initiated the Davis Cup?**

7. When?

8. **How many bottles of champagne will the Davis Cup trophy hold?**

9. How many teams entered for the first Davis Cup tournament?

10. **What was the result?**

11. Who was the first woman competitor at Wimbledon to play in a dress that was not ankle length?

12. **What constitutes the Grand Slam?**

13. Who was the first woman to win the Grand Slam?

14. **When?**

15. Who were the first brother and sister to win a mixed doubles Wimbledon championship in 1980?

ANSWERS **1.** Ricardo (Pancho) Gonzales and Charlie Pasarell **2. Gonzales 3. Boris Becker 4. 17 years 7 months 5.** Kevin Curran **6. Wealthy U.S. Harvard student Dwight Filley Davis 7.** 1900 **8. Thirty seven 9.** Two – USA and Britain **10. USA won 3-0 11.** American May Sutton **12. Four tournaments: Wimbledon, French, Australian and American Opens 13.** Maureen Connolly **14. 1953 15.** Tracey and John Austin

# THE ULTIMATE SPORTS FACT AND QUIZ BOOK

# *Quiz* 02 TENNIS

1. Who was the first black player to win Wimbledon?

2. **When?**

3. Who did he beat in the final?

4. **How many successive Wimbledon singles titles did Bjorn Borg win?**

5. Who did he beat to win his first Wimbledon title?

6. **What year was that?**

7. Who was Borg's unseeded 1977 Wimbledon final opponent?

8. **How many sets were played in that final?**

9. When did Martina Navratilova defect from the Czech team to America?

10. **How old was she at the time?**

11. When did she win her first Wimbledon singles title?

12. **Name her opponent in that final.**

13. How many previous matches had Navratilova lost to that opponent?

14. **How many Wimbledon singles titles did Navratilova win during her career?**

15. Whose record did she beat?

# *Quiz* 03

## TENNIS

1. Monica Seles was the youngest winner of a Grand Slam event since 1887. In what year did she achieve this feat?

2. **How old was she?**

3. Which Grand Slam tournament did she win?

4. **Who was Seles' opponent in the final?**

5. In what tournament was she stabbed by a spectator?

6. **How long was she out of competitive tennis?**

7. At Wimbledon in 1991, Martina Navratilova was beaten in the quarter-finals by a competitor 19 years her junior. Who was she?

8. **How old was her opponent?**

9. Who was the first ever player to be defaulted from a Grand Slam tournament?

10. **Which tournament was this?**

11. Who was his opponent?

12. **Why was he defaulted?**

13. In which set of their match did this happen?

14. **Which country defeated Britain in the 1992 Davis Cup?**

15. To which bottom group was Britain subsequently demoted?

# Quiz 04

## TENNIS

1. When did Andre Agassi win his first Wimbledon singles title?

2. **Who was his opponent in the Final?**

3. How many sets were played in that Final?

4. **Who was the 1971 Wimbledon women's singles champion of aboriginal origins?**

5. After marrying and then giving birth to a daughter, she came back to win a second Wimbledon title. In what year?

6. **Who won the US women's singles title in 1951 before she was 17?**

7. Between 1951 and 1954 how many Grand Slam events did she win?

8. **What ended her short career?**

9. Who at the age of fifteen in 1887 won the first of five Wimbledon titles?

10. **Who were known as the Australian 'boy wonders' in the 1950s?**

11. Who are the two American black sisters hoping for Grand Slam victories?

12. **Who is the only man to have won the Grand Slam twice?**

13. What was his nationality?

14. **Who knocked Tim Henman out of the Sydney Adidas International in 1998?**

15. The same player knocked out a famous American from the Australian Open nine days later. Who went home?

ANSWERS 1. 1992 2. **Goran Ivanisevic** 3. Five sets, resulting 6-7, 6-4, 6-4, 1-6, 6-4 4. **Evonne Goolagong** 5. 1980 6. **Maureen Connolly** 7. Ten 8. **Her leg was broken in a riding accident** 9. Charlotte Dod 10. **Len Hoad and Ken Rosewall** 11. Venus and Serena Williams 12. **Rod Laver** 13. Australian 14. **Karol Kucera** 15. Pete Sampras

# THE ULTIMATE SPORTS FACT AND QUIZ BOOK

## *Quiz* 05 — TENNIS

1. Who with a 5-1 lead in the final set of the 1993 women's Wimbledon final double faulted and lost the match?

2. **Who took the title?**

3. Who was the first Englishman to reach the Wimbledon quarter-finals in 1996 for 23 years?

4. **Who was the 1973 quarter-finalist?**

5. Who in 1997 became the youngest ever woman to achieve the Grand Slam?

6. **Who in January 1998 became the first player in 30 years to win three matches in the same Grand Slam tournament from being two sets down?**

7. Where was that tournament?

8. **Who won the Australian Open men's singles title in 1998?**

9. Who was his opponent in the final?

10. **Who was the youngest female player to successfully defend a Grand Slam title in 1998?**

11. Where was it played?

12. **Who did she beat in that final?**

13. How much did she win in retaining that title?

14. **Who was the last British woman to be ranked in the World top ten?**

15. What was her sporting job in the late 1990s?

# *Quiz* 06     **TENNIS**

1. Who said he would fly if he won his first Grand Slam title in Australia?

2. **What happened when he did win?**

3. What were his winnings?

4. **Which 17 year old American reached the 1998 US Open final?**

5. Who beat Martina Hingis to win the Pan Pacific title in Tokyo in February 1998?

6. **What was the winner's World ranking at that time?**

7. Which former tennis player invested £4 million in a Third Division football club?

8. **Which American started the 1998 New Year by beating his old rival Pete Sampras at the Sybuse Open in San Jose?**

9. How many sets did he drop in winning that tournament?

10. **Who did Agassi marry in 1997?**

11. For how many weeks did Steffi Graf hold her No. 1 World ranking before her serious knee injury in June 1997?

12. **Who took over her No. 1 spot?**

13. How much prize money did Martina Navratilova win during her career? To the nearest million!

14. **How many years did she compete on the tennis circuit?**

15. Who was the British men's No. 1 from 1946 to 1955?

# Quiz 07

## TENNIS

1. What was the Christian name of Tony Mottram's son Buster?

2. **Buster's mother was a British Wightman Cup player. What was her maiden name?**

3. Who was Britain's No. 1 at the start of 1998?

4. **Where was he born?**

5. Which title did he win in February 1998?

6. **Apart from the £100,000 prize money for this win, what was his other prize?**

7. Can he keep this award?

8. **Has anybody won one of these for keeps?**

9. Who rose to a No. 4 World ranking in February 1998 after winning the Guardian Direct Cup Final?

10. **What is his nationality?**

11. Who in March 1998 achieved his No. 1 World ranking for the 100th successive week?

12. **Who achieved 157 consecutive weeks as World No. 1 from September 1985 to September 1988?**

13. Who led the big servers' league in March 1998?

14. **What was his recorded speed?**

15. Where did he set the record?

ANSWERS **1.** Christopher **2. Joy Gannon 3.** Greg Rusedski **4. Canada 5.** ECC Championship **6. A £1 million diamond encrusted tennis racquet 7.** Not unless he achieves three victories in five years **8. Ivan Lendl 9.** Yevgeny Kafelnikov **10. Russian 11.** Pete Sampras **12. Ivan Lendl 13. Greg Rusedski 14. 149 mph 15.** The Champions Cup semi finals at Indian Wells

# Quiz 08    TENNIS

1. When Greg Rusedski set his 149 mph service record, what was his reward?

2. **Who was Andre Agassi praising when he said: "He has a lot of Stefan Edberg in his game. He's a joy to watch."?**

3. Who became the World No. 1 for the first time on March 30, 1998?

4. **In which country was he born?**

5. Who did he displace as No. 1?

6. **How long did he remain in the No. 1 spot?**

7. Who took over the No. 1 place from him?

8. **What was the margin of Britain's Davis Cup victory over the Ukraine in April 1998?**

9. How much was the Wimbledon men's singles championship prize in 1998?

10. **What did the 1998 first round losers take home?**

11. How many times did Roger Taylor reach the Wimbledon singles semi-finals?

12. **In which years?**

13. Who topped the World men's rankings for 160 weeks between 1974 and 1977?

14. **Who conquered a childhood illness to win the Wimbledon women's singles title in 1951?**

15. How many times did she win the US Open title?

# Quiz 09     TENNIS

1. Virginia Wade became Wimbledon singles champion in 1968 by beating whom in the final?

2. **Who won the triple crown – men's singles, doubles and mixed doubles – in his only Wimbledon appearance?**

3. In which year did he achieve this?

4. **Thirty four years later, the same man played singles against two women in the 'Battle of the Sexes'. Who were the two ladies?**

5. Who won those matches?

6. **Who was the first player to win the Grand Slam?**

7. In what year?

8. **Why did 'Gorgeous Gussie' Moran cause such a stir at the 1949 Wimbledon?**

9. When did the International Lawn Tennis Federation agree that tennis should become 'open', discarding amateur and professional labels?

10. **Who won the first Wimbledon Open singles title?**

11. Which British player won a hat-trick of Wimbledon singles titles in the 1930s?

12. **Who was the first Spanish woman to win a Wimbledon singles title?**

13. When was this?

14. **Who did she beat in the final?**

15. Which other Spanish competitor won the US Open in the same year?

ANSWERS 1. Billie-Jean King 2. **Bobby Riggs** 3. 1939 4. **Margaret Court and Billie-Jean King** 5. Riggs beat Court but lost to King 6. **Donald Budge** 7. 1938 8. **She wore frilly lace panties under a very short skirt** 9. 1968 10. **Rod Laver and Billie-Jean King** 11. Fred Perry 12. **Conchita Martinez** 13. 1994 14. **Martina Navratilova** 15. Sánchez Vicario

# *Quiz* 10     TENNIS

1. Who won the 1998 US Open singles title?

2. **How far did he progress in the 1998 Italian Open?**

3. Who was his opponent?

4. **Where was the venue for the US Open before Flushing Meadow?**

5. Who partnered Britain's Ann Jones in 1969 when she won the Wimbledon mixed doubles title?

6. **Who said on winning the 1998 Italian Open: "It was a beautiful day for tennis and the Lord just took over."?**

7. Who did he beat in straight sets?

8. **Who in 1989 became the youngest player to win a men's singles title in a Grand Slam event by winning the French Open?**

9. How old was he?

10. **Who was his opponent?**

11. Who was the previous American winner of the French Open?

12. **In what year?**

13. In 1989, the same year as Chang, a 17 year old from Spain also won the women's singles title in the French Open. Who was she?

14. **Who did she beat?**

15. Who at the age of 16 defeated Martina Hingis in the 1998 German Open?

ANSWERS **1.** Pat Rafter **2. He was eliminated in the first round 3.** Holland's Sjeng Schalken **4. Forest Hills 5.** Fred Stolle **6. Michael Chang 7.** Pete Sampras **8. Michael Chang 9.** Seventeen **10. Stefan Edberg 11.** Tony Trabert **12. 1955 13.** Arantxa Sanchez **14. Steffi Graf 15.** Anna Kournikova of Russia

# *Quiz* 11    TENNIS

1. Who was the first Englishman to reach the Wimbledon singles semi-finals since Roger Taylor in 1973?

2. **Who did he meet in the semi-final of 1998?**

3. What was the result?

4. **How many sets had Sampras lost during the tournament before that?**

5. Who was playing his third Wimbledon final against him?

6. **What was the result?**

7. Who did Andre Agassi beat in a five-sets final in 1992?

8. **Sampras equalled Bjorn Borg's five Wimbledon singles titles but why was Borg's achievement more astounding?**

9. Who became the first player to win the Wimbledon singles and doubles in the same year (1998) for ten years?

10. **Who performed the feat in 1988?**

11. Who was the losing finalist in the 1988 Wimbledon singles?

12. **Who was Novotna's doubles-winning partner at Wimbledon 1998?**

13. Who were Wimbledon men's doubles champions for five consecutive years leading up to the 1998 tournament?

14. **Who beat them in the 1998 men's doubles final?**

15. Who was the British women's No. 1 who reached the singles fourth round for the first time?

ANSWERS 1. Tim Henman   2. **Pete Sampras**   3. Sampras won in four sets
4. **None**   5. Goran Ivanisevic   6. **Sampras won in five sets**   7. Goran Ivanisevic
8. **Borg won in consecutive years**   9. Jana Novotna   10. **Steffi Graf**
11. Nathalie Tauziat   12. **Martina Hingis**   13. Mark Woodforde and
Todd Woodbridge   14. **Jacco Eltingh and Paul Haarhuis**   15. Sam Smith

# SNOOKER

# THE ULTIMATE SPORTS FACT AND QUIZ BOOK

## *Quiz 01*  SNOOKER

1. Who won the first World Snooker Championship?

2. **In what year?**

3. How long did he remain undefeated World champion?

4. **Who took the title from him?**

5. Who was the 1948 champion?

6. **What relation was Fred Davis to Joe Davis?**

7. Why did only two players enter the 1952 World Championship?

8. **Who were those two entrants?**

9. Who won and what was the score – 94-49, 55-49 or 36-35?

10. **Name the Irishman who won the World Championship in 1972.**

11. How many times had he already competed for the World title?

12. **How did he earn his nickname Hurricane?**

13. Who did he beat in that 1972 final?

14. **When was the Championship first contested over two weeks instead of a year?**

15. What is the maximum snooker break?

ANSWERS **1.** Joe Davis **2. 1927 3.** Until 1947 **4. Walter Donaldson
5.** Fred Davis **6. Younger brother 7.** There was a rift between the pros and the Billiards Association **8. Horace Lindrum and Clark McConachy
9.** Lindrum won 94-49 **10. Alex Higgins 11.** It was his first attempt
**12. He rushed through his game 13.** John Spencer **14. 1973 15.** 147

# *Quiz* 02    SNOOKER

1. How many World titles did Ray Reardon win?

2. **When did he win his last title?**

3. Who was his opponent in the final of the 1976 World Championships?

4. **When did the BBC's blanket television coverage of the World Championship start?**

5. Who in 1997 became president of the World Professional Billiards and Snooker Association?

6. **Who won the 1983 UK Championship?**

7. What was the final score?

8. **Who won the 1997 World Championship?**

9. Who did he beat in the final?

10. **How many World titles did Stephen Hendry hold in 1997?**

11. Who beat Hendry in the 1998 Benson & Hedges Masters at Wembley?

12. **What was the score?**

13. How was the final frame won?

14. **A week later that winning player lost in Aberdeen. Who beat him?**

15. What was his victor's World ranking at the time?

15. 90th
11. Mark Williams   12. 10-9   13. On a re-spotted black   14. Peter Lines
6. Alex Higgins   7. 16-15   8. Ken Doherty   9. Stephen Hendry   10. Six
ANSWERS 1. Six   2. 1978   3. Alex Higgins   4. 1978   5. Lord Archer

# *Quiz* 03    SNOOKER

1. Who won the World Professional Billiards Championship in 1980?

2. **How old was he?**

3. When did Steve Davis win his first World Snooker Championship?

4. **Who was his opponent in the Final?**

5. What was the score – 18-17, 18-15 or 18-12?

6. **How much did Davis win in that final – £5,000, £20,000 or £50,000?**

7. How many World Championships did Steve Davis win in his career?

8. **Who made the fastest ever maximum break in the 1997 World Championship?**

9. What was his time?

10. **Who became the youngest ever World Champion in 1990?**

11. Who did he beat in the final?

12. **How many World titles did Stephen Hendry win between 1990 and 1997?**

13. When did Terry Griffiths win his World Championship?

14. **Who did he play in the Final?**

15. When was drug testing first initiated by the WPBSA?

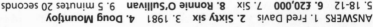

ANSWERS 1. Fred Davis  2. Sixty six  3. 1981  4. Doug Mountjoy
5. 18-12  6. £20,000  7. Six  8. Ronnie O'Sullivan  9. 5 minutes 20 seconds
10. Stephen Hendry  11. Jimmy White  12. Six  13. 1979
14. Dennis Taylor  15. 1985

# Quiz 04

## SNOOKER

1. Who won the 1998 Embassy World Championship?

2. **Who did he beat in the final?**

3. During the contest the record was broken for the most century breaks in a tournament. Who has previously held that record?

4. **What was the number of that previous record number of century breaks?**

5. What is the new record number of centuries?

6. **With whom did the new record holder share the prize for the highest break in the 1998 World Championship?**

7. What was the break?

8. **How many times has Jimmy White contested the World Championship?**

9. How many times has he won it?

10. **In how many finals has he been runner-up?**

11. How many times did White lose in the final to Stephen Hendry?

12. **Maria Catalano, a teenager on the women's circuit, is the cousin of which UK snooker champion?**

13. Which former Arsenal schoolboy footballer scored a record of two century breaks in his 1998 debut at The Crucible?

14. **Why did he end a promising football career?**

15. Who was the oldest competitor in the 1998 World Championship?

ANSWERS 1. John Higgins  2. **Defending champion Ken Doherty**  3. Stephen Hendry  4. **Twelve**  5. Fourteen  6. **Jimmy White**  7. 143  8. **Eighteen**  9. None  10. **Six**  11. Four times  12. **Ronnie O'Sullivan**  13. Alfie Burden  14. **He suffered a broken leg**  15. Steve Davis, aged 40

# Quiz 05 SNOOKER

1. Stephen Hendry went ahead of Steve Davis in the all-time ranking list in 1998 for winning the most titles. What was that record?

2. **Where was Davis' record broken?**

3. Who did Hendry beat to achieve that record?

4. **When was the first World Professional Billiards Tournament held?**

5. Who was the first champion?

6. **When was the first World Professional Snooker Championship held?**

7. Who was the winner?

8. **How many points is a cannon worth in billiards?**

9. Who is the snooker ladies' champion?

10. **Who described himself as 'the Jack Nicklaus of snooker'?**

11. Who was Stephen Hendry's 'idol turned rival'?

12. **Why did Welshman Mark Williams nickname Peter Ebdon 'Psycho'?**

13. Who made a billiards break of 4,137 in 175 minutes?

14. **What was his nationality?**

15. How much did Joe Davis pay for the cue which he used throughout his career?

15. 7s 6d (37p today's money)
shouted to spur himself on   13. Walter Lindrum   14. Australian
9. Alison Fisher   10. Steve Davis   11. Jimmy White   12. Because he
4. 1870   5. William Cook   6. 1927   7. Joe Davis   8. Two points
ANSWERS 1. Twenty nine   2. Thailand Masters in Bangkok   3. John Parrott

# BRITISH FOOTBALL

# Quiz 01

## BRITISH FOOTBALL

1. Which league club did England captain Billy Wright began his career at in 1941?

2. **How many times did Wright play for England?**

3. How many times did he captain his country?

4. **Which club did Wright manage after he retired from playing?**

5. Who from Theatreland was his wife?

6. **With which league club did England captain Stan Cullis begin his playing career between the two World Wars?**

7. How many times did he play for England, excluding wartime caps?

8. **With which club did he become secretary-manager after World War Two?**

9. How many times did that club win the FA Cup under his control?

10. **How many League Championships did they win under him?**

11. Which club did Cullis manage next?

12. **Which club finished runners-up in the First Division four times in the first six years after World War Two?**

13. Did they ever win the League Championship during that period?

14. **Who won the title twice during that period?**

15. Who won the FA Cup in 1939 and held it for seven years?

ANSWERS 1. Wolverhampton 2. 105 3. 90 4. Arsenal 5. Joy Beverley of The Beverley Sisters pop group 6. Wolverhampton again 7. Twelve 8. Wolverhampton 9. Twice 10. Three 11. Birmingham City 12. Manchester United 13. Once 14. Portsmouth 15. Portsmouth

# Quiz 02

## BRITISH FOOTBALL

1. Who were first champions of the Football League in the 1888-89 season?

2. **Who were first team to win the First Division title on its formation in 1892-93?**

3. Who were the champions five times in the next seven seasons?

4. **When was the start of the First Division as it is today?**

5. Who were the first champions of the new First Division?

6. **The Second Division in its original form began in what year?**

7. Who were the first champions in that season?

8. **Who won the old Second Division championship in its last season of 1991-92?**

9. Who were the last champions of the original First Division in its closing season of 1991-92?

10. **Who in 1996 won the FA Charity Shield for the third time in four seasons?**

11. Who were their beaten opponents?

12. **What was the score?**

13. Who skippered the winning side in that match?

14. **When was the first Charity Shield contested?**

15. Who were the winners on that occasion?

# *Quiz* 03

## BRITISH FOOTBALL

1. Which player holds the record for an unbroken run by taking part in the League in the first nine post-war seasons, 1946-55?

2. **How many matches did he play in that run?**

3. Including FA Cup appearances for his club during that spell, how many times was he ever-present?

4. **Did Rangers or Celtic win the Scottish FA Cup Final in 1997?**

5. Which teams contested that Final?

6. **What was the result?**

7. How many times have Kilmarnock won the Scottish FA Cup?

8. **Who beat Kilmarnock after a replay to win the Scottish Cup in 1957?**

9. Anyone over the age of 130 will remember vividly the first winners of the Scottish Cup in 1874! What was the team?

10. **Who won the Scottish Cup in three consecutive years from 1982-84?**

11. Did any of these matches go to extra time?

12. **Which club have won the Scottish Cup most times?**

13. How many times have they won it up to 1998?

14. **Rangers come second in the Cup winners' list with how many successes?**

15. The Welsh Cup was first competed for in 1878. Who were the winners?

ANSWERS 1. Harold Bell (Tranmere Rovers) 2. 401 3. 459 4. Neither 5. Falkirk and Kilmarnock 6. Kilmarnock won 1-0 7. Twice – in 1920 and 1929 8. Falkirk 9. Queen's Park 10. Aberdeen 11. All three 12. Celtic 13. Thirty 14. Twenty-seven 15. Wrexham

# Quiz 04

## BRITISH FOOTBALL

1. Which former player and manager was honoured in 1998 at Liverpool with a statue?

2. **Which club won the Charity Shield three times between 1988-90?**

3. One club won the Shield in four consecutive years before that. Can you name them?

4. **Which goalkeeper played in 394 successive Football League matches between 1981 and 1990?**

5. For how many clubs did he play during that period?

6. **Can you name them?**

7. Which Liverpool player made 366 consecutive First Division appearances from 1974-83?

8. **Who were the last club to win the League Championship the year after winning promotion?**

9. What years were those?

10. **Which England international player won eight Championship medals in three different countries?**

11. With which English club did he win two of those medals?

12. **With which non-English club did he win five of them?**

13. Those five successes were in 1990, 1991, 1993, 1994 and 1995. But what happened in 1992?

14. **With which club did he win that medal?**

15. Which England international player won Championship medals with Leeds and Blackburn in the 1990s?

# Quiz 05 BRITISH FOOTBALL

1. On April 27, 1974, the match between Manchester United and Manchester City was abandoned late in the second half. Why?

2. **How many minutes remained to be played?**

3. The score of United 0 City 1 was allowed to stand with what consequence?

4. **Who scored that single goal of that match?**

5. How long were Manchester United in the Second Division?

6. **In what position did Manchester United finish in their first season in the First Division (1975-76)?**

7. How many times between seasons 1972-73 and 1990-91 did Liverpool fail to finish in the top two in the old First Division?

8. **In which season was that?**

9. Who were champions in that season?

10. **How many times did Liverpool win the Championship during that 19-year period?**

11. The 1988-89 League Championship ended with two teams at the top on equal points. Who were they?

12. **Which team won the title on goal difference?**

13. Two players who each scored 21 goals for England later became a racehorse trainer and an owner respectively. Who were they?

14. **Jimmy Greaves played 57 times for England. How many goals did he score for them?**

15. Who scored 28 goals for England in only 23 games?

# Quiz 06

## BRITISH FOOTBALL

1. Which team failed to win an away League match the season after winning the Championship?

2. **In what year was that Championship won?**

3. The following season was the start of the FA Premier League. How many clubs played in that first season?

4. **Manchester United won the title by how many points?**

5. Who finished second on 74 points?

6. **When did the competition become known as the FA Carling Premiership?**

7. How many London clubs played in the first year of the Premier League?

8. **One of these was relegated. Who?**

9. Which was the London club that won promotion to keep the Capital's representation at six?

10. **Who was transferred by Nottingham Forest for £8.5 million in June 1995?**

11. Which club did he join?

12. **Who paid £7 million for him in May 1997?**

13. Who was the player involved in a record all-Scottish transfer deal of £4 million?

14. **Who were the clubs involved?**

15. Who sold Chris Waddle to Marseille in 1989?

# *Quiz* 07

## BRITISH FOOTBALL

1. Which Liverpool player was fined £2,000 for exceeding 45 disciplinary points during the 1995-96 season?

2. **Who in 1996 was fined £2,000 for refusing to leave the field when sent off in a reserve game?**

3. What post did he hold at the time with the club?

4. **Which player did UEFA fine £900 'for wearing a politically motivated under-shirt' during a Cup Winners' Cup tie?**

5. What was England's biggest win over Scotland?

6. **Where and when did that take place?**

7. What was Scotland's biggest win over England?

8. **Where and when was that?**

9. England's biggest win over Wales was at Cardiff in 1896. What was the score?

10. **How many times did Glenn Hoddle play for England?**

11. He won those caps while playing for Tottenham and which other club?

12. **Harry Hibbs kept goal for England 25 times. Who were his club?**

13. How many times did Kevin Keegan play for England?

14. **He won those caps when playing for three different clubs. Can you name them?**

15. Which Rangers player made 40 appearances for Scotland from 1957-63?

ANSWERS 1. Neil Ruddock  2. **Gordon Strachan (Coventry City)**  3. Assistant manager  4. **Robbie Fowler**  5. 9-3  6. **Wembley, April 1961**  7. 7-2  8. **Glasgow, March 1878**  9. 9-1  10. **Fifty-three**  11. Monaco  12. **Birmingham**  13. Sixty-three  14. Liverpool, SV Hamburg and Southampton  15. Eric Caldow

# *Quiz* 08

## BRITISH FOOTBALL

1. Which Italian club did Ian Rush join?

2. **Duncan Ferguson was with which club when he first played for Scotland?**

3. From which club did Aston Villa sign David Platt?

4. **From which country did Graeme Souness return to take over as Southampton's manager?**

5. Who succeeded Jack Charlton as manager of Sheffield Wednesday?

6. **For which club did Kevin Hector score seven goals in one game?**

7. What were Queens Park Rangers known as before their present name?

8. **Who are The Cobblers?**

9. Which former England goalkeeper was once manager of Barnet?

10. **From whom did Roy Hodgson take over as manager of Blackburn in 1997?**

11. Which Scottish League club plays at Cliftonhill Stadium?

12. **And where is Glebe Park home to?**

13. Which club qualified for European competition by winning the League of Wales Championship in 1997?

14. **England scored only one goal in Euro 92. Who scored?**

15. From which Brazilian club did Middlesbrough sign Juninho?

ANSWERS 1. Juventus  2. **Dundee United**  3. Crewe Alexandra
4. **Turkey**  5. Howard Wilkinson  6. **Derby County**  7. St. Jude's Institute
8. **Northampton Town**  9. Ray Clemence  10. **Ray Harford**
11. Albion Rovers  12. **Brechin City**  13. Barry Town  14. **David Platt**
15. São Paulo

# Quiz 09

## BRITISH FOOTBALL

1. Who is the youngest-ever player to represent Scotland in a full international?

2. **He joined which English League club straight from school?**

3. Which was Tommy Lawton's first professional club?

4. **How old was he when he first played for England?**

5. Who was the first Third Division player to be chosen for England?

6. **From which club did Tottenham sign Danny Blanchflower?**

7. Celtic were fined £100,000 in 1994 for poaching whose manager?

8. **Peter Shilton made his 1,000 League appearance when with which club?**

9. Which Manchester United player scored twice on his debut?

10. **He got those goals in a Coca-Cola Cup tie. Who were the opponents?**

11. Three days later, he made his League debut and scored again. Against which club?

12. **Who became the youngest player to appear for Wales in June 1998?**

13. Who were the opposition?

14. **He got his first cap at the age of 17 years 226 days. That was 66 days younger than the previous record holder. Who was that?**

15. Who made his League debut for Newcastle against QPR in 1985?

# Quiz 10    BRITISH FOOTBALL

1. From whom did Kevin Keegan take over as Fulham manager in May 1998?

2. **Who were the only team to beat Arsenal at home and away during the 1997-98 season?**

3. Who inflicted the worst defeat of the 1997-98 season on Arsenal and what was the score?

4. **Who finished as top scorer in the First Division in 1997-98?**

5. Only two teams in the Football League have been champions of every division. Can you name them?

6. **Which club holds the record of having been unbeaten through a single League season of 30 games?**

7. There were only five 'ever-present' players in the Premiership in the 1997-98 season. Name two of them.

8. **One other Premiership player was involved in every game, but he played substitute in one of them. Name him.**

9. Three players each scored 18 Premiership goals in the 1997-98 campaign. Can you name them?

10. **Who did Ron Atkinson replace as manager of Sheffield Wednesday?**

11. Which of the six seasons of the Premier League up to 1998 had the best results for average goals per game?

12. **Who was the Premiership club leading scorer in all first-class games in 1997-98?**

13. How many did he score?

14. **Which was the only Premiership club to receive just one red card in 1997-98?**

15. How many red cards were shown in the 1997-98 Premiership season – 68, 78 or 88?

ANSWERS **1.** Ray Wilkins **2. Liverpool 3.** Liverpool beat them 4-0
**4. Pierre Van Hooijdonk (Nottingham Forest) 5.** Burnley and Wolves
**6. Burnley 1920-21 7.** Per Frandsen (Bolton), Des Walker (Sheffield
Wednesday), Paul Jones (So'ton), Kevin Miller (Crystal Palace), Neil Sullivan
(Wimbledon) **8. Steve Carr (Spurs) 9.** Dion Dublin (Coventry), Michael
Owen (Liverpool), Chris Sutton (Blackburn) **10. David Pleat 11.** 1997-98
**12. Andy Cole 13.** Twenty-five **14. Manchester United 15.** 68

# Quiz 11

## BRITISH FOOTBALL

1. Who was the amateur signed by Leeds United at the age of 15 who went on to play for Wales at the age of 18 years 71 days?

2. **Which Italian clubs did he also play for?**

3. Who played 68 times for Wales between 1951 and 1966?

4. **Who is the most-capped Welsh footballer?**

5. Name the Welshman for whom Arsenal paid a record £14,500 in 1938.

6. **Name the Scotsman Derby County paid £15,000 for nine years later.**

7. Which Scottish club sold him?

8. **Which London League club were unbeaten at home in 59 consecutive games from 1964-67?**

9. How many times did Liverpool win the League Championship under Bob Paisley's management?

10. **Who are the only club to have won the League Championship, the League Cup and the European Cup in the same season?**

11. Which season was that?

12. **Who was their manager at the time?**

13. Who played 620 times for Tottenham in 16 years with the club?

14. **Which England player was sent off three times in 1997-98 when playing for his club?**

15. Who scored 25 years as a manager with eight League clubs in 1998?

ANSWERS 1. John Charles  2. **Juventus and Roma**  3. Ivor Allchurch
4. **Neville Southall**  5. Bryn Jones  6. **Billy Steel**  7. Morton  8. **Millwall**
9. Six  10. **Liverpool**  11. 1983-84  12. **Joe Fagan**  13. Gary Mabbutt
14. **David Batty**  15. Jim Smith (Derby)

# *Quiz* 12

## BRITISH FOOTBALL

1. Who was sent off from the substitutes' bench for arguing on the touchline with the referee and assistant over a penalty award in a Premiership match at Coventry?

2. **Who was the First Division defender who admitted a drugs misconduct charge at an FA hearing in 1998?**

3. Which club plays at Moss Rose?

4. **Who managed Sunderland when they beat Leeds in the 1973 FA Cup Final?**

5. Which team played in three consecutive FA Cup Finals at Wembley in the 1980s?

6. **In how many FA Cup Finals did Neville Southall keep goal for Everton?**

7. Who was voted PPA Young Player of the Year in 1992 and 1993?

8. **When did a crowd of 62,432 watch a match between two Second Division sides in 1998?**

9. What was the result?

10. **Who said: "I realise now that the important thing in a match is staying on the field"?**

11. Who was Bruce Rioch discussing when he spoke of one of his signings for Arsenal: "He doesn't have an O Level or an A Level, he has an honours degree in football intelligence"?

12. **From which Italian club did Arsenal sign that player?**

13. Which defender announced his retirement in 1998, having won 83 caps for the Republic of Ireland?

14. **Who set a Premiership record by scoring in seven consecutive matches?**

15. Aston Villa manager John Gregory's byword for success is KISS, which he constantly urges his players to keep doing. What does it stand for?

ANSWERS **1.** Tim Flowers (Blackburn) **2. Shane Nicholson (West Brom)**
**3.** Macclesfield **4. Bob Stokoe 5.** Everton **6. Four 7.** Ryan Giggs
**8. The Auto Windscreens Final, Bournemouth v Grimsby, at Wembley**
**9.** Grimsby won 2-1 after extra time **10. Vinnie Jones 11.** Dennis Bergkamp
**12. Inter Milan 13.** Paul McGrath **14. Mark Stein (Chelsea)**
**15.** 'Keep It Simple, Stupid!'

# *Quiz* 13     BRITISH FOOTBALL

1. Who was the voted Man of the Match after the Chelsea-Middlesbrough Coca-Cola Cup Final of 1998?

2. **Who in 1988 was fined £750 by the FA for dropping his shorts and 'mooning' during a testimonial match?**

3. Which was the first English club to achieve an FA Cup–League double this century?

4. **Which former member of the Arsenal 1971 Double-winning side said: "For me, that squad was as near perfection as you could get"?**

5. Who was the first black player to captain England?

6. **Where and when was that?**

7. Who in April 1998 along with her husband became the major shareholder at Norwich City?

8. **How many steps must the winners climb at Wembley to receive the Cup?**

9. To which club was Hope Powell appointed manager in April 1998?

10. **How many Barnsley players were sent off in their 3-2 defeat by Liverpool in March 1998?**

11. Who was the referee in that match who also walked off in the second half because of spectator trouble?

12. **Why have Leeds United players the highest regard for John Hackett?**

13. Who made his 600th League appearance in a Premiership match in March 1998?

14. **Who was manager Gordon Strachan describing: "The poor bloke looks more like he's made 6,000 appearances. I don't know how many times he's had his nose broken"?**

15. Who captained Newcastle when they last won the FA Cup?

# Quiz 14    BRITISH FOOTBALL

1. Who scored his 100th goal in League matches for his first club at the age of 20 years 9 months?

2. **He signed for which Italian club at the age of 21?**

3. He scored his 200th League goal at the age of 23 years 290 days. Who achieved a similar feat at exactly the same age to the day 30 years earlier?

4. **On behalf of which QPR player did Jamaica play in a testimonial match before going to the World Cup 1998?**

5. How many League Championships did Liverpool win with Kenny Dalglish as manager?

6. **Which English club was founded in 1862 and is the oldest League club in the world?**

7. How many original members of the Football League were there when it was formed in 1888?

8. **Who was the Portsmouth half-back who played 48 times for England?**

9. Who is the only player to have been on the winning side in the Finals of the World Cup, European Cup, FA Cup and League Championship?

10. **Who became the first American to play in a Wembley final?**

11. What was the occasion?

12. **What fines were imposed when a First Division match between Manchester United and Arsenal in 1990 dissolved into a brawl?**

13. Who scored the last-minute goal for Arsenal that won the FA Cup against Manchester United in 1979?

14. **Which three players were cleared of match-fixing charges in the 1990s?**

15. How many Scottish Cups and League Cups did Walter Smith win as manager of Rangers?

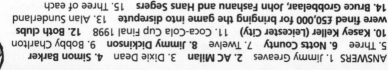

ANSWERS 1. Jimmy Greaves  2. AC Milan  3. Dixie Dean  4. Simon Barker  5. Three  6. Notts County  7. Twelve  8. Jimmy Dickinson  9. Bobby Charlton  10. Kasey Keller (Leicester City)  11. Coca-Cola Cup Final 1998  12. Both clubs were fined £50,000 for bringing the game into disrepute  13. Alan Sunderland  14. Bruce Grobbelaar, John Fashanu and Hans Segers  15. Three of each

# THE ULTIMATE SPORTS FACT AND QUIZ BOOK

# Quiz 15 — BRITISH FOOTBALL

1. For what Yugoslav team did Charlton goalkeeper Sasa Ilic play before moving to England?

2. **In which East Sussex town was he playing non-League football before signing for Charlton?**

3. Who is the Wolves striker who played for the Republic of Ireland in 1998 at the age of 17?

4. **Who was the England player Ron Atkinson was discussing when he said: "The only time he goes forward is to toss the coin"?**

5. Graeme Souness once said of a famous fellow-Scot: "I can think of only two who could go ahead of him – Pele and possibly Cruyff." Who was he praising?

6. **Who captained England, then managed Bolton and Leeds?**

7. Geoff Hurst played first-class cricket with which county?

8. **Who was England's first black international?**

9. Who was England's first captain under manager Terry Venables?

10. **A set of stamps issued in 1996 commemorated five British footballers. Who were they?**

11. Who was the 'baby' of England's 1966 World Cup squad?

12. **Bobby Robson and Alf Ramsey left the same League club to take over as England manager. Name the club.**

13. How many times has the English League-FA Cup Double been achieved in the 20th Century?

14. **Arsene Wenger achieved the Double for Arsenal after how many months as their manager?**

15. Which was the first English club to perform the Double in 1889?

# Quiz 16

## BRITISH FOOTBALL

1. In which two years did Manchester United achieve the Double?

2. **Name the Scot who has won medals for the Scottish Cup, League Championship, Coca-Cola Cup and European Champions League.**

3. Who scored Arsenal's goals when they beat Liverpool 2-1 in the 1971 FA Cup Final after extra time?

4. **Which former Liverpool and England star now suffers from Parkinson's Disease?**

5. Who was Arsenal's manager in their 1971 Double year?

6. **What was the score when Hearts met Rangers in the 1996 Scottish Cup Final?**

7. Who was the Charlton player who scored for both sides in the 1946 FA Cup Final?

8. **Charlton lost then but won the Cup the following year by a single goal. Who scored it?**

9. Name England's first black captain at Under-21 level.

10. **Who was the first black British international footballer?**

11. Which country did he play for and what year?

12. **Who said: "When the seagulls follow the trawler, it is because they think that sardines will be thrown into the sea"?**

13. Who told radio listeners just before the 1998 World Cup: "The spirit comes back. This physical body is just an overcoat"?

14. **Which soccer star was found guilty of dangerous driving when he wrote off his £103,000 Ferrari by hitting a motorway bridge?**

15. Who was the last player to score a hat-trick in the FA Cup Final and in which year?

# *Quiz* 17     BRITISH FOOTBALL

1. Who was the first player to complete 100 appearances for England?

2. **Who played 119 matches for Northern Ireland?**

3. How old was he when he retired at the end of the 1986 World Cup?

4. **Who were beaten 13-2 by Tottenham in an FA Cup fourth-round replay in 1960?**

5. Who did Newcastle beat 13-0 in a Division Two match in 1946?

6. **Who was voted Nationwide League Player of the Year 1998?**

7. Of the first ten teams promoted to the top division since the end-of-season play-offs system was introduced, how many have been relegated the following season?

8. **Who went out after four seasons in the top flight?**

9. Who were the two survivors by the end of season 1997-98?

10. **What is the middle name of Derby County's defender from Argentina, Horacio Carbonari?**

11. Which team went from the Fourth Division of the Football League to the First Division in four years?

12. **Which player suffered relegation from the Premiership with both Swindon Town and Manchester City?**

13. And which club did he play for when they missed out on Premiership promotion in the end-of-season play-offs?

14. **Who was Graeme Souness' last signing for Southampton?**

15. From which club was he signed and for what fee?

# FOOTBALL AROUND THE WORLD

# *Quiz* 01 FOOTBALL AROUND THE WORLD

1. When was the first Women's World Championship?

2. **Which nation hosted this Championship?**

3. Who beat Norway 2-1 in the 1991 Final?

4. **Which great Russian footballer played ice hockey for Moscow Dynamo?**

5. Which Italian club did Ruud Gullit leave on a free transfer to join Chelsea?

6. **When Gullit was voted World and European Footballer of the Year in 1987, to whom did he dedicate his European award?**

7. Where was Gullit born?

8. **Who won the CONCACAF Gold Cup tournament in the United States in 1998?**

9. Who beat Brazil 1-0 in that tournament?

10. **Brazil salvaged third place by a single-goal win over Jamaica in the play-off. Who scored the goal?**

11. Who were European Championship winners in 1996?

12. **How many times had they then won the title?**

13. Germany were losing 1-0 in the Wembley final until 20 minutes from time. Who then came on as substitute to make the score 1-1 after 90 minutes?

14. **Who scored Germany's winning goal in the fourth minute of extra time?**

15. Who was the leading scorer of Euro 96 with five goals?

# *Quiz* 02  FOOTBALL AROUND THE WORLD

1. Who made a record 103 appearances for West Germany?

2. **Who was Bayern Munich's captain in their European Cup-Winners' Cup triumph in 1967?**

3. Who were the beaten finalists that year?

4. **Which Argentinian made his international debut at the age of sixteen?**

5. Which Italian club did he lead in 1987 to a League and Cup double?

6. **Which Brazilian made his international debut at the age of sixteen?**

7. With which North American team did he play after his first 'retirement'?

8. **What government position was he given in 1994?**

9. Who was the Argentinian who played for Juventus and Napoli and was capped by both Argentina and Italy?

10. **Who once scored a hat-trick in the World Cup for Germany and was twice European Footballer of the Year?**

11. Who was the Uruguayan international who won three European Cup medals with Real Madrid?

12. **Which other nation did he play for in the World Cup?**

13. Which club plays at the Estadio Da Luz in Portugal?

14. **Where is the Ernst-Happel Stadium?**

15. Which team had Manchester United just beaten before the Munich air crash on their way home?

15. Red Star Belgrade
11. Jose Santamaria  12. **Spain**  13. Benfica  14. **Vienna**
**Minister for Sport**  9. Omar Sivori  10. **Karl-Heinz Rummenigge**
4. **Diego Maradona**  5. Napoli  6. **Pele**  7. New York Cosmos  8. **Brazil's**
ANSWERS 1. Franz Beckenbauer  2. **Beckenbauer**  3. Rangers

# Quiz 03  FOOTBALL AROUND THE WORLD

1. With which Japanese club did Gary Lineker end his playing career?

2. **Which Dutch club introduced the 'Total Football' system of play?**

3. What is the name of the national stadium in Mexico City?

4. **In which city is the Luzhniki Stadium?**

5. Who beat Arsenal in the 1994 Cup-Winners' Cup Final?

6. **Who was the president of FIFA for 24 years until 1998?**

7. Who was the Englishman from whom he took over the position 24 years earlier?

8. **In which country was the Portuguese star Eusebio born?**

9. Eusebio scored twice in Benfica's glorious 5-3 win in the European Cup Final of 1962. Who did they beat?

10. **How many times have Real Madrid won the European Cup?**

11. What is the name of their home ground?

12. **What is the name used when referring to the confederation of North and Central American countries?**

13. By what name was Manoel Francisco dos Santos better known?

14. **What was the cause of his premature death?**

15. How many times was Johan Cruyff voted European Footballer of the Year?

# *Quiz* 04  FOOTBALL AROUND THE WORLD

1. Who beat Sampdoria 1-0 in the European Cup final of 1992?

2. **Who was their manager for this victory and also for four of their Spanish League championships?**

3. Where was that 1992 European Cup triumph achieved?

4. **Who were hosts for the 1996 African Nations Cup?**

5. Who were the winners that year?

6. **Who won the European Cup in 1979 and 1980?**

7. What was the score in those finals against Malmo and Hamburg?

8. **Who is the former Brazilian star who as a scout discovered Ronaldo?**

9. Which was Ronaldo's first European club?

10. **He was then sold for £12.9 million. To whom?**

11. Who was the prolific German goalscorer who said: "There was no secret to my goals. Every time I played I thought I would score. It was instinct"?

12. **With which club did he win three European Cup medals?**

13. How many goals did he score for West Germany in 62 games?

14. **Which legendary player had spells late in his career with Los Angeles Aztecs, Fort Lauderdale Strikers and San Jose Earthquakes?**

15. Which former Derby County and Sheffield United forward steered Benfica to three Portuguese championships as their manager?

ANSWERS **1.** Barcelona **2. Johan Cruyff 3.** Wembley Stadium **4. South Africa 5.** South Africa **6. Nottingham Forest 7.** 1-0 both games **8. Jairzinho 9.** PSV Eindhoven **10. Barcelona 11.** Gerd Muller **12. Bayern Munich 13.** 68 **14. George Best 15.** Jimmy Hagan

# *Quiz* 05 FOOTBALL AROUND THE WORLD

1. Who was the Italian star banned from playing for two years for alleged involvement in a bribery case?

2. **Which club released him as a youngster and bought him back after he had starred at World Cup level?**

3. Who held England to a 0-0 draw then lost 6-0 five days later?

4. **Who hit them for six?**

5. Who is the English football official who was awarded the FIFA Order of Merit in 1998?

6. **"This is the greatest moment of my life," said an international after scoring the winning goal in a European Cup-Winners' Cup Final?**

7. Who were the losing side in that match?

8. **Who was voted Holland's Player of the Year for 1998?**

9. Who did Inter Milan beat in the 1998 UEFA Cup Final?

10. **Who was voted Player of the Match for that final?**

11. Name the manager of Atletico Madrid appointed in 1995 who amazingly held the post for three years.

12. **What is the name of the Spanish club's sack-'em-all president?**

13. Who was manager of Norwich when they won the UEFA Cup in 1993?

14. **Who did they beat in the Final?**

15. Who won the Italian League championship in 1998 for the first time in 40 years?

ANSWERS 1. Paolo Rossi   2. Juventus   3. Saudi Arabia   4. Norway
5. Sir Bert Millichip   6. Gianfranco Zola   7. VfB Stuttgart   8. Jaap Stam,
then with PSV Eindhoven   9. Lazio   10. Ronaldo   11. Raddy Antic
12. Jesus Gil   13. Mike Walker   14. Bayern Munich   15. Lazio

# Quiz 06 FOOTBALL AROUND THE WORLD

1. Who was named Republic of Ireland's International Player of the Year in 1997?

2. **Who was named their Young Player of the Year?**

3. Who won the Spanish League and Cup in 1998?

4. **It was the first time they had done the double in how many years?**

5. Name the striker who has won championship medals in Scotland, Denmark, Italy and Germany.

6. **His elder brother Michael was a member of whose World Club Cup winning team?**

7. Who was the Dutchman who won awards as FIFA, European and World Player of the Year while with Milan?

8. **With which club did he win the European Golden Boot?**

9. Who is the American who signed for English and Turkish clubs?

10. **Who was manager of Galatasaray when Friedel kept goal there?**

11. Who is the Nigerian forward who played in the Italian League after recovering from heart surgery?

12. **From which club did Lazio sign Marcelo Salas, the Chilean?**

13. Who won the vote as Jamaica's Sports Personality of the Year ahead of cricketer Courtney Walsh?

14. **What record did Blendi Nollbani set up when playing against England on April 26, 1989?**

15. Which country was he playing for?

# Quiz 07 FOOTBALL AROUND THE WORLD

1. Which was the first foreign side to beat England at Wembley?

2. **What year was that?**

3. What was the scoreline?

4. **Which Argentinian club plays at the Bombonera Stadium in Buenos Aires?**

5. When was the North American Soccer League founded – 1957, 1962 or 1967?

6. **Who played for New Zealand in their only World Cup finals appearance in 1982 and then won a West German Championship medal 11 years later?**

7. Which German team did he play for?

8. **Which player from Cameroon was voted African Footballer of the Year in 1976 and 1990?**

9. Who scored four goals for Real Madrid in the 1960 European Cup Final?

10. **Who were the opposition that day and what was Real Madrid's final winning score?**

11. Where was that game played?

12. **Who scored 83 goals for Hungary?**

13. Who was coach of Juventus when they won seven Italian League titles and two Italian Cups, in addition to many other cup triumphs?

14. **In which year did Ossie Ardiles earn a World Cup winners' medal?**

15. Name the Argentinian teammate of Ardiles who signed along with him for Tottenham.

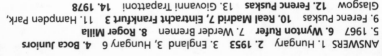

15. Ricardo Villa

Glasgow 12. Ferenc Puskas 13. Giovanni Trapattoni 14. 1978
9. Ferenc Puskas 10. Real Madrid 7, Eintracht Frankfurt 3 11. Hampden Park,
5. 1967 6. Wynton Rufer 7. Werder Bremen 8. Roger Milla
ANSWERS 1. Hungary 2. 1953 3. England 3, Hungary 6 4. Boca Juniors

# CRICKET

# Quiz 01        CRICKET

1. Who is coach of the South African Test team?

2. **Which English county did he play for?**

3. Did he ever score a century for England against Australia?

4. **If so, how many?**

5. Who were 1997 County Champions?

6. **Was this their first County Championship?**

7. What was the first county one-day knockout competition known as?

8. **Who were the first holders in 1963?**

9. Which was the only county to win the trophy three years running from 1970-72?

10. **Who became sponsors of the competition in 1981?**

11. The trophy was won that year for the only time by which county?

12. **Essex won the trophy in 1997 by nine wickets, against which county?**

13. Who was Essex captain on that occasion?

14. **What is the world's highest first-class individual score?**

15. Who was the batsman?

ANSWERS 1. Bob Woolmer  2. **Kent**  3. Yes  4. **Three**  5. Glamorgan
6. **No – they also won in 1969**  7. Gillette Cup  8. **Sussex**  9. Lancashire
10. **NatWest**  11. Derbyshire  12. **Warwickshire**  13. Paul Prichard
14. **501 not out**  15. Brian Lara

# Quiz 02 CRICKET

1. What is the highest ever individual Test score?

2. **Who was the batsman?**

3. Who was the previous record holder?

4. **What was his score?**

5. Who scored the highest ever Test innings for England?

6. **What was that score?**

7. Who were the opposition?

8. **On which ground was that score compiled?**

9. What was the highest first class innings total: 1107 or 1017?

10. **Which was the team amassing that score: Victoria or New South Wales?**

11. What was Don Bradman's highest individual score?

12. **The highest single innings total in a county match was 887 in a Yorkshire v Warwickshire match. Who made that score?**

13. The highest Test match innings total in Ashes series was 903-7 declared. Who were the country?

14. **Who were they playing?**

15. Was the match at The Oval or Lord's?

ANSWERS 1. 375 2. Brian Lara 3. Garry Sobers 4. 365 not out
5. Len Hutton 6. 364 7. Australia 8. The Oval 9. 1107 10. Victoria
11. 452 not out 12. Yorkshire 13. England 14. Australia 15. The Oval

# *Quiz* 03     CRICKET

1. Who holds the world record for the most first-class hundreds?

2. **How many centuries did he score?**

3. Which county did he play for?

4. **Which Yorkshireman scored the most centuries?**

5. Was that total 131, 141 or 151?

6. **Whose record did he beat?**

7. Which Middlesex player scored the highest number of centuries – Patsy Hendren or Denis Compton?

8. **Who scored most hundreds (167) whilst a Gloucestershire player?**

9. Who is the West Indies' scorer of most first-class centuries?

10. **Name the wicket-keeper with 102 centuries to his credit.**

11. Which county did he play for?

12. **Only one player has ever scored two innings of more than 400. Name him.**

13. He played for which Australian state?

14. **Which English county has a badge featuring six martlets?**

15. How many times have they been Sunday League champions?

ANSWERS 1. Jack Hobbs 2. **197** 3. Surrey 4. **Geoffrey Boycott** 5. 151
6. **Herbert Sutcliffe** 7. Patsy Hendren 8. **Walter Hammond** 9. Viv Richards
10. **Leslie Ames** 11. Kent 12. **Bill Ponsford** 13. Victoria 14. Sussex
15. Once

# Quiz 04

## CRICKET

1. How many times have Somerset won the County Championship?

2. **Have they ever been Sunday League champions?**

3. Which county's badge is a Tudor rose?

4. **Have they ever won the County Championship?**

5. How many times have they been Sunday League champions?

6. **Which county's badge portrays a running fox?**

7. How many times have they won the County Championship?

8. **Their 1998 vice-captain Chris Lewis has played for two other counties. Who are they?**

9. The record for the most runs in one day is 721. Which team did the deed?

10. **Who were the unfortunate fielding side?**

11. Where was that match played?

12. **What is Garry Sobers' middle name?**

13. Sobers played for the West Indies 93 times – or was it 103?

14. **Who was Sonny Ramadhin's spin-bowling partner against England in the 1950s?**

15. Who played 121 times for the West Indies?

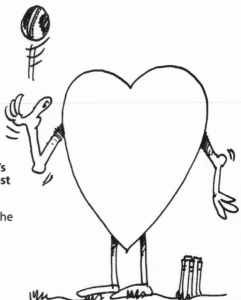

# Quiz 05 CRICKET

1. Which former fast bowler was given an MBE one month before his 90th birthday?

2. **Was he then the oldest living Test cricketer?**

3. Which England captain was born on April 1, 1957?

4. **How many Test caps did he win? Was it 97, 107 or 117?**

5. Who holds the record for the most Test appearances for England?

6. **How many times?**

7. Who holds the world record for most Test appearances?

8. **What is that record – 146 or 156 appearances?**

9. Who became the Bishop of Liverpool in 1975?

10. **Which county did he play for?**

11. Which cricket-mad billionaire received an honorary knighthood in 1986?

12. **Of which county was he President in 1996-97?**

13. When did he become a full knight as a naturalised British subject?

14. **Who is South Africa's leading Test wicket taker?**

15. Who was the off-spinner whose record he broke?

# *Quiz* 06  CRICKET

1. Who is the only player to have captained England more than 50 times?

2. **Who scored 1,294 first-class runs in June 1949?**

3. Who scored 3,816 first-class runs in one season?

4. **What year was it?**

5. Who finished second that year with 3,539 runs?

6. **The previous record of 3,518 was set by T.W. Hayward in 1906. Which county did he play for?**

7. Who holds the record for most sixes in a season?

8. **Was that in 1980, 1985 or 1990?**

9. Did he hit more or fewer than 80 sixes in that season?

10. **Who was the first player to score 36 off one six-ball over?**

11. With which English county was he playing at the time?

12. **Who was the unfortunate bowler and for which county?**

13. Six sixes in one over has since been achieved only once. Who was the batsman?

14. **Where and when was that?**

15. Those sixes were scored in the fastest double hundred innings on record. How many minutes did it take?

ANSWERS 1. Michael Atherton  2. **Len Hutton**  3. Denis Compton  4. 1947
5. **Bill Edrich**  6. **Surrey**  7. Ian Botham  8. **1985**  9. Exactly 80
10. **Garry Sobers**  11. Nottinghamshire  12. **Malcolm Nash (Glamorgan)**
13. Ravi Shastri  14. **Bombay, 1984-85**  15. 113 minutes

# *Quiz* 07 — CRICKET

1. The former West Indies captain Richie Richardson played for which English county?

2. **Umpire Dickie Bird played for two counties. Who were they?**

3. In how many Test matches did Dickie umpire?

4. **Who was the umpire with the previous highest Test duties totalling 48?**

5. England's lowest innings total against Australia in a home series was 52 in 1948. On which ground?

6. **Who played in 58 consecutive Tests for New Zealand?**

7. Who captained West Indies the most times?

8. **For which English county did he play?**

9. Who captained England 41 times?

10. **Who was the former England wicket-keeper found hanged at his home in January 1998?**

11. Worcestershire captain Tom Moody played for which other county?

12. **Nick Knight has played for two counties. Name them.**

13. Three Langridges have played for which county?

14. **Who took most wickets for England in a series against Australia?**

15. Who scored 974 runs in seven innings in a Test series against England?

ANSWERS 1. Yorkshire 2. Yorkshire and Leicestershire 3. Sixty six 4. Frank Chester 5. The Oval 6. John Reid 7. Clive Lloyd 8. Lancashire 9. Peter May 10. David Bairstow 11. Warwickshire 12. Essex and Warwickshire 13. Sussex 14. Jim Laker 15. Don Bradman

# *Quiz* 08    CRICKET

1. Ian Botham played for how many English counties?

2. **Name them.**

3. Botham also played first-class cricket for an Australian state. Which one?

4. **An Australian captain also played with Botham for that state. Who was he?**

5. How many Australian Test players were 1998 county captains?

6. **Who were they?**

7. Who is the umpire nicknamed 'Pasty'?

8. **With which county did he end his playing career?**

9. For which country did Martin Crowe play?

10. **He also played for which English county?**

11. Who made a maiden Test century for England in 1998?

12. **Which county does he captain?**

13. Who was top of England's Test bowling averages against the West Indies in the 1998 series?

14. **Who was top of the Test batting averages in that series?**

15. Who headed the West Indies bowling averages in that series?

ANSWERS 1. Three  2. Somerset, Worcestershire and Durham
3. Queensland  4. Allan Border  5. Two  6. David Boon (Durham) and
Tom Moody (Worcestershire)  7. M.J. Harris  8. Nottinghamshire
9. New Zealand  10. Somerset  11. Mark Ramprakash  12. Middlesex
13. Angus Fraser  14. **Mark Ramprakash**  15. Curtly Ambrose

# *Quiz* 09    CRICKET

1. Why was the First Test between England and the West Indies called off on the first day?

2. **How many England wickets had fallen by the time the match was abandoned?**

3. Where was that match?

4. **Who was the England coach on that tour?**

5. For which county did he play?

6. **Which South African played for Middlesex in 1997?**

7. Who had been Middlesex's original choice as overseas player that year?

8. **Why the substitution?**

9. Whose best bowling was 9-57 for England in 1994?

10. **Who were the opposition?**

11. Where was that Test played?

12. **Who was captain of England from 1986 to 1988?**

13. When did he give up the captaincy of Middlesex?

14. **Name the county cricketer whose father and brother played for England?**

15. Who was the Essex bowler to tour the West Indies with England in 1998?

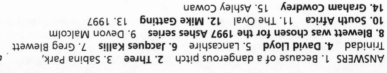

ANSWERS 1. Because of a dangerous pitch   2. **Three**   3. Sabina Park, Trinidad   4. **David Lloyd**   5. Lancashire   6. **Jacques Kallis**   7. Greg Blewett   8. **Blewett was chosen for the 1997 Ashes series**   9. Devon Malcolm   10. **South Africa**   11. The Oval   12. **Mike Gatting**   13. 1997   14. **Graham Cowdrey**   15. Ashley Cowan

# Quiz 10     CRICKET

1. Who was the only player to have scored two double hundreds in a match?

2. **For which county did he open the batting?**

3. Who scored most hundreds in a season?

4. **How many centuries did he score that season?**

5. Who is listed second for most hundreds iin a season?

6. **How many did he score?**

7. Who holds the individual record for scoring most runs in a day?

8. **For whom was he playing?**

9. Who succeeded Courtney Walsh as captain of the West Indies?

10. **Who was his vice-captain in the 1998 series with England?**

11. Who took eight for 38 in an England first innings in 1997?

12. **Where was that?**

13. Who was the England player to be given out 'handled the ball' in 1993?

14. **Who were England playing in that Test?**

15. Name the Middlesex bowler who took all ten wickets in an innings against Derbyshire in 1994.

ANSWERS 1. Arthur Fagg **2. Kent** 3. Denis Compton **4. Eighteen** 5. Jack Hobbs **6. Sixteen** 7. Brian Lara (390 not out) **8. Warwickshire** 9. Brian Lara **10. Carl Hooper** 11. Glenn McGrath **12. Lord's** 13. Graham Gooch **14. Australia** 15. Richard Johnson

# Quiz 11     CRICKET

1. Who in a 1996 match scored a century and took four wickets with consecutive balls for Hampshire?

2. **Which touring side were their opponents?**

3. Who once scored 499 in an innings?

4. **Whose innings of 452 not out was once a world record?**

5. Whose highest score is 405 not out?

6. **For whom was he playing when compiling that total?**

7. In which country was Usman Afzaal of Nottinghamshire born?

8. **In which country was Martin McCague of Kent born?**

9. Who was the Player of the Series for England against Australia in 1997?

10. **Who was the first Australian wicket-keeper to claim 100 victims in Tests against England?**

11. Which other Australian wicket-keeper has emulated that feat?

12. **Only one other wicket-keeper, an Englishman, has claimed 100 victims in Tests between England and Australia. Who is it?**

13. Who are the two brothers who play for Derbyshire and Essex?

14. **Where is the Queen's Park Oval?**

15. Where is Trust Bank Park?

ANSWERS 1. Kevan James 2. **India** 3. Hanif Mohammad 4. **Don Bradman** 5. Graeme Hick 6. **Worcestershire** 7. Pakistan 8. **Northern Ireland** 9. Graham Thorpe 10. **Rodney Marsh** 11. Ian Healy 12. **Alan Knott** 13. Adrian and Robert Rollins 14. **Port-of-Spain, Trinidad** 15. Hamilton, New Zealand

# Quiz 12     CRICKET

1. Who is the England player whose father played for the West Indies?

2. **Who is the England player whose grandfather played for the West Indies?**

3. Who took a record three hat-tricks during the summer of 1996?

4. **Which county was he playing for at the time?**

5. For which county did he first play?

6. **Who was presented with South Africa's highest sporting honour, the Gold Medal, in 1997?**

7. Who made the presentation?

8. **Who was voted 1997 Young Cricketer of the Year by both the cricket writers and his fellow professionals?**

9. Who won the gold medal award for Essex in the 1997 NatWest Trophy final?

10. **Where was he born?**

11. Who is the first Englishman to score a double century on his championship debut?

12. **Who is the youngest batsman to score a half century in the Sunday League?**

13. Who was the first batsman to score 100 hundreds in a career?

14. **Who is the only bowler to have taken all 10 wickets in an innings twice in the same season?**

15. His team-mate also took ten wickets in an innings in the same season. Who was he?

# *Quiz* 13          CRICKET

1. First-class umpire Trevor Jesty played for how many counties?

2. **Can you name them?**

3. Name the two brothers who have both umpired Test matches.

4. **Which county did they play for?**

5. Has either of them played for England?

6. **Who is the Test umpire known for his superstition about the 'Nelson' score of 111, 222, 333 and so on?**

7. How does he acknowledge those totals?

8. **Which county did he play his cricket with?**

9. Which England player in the 1998 series against South Africa is the son of an old Kent player?

10. **He once scored the fastest Sunday League century off how many balls?**

11. Who returned the best first-class bowling figures of 13 for 79 in 1997?

12. **Which county were the opposition?**

13. Which Welsh-born former opening batsman for England retired at the end of 1997 season?

14. **What job did he take up in cricket administration in 1998?**

15. How many times did he play for England?

ANSWERS 1. Three 2. Hampshire, Surrey, Lancashire 3. Ken and Roy Palmer
4. Somerset 5. Ken once 6. David Shepherd 7. Standing on one leg or
'skipping' until the score changes 8. Gloucestershire 9. Mark Ealham
10. Forty-four 11. Peter Martin for Lancashire 12. Middlesex
13. Hugh Morris 14. Technical director of the ECB 15. Three

# Quiz 14     CRICKET

1. Who topped the English first-class batting averages for 1997?

2. **Was his average over or below 70?**

3. Where was he born?

4. **Who is the youngest batsman ever to score 50 first-class centuries?**

5. Whose best bowling figures of 7 for 28 were earned in a 'Roses' match at Headingley in 1995?

6. **Who is the current county cricketer whose father played for Yorkshire and England?**

7. Name the current county cricketer who was born in Barbados and has played 17 times for England?

8. **Who once bowled an 18-ball over against Middlesex in 1982?**

9. Who has scored the most runs in the history of one-day Test matches?

10. **Is that total more or less than 8,000?**

11. Is his average for those runs more or less than 40?

12. **Who scored 1,000 runs in an English season in only seven innings?**

13. This equalled the record held by which other cricketing legend?

14. **Where in the Caribbean was B.C. Lara born?**

15. What does the second initial 'C' stand for?

ANSWERS 1. Graeme Hick (Worcestershire) 2. 69.27 3. Zimbabwe 4. Graeme Hick 5. Darren Gough 6. Ryan Sidebottom (Yorkshire) 7. Gladstone Small 8. Gladstone Small 9. Desmond Haynes 10. 8,648 11. 41.37 12. Brian Lara 13. Don Bradman 14. Port-of-Spain, Trinidad 15. Charles

# *Quiz* 15    CRICKET

1. Which current English first-class cricketer heads the list for most catches?

2. **Do those catches total more or less than 500?**

3. Who came next in that list of catchers with 417?

4. **Who headed the wicket-keepers' list of most catches before 1998?**

5. Do those catches total more or less than 900?

6. **Steve Rhodes is second in the list of stumpings up to the same deadline with 108. Who is above him?**

7. What was Graham Gooch's highest Test innings?

8. **Where and against whom was that innings?**

9. Which Test team were dismissed for 26 in a series played in 1954-55?

10. **Who were the opposition and where was the match played?**

11. Which Test team were twice dismissed for 30 in an innings in matches 28 years apart?

12. **Who were the opponents on those occasions?**

13. Who holds the Middlesex record for the highest individual innings in first-class games?

14. **What was his not-out score?**

15. Who were the opponents in that 1949 match?

# Quiz 16 CRICKET

1. Who took most wickets for Australia in the Ashes series of 1997 in England?

2. **How many wickets did he take?**

3. Who won the women's World Cup in December 1997?

4. **Who were the defending champions?**

5. Who beat England in the semi-finals?

6. **Who was England women's captain in the 1997 World Cup?**

7. Who scored the slowest double century in Test history during the 1980s?

8. **Who was he playing against?**

9. Was that double century scored in more or less than 12 hours?

10. **The slowest double century in Ashes matches between England and Australia was scored by which Australian?**

11. Did he occupy the crease more than ten hours?

12. **What should a new ball weigh?**

13. What width should the wickets be?

14. **What is the maximum length permitted for a cricket bat?**

15. What is the maximum width?

ANSWERS 1. Glenn McGrath 2. 36 3. Australia 4. England
5. New Zealand 6. Karen Smithies 7. D.S.B.P. Kuruppu (Sri Lanka)
8. New Zealand 9. 12hrs 57mins 10. Bobby Simpson 11. 10hrs 8mins
12. Between 5 1/2 and 5 3/4ozs 13. 9ins 14. 38ins 15. 4 1/4ins

# Quiz 17    CRICKET

1. Which England bowler took his 100th Test wicket against the West Indies in 1995?

2. **Whose wicket did he capture?**

3. Which counties has his brother Alastair played for?

4. **Graham Cowdrey shared a Kent record partnership for any wicket with whom in 1995?**

5. What was the stand worth?

6. **Against which county?**

7. Name the Kent player who held a World record eight catches in an innings and scored 113 not out against Middlesex at Lord's in 1991.

8. **How many times has he played for England?**

9. Which Glamorgan player was one of the five 1997 Wisden Cricketers of the Year?

10. **Who was the Northamptonshire player nicknamed 'Ollie'?**

11. How many Test caps did he win before his car accident?

12. **Brothers A. and G.W. Flower have both played for which Test country?**

13. Name another pair of brothers who have been capped for that country.

14. **How many times did Ian Botham play for England?**

15. Who has played most times for India with 131 appearances?

# WHO SAID THAT?

# Quiz 01 WHO SAID THAT?

1. Which learned old cricketer said: "I hate defensive strokes. You only get three of them"?

2. **Alan Shearer was praising which club: "They are a very good side with a very good manager and they deserved to win both"?**

3. Which former teammate said: "Gazza will always attract the headlines. It was the same for Alex Higgins, Jimmy White and Ian Botham. The public profess to love them but when things go wrong, they are dug up and slaughtered"?

4. **Which golfer uttered these words of wisdom: "I can't wait to wake up in the morning to hear what I have to say"?**

5. On signing for Arsenal, who said: "I could have gone to Inter Milan but I love it here – the club, the people and I love London"?

6. **On winning seven Olympic medals, who said: "They weighed a lot. It was hard to stand up straight wearing them all"?**

7. On being appointed Minister of Sport: "It's a bit like going to heaven without having to die first." Who was it?

8. **Whose glowing tribute is this: "Dennis Bergkamp is better than Ronaldo"?**

9. Whose thoughts on Michael Owen are these: "He's worlds apart from me at that age – I was a late developer. He has more talent but maybe I was a more natural goalscorer"?

10. **Which World Cup team coach said this of what makes a good footballer: "You have to have a lot of stamps in your passport to show you have travelled and played the game a lot"?**

# Quiz 02 WHO SAID THAT?

1. Which boxer after defeating Joe Frazier said: "It was next to death, the closest thing I know of to dying"?

2. **Aston Villa's Mark Bosnich was praising which fellow goalkeeper: "He is worth thirty points a season to his club"?**

3. Wicket-keeper Jack Russell was describing which overseas fast bowler: "Totally ruthless, but you couldn't meet a nicer bloke"?

4. **Which Wales and Swansea rugby player said of soccer: "I don't follow any football team but I liked David Beckham because I wanted to grow my hair like his"?**

5. Who did Middlesbrough's assistant manager have in mind when he said: "He's as good as Juninho"?

6. **Which American golf hero of the 1970s said: "Happiness is knowing that even your worst shot is still going to be pretty good."?**

7. Which fiery Yorkshire bowler said: "They set me up as an untameable Northern savage who ate broken glass and infant batsmen for breakfast"?

8. **Which England football manager said: "You never play as badly when you lose as people say. You never play as well when you win as people say"?**

9. Which National Hunt jockey on winning the Grand National said: "I rode this race for all the people in hospital. My winning shows that there is always hope, and all battles can be won"?

10. **Who was the Manchester United manager referring to when he said: "He is so mild-mannered when the volcano inside him isn't erupting"?**

# *Quiz* 03   WHO SAID THAT?

1. Which football manager upset female fans by saying: "Women should be in the kitchen, the discotheque and the boutique, but not in football"?

2. **After going through the card at an Ascot meeting, which jockey said: "I thought one day I might do it at a small meeting, but on such a competitive card is beyond me. God was on my side"?**

3. Which fellow snooker player was Bill Werbenuik describing: "He was the worst poker player you can possibly imagine. It was the closest I ever got to stealing"?

4. **Which prolific England goalscorer said: "It is easy to beat Brazil. Just stop them getting twenty yards from your goal"?**

5. Who was jockey Jimmy Lindley describing: "The Americans used to say that a cavalry officer would ride a horse until it dropped dead and then an Apache would come along and get it to go another twenty miles. That was the way he rode"?

6. **Who said of Paul Gascoigne: "He is accused of being arrogant, unable to cope with the Press and a boozer. Sounds like he's got a chance to me"?**

7. Who was Kris Akabusi describing after the 4 x 400 metres relay at the 1991 World Championships: "He may be World champion but he's only a kid when it comes to relay"?

8. **Which cricketer was Frances Edmonds, author and wife of Phil Edmonds, describing thus: "It's difficult to be more laid back without being actually comatose"?**

9. On being a substitute, which former World Footballer of the Year said: "At the moment I feel like a Ferrari being driven by a traffic warden"?

10. **Whose self-assessment was this: "Even as a young girl, I knew I was going to be the greatest tennis player in the World one day"?**

# *Quiz* 04    WHO SAID THAT?

1. Who after the Hillsborough tragedy said: "Football is irrelevant now. Nobody is even asking after the other scores"?

2. **Which horse was owner Richard Burridge describing after the 1989 Gold Cup victory: "The emotion that horse generates is unbelievable. We all love him dearly"?**

3. Which fellow golfer was American Ray Floyd describing: "What an unleashing of power. I watched him hit a few balls and went home with a bad back"?

4. **Whose game was Lee Trevino describing: "He hits the ball further than I go on my holidays"?**

5. Which former football manager said: "Trevor Brooking floats like a butterfly and stings like one too"?

6. **Who described a goal by Tony Yeboah as: "It was in the net in the time it takes a snowflake to melt on a hot stove"?**

7. Which Olympic ski-jumper said: "Everybody back home thinks I'm crazy. They're probably right"?

8. **Which commentator, describing Shergar's four-length Irish Derby win, said: "He's only in an exercise canter"?**

9. Who was an England striker describing when he said: "He has about as much personality as a tennis racket"?

10. **Who was boxer Billy Hardy praising when he said: "He's got a kick like a mule. He's certainly got something special in his hands"?**

# *Quiz 05*    WHO SAID THAT?

1. Which legendary footballer said: "A penalty is a cowardly way to score a goal"?

2. **Who said of Kevin Keegan: "He never stole the blackboard duster. If he hadn't taken up football, he'd have been a university intellect"?**

3. Who on winning the US Masters said: "Winning here will do a lot for the game of golf. It will draw people in who haven't even thought of playing. It will do a lot for the minorities"?

4. **Who after the death of Ayrton Senna at Imola in 1994 said: "If we start believing that motor racing isn't dangerous, then we are stupid. It is almost as if God has held His hand over Formula One. At Imola, He took it away"?**

5. Who on arriving in England to play for Chelsea said: "I didn't come here on holiday to enjoy myself. I came here to play and become a legend in London"?

6. **Which former England Test cricket captain said: "The cover drive is the most beautiful stroke in batsmanship. Does that throw any light on why I am a self-admitted lover of all things British and traditional"?**

7. Which Australian batsman said of Garry Sobers: "With his long grip of the bat, his high backlift and free scoring, Sobers consistently hits the ball harder than anyone I can remember"?

8. **Who is the former football manager who said of his chairman: "He was a multi-millionaire when I came back here. With all the players I bought, I tried to make him just an ordinary millionaire"?**

9. Who said of racing motor-cyclists: "While the necessity to ride as near to the limit as possible remains the same, you have to be a very special kind of lunatic to do so"?

10. **Which legendary black athlete said of the Olympic Games: "The road to the Olympics goes far beyond Lake Placid or Moscow, ancient Greece or Nazi Germany. It leads in the end to the best within us"?**

# Quiz 06  WHO SAID THAT?

1. Who on conceding a 2 1/2ft putt to Tony Jacklin at the 18th said: "I don't think you would have missed but in these circumstances, I would never give you the opportunity"?

2. **Who on winning the PGA Championship said: "The most pleasing thing of the day is to see Ernie Els in the runners-up spot"?**

3. Who was former boxing champion Barry McGuigan praising when he said: "By the end he was throwing combinations and pulling off moves some pros spend ten years trying to perfect and still fail"?

4. **Who after losing to Martina Navratilova said: "My legs were a bit rubbery. I tried to get my rhythm back but my feet were lazy. I just kept saying 'Feet get moving but they wouldn't listen'"?**

5. Which champion jumps jockey offered this advice to young jockeys: "Unless you love the game and horses, don't do it. You fall, get kicked and break bones"?

6. **Who on his return to the England cricket squad said: "You can't change your character but you can listen, learn and take a look at yourself. That's what I've been doing and I am a calmer, more relaxed and focused cricketer now"?**

7. Which soccer manager said on losing out in the play-offs of 1998: "It's my job to make sure we get to the Premiership in four years. We are a bit short of time but it will make it more fun"?

8. **Which World Player of the Year, looking to the 1998 World Cup squad, said: "I watched my first World Cup at home in Bento Ribeiro in 1982. I was five and I cried when Paolo Rossi knocked out Brazil with a hat-trick"?**

9. Stating his claim to be the next Ryder Cup captain, who said: "I want the job and would take it right now if it was offered to me"?

10. **Which former National Hunt champion jockey offered these words of wisdom: "A lot of horses don't fall so much as the jockeys on top wrestle them to the ground"?**

ANSWERS 1. Jack Nicklaus in 1969 when the Ryder Cup was shared 2. **Colin Montgomerie** 3. Daniel Day-Lewis's acting in The Boxer film after he had coached him 4. **Tracey Austin** 5. Jonjo O'Neill 6. **Dominic Cork** 7. Kevin Keegan (Fulham) 8. **Ronaldo** 9. Ian Woosnam 10. **John Francome**

# *Quiz* 07 — WHO SAID THAT?

1. Which former England manager said: "For me, young Michael Owen is the jewel in England's crown. He is as good now as Ronaldo was at eighteen"?

2. **Which cricket commentator described West Indian bowler Curtly Ambrose as "like an animated lamp-post"?**

3. Who said of England in 1988: "The first thing that went wrong was half-time. We could have done without that"?

4. **Who said of W.G. Grace: "I remember sitting on his knee with my sisters and pulling his beard"?**

5. Which Scottish footballer who played cricket three times for Scotland said: "If I thought I could have made the same amount of money playing cricket as I have in football, I would have done so"?

6. **Which ex-jockey gave said of women jockeys: "They crouch forward and don't slip the reins. If a horse makes a mistake, there is no give and they are pulled over his head"?**

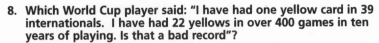

7. Which former German captain told his players: "If you weren't footballers, you would be tramps sleeping under a bridge"?

8. **Which World Cup player said: "I have had one yellow card in 39 internationals. I have had 22 yellows in over 400 games in ten years of playing. Is that a bad record"?**

9. Which cricket tourist described Chris Lewis as "definitely the best all-rounder in England – and has been for a few years now"?

10. **After shooting an 11-under-par round of 61 in the German Open, who seriously said: "I could have shot a 57 today"?**

# THE ULTIMATE SPORTS FACT AND QUIZ BOOK

# *Quiz* 08    WHO SAID THAT?

1. Who was the Raging Bull ex-boxer who said: "My third wife divorced me because the only thing I said to her was: 'Darling, your stockings are wrinkled'. How the hell did I know she wasn't wearing any"?

2. **Who said: "Arsenal are my club now. There is more potential here than any other club in Europe. I wouldn't leave for a million pounds a year"?**

3. Which other foreign striker with a London club said: "I am not leaving – they can't send me back. I have four years to run on my contract. They would need police help to remove me"?

4. **Discussing FIFA's decision to outlaw the tackle from behind in the World Cup, who said: "Tell Jack Charlton or Norman Hunter that you can't tackle properly from behind and win the ball"?**

5. Which Scottish golfer said: "You do get fed up answering questions about a Major. I am the highest-ranked player not to have won one. I'd like to get that monkey off my back"?

6. **Who was the England football manager who after a 2-2 home draw with Holland opened a news conference by singing Buddy Holly's hit: "Oh misery, misery, what's going to become of me"?**

7. Who was South African captain Hansie Cronje describing when he said: "He is the catalyst for the remainder of the field. If he has a good day, it lifts the whole team"?

8. **Which football club manager said about retirement: "Oh no, I'm far too young. I've still got a lot of trouble to cause yet"?**

9. Which Rugby League star has these ambitions: "To score more tries than Billy Boston, to win the lottery and to grow another inch so that I can dunk a basketball"?

10. **Which former pupil did the headmaster of Hawarden High School, have in mind: "We could see he was touched by greatness but he was never arrogant, never cocky"?**

ANSWERS **1.** Jake La Motta **2. Marc Overmars 3.** Gianfranco Zola of Chelsea **4. Bobby Robson 5.** Colin Montgomerie **6. Graham Taylor 7.** Jonty Rhodes **8. Alex Ferguson 9.** Martin Offiah **10. Michael Owen**

# THE ULTIMATE SPORTS FACT AND QUIZ BOOK

## *Quiz 09*  WHO SAID THAT?

1. Wimbledon boss Joe Kinnear said this about whom: "I'm not saying the old team were sterile but they did grind out results, where this lot just give you a headache from the start. An absolutely awesome side"?

2. **Which London Marathon winner said: "Wine is an important part of my life. I probably drink four bottles a week. I find it relaxes me and sets me up for a race"?**

3. Who said: "Jaap Stam is a great signing for Manchester United. He can win the Champions' League for Alex Ferguson. It is the Holy Grail for Alex and United"?

4. **After the First Test against West Indies in 1998 was called off because of the dangerous pitch, who said: "It was like a war zone out there"?**

5. Who led Scotland to a 1990 Rugby Grand Slam but said eight years later: "I'm not paying £30 to watch Scotland under-perform"?

6. **Who said of Liverpool's Tommy Smith: "He was never a young man. He was 18 years old when he was born"?**

7. Which ex-cricketer described the Cresta Run thus: "It is more terrifying than facing a rampant Curtly Ambrose, or facing Mike Gatting in the dressing room having run him out"?

8. **Which snooker champion said: "I used to be a nippy winger but decided my future lay in snooker when a great big full-back kicked me ten feet in the air"?**

9. Which Chelsea player said: "My reputation is affecting referees. Thank God we are playing abroad tonight where the refs don't know me"?

10. **Who on being appointed managing director of Birmingham City said: "Please don't call us Bummingham Titty"?**

# BOXING

# *Quiz* 01     **BOXING**

1. Who is the 'Golden Boy' who retained his WBA title in El Paso in June 1998?

2. **Who did he put down three times in one round before the contest was stopped?**

3. In which round was the bout stopped?

4. **This was the champion's 28th professional bout. How many has he lost?**

5. How many World titles has he won as a professional?

6. **Which former World champion said of him: "He is a combination of Sugar Ray Leonard and Tommy Hearns – even though he is perhaps not as good as either in his heyday"?**

7. Who retained his WBA featherweight crown on the same bill by stopping Genaro Rios in the eighth round?

8. **Who is the WBO champion that the WBA man wants to meet for a unification contest?**

9. What award did Lennox Lewis receive in the 1998 Queen's Birthday Honours?

10. **What boxing title did he hold at the time?**

11. With which national team did Lennox Lewis compete at the 1988 Olympic Games in Seoul?

12. **Did he win a medal in Seoul?**

13. Lewis says he is "so proud to be British". Where in Britain was he born?

14. **What is the accepted meaning of the expression 'The Real McCoy'?**

15. Where did the name come from?

**ANSWERS** 1. Oscar De La Hoya   2. **Patrick Charpentier (France)**   3. Third
4. **None**   5. Four   6. **Barry McGuigan**   7. Genaro Rios (Nicaragua)
8. **Prince Naseem Hamed (Britain)**   9. An MBE   10. **WBC heavyweight title**
11. Canada   12. **Gold**   13. East London   14. **A master of trickery and kidology**
15. After Kid McCoy, World welterweight champion at the turn of the Century

# *Quiz* 02     BOXING

1. Why did Kid McCoy powder his face white before the bout in which he won a World title?

2. **Anyone over 100 should be able to answer this! Who was the first British-born boxer to win the World heavyweight title?**

3. How old was he at the time – 24, 30 or 34?

4. **Who did he beat to win the title?**

5. Who retired as undefeated World heavyweight champion in 1956?

6. **From whom did he take the title?**

7. Who was the Englishman he fought in a title bout in 1955?

8. **What was the result of that contest?**

9. Name the British boxer with an unbeaten record after winning the WBO Inter-Continental cruiserweight championship in 1998.

10. **Which city does he come from?**

11. Who was Mike Tyson's first opponent following the former champion's release from jail?

12. **How many rounds did that fight last?**

13. What was the World champion's name before he became Muhammad Ali?

14. **Who was the Yorkshireman he beat in five rounds in 1976?**

15. Why did that contest take place in Munich?

ANSWERS 1. To 'convince' his opponent he was suffering from consumption!
2. **Bob Fitzsimmons** 3. 34 4. **James J. Corbett** 5. Rocky Marciano
6. **Jersey Joe Walcott** 7. Don Cockell 8. **Marciano won, the referee stopping the fight in the ninth round** 9. Kelly Oliver 10. Lincoln 11. Peter McNeeley
12. **Tyson won in 89 seconds** 13. Cassius Clay 14. **Richard Dunn**
15. The British Boxing Board would not sanction the contest in Britain

# *Quiz* 03     BOXING

1. What vacant title did Jon Jo Irwin win in May 1998?

2. **Who did he beat on points?**

3. Irwin won his first two title fights before losing the crown in 1996 to whom?

4. **Who took nine rounds to defeat Juan Carlos Gimenez in a WBO championship bout in Cardiff in April 1998?**

5. In which weight division did he win that title?

6. **Who held the World heavyweight title from 1899 until his retirement as undefeated champion in 1905?**

7. He returned to the ring for a World title fight five years later to challenge whom?

8. **The referee stopped the fight in the champion's favour in which round?**

9. Who was the champion famed for his 'bolo punch'?

10. **What was his nationality?**

11. How did he develop the bolo?

12. **Name the heavyweight who has held the British, European, Commonwealth and Australian titles?**

13. Where was he born?

14. **He went the distance twice with which World champion?**

15. He also held another American holder of the World crown to a points decision. Who was that?

ANSWERS **1.** British Featherweight **2. Esham Pickering 3.** Colin McMillan **4. Joe Calzaghe 5.** Super-middleweight **6. James J. Jeffries 7.** Jack Johnson **8. Fifteenth 9.** Kid Gavilan **10. Cuban 11.** He acquired it from working in the sugar cane fields **12. Joe Bugner 13.** Hungary **14. Muhammad Ali 15.** Joe Frazier

# *Quiz* 04　　BOXING

1. Who did Brian London challenge for the World heavyweight title in 1959?

2. **How many rounds did London last – one, seven or eleven?**

3. Brian London again fought for the World title seven years later in London. Who was his opponent?

4. **How many rounds did he last this time – three, six or nine?**

5. Who was paid to be 'knocked out' by a pizza in a TV commercial?

6. **Who won the WBC super-middleweight title in March 1998?**

7. Who did he beat for the title?

8. **Where in Britain did that contest take place?**

9. Who was the referee who said: "Chris Eubank is too brave for his own good. It brings tears to my eyes to see him like that. Someonne should try to persuade him to pack it in"?

10. **Who was Eubank's opponent in that bout in April 1998?**

11. At what weight was that boxer defending his WBO title?

12. **Francis was the referee in September 1991 when Eubank fought whom?**

13. Herbie Hide beat Damon Reed of Kansas in how many rounds in a Manchester title fight?

14. **What championship was at stake?**

15. The bout ended in how many seconds – 52, 102 or 152?

# THE ULTIMATE SPORTS FACT AND QUIZ BOOK

# Quiz 05    BOXING

1. Mike Tyson made a meal out of whose ear?

2. **What was the Year of the Ear?**

3. Which boxing authority revoked Tyson's licence after the incident?

4. **In which American venue did the ear-munching take place?**

5. Evander Holyfield was prepared to defend two titles against Henry Akinwande in June 1998. What are they?

6. **Why was their fight called off at the last moment?**

7. Which heavyweight title did Lennox Lewis possess at the time?

8. **Who was the former London barrow-boy who won the World flyweight championship?**

9. What nationality was the previous champion, Rinty Monaghan?

10. **Two Scots held the flyweight title before Monaghan. Can you name them?**

11. Which Scot held the World flyweight title in the 1960s?

12. **The light-middleweight division was created in 1962. What is the weight limit?**

13. Who was the British holder of the World light-middleweight title in 1979 and 1980?

14. **Which twins, born in London in 1934, both became boxers?**

15. Henry Cooper won two ABA titles before turning professional. At what weight did he win those championships?

# THE ULTIMATE SPORTS FACT AND QUIZ BOOK

# Quiz 06 BOXING

1. Who is the only boxer to have won three Lonsdale Belts outright?

2. **How many times did he fight for the World heavyweight title?**

3. What was the result of the London fight with Muhammad Ali?

4. **The referee stopped that bout in which round?**

5. Terry Downes challenged for world titles at two weights. What were they?

6. **At which weight did he win the World crown in 1961 in London?**

7. He fought the same American opponent three times for that title. What was the final 'score'?

8. **Downes challenged for the World light-heavyweight title in 1964 in Manchester. Who beat him?**

9. John Conteh fought four times for the WBC light-heavyweight title between 1974 and 1977. How many of these did he win?

10. **How did he lose the title?**

11. A year later in Belgrade, he challenged the new champion Mate Parlov. What happened?

12. **The next two years, Conteh fought Matthew Saad Muhammad (formerly Matt Franklin) twice for the title. What happened?**

13. Who failed to regain his WBO super-middleweight crown in October 1997?

14. **Who when urged to retire said: "A winner never quits and a quitter never wins"?**

15. Why was Henry Akinwande disqualified against Lennox Lewis in a WBC title fight in July 1997?

# Quiz 07

## BOXING

1. Who is the Coventry super-featherweight who won the WBO Inter-Continental title?

2. **Who was his trainer, a former British flyweight champion?**

3. Who was America's only Olympic champion at Barcelona in 1992?

4. **Which British heavyweight owes his first name to the fact that his father was a big football fan?**

5. Who did he beat in 1998 in a British title eliminator?

6. **Which unbeaten American light-middleweight was jailed for 15 years for rape?**

7. Who won the Olympic heavyweight championship in 1972, 1976 and 1980?

8. **What was his nationality?**

9. Who was the Olympic heavyweight gold medallist in Tokyo in 1964?

10. **And who won it in 1968 in Mexico?**

11. Two American brothers won gold medals at different weights in Montreal in 1976. Who were they?

12. **Which former stable lad became a champion boxer?**

13. What title did he win?

14. **Against whom did he retain his title on split points?**

15. Name the boxing promoter who said: "I watch any sport. I love sport. I even like synchronised swimming!"

# *Quiz* 08    BOXING

1. Name the former British and World champion who used to enter the ring to the accompaniment of The Beatles' song: "When I'm 64"?

2. **Who was the only boxer to beat Gary Mason in his 36-fight career?**

3. Mason was stopped in which round in that Wembley fight?

4. **Who said: "Oscar De La Hoya is one of boxing's great showmen. Bringing him and Naseem Hamed together is a mouthwatering prospect"?**

5. Dean Pithie's greatest claim to fame as an amateur boxer was the defeat of whom?

6. **Muhammad Ali had 61 professional bouts. How many did he lose?**

7. Why was he lost to boxing for three years?

8. **Who did he beat in the 'Rumble in the Jungle' in Zaire in 1974?**

9. Who did Prince Naseem Hamed beat to win the WBO World featherweight title?

10. **What year was that?**

11. Name the Irishman who won the World featherweight title in 1985.

12. **Who did he beat?**

13. Was the champion from Panama was making his 12th or 15th or 20th defence of his title?

14. **Where in London did the fight take place?**

15. Which famous ex-boxer is cousin of the super-middleweights Paul and Michael Bowen?

ANSWERS 1. Dennis Andries  2. Lennox Lewis  3. Seventh  4. Frank Warren  5. Prince Naseem Hamed  6. Five  7. He refused to serve in Vietnam on religious grounds  8. George Foreman  9. Steve Robinson  10. 1995  11. Barry McGuigan  12. Eusebio Pedroza  13. 20th  14. Loftus Road (QPR ground)  15. Nigel Benn

# Quiz 09

## BOXING

1. Who is the first woman to be granted a manager's licence by the British Boxing Board of Control?

2. **Which woman boxer won the right for a fighter's licence after appealing to an industrial tribunal against a BBB of C decision?**

3. Who forced Naseem Hamed to take three counts in a WBO World featherweight bout in December 1997?

4. **Naseem finally won that contest in which round?**

5. Where was that contest staged?

6. **Who was the British boxer who backed himself at 5-1 to win $25,000 in a title bout in America in 1986?**

7. Who was the defending champion?

8. **What was the title?**

9. The challenger won to upset the odds in how many rounds?

10. **Who won the World middleweight title from Sugar Ray Robinson at Earls Court in 1951?**

11. How long did he retain the title?

12. **Who took the title from him?**

13. In which round?

14. **What happened to the victor 15 years later?**

15. Who was the ABA heavyweight champion in 1980 who went on to fight World titles?

ANSWERS 1. Tania Follett  2. **Jane Couch**  3. Kevin Kelly (New York)
4. **Fifth round**  5. Madison Square Garden  6. **Lloyd Honeyghan**
7. Don Curry  8. **Undisputed Welterweight Championship of the World**
9. Six  10. **Randolph Turpin**  11. Sixty-four days  12. **Sugar Ray Robinson**
13. Tenth  14. **He committed suicide**  15. Frank Bruno

# THE ULTIMATE SPORTS FACT AND QUIZ BOOK

# *Quiz* 10

## BOXING

1. Who was the youngest heavyweight champion of the World?

2. **Who did he beat in 1986 to win the WBC title?**

3. How old was the new champion?

4. **Four months later he won the WBA belt by beating whom?**

5. Five months later he completed the treble by winning the IBF title. Who was his victim this time?

6. **In which round did the referee rescue Bruno from Tyson this second time?**

7. Gene Tunney lost only one pro fight. Who beat him?

8. **What title was at stake in that fight?**

9. Which British boxer met Mike Tyson in the open air at Las Vegas in 1989?

10. **In which round was the challenger halted?**

11. Who met Lennox Lewis in 1993 in his first defence of the WBC heavyweight title he won outside the ring?

12. **Who won that bout on points?**

13. Who was Lewis' second challenger for his title?

14. **In which round was the challenger halted?**

15. Who did Mike Tyson challenge for his WBC title in Las Vegas in 1996?

# THE ULTIMATE SPORTS FACT AND QUIZ BOOK

# *Quiz* 11    BOXING

1. Who beat Jack Dempsey twice in World heavyweight title contests?

2. **Nigel Benn and Chris Eubank contested the World super-middleweight contest in Manchester in 1993. What was it billed as?**

3. What title did Eubank hold at the time?

4. **And what title was Benn defending?**

5. What was the verdict?

6. **Who in that fight was penalised a point for a succession of low blows?**

7. Who won the WBA heavyweight title from Evander Holyfield in 1992?

8. **Who won the WBA title from Riddick Bowe in 1993?**

9. What caused a temporary interruption during that contest?

10. **Who died from brain injuries after losing his British super-bantamweight title in 1994?**

11. Who did Frank Bruno outpoint at Wembley to win the WBC World title in 1995?

12. **From whom had McCall won the crown the previous year?**

13. Who in 1995 was the first boxer to beat Chris Eubank?

14. **What title was at stake?**

15. What happened in their second meeting that year in Cork?

ANSWERS 1. Gene Tunney 2. **'Judgment Day'** 3. WBO 4. **WBC** 5. Draw 6. **Nigel Benn** 7. Riddick Bowe 8. **Evander Holyfield** 9. A parachutist landed in the ring 10. **Bradley Stone** 11. Oliver McCall 12. **Lennox Lewis** 13. Steve Collins 14. **WBO super-middleweight championship** 15. Collins won on a split decision

# OLYMPIC GAMES

# *Quiz* 01 OLYMPIC GAMES

1. Why did the crowd sing "When Irish Eyes Are Smiling" at Melbourne in 1956?

2. **Which British swimmer won gold after training in America for the 1976 Games?**

3. In 1984, who equalled Jesse Owens' achievement of 1936 with four gold medals in the 100 and 200 metres, long jump and relay?

4. **Which British team won the first Olympics hockey game in 1908?**

5. Who performed floor exercises to the 'Mexican Hat Dance' in Mexico in 1968?

6. **In what year was women's judo added to the official Olympic programme?**

7. In Seoul in 1988, which athlete gained the most attention, but for all the wrong reasons?

8. **Why was the gold medal, won by shooter Xu Haifeng at Los Angeles in 1984, so significant for China?**

9. Which was the first equestrian event to be included in the Games?

10. **Who was the first Olympian to swim the English Channel?**

11. For what was swimmer and medallist Johnny Weissmuller also famous?

12. **In what event in 1948 did Sri Lanka win their first-ever Olympic medal?**

13. What were the three demonstration sports introduced at Seoul in 1988?

14. **In what year did archery and men's handball return to the Olympic programme?**

15. Who were the surprise bronze medallists in the soccer competition at Mexico City in 1968?

ANSWERS **1.** Ron Delaney (Ireland) won the 1500 metres **2. David Wilkie 3.** Carl Lewis (USA) **4. Scotland beat Germany 4-0 5.** Vera Caslavska, who won four golds **6.** 1992 **7.** Ben Johnson, disqualified for failing a drugs test **8. It was China's first-ever Olympic title 9.** Showjumping **10. Edward Temme (GB) 11.** He played Tarzan in films **12. Silver in the 400 metres hurdles 13.** Baseball, taekwondo and women's judo **14.** 1972 **15.** Japan

# *Quiz* 02    OLYMPIC GAMES

1. How many rings make up the Olympic logo?

2. **Who was the first-ever female Olympic champion?**

3. When was table tennis made an Olympic sport?

4. **When was the only occasion that cricket was played at the Games?**

5. Who were the finalists?

6. **How did Lia Manoliu, an athlete from Romania, find her way into the history books?**

7. Why did the spectators jeer as Frank Shorter (USA) won the 1972 Munich Marathon?

8. **At the 1964 Tokyo Games, why did the band play the Japanese national anthem to honour Abebe Bikila, the Ethiopian Marathon winner?**

9. What in sailing is a 'Tornado'?

10. **Who holds the record for winning seven golds?**

11. Where and when was that?

12. **When was the first dead-heat in Games swimming?**

13. For how many years was the tug-of-war part of the Olympics?

14. **Who became the first competitor in Olympic history to win medals at a summer and winter Games in the same year (1988)?**

15. What did she win?

# THE ULTIMATE SPORTS FACT AND QUIZ BOOK

## *Quiz* 03  OLYMPIC GAMES

1. Which 800 metres gold medallist in 1972 always wore an old golf cap while he ran?

2. **In 1988, how many gold medals did Kristin Otto (GDR) win?**

3. Did any other competitor better this achievement at Seoul in 1988?

4. **Which sport was she famous for?**

5. Which horse became a household name in 1952 and was even rumoured to be able to write his own name?

6. **Who rode him to victory in the showjumping?**

7. In 1972, which female gymnast captivated the world?

8. **Can you recall the gymnast who scored the first-ever maximum ten points at Montreal in 1976?**

9. Was she then aged 14, 16 for 18?

10. **What is team handball?**

11. How is a goal scored?

12. **What are 'tatamis'?**

13. Who won the men's 10,000 metres in 1992?

14. **Was he from Morocco, Kenya or Ethiopia?**

15. How many runners take part in the final of the men's 10,000 metres?

ANSWERS 1. David Wottle (USA) 2. **Six** 3. She was the most successful 4. **Swimming** 5. Foxhunter 6. **Harry Llewellyn** 7. Olga Korbut 8. **Nadia Comaneci** 9. 14 10. **A hybrid of basketball and soccer** 11. The ball is thrown past a goalkeeper and into a goal 12. **Rectangular mats used in judo** 13. Khalid Skah 14. **Morocco** 15. 20

# *Quiz* 04   OLYMPIC GAMES

1. What did javelin thrower Ozolina (1964) and the entire Japanese wrestling team (1980) have in common?

2. **In 1984, which similar event replaced the women's five-event pentathlon?**

3. Do equestrian regulations require horses to be at least five, six or seven years old?

4. **In the individual jumping event, how many faults are given for a second refusal?**

5. What is the penalty if either a horse or rider falls?

6. **Which event did Linford Christie (GB) win in 1992?**

7. Who took the gold in 1996?

8. **Who was the men's 400 metres champion in 1992?**

9. How did he then become a Continental celebrity?

10. **Who won the women's javelin throw in 1984?**

11. Was she born in Scotland, America or Jamaica?

12. **What are the age restrictions for boxers?**

13. What is the lightest boxing weight category?

14. **And the heaviest?**

15. In 1992, why did Irish pubs sell beer at 1956 prices?

Carruth's boxing gold. Ron Delaney was Ireland's first champion in 1956
14. **Super-heavyweight – unlimited weight** 15. To celebrate Michael
12. **Must be aged between 17-35** 13. Light-flyweight – 48 kilograms
star in a European TV commercial 10. **Tessa Sanderson (GB)** 11. Jamaica
7. Donovan Bailey (Canada) 8. **Quincy Watts (USA)** 9. Nike chose Watts to
2. **Seven-event heptathlon** 3. Seven 4. **Six** 5. Eight faults 6. **100 metres**
ANSWERS 1. They all had their heads shaved following poor performances

# *Quiz* 05 OLYMPIC GAMES

1. Which oarsman won four gold medals in consecutive Olympics?

2. **In which years did he achieve this?**

3. With whom did he share victory in the coxless pairs in 1992 and 1996?

4. **For what did Benjamin Spock, a medical student and member of the USA champion rowing crew in 1924, later become famous?**

5. Was the young German coxswain, Klaus Zerta, gold medallist in 1960, aged 12, 13 or 14 years?

6. **Does this make him the youngest male in Olympic history to win a medal?**

7. What was the unfortunate experience of 800 metres runner Wyn Essajas, the first person to represent Surinam, in 1960?

8. **What happened when he arrived for his heat in the afternoon?**

9. For what did Steve Ovett win a gold for Britain in 1980?

10. **Who won the silver medal?**

11. Did Ovett take the gold for the men's 1500 metres in the same year?

12. **Who was the champion?**

13. What happened in the men's 1500 metres final in 1984?

14. **Did Great Britain win any medals in the men's 1988 1500 metres?**

15. How many laps are run in the men's 5,000 metres – is it 12½, 13 or 13½?

# Quiz 06   OLYMPIC GAMES

1. Does the women's javelin weigh 400, 600 or 800 grams?

2. **When was this event first held?**

3. In 1964, who were the two British 'Marys' to compete in the pentathlon?

4. **What events make up three-day eventing?**

5. Who won the individual three-day event in 1984 and 1988?

6. **How many members does a three-day event team require?**

7. How did Cornishman V, a medal-winning horse, also achieve fame?

8. **What are the foil, the epee and the sabre?**

9. In fencing, what is the name for the position taken before combat begins?

10. **In the men's 100 metres, how many false starts are allowed by each runner?**

11. What happens if a runner has a second false start?

12. **Which British athlete was disqualified in the men's 100 metres final in 1996?**

13. Who is the 100 metres champion depicted in the film 'Chariots of Fire'?

14. **Who was the next British sprinter to win the men's 100 metres?**

15. Do you remember which year?

ANSWERS 1. 600 grams 2. 1932 3. Mary Rand and Mary Peters 4. Dressage, endurance and show jumping 5. Mark Todd (NZ) 6. Four 7. He starred in two films – 'Dead Cert' (1974) and 'International Velvet' (1978) 8. Types of sword used in fencing 9. En garde position 10. One 11. Disqualification 12. Linford Christie 13. Harold Abrahams (GB) in 1924 14. Alan Wells 15. 1980

# *Quiz* 07  OLYMPIC GAMES

1. Which year did South Africa return to the Olympics?

2. **For how many years had they been absent?**

3. How many medals did they win altogether in that year?

4. **Did they better their last appearance in 1960?**

5. After the 1960 Games, which legendary boxer turned professional and changed his name?

6. **Did he box as a middleweight, light-heavyweight or heavyweight?**

7. In 1960, which country beat India in the hockey final for the first time since 1928?

8. **What was the score?**

9. Besides South Africa, two other countries were banned from the 1964 Games. Indonesia was one, what was the other?

10. **In 1964, in which event did Mary Rand win Britain's first-ever gold medal in women's athletics?**

11. In the same year, what medal did Ann Packer win for Britain?

12. **In which athletics event?**

13. How many gold medal winners in Olympic tennis were also successful at Wimbledon?

14. **In 1988, which female Olympic champion also won the tennis Grand Slam?**

15. Who was only 16 in 1992 when she won the gold medal in tennis?

# *Quiz* 08    OLYMPIC GAMES

1. Where were the 1996 Olympic Games held?

2. **Why was 1996 a special date for the Olympics?**

3. Which five sports have all been included in the Games since 1896?

4. **When was women's soccer included in the Olympic programme?**

5. Who were the champions?

6. **Did Italy, Brazil or Nigeria win the men's football gold in 1996?**

7. What is remarkable about Eddie Eagan's Olympic achievement?

8. **Which events did he win?**

9. When were canoeing competitions first held?

10. **Who won swimming gold medals for Ireland in 1996?**

11. Did she win two, three or six?

12. **In which events?**

13. When did synchronised swimming become an Olympic event?

14. **What changes were made to this event for 1996?**

15. Which team won the gold in that event in 1996?

ANSWERS 1. Atlanta, USA 2. **100th anniversary of the rebirth of the Modern Olympics** 3. Cycling, fencing, gymnastics, swimming and athletics 4. **1996 Olympics** 5. USA 6. **Nigeria** 7. He is unique in winning gold medals in both summer and winter Games 8. **1920 light-heavyweight boxing title and member of 1932 winning 4-man bob** 9. 1936 10. **Michelle Smith** 11. Three 12. **400 metres freestyle, 200 and 400 metres individual medley** 13. 1984 14. **Solo and duet events were replaced by a single team event** 15. USA

# *Quiz* 09    OLYMPIC GAMES

1. Who wore golden running shoes in Atlanta in 1996?

2. **In which events?**

3. Did he win any medals?

4. **Was he part of the 4 x 400 metres relay team?**

5. Who won the 4 x 400 metres relay?

6. **Did America, South Africa or Canada take the 4 x 100 metres gold?**

7. When was the obstacle race contested as an Olympic event?

8. **What was it?**

9. Where will the Games be held in 2,000?

10. **How many times have Australia been host to the Games?**

11. Which city?

12. **How many times have the Games been cancelled?**

13. When did this happen?

14. **Why were they cancelled?**

15. In which city did the Spanish Games take place in 1992?

ANSWERS 1. Michael Johnson (USA) 2. **200 and 400 metres** 3. Gold in both 4. **No, he was injured** 5. USA 6. **Canada** 7. Yes, in 1900 8. **A water event in which they climbed over a pole, a row of boats and then swim under another row of boats** 9. Sydney, Australia 10. **Once in 1956** 11. Melbourne 12. **Three times** 13. 1916, 1940 and 1944 14. **Because of war** 15. Barcelona

# *Quiz* 10    OLYMPIC GAMES

1. How many times has Germany hosted the Olympics?

2. **When?**

3. Which Olympic swimming event was won by Eleanor Holm in 1932?

4. **How did she again find fame in 1938?**

5. Who was her co-star?

6. **Which country dominates the 110 and 400 metres hurdles?**

7. How many hurdles must contestants jump in the 110 metres?

8. **Champion in 1976 and 1984, who broke the World record time for 400 metres hurdles?**

9. How did the 3,000 metres steeplechase get its name?

10. **Which country has won every steeplechase event it has entered?**

11. In walking events, why are Olympic winning times not eligible for World records?

12. **When did Poland win their first gold medal in the 50,000 metres walk?**

13. Why did 1988 gold medallist Vyacheslav Ivanenko take up the 50,000 metres walk?

14. **How did he become good enough to represent his country?**

15. Did he win in record time?

# *Quiz 11* OLYMPIC GAMES

1. What is the distance of the Marathon?

2. **What concoction was administered to Thomas Hicks, Marathon winner in 1904?**

3. Could an athlete take this today?

4. **When was the Marathon first run at night?**

5. Was 1952, 1960 for 1968 the first Marathon to be won by a black African?

6. **Who was the gold Marathon medallist in 1960 and 1964?**

7. Who was the only other person to win two Olympic Marathons?

8. **When did he win?**

9. How did Ecuador win their only medal, a gold, in 1996?

10. **How did Hong Kong win their single gold in 1996?**

11. Who took a swimming silver in 1984, retired in 1988 and then won a gold in 1992?

12. **In which event?**

13. Who won the gold medal in 1992 and 1996 for both 50 and 100 metres freestyle?

14. **When was women's diving introduced to the Games?**

15. What did Jam Hardy do in 1904 to help swimmers keep to a straight course?

# Quiz 12 OLYMPIC GAMES

1. Which cycling event was introduced in 1996?

2. **Does cyclist Chris Boardman's 1992 4,000 metres pursuit record time still stand?**

3. When was this record broken?

4. **By whom?**

5. Which two Olympic heavyweight boxing champions also won World professional titles?

6. **What is the Val Barker Cup?**

7. How is it awarded?

8. **Which nation won the most Games medals in 1996?**

9. How many did they win?

10. **How many golds?**

11. Did Great Britain win 15, 25 or 40 medals in 1996?

12. **Was this more or fewer than in 1992?**

13. How many medals did Great Britain win in 1992?

14. **And in 1988?**

15. Back in 1984, did Great Britain win 20, 25 for 27 medals?

ANSWERS 1.Mountain-bike racing **2. No** 3. 1996 **4. Andrea Collinelli (Italy)** 5. Joe Frazier (USA, 1964) and George Foreman (USA, 1968) **6. A boxing award** 7. To the competitor judged to be the best stylist at the Games **8. USA** 9. 101 **10. 44** 11. 15 **12. Fewer** 13. 20 **14. They won 24 medals** 15. 27

# Quiz 13 OLYMPIC GAMES

1. With which event do you associate the 'Fosbury Flop'?

2. **What is it?**

3. Who introduced this technique?

4. **Was this in 1964, 1968 or 1972?**

5. Was this technique successful?

6. **How high did he jump?**

7. In the pole vault event, what is the pole made of?

8. **Between 1896 and 1968, which nation won every Olympic pole vault competition?**

9. Which country took the gold in 1972?

10. **Which travels faster, a shuttlecock, a tennis ball or a volleyball?**

11. Which country won the mixed badminton doubles in 1996?

12. **Who were the previous champions?**

13. What feats did athletes have to perform for the pentathlon in the Ancient Olympics?

14. **What does the modern pentathlete have to do?**

15. Why was the order of events in the pentathlon changed in 1992?

ANSWERS 1. High jump 2. **A jumping technique in which the athlete clears the barrier head first with his back to the bar** 3. Dick Fosbury (USA) 4. **1968** 5. Yes, he won a gold medal 6. **Seven feet four and a quarter inches – an Olympic record** 7. Any material or combination of materials 8. **USA** 9. East Germany 10. **Shuttlecock** 11. South Korea 12. **None, this event was held for the first time in 1996** 13. Run, jump, throw a javelin, throw a discus and wrestle 14. **Fence, swim, shoot, run and ride** 15. Riding was moved from the first to the last event, as it caused too many injuries to be held at the start

# THE ULTIMATE SPORTS FACT AND QUIZ BOOK

# *Quiz* 14  OLYMPIC GAMES

1. Who was the Welsh P.E. teacher who won a gold medal in 1964?

2. **Which event did he win?**

3 .Whose long jump Olympic and World record stood for 22 years 316 days?

4. **How far did he jump?**

5. Did he break the record in 1968, 1972 for 1976?

6. **Who was known as Flojo?**

7. What did she win in 1988?

8. **Who was the first person to record a 200–400 metres double win in the Olympics?**

9. In which year?

10. **Which women's athletic event was held for the first time in 1996?**

11. In which other event did Jesse Owens and Carl Lewis, both Olympic champion sprinters, gain gold medals?

12. **How many long jump gold medals has Carl Lewis won?**

13. Over which years?

14. **Did Liz McColgan (GB) finish fourth, fifth or sixth in the 1992 final of the 10,000 metres?**

15. Did the winner of this event represent China, France or Portugal?

ANSWERS 1. Lynn Davies 2. **Long jump** 3. Bob Beamon (USA) 4. **29 feet 21/2in (8.90m)** 5. 1968 6. **Florence Griffith Joyner (USA)** 7. Three gold medals and one silver 8. **Valerie Brisco-Hooks (USA)** 9. 1984 10. **5,000 metres** 11. Long jump 12. **Four** 13. 1984-1996 14. **Fifth** 15. Fernando Ribeiro (Portugal)

# Quiz 15 OLYMPIC GAMES

1. Who was the first Portuguese woman to win an Olympic medal?

2. **Did she win gold, silver or bronze in the 1984 Marathon?**

3. Why was the 1984 women's Marathon a special event?

4. **Wearing a white painter's cap back to front, who won this inaugural event?**

5. Did Rosa Mota's name feature again in the women's Marathon?

6. **Who won a gold medal for Great Britain in the 400 metres hurdles?**

7. Which year?

8. **In archery, is the inner ring of the target coloured red, blue or gold?**

9. How many points is this zone worth?

10. **In 1988 and 1992, were Great Britain among the medal takers in the archery event?**

11. When was underwater swimming banned from breaststroke competitions?

12. **Why was it banned?**

13. Which event did double-gold swimmer Kieren Perkins win in 1992 and 1996?

14. **Why did he take up swimming?**

15. Which country did he represent?

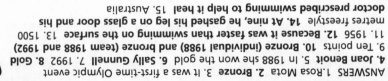

ANSWERS 1. Rosa Mota 2. **Bronze** 3. It was a first-time Olympic event 4. **Joan Benoit** 5. In 1988 she won the gold 6. **Sally Gunnell** 7. 1992 8. **Gold** 9. Ten points 10. Bronze (individual 1988) and bronze (team 1988 and 1992) 11. 1956 12. **Because it was faster than swimming on the surface** 13. 1500 metres freestyle 14. **At nine, he gashed his leg on a glass door and his doctor prescribed swimming to help it heal** 15. Australia

# *Quiz* 16  OLYMPIC GAMES

1. Which sport do you associate with the 'submarine start'?

2. **What is it?**

3. Are backstrokers still allowed to use this technique?

4. **In 1976, which nation won 12 of the 13 men's swimming events?**

5. Who was the exception?

6. **What did he win?**

7. What was his nationality?

8. **Who won gold medals for Great Britain, swimming 100 metres breaststroke in 1980 and 1988?**

9. What is the order of strokes in the individual medley?

10. **Who broke the World record, swimming breaststroke for Great Britain, in 1960?**

11. How many men make up a water polo team?

12. **Who were the 1996 water polo champions?**

13. What is the depth of the water for water polo games?

14. **Who holds the record for winning the most gold medals in one day?**

15. How many did he win?

ANSWERS **1.** Swimming – backstroke **2. A swimming start in which the swimmers can remain submerged for up to 35 metres 3.** No, any backstroker under water after 15 metres would be disqualified **4.** USA **5.** David Wilkie **6. 200 metres breaststroke 7.** Scottish **8. Duncan Goodhew (1980) and Adrian Moorhouse (1988) 9.** Butterfly, backstroke, breaststroke and freestyle **10. Anita Lonsbrough 11.** Seven **12. Spain 13.** Approx two metres **14. Vitaly Scherbo 15.** Four (in gymnastics)

# *Quiz* 17   OLYMPIC GAMES

1. In which single Olympic event were the most nations represented?

2. **How many nations took part?**

3. How old was the oldest female competitor ever in the Games?

4. **What was her name?**

5. Did she represent America, Great Britain or Australia?

6. **In which event did she compete?**

7. Which nation has taken the most medals in Olympic swimming events?

8. **Which country has won the most medals for Olympic equestrian events?**

9. Did the British ladies get a medal in 1992 in 4 x 400 metres relay?

10. **Name one of the four members of the team.**

11. Who was the first black woman from any country to earn an Olympic gold medal?

12. **What did she win?**

13. When was this?

14. **Who from Great Britain was the middleweight boxing champion in 1968?**

15. What age was featherweight champion Richard Gunn of Great Britain, the oldest fighter ever to win an Olympic championship?

ANSWERS 1. Men's Marathon 1992 2. 72 3. 70 years 5 days 4. Lorna Johnstone 5. Great Britain 6. Dressage (1972) 7. USA 8. Germany 9. Bronze 10. Smith, Douglas, Stoute, Gunnell 11. Alice Coachman 12. High jump 13. 1948 14. Chris Finnegan 15. 37 years

# THE ULTIMATE SPORTS FACT AND QUIZ BOOK

# *Quiz 18*  OLYMPIC GAMES

1. What is the modern name for the event known as 'hop, step and jump'?

2. **Who won three gold medals in the triple jump in 1968, 1972 and 1976?**

3. Did he compete in 1980?

4. **Why did Mike Conley (USA), who won a silver for the triple jump in 1984, not make the US team in 1988?**

5. Competing in a bodysuit in 1992, how did he get on?

6. **What is a 'shot' as used in the shot putt?**

7. How did Britain's Goliath, Geoff Capes, perform in the shot putt in 1976 and 1980?

8. **What is the weight of the women's shot?**

9. Who won the women's 1996 Olympics gold in the shot putt?

10. **What are the seven events which make up the women's heptathlon?**

11. Who was runner-up in the Los Angeles women's heptathlon, but went on to win gold in Seoul and Barcelona?

12. **How was Zola Budd, a South African and banned internationally, able to continue her running career in 1984?**

13. How did she manage this?

14. **Did she compete in the 1984 Olympics?**

15. What was her trademark as a runner?

ANSWERS **1.** Triple jump **2.** Viktor Saneyev **3.** Yes, he won the silver **4.** The judges at the Olympic trials ruled that his shorts grazed the sand 41/4in before his feet **5.** He won the gold **6.** A 16lb ball of iron or brass **7.** He was unplaced **8.** Four kilograms (8lbs 143/4 ozs) **9.** Astrid Kumbernuss (Germany) **10.** Day One – 100 metres hurdles, high jump, shot putt and 200 metres dash. Day Two – long jump, javelin and 800 metres run **11.** Jackie Joyner (USA) **12.** She became a British citizen **13.** Her grandfather was British, so her family moved to Britain **14.** Yes, she was seventh in the 3,000 metres final **15.** She always ran barefoot

# THE ULTIMATE SPORTS FACT AND QUIZ BOOK

# Quiz 19  OLYMPIC GAMES

1. Which is the only track and field event in which a World record has never been set in the Olympics?

2. **Does the men's discus weigh one, two or three kilograms?**

3. From which country does the discus throw originate?

4. **Which nation has dominated the Olympic discus championship?**

5. Who was the World champion in 1996?

6. **Which country was he from?**

7. Which event was discontinued in 1924 after only 15 out of 38 runners finished?

8. **Why was this event so disastrous?**

9. What happened to those who failed to finish?

10. **Who was the first South American and first black swimmer to win a gold medal by taking the 100 metres butterfly?**

11. Which country did he represent?

12. **When was this?**

13. In the same games, who became the first black competitor to win a wrestling gold?

14. **In 1992, which continent won everything on the track over 400 metres?**

15. Who was the outstanding female athlete at Seoul?

# Quiz 20 OLYMPIC GAMES

1. Who was the only athlete ever to win the same Olympic track and field event four consecutive times?

2. **Which event did he win?**

3. When was he champion?

4. **Where was the Olympic stadium which was first used in 1932 and again 52 years later?**

5. What was the stadium called?

6. **Which nation announced a last-minute boycott of the 1984 Games?**

7. What is the 'hammer'?

8. **Who won Finland's first gold medal for 20 years in the javelin throw?**

9. Was this in 1980, 1984 or 1988?

10. **Did British World record holder Steve Backley win a medal for his javelin throws in 1992?**

11. How many events do athletes contest in the decathlon?

12. **Who was record-making Bob Mathias?**

13. At what age did he achieve this?

14. **Who was the British decathlon champion in 1980 and 1984?**

15. For how many years did Daley Thompson hold the decathlon World record?

14. Daley Thompson 15. Eight

ANSWERS 1. Al Oerter (USA) 2. Discus throw 3. 1956, 1960, 1964 and 1968 4. Los Angeles 5. The Memorial Coliseum 6. Soviet Union 7. A 16lb metal sphere attached to a grip with a length of spring steel wire 8. Arto Harkonen 9. 1984 10. Yes, silver 11. Ten 12. The youngest decathlon winner of a men's track and field gold medal in Olympic history 13. 17

# Quiz 21   OLYMPIC GAMES

1. In 1996, which country won the women's high jump?

2. **Did Bulgaria win three, five or seven gold medals in 1996?**

3. Did Germany, Norway or Nigeria win the women's 1996 long jump?

4. **Had the winner previously won a medal in this event?**

5. In which other event did that winning country get a gold medal in 1996?

6. **Which women's track and field event was held for the first time in 1996?**

7. Which country was victorious?

8. **Two female British javelin throwers were successful in the 1980s. Fatima Whitbread was one, who was the other?**

9. Did Fatima Whitbread ever become Olympic champion?

10. **Did she win any medals?**

11. Which country took the gold for the first time in 1996 in the women's javelin?

12. **Which is the only Olympic sport in which men and women compete against each other in individual events?**

13. Which rider won six gold medals between 1964 and 1988?

14. **In the dressage team event, which nation has won a medal at every Olympics?**

15. In the individual jumping event, how are riders who exceed the time limit penalised?

# *Quiz* 22    OLYMPIC GAMES

1. Why was the men's 100 metres final in 1968 unique?

2. **Why were Tommie Smith and John Carlos (USA) expelled from the Olympic village in 1968?**

3. Why did black African nations threaten to boycott the 1968 Games?

4. **Did South Africa join the Games?**

5. Why did the IOC ban Rhodesia from the 1972 Games?

6. **Why were the favourites, USA, unable to field a 4 x 400 metres relay team in 1972?**

7. What was the shock result of the 1972 basketball event?

8. **What was the spectacular feature of the 1992 opening ceremony?**

9. Who performed this?

10. **In 1956, when the main Olympic programme was held in Melbourne, where were the equestrian events held?**

11. Why was this?

12. **Where was the main venue for the Melbourne Games?**

13. In the diving competition, what is a 'pike'?

14. **Who was the men's springboard and platform diving champion in 1984 and 1988?**

15. What was the 'Dive of Death'?

ANSWERS 1. All finalists were black, not known prior to 1968 2. For a 'Black Power' protest during the US anthem 3. The IOC had decided to readmit South Africa 4. No, the IOC reversed its decision 5. After pressure from black African nations 6. US gold and silver medallists in the 400 metres were banned after a 'Black Power' protest 7. Soviet Union defeated America 8. The Olympic flame was lit by shooting an arrow at the torch tower 9. Paraplegic archer Antonio Rebolle 10. Stockholm, Sweden 11. Because of Australia's strict animal quarantine laws 12. Melbourne Cricket Ground 13. Body bent at the waist with legs straight 14. Greg Louganis (USA) 15. A reverse three-and-a-half somersault in the tuck position, which had killed two divers

# Quiz 23 OLYMPIC GAMES

1. How old was Aileen Riggin (USA) when she won a gold medal for springboard diving in 1920?

2. **And how old was she when she won six age-group titles at the World Masters Swimming Championships?**

3. Has USA, Cuba or China dominated the women's diving events since 1988?

4. **In 1992, which country competed but failed to win a medal for the first time in the history of the diving event?**

5. In the platform diving event, is the board nine, ten or eleven metres above the water?

6. **How many medals were awarded in the first Games of 1896?**

7. And how many, a century later, in 1996?

8. **In 1896, how many countries were represented?**

9. And in 1996?

10. **Has rugby ever been contested as an Olympic event?**

11. Who are the reigning Olympic champions at rugby?

12. **What happened when the gold medallists visited Britain in 1924 to play Harlequins and Blackheath?**

13. Who is the oldest man to win the Olympic 100 metres?

14. **How old was he when he won the gold in 1992?**

15. In the same race, who was the first black African to win a medal in that event?

# Quiz 01   OLYMPIC GAMES
## TRUE OR FALSE?

1. The 1964 Olympic Games were held in Tokyo.

2. **The pentathlon was first introduced in 708 BC.**

3. Tennis was reintroduced as an Olympic event (for the first time since 1924) at Los Angeles in 1984.

4. **In 1896, France did not enter the Olympic Games.**

5. In Paris in 1900, America's F.W. Jarvis broke the 400 metres World record.

6. **A total of 121 nations competed in Munich for the 1972 Games.**

7. The first photo-finish took place in 1936 to decide the winner of the 100 metres.

8. **Between 1912 and 1952, Sweden won every men's modern pentathlon gold.**

9. In 1896, the 100 and 1,200 metres swimming championships were held in the open sea at Phaleron.

10. **Croquet has never been contested as an Olympic sport.**

11. Equestrian three-day eventing actually covers four days.

12. **Swimmer Clarence 'Buster' Crabbe (USA), 400 metres gold medallist in 1932, became 'Flash Gordon' and 'Buck Rogers' in children's serials.**

13. Top scorer in Olympic soccer history was Ferenc Bene (Hungary). He scored nine goals.

14. **Philip Neame (GB) is the only holder of the Victoria Cross to win an Olympic gold medal (1924 running deer team).**

15. The longest race ever held in the Games, at any sport, was the 1912 cycling road race over a distance of 320 kilometres.

ANSWERS 1. True 2. **True** 3. False. Tennis was reintroduced at Seoul in 1988 4. **False. France was one of only nine to enter** 5. False. He broke the 100 metres record 6. **True** 7. False – the camera was first used in 1932 8. **False. Germany won it in 1936** 9. True 10. **False, but only once in 1900 when all the competitors were French** 11. True. The dressage now occupies two days 12. **True** 13. False – he top scored with 12 14. **True** 15. True

# THE ULTIMATE SPORTS FACT AND QUIZ BOOK

# Quiz 02 OLYMPIC GAMES TRUE OR FALSE?

1. Equestrian regulations require riders to be at least 18 years old for the dressage event.

2. **Amateur boxing matches consist of three three-minute rounds.**

3. Swimming dominated the first week of the 1972 Games, with 30 World records bettered or equalled.

4. **Until 1976, East Germany had never won a women's swimming event.**

5. In 1936, the Games were held in Munich.

6. **In 1976, Princess Anne fell at fence 19 on the cross-country course.**

7. Harry Llewellyn and Foxhunter won Britain's only gold medal at Helsinki 1952.

8. **David Hemery was Britain's champion 200 metres runner in 1968.**

9. In 1952, Emil Zatopek won gold medals in 5,000 and 10,000 metres and Marathon.

10. **Ed Moses took up hurdling only four months before winning gold in the 400 metres hurdles in 1976.**

11. At Los Angeles in 1984, 12 competitors were disqualified for doping offences.

12. **NBA star Michael Jordan, who appeared at the 1972 Games, plays for Orlando Magic.**

13. The oldest medallist at the 1992 Games was Swedish shooter Ragnar Skanakar, at 58 years 48 days.

14. **In 1924, more than half the starters did not finish the 10,000 metres due to the temperature rising over 40 degrees.**

15. Soccer was the first team game to be included in the Olympics.

# THE ULTIMATE SPORTS FACT AND QUIZ BOOK

## *Quiz* 03    OLYMPIC GAMES
### *TRUE OR FALSE?*

1. In 1912, one wrestling bout in the Greco-Roman middleweight class lasted for 11 hours 40 minutes.

2. **The heaviest Olympic competitor ever was the 1972 super-heavyweight bronze medallist, Chris Taylor (USA), who weighed nearly 190 kilograms (over 30 stone)**

3. Softball was introduced as an official medal sport in 1988.

4. **In 1904, Frank Kungler (USA) won medals at three sports in the same Games.**

5. Men's diving was introduced in 1904.

6. **Tennis player Goran Ivanisevic was the Olympic champion in 1996.**

7. The Games have been held twice in Sweden.

8. **In 1960, the Italian Games were held in Naples.**

9. Carl Lewis (USA) holds the Olympic record for the 100 metres.

10. **China won 16 gold medals in 1996.**

11. The only Olympic cycling medallist to win the Tour de France was Joop Zoetemelk (Netherlands) in 1968.

12. **The 1908 middleweight boxing champion, John Douglas (GB), later captained the England cricket team against Australia in 1911.**

13. American boxers dominated the 1992 Olympics.

14. **In 1924, lane dividers were introduced in the swimming pool.**

15. In 1928, women were allowed to compete in track and field events.

and 2 silvers **14. True 15.** True
**Rome 9.** True **10. True 11.** True **12. True** 13. False – the Cubans took 7 golds
**Agassi won the gold 7.** False – once in 1912 **8. False – they were held in**
ANSWERS 1. True **2. True** 3. False – 1996 **4. True** 5. True 6. False – Andre

# Quiz 04 — OLYMPIC GAMES TRUE OR FALSE?

1. In walking races, the contestants must keep at least one foot in contact with the ground.

2. **South Africa won five medals in the 1996 Olympics.**

3. In high jump events, the crossbar is four metres long.

4. **Badminton became an Olympic event in 1996.**

5. Shuttlecocks travel at speeds in excess of 150mph.

6. **In the riding section of the pentathlon, the rider can choose his mount.**

7. Olympic swimming pools must be 50 metres long.

8. **Table tennis is played on a table nine feet long.**

9. In 1996 Syria's only gold was won in the women's heptathlon.

10. **In 1992, Thailand did not win a medal.**

11. The first married couple to win gold medals were Emil and Dana Zatopek in 1952.

12. **In the 1988 men's Marathon, 98 out of 118 runners finished.**

13. Carl Lewis was born on July 1, 1961.

14. **Polo was discontinued as an Olympic event in 1948.**

15. In 1996, China won a total of 50 medals.

ANSWERS 1. True 2. True 3. True 4. False – 1992 5. True 6. False, horses are picked by lot 7. True 8. True 9. True 10. False – Thailand won a bronze 11. True 12. True 13. True 14. False – 1936 15. True

# *Quiz* 01 OLYMPIC GAMES *AGAINST THE ODDS*

1. Why did sprinter Wilma Rudolph (USA) captivate the stadium in 1960?

2. **Did she win any medals?**

3. Which British swimmer was mocked by his schoolmates after an accident left him bald and because he was dyslexic?

4. **What was his Olympic achievement?**

5. What happened to Constantinidhis (Greece) during the 87 kilometres cycling race in 1896.

6. **He still won the gold. How?**

7. Why is the life story of Oliver Halassy, Olympic water polo player, 'inspiring'?

8. **Who, told that she was too old at 30 with two children, defied the odds by winning golds in the 1948 Olympics?**

9. How many did she win?

10. **Who became Olympic triple jump champion in 1964 after an operation on his knee two months earlier?**

11. What was the courageous performance from diver Mizki King at the Mexico Olympics in 1968?

12. **How did US gymnast George Eyser make Olympic history?**

13. What was Jeff Blatnick's achievement in the 1984 Games?

14. **Why was Mimoun (France) known as the 'Olympic bridesmaid'?**

15. Did he ever take the gold?

ANSWERS 1. One of 22 children and had suffered from polio as a child 2. Three golds 3. Duncan Goodhew 4. He won gold in 1980 in 100 metres breaststroke 5. He crashed twice, severely injured himself and his bicycle 6. He borrowed another bike! 7. He only had one leg 8. Fanny Blankers-Koen 9. Four 10. Josef Schmidt (Poland) 11. She fractured her arm on the springboard but completed her dives 12. In 1904, he won six medals (three golds) – with a wooden leg! 13. He recovered from cancer to take gold in Greco-Roman wrestling 14. In 1948 and 1952, he came second to Zatopek in the 5,000 and 10,000 metres 15. in 1956, he beat Zatopek to take the gold in the Marathon

# *Quiz* 02 OLYMPIC GAMES AGAINST THE ODDS

1. Why was a German competitor in the three-day team event in 1936 hailed as a hero?

2. **Was he able to compete in the jumping competition the next day?**

3. What happened this time?

4. **Did the German team win a medal?**

5. What happened to Bill Roycroft of Australia as he competed in the three-day event in 1960?

6. **How long did he spend in hospital?**

7. Were his efforts worthwhile?

8. **Why did Hungarian Endre Kabos want to prove himself in the fencing in 1936?**

9. Did he prove himself?

10. **Why is it astonishing that Fatima Whitbread won silver in 1988 throwing the javelin?**

11. What happened to Paul Gonzalez (USA) in the first round of his boxing bout in 1984?

12. **Did he manage to continue boxing?**

13. How did Doug Herland make his mark on Olympic history in 1984?

14. **Why was this remarkable?**

15. In the 1980 team fencing event, how did Soviet fencer Vladimir Lapitsky have a narrow escape to win a silver medal?

ANSWERS **1.** Konrad von Wangenheim fell and broke his collarbone in the steeplechase, but finished the course **2. Yes, his sling was removed just before he mounted 3.** The horse fell and landed on von Wangenheim, who again remounted **4. Yes, they won the gold, and the stadium gave him a standing ovation 5.** He had concussion and a broken collarbone after a fall **6. One day. He defied doctor's order and competed the following day 7.** Yes – Australia came first **8. Fellow students teased him about the fencing outfit** he got as a birthday gift **9.** He won a gold medal **10.** In 1987, she had a **trapped nerve in her throwing shoulder, a foot injury, an abscess in her back, hamstring problems, glandular fever and was in a car crash 11.** He sustained a hairline fracture above his right wrist **12. Yes – and went on to win a gold medal 13.** He was coxswain for the bronze-winning US coxed pairs **14. He was born with broken hips, broken ribs and a broken collarbone, as a result of brittle-bone disease. 15.** His chest was accidentally run through by his opponent's sword, which just missed his heart

# *Quiz* 03 OLYMPIC GAMES AGAINST THE ODDS

1. What happened to British runner Derek Redmond in 1988 less than two minutes before his opening heat?

2. **Did he compete in 1992?**

3. What happened?

4. **Why did the crowd of 65,000 give the young runner a standing ovation?**

5. Following Coe's gold in the 1500 metres in 1980, why were experts predicting in 1983 that his championship days were over?

6. **Were his running days over?**

7. What was Murray Halberg's winning achievement in 1960?

8. **Why was this particularly remarkable?**

9. To qualify for the 1988 judo competition (extra-lightweight), how did Kim Jae-yup lose 13 pounds in 20 days?

10. **Was this frugal diet fit for a champion?**

11. Why did right-handed Karoly Takacs, a champion shooter, have to learn how to shoot with his left hand?

12. **Was he successful?**

13. What non-sporting event stole the headlines of Munich 1972?

14. **What happened to the Israeli team?**

15. Did the Games continue?

ANSWERS 1. A leg injury forced him to withdraw and undergo major surgery 2. Yes 3. He tore a hamstring and was unplaced 4. **He refused a stretcher and finished the race in agony** 5. He spent months in hospital recovering from toxoplasmosis, a rare and sometimes fatal infection 6. **Hardly! He won the 1500 metres gold in 1984** 7. He won the gold in the 5000 metres in 1960 8. **He paralysed his left arm playing rugby, and had to learn how to walk, run, dress and feed himself** 9. He ate one meal per day of porridge with raw fish slices 10. **Yes, he won the gold medal** 11. A grenade exploded in his right hand on army duty, so he taught himself to shoot with this left hand 12. **He won a gold medal in 1948** 13. Arab terrorists broke into the Israeli team headquarters in the Olympic village 14. **Nine members were murdered by the terrorists** 15. The Games resumed, following a memorial service

# *Quiz* 04   OLYMPIC GAMES *AGAINST THE ODDS*

1. What did Swiss-born tennis champion Norris Williams win for America in 1924?

2. **Why was he hailed a hero in 1912?**

3. Did he win other tennis titles?

4. **How did Donald Thompson, from Middlesex, prepare for the 50,000 metres walk to be held on a hot, sticky day in Rome 1960?**

5. What was the temperature in Rome 1960 on the day of the race?

6. **Were his efforts worthwhile?**

7. Why could Gail Devers never imagine herself as an Olympic runner?

8. **In which Olympics did she participate?**

9. Did she perform well?

10. **Did she run in 1996?**

11. Who lost the vision in his left eye, but went on to win four gold medals?

12. **Which events did he win?**

13. Who was Miller Anderson?

14. **What happened to him?**

15. How did he perform in the springboard diving event in 1948?

ANSWERS 1. Gold 2. **He survived the sinking of the Titanic, swimming in icy water for over an hour** 3. **Wimbledon in 1920** 4. He took heaters and boiling kettles into his bathroom to raise the temperature to 38 degrees centigrade 5. **30.5 degrees centigrade** 6. **He won the gold** 7. in 1990, she was diagnosed with Graves' disease and began radiation therapy 8. **1992** 9. She won the 100 metres gold 10. **Yes, and won gold again** 11. **Tamas Darnyi of Hungary** 12. **1988 and 1992 200 and 400 metres individual medley** 13. Member of the US diving team of 1948, having been shot down in World War II and his leg almost torn off 14. An operation left **him with silver plates in a thigh bone** 15. He won a silver medal

# *Quiz* 01　WINTER OLYMPIC

1. How many times have the Winter Olympics been held in France?

2. **Where were the French locations?**

3. Which year was the first Winter Games?

4. **Who was the first-ever Olympic winter gold medallist?**

5　What did he win?

6. **Where were the Games held in 1952?**

7. Which couple won a maximum nine sixes in the 1984 ice dancing event?

8. **Which team won the gold medal in ice hockey in 1994?**

9. Who was the British men's figure skating champion in 1976?

10. **What is the biathlon?**

11. Did women first compete in the biathlon in 1988, 1992 or 1998?

12. **Which were the last Winter Games to be held in the same year as the Summer Games?**

13. Where were the 1998 Winter Olympics held?

14. **What did British figure skater Robin Cousins win in 1980?**

15. How many other medals did Britain win that year?

ANSWERS **1.** Three **2.** Chamonix, Grenoble and Albertville **3.** 1924
**4. Charles Jewtraw (USA) 5.** 500 metres speed skating **6. Norway**
**7.** Jayne Torvill and Christopher Dean **8. Sweden 9.** John Curry
**10. Combination of skiing and shooting 11.** 1992 **12.** 1992
**13.** Nagano, Japan **14. He won gold** 15 It was Britain's only medal

# *Quiz* 02   WINTER OLYMPICS

1. Where will the 2002 Winter Games be held?

2. **Who ice-danced to Ravel's 'Bolero' in 1984?**

3. When were the first Winter Games to be held in Eastern Europe?

4. **Where were they held?**

5. Who was 'Eddie the Eagle'?

6. **What did he do?**

7. Which famous French soccer star lit the flame at the 1992 Winter Olympics?

8. **Which nation won 26 medals at the 1992 Winter Olympics?**

9. How many times have Norway hosted the Games?

10. **Which has been the southernmost location for the Winter Games?**

11. What did the four Italian Huber brothers achieve in 1994?

12. **When was curling introduced as a demonstration sport?**

13. When did curling become a medal event?

14. **Is snowboarding a medal event?**

15. Which Olympic luger had a famous brother who won the 1980 Olympic 800 metres?

ANSWERS 1. Salt Lake City, USA 2. **Torvill and Dean** 3. 1978 4. Sarajevo 5. British ski jumper, Michael Edwards 6. **He finished last in both jumps, but kept the media and crowds amused with his antics** 7. Michel Platini 8. **Germany** 9. Twice 10. Nagano, Japan 11. They all won medals 12. 1992 13. 1998 14. Yes, new in 1998 15. Nick Ovett, brother of Steve

# RUGBY

# Quiz 01  RUGBY UNION

1. Which year did Lawrence Dallaglio make his England debut?

2. **In which match?**

3. Which international squad staged a sit-down protest during training in 1996?

4. **Why?**

5. In what year did Scotland win their first Grand Slam for 59 years?

6. **Who was the player who kicked 46 points and scored a try in the Scottish total of 86 points in winning that title?**

7. Which BBC commentator played 29 internationals for Wales in the 1950s?

8. **Which injured England player did Jeremy Guscott replace when making his debut for the British Lions in 1989?**

9. Which Gloucester fly-half played in the New Zealand Under-19 cricket team?

10. **How many times did Will Carling captain England?**

11. How many of those games did England win?

12. **How many Grand Slams did England win under his captaincy?**

13. Which years?

14. **Which club does he represent?**

15. In what position does he play?

# *Quiz* 02    RUGBY UNION

1. How many clubs form the English League One?

2. **Which is the oldest club in League One?**

3. When was that club formed?

4. **Who took over as player-coach at Sale for the 1996-97 season?**

5. Where was his previous post?

6. **Who captained the England A team to five victories in 1995-96?**

7. Which club does he captain?

8. **Who played for South Africa's Eastern Province Under-21 squad before his England career began?**

9. Which League One team was he playing for in 1998?

10. **Which club's colours are light blue, magenta, chocolate, trench grey, black and light green?**

11. Which flanker has represented England at every level except as a schoolboy?

12. **Which team does he captain?**

13. For which senior club did Liam Botham, son of Ian, first play?

14. **Which cricket county did he also first play for?**

15. Which club won the Pilkington Cup in 1966?

ANSWERS 1. Twelve 2. Sale 3. 1861 4. John Mitchell 5. Waikato, New Zealand 6. Tony Diprose 7. Saracens 8. Mike Catt 9. Bath 10. Harlequins 11. Lawrence Dallaglio 12. Wasps 13. West Hartlepool 14. Hampshire 15. Bath

# *Quiz* 03    RUGBY UNION

1. How many times was Rob Andrew capped for England?

2. **How many caps did Will Carling earn?**

3. Which club celebrated a tenth consecutive Pilkington Cup victory in 1995-96?

4. **Which club did they defeat?**

5. What was the score?

6. **How many times did New Zealand's Chris Cullen score in the 1996 Hong Kong Sevens?**

7. In how many matches?

8. **Which country won the title for the third consecutive year?**

9. When were Barbarians the winners of the Hong Kong Sevens?

10. **Which member of the Royal Family played flanker for Scottish Schoolboys in the 1995-96 season?**

11. Which 17-stone Irish prop forward was banned from playing for 26 weeks after being judged guilty of dangerous play in the 1996 France v Ireland match?

12. **What was the French winning score in that match – 45-10, 45-20 or 55-10?**

13. When and where did Will Carling play his last match as England captain?

14. **Who were the opposition?**

15. What was the significance of that win?

# *Quiz* 04    RUGBY UNION

1. For which club did Rob Andrew play before moving into his present post?

2. **Who took over the captaincy when he left that first team?**

3. To which lower division club did Andrew move?

4. **What title was he given?**

5. Who is the Newcastle chairman who persuaded him to join the club?

6. **At Cambridge, Andrew won Blues for rugby and which other sport?**

7. Which Scottish forward with Newcastle is an accomplished one-day eventer and clay pigeon enthusiast?

8. **How many caps had he won by the end of the 1997-98 international season?**

9. Which is the oldest rugby club in the World?

10. **What was England's worst rugby defeat?**

11. When was that?

12. **Why was an inexperienced team chosen?**

13. Who was the youngest England fly-half for 71 years picked to play in that match?

14. **How old was he?**

15. Who captained that disastrous England team?

# *Quiz 05*    **RUGBY UNION**

1. In what year was the RFU founded – 1850, 1871 or 1901?

2. **How many founder members were there – 10, 33 or 21?**

3. A schoolboy was reputed to have initiated the game of rugby by picking up the ball and running with it. His name?

4. **Which school did he attend?**

5. What year was the game first played?

6. **When did the first All-Blacks team tour Britain?**

7. In their 32-match tour, how many games did they win?

8. **Which team defeated them?**

9. How many tries did they concede during the tour – 7, 17 or 27?

10. **Why was Twickenham known as 'The Cabbage Patch' in its early days?**

11. How much did the land cost? Was it approximately £5,500, £25,500 or £50,500, ?

12. **What year was the ground purchased?**

13. When was the first game played there?

14. **Who played in that first game?**

15. What was the result?

# *Quiz* 06 **RUGBY UNION**

1. When was the first international match at Twickenham?

2. **Who did England play?**

3. Before this match, what was England's record against Wales?

4. **What was the score in that inaugural match at Twickenham?**

5. Adrian Stoop planned England's victory. Which club team did he captain?

6. **In what year was the first Five Nations Championship played?**

7. Who were the winners?

8. **In which match did Gareth Edwards make his debut for Wales?**

9. How old was he when he was made captain a year later?

10. **Wales dominated British rugby in the 1970s. Can you name five of the big Welsh names of that era?**

11. In which year did the Lions win their first series against the All-Blacks in New Zealand?

12. **In 1973, which of the Welsh wizards scored what was described as "the greatest try of all time" for the Barbarians against the All-Blacks?**

13. Where was the game played?

14. **What was the score?**

15. Between 1969 and 1979, how many times did Wales finish top or joint top of the Five Nations Championship?

ANSWERS 1. 1910 2. **Wales** 3. They had lost every match to Wales for 11 years 4. England won 11-6 5. **Harlequins** 6. 1910 7. England 8. **In Paris against France on April 1, 1967** 9. 20 years 7 months 10. JPR Williams, Gerald Davies, Barry John, Gareth Edwards, Mervyn Davies 11. 1971 12. Gareth Edwards 13. Cardiff Arms Park 14. **Barbarians won 23-11** 15 All bar three

# *Quiz* 01   RUGBY LEAGUE

1. Which former Great Britain Rugby League star joined Bedford RU club in the 1996-97 season?

2. **Which other club did he sign for in his 'double code' move?**

3. From which club did Bedford sign him?

4. **What nickname does he have from his many fans?**

5. Which team was beaten in the 1996 Challenge Cup after a successful run of 43 matches over nine years?

6. **Who beat them?**

7. What was the score?

8. **In the 1992 World Cup Final, Great Britain led Australia by 6-4 at half time. Who won?**

9. What was the final score?

10. **In 1966, in an attempt to popularise the game, the law limiting possession was changed to how many tackles?**

11. In 1972, the law was again changed to allow how many tackles?

12. **Who was the Welsh RU fly-half and British Lions captain who changed code to join Salford?**

13. What year was that?

14. **What was the fee paid by Salford – £6,000, £16,000 or £60,000?**

15. Which RL official was appointed chairman of the newly formed national Sports Cabinet in July 1998?

ANSWERS 1. Martin Offiah 2. London Broncos 3. Wigan 4. 'Chariots' 5. Wigan 6. Salford 7. 26-16 8. Australia 9. 10-6 10. Four 11. Six 12. David Watkins 13. 1967 14. £16,000 15. Sir Rodney Walker, also chairman of the RL

# *Quiz* 02  RUGBY LEAGUE

1. Who was the first woman to referee a rugby league Varsity Match?

2. **When?**

3. How many Super League teams have animals, birds or fish in their names – seven, eight or nine?

4. **Name four of them.**

5. Who were the 1997 Super League champions?

6. **Who is the rugby league club coach with the same name as a former England soccer international?**

7. Which club does he coach?

8. **When was the Rugby League County Championship abolished?**

9. How long had it been contested?

10. **In what year did the Rugby League introduce the sin bin?**

11. In which year did the Rugby League increase points for a try from three to four?

12. **Which club won the Challenge Cup Final in May 1998?**

13. Who were the favourites to win the cup?

14. **What was the result?**

15. Who was the first rugby league player to be transferred for £100,000?

ANSWERS 1. Julia Lee, a day-nursery teacher   2. **March 1999**   3. Seven   
4. **Bradford Bulls, Castleford Tigers, Leeds Rhinos, London Broncos, Sheffield Eagles, Warrington Wolves**   5. Bradford Bulls   
6. **Tony Currie**   7. London Broncos   8. 1982   9. 87 years   10. **1983**   
11. 1983   12. **Sheffield Eagles**   13. Wigan   14. 17-8   15. Joe Lydon in 1986

# *Quiz* 03    RUGBY LEAGUE

1. What height is the crossbar from the ground?

2. **How far apart are the goalposts?**

3. What is the maximum distance from goal-line to goal-line?

4. **What was the league's original title?**

5. In what year was the Rugby League Cup Final first played at Wembley Stadium?

6. **Which was the first Rugby League team to take part in the Middlesex Sevens?**

7. What year was that?

8. **Where did they finish in the tournament?**

9. Which Great Britain Test player has a cousin in the England rugby union squad?

10. **With which club does his cousin play?**

11. Who set up a record between 1954 and 1964 of 52 international appearances for Great Britain and England?

12. **He played for five different Yorkshire and Lancashire clubs during his career. How many can you name?**

13. Who was the legendary full-back between the two World Wars who topped a century of goals every year for 19 consecutive seasons?

14. **What was his career total of goals – 2, 459, 2, 759 or 2,959?**

15. Another legendary figure scored 475 tries for Wigan between 1953 and 1968. Who was he?

# ATHLETICS

# *Quiz* 01    ATHLETICS

1. Name the 100 metres World record holder who became 60 metres indoor World record champion in Madrid in February 1998.

2. **What was his time in Madrid?**

3. Which middle distance runner who held 12 World records acted as fitness trainer to Conservative leader William Hague?

4. **When did Roger Bannister run the first four minute mile?**

5. Who were his two teammates who helped him to achieve his dream?

6. **What was his time?**

7. Who recorded 3 mins 58 secs in Finland 46 days later?

8. **Who won a silver medal in Lisbon in 1998 in her first ever attempt at 10,000 metres?**

9. Whose seven-year British record did she destroy?

10. **What was her time?**

11. Which British field events athlete has been awarded an MBE and an OBE?

12. **Who had to wait four years to receive his bronze medal for a 100 metres race run in 1994?**

13. Why the delay?

14. **Which British champion athlete had a twin sister?**

15. Where did Brendan Foster set his 3,000 metres World record?

ANSWERS **1. Maurice Green** **2.** 6.39 secs **3. Sebastian Coe** **4. May 6, 1954** **5.** Chris Chataway and Chris Brasher **6.** 3 mins 59.4 secs **7.** John Landy **8. Paula Radcliffe** **9.** Liz McColgan's **10. 30 mins 48.58 secs** **11.** Javeline thrower Tessa Sanderson **12. Frankie Fredericks** **13.** Horace Dave-Edwin finished third but was later disqualified **14. Lillian Board** **15.** Gateshead (in August 1974)

# *Quiz* 02     ATHLETICS

1. Who ran the first sub-3.50 mile in 1975?

2. **What was his time?**

3. How old was Daley Thompson when he scored a best ever British total of 7,684 decathlon points in 1976?

4. **How many gold medals did Britain win at the 1998 European Indoor Championships?**

5. What medal did Ashia Hansen win in the women's triple jump?

6. **Her World record was the first British success in track and field for 18 months, two years or four years?**

7. Whose gold-winning triple jump of 17.43 metres was his best since 1995?

8. **Who took the silver medal behind the Englishman in that event?**

9. What medal did John Maycock win at that meeting?

10. **Who is the former World indoor mile record holder who coaches John Maycock?**

11. Name the Oxford blue who ran for Britain before being awarded two VC's and a Military Medal in the First World War?

12. **Name the former 5,000 metres World record holder who became involved in reforming British athletics.**

13. Who was the first 3,000 metres steeplechase World record holder?

14. **Where was the event?**

15. Was his time more or less than 8 mins 50 secs?

ANSWERS 1. New Zealander John Walker 2. **3 mins 49.4 secs** 3. Seventeen 4. **Three** 5. Gold 6. **Two years** 7. Jonathan Edwards 8. **Charles Friedek** (Germany) 9. Gold 10. **Peter Elliott** 11. Noel Godfrey Chavasse 12. **David Moorcroft** 13. Hungarian Sandor Rozsnyoi 14. **1954 European Championships in Berne** 15. 8 mins 49.6 secs

# *Quiz* 03 ATHLETICS

1. Who earned the cheers at White City on October 13, 1954 when he beat European title-holder Vladimir Kuts in the final stride of the 5,000 metres?

2. **Who was the Irish woman athlete who won two gold medals at the 1998 World Cross-country Championships?**

3. What were her winning races?

4. **Who took the silver in the long course event?**

5. What made the Irishwoman's victories unique?

6. **At the same meeting, who led Kenya to its 13th successive team title?**

7. Who ran the first four minute mile in the United States?

8. **When?**

9. Gordon Pirie broke the 5,000 metres World record in 13 mins 26.8 secs, 13 mins 30.8 secs or 13 mins 36.8 secs in 1956?

10. **Who did he beat?**

11. How many World records did Gordon Pirie beat in his career?

12. **Who won the 1958 'Mile of the Millennium' in Dublin?**

13. What was his time?

14. **Who knocked nearly eight seconds off the World 10,000 metres record in London in 1973?**

15. Whose record did he break?

ANSWERS **1.** Chris Chataway **2. Sonia O'Sullivan** **3.** Long course (8 kms) and short course (4 kms) **4. Paula Radcliffe** **5.** They were run on a desert course in 30ᵒC (86ᵒF) heat **6. Paul Tergat** **7.** Jim Bailey **8. May 5, 1956** **9.** Gordon Pirie **10. Russian Vladimir Kuts** **11.** Five **12. Herb Elliott** **13.** 3 mins 54.5 secs **14. Dave Bedford** **15.** Lasse Viren's

# Quiz 04     ATHLETICS

1. Who was the first man to run 100 metres in ten seconds?

2. **When was that?**

3. Whose 8.21 metres leap in 1960 broke the long jump record set by Jesse Owens in the 1930s?

4. **Who promised that if Gateshead Council laid an all-weather track he would break the World 3,000 metres record on it?**

5. When was his run – and in what time?

6. **Did he break the record?**

7. Who ran across America from Los Angeles to New York in 65 days?

8. **How many miles did he run?**

9. What record did he break?

10. **Which year?**

11. Where did the sport of Orienteering originate?

12. **Name the English international distance runner who, as a schoolboy, started his career in Orienteering.**

13. Which English international athlete helped to bring the sport to Britain?

14. **Who broke Ingrid Kristiansen's 13 year old Marathon record time of 2 hrs 21 mins 06 secs?**

15. By how many seconds did she beat the record – 59, 39 or 19?

**ANSWERS 1.** German sprinter Armin Hary **2. June 1960 (in Zurich)**
**3.** Ralph Boston **4. Brendan Foster 5. August 1974 in 7 mins 35.2 secs
6. Yes 7.** Bruce Tulloch **8. 2,876 miles 9.** The World's longest run
**10** 1969 **11.** Sweden **12. Gordon Pirie 13.** John Disley
**14. Kenyan Tegla Loroupe 15.** Nineteen seconds

# Quiz 05 ATHLETICS

1. Who were the English 1998 twelve-stage road relay club champions?

2. **Which club were the defending champions?**

3. Who was the first sprinter to break the ten seconds barrier for the 100 metres?

4. **Where and when was he competing?**

5. What was his time?

6. **Which woman athlete won the 1998 Flora London Marathon?**

7. How many previous Marathons had she run?

8. **What nationality is she?**

9. Who finished second to her 28 seconds later?

10. **Who was the winner of the 'World's Fastest Woman' race staged in China in May 1998?**

11. Where did Li Xuemel, the Chinese champion, finish?

12. **The winner's time of 10.71 secs over 100 metres was still outside the record. Who holds it?**

13. Who were the first 4 x 400 metres relay team to break the three minute barrier?

14. **When and where?**

15. Who broke 18 World records but never won an Olympic gold medal?

ANSWERS 1. Birchfield Harriers 2. **Salford Harriers** 3. Jim Hines
4. **American Athletics Union Championships in 1968** 5. 9.9 secs
6. **Catherina McKiernan** 7. Only one (in Berlin) 8. **Irish** 9. Liz McColgan
10. **Marion Jones of USA** 11. Fourth 12. **Florence Griffith-Joyner**
13. USA (Bob Frey, Lee Evans, Tommie Smith and Theron Lewis)
14. **Los Angeles in July 1966** 15. Australian Ron Clarke

# *Quiz* 06  ATHLETICS

1. How many men entered the 1998 London Marathon – more than 15,000, 25,000 or 30,000?

2. **Who was the winner?**

3. Where did the 1997 winner, Antonio Pinto of Portugal, finish?

4. **Who broke her own British pole vault record at her first 1998 attempt?**

5. What height did she clear?

6. **When were the Asian, Pan American and Mediterranean Games first held – 1951, 1961 or 1991?**

7. Which Olympic gold medallist became coach of former European junior 200 metres champion, Katharine Merry?

8. **When were synthetic tracks first used for major athletics events?**

9. Who won the Commonwealth Games and the Boston Marathons in 1970?

10. **Who was the record-breaking British athlete who died of cancer at the age of 22?**

11. Where were women allowed to compete in a mixed athletics meeting for the first time in 1998?

12. **Who in 1970 won both the senior and junior Southern cross-country championships within 20 minutes of each other?**

13. Who ran the Detroit Marathon backwards in 1982?

14. **What was his time?**

15. Who set an unofficial world beating record for the women's 5,000 metres in South Africa in 1984?

ANSWERS 1. 30,663  2. Abel Anton (Spain)  3. Third  4. Janine Whitlock
5. 4.25 metres  6. 1951  7. Linford Christie  8. 1968  9. Ron Hill
10. Lillian Board  11. Qatar in the Arabian Gulf  12. Dave Bedford
13. Scott Welland  14. 4hrs 7mins 54secs  15. Zola Budd

# *Quiz* 07     ATHLETICS

1. Who ended Ed Moses' run of 122 wins in 122 races in Madrid in June 1987?

2. **Who defeated Olympic and World 100 metres champion Carl Lewis in the 1987 World Championships in Rome?**

3. Who in 1990 became the first British athlete in 17 years to set a World record at home?

4. **Which record did that athlete beat?**

5. Who broke his own 27th world pole vault record by clearing 6.10 metres in August 1991?

6. **Britain won two gold medals in the 1991 Tokyo World Championships. In which events?**

7. How many medals did Britain earn at the 1993 World Championships in Stuttgart?

8. **Two of these medallists had already won Olympic gold a year earlier. Who were they?**

9. In which event in Stuttgart did Sally Gunnell break a World record?

10. **Who broke the 100 metres men's record to win a gold medal at the same meeting?**

11. Whose World record triple jump distance did Jonathan Edwards surpass in the 1995 European Games?

12. **Why didn't Jonathan Edward's jump of 18.43 metres count as a World record?**

13. What was his record breaking jump two months later in the World Championships?

14. **Who had his third in a row victory in the 1996 London Marathon?**

15. When were the first European Games held?

# MIXED BAG
## THE TEST FOR SPORTING KNOW-ALLS

# *Quiz 01*    MIXED BAG

1. In which sport do the Leeds Rhinos and London Broncos compete?

2. **Which British basketball team is backed by American pharmaceutical millionaire Bill Cook?**

3. Name the blind middle-distance runner who won 27 gold medals in European and World Paralympic Games between 1983 and 1994.

4. **How many times had Lisa Lomas won the English women's table tennis title before her retirement in 1998?**

5. Russia's Skaidrite Smildzinya was elected Miss Basketball at the 1964 World Championships. How tall was she?

6. **Who ended Russian swimmer Alex Popov's run of 12 successive title wins at the 1998 Perth World Championships?**

7. Who won four times at Badminton's three-day eventing between 1971 and 1981?

8. **On which children's game is the triple jump thought to have been based?**

9. Which South African spin bowler delivered 137 consecutive balls to England batsmen in Durban in 1957 without conceding a run?

10. **Who won the singles title at the first World Bowls Championships in 1966?**

11. Who was the first foreign golfer to win the US Open in 1981?

12. **Which baseball player had 2,130 consecutive games for the New York Yankees?**

13. Karen Brown, the World's most capped hockey player, had been awarded how many caps for England and Great Britain in 1998 – 223, 243 or 273?

14. **Who won Belgium's cycling Tour of Flanders in April 1998 for the third time in six years?**

15. Who owned the first, second, fourth and fifth placed horses in the 1932 St Leger?

# *Quiz* 02     MIXED BAG

1. Who won yachting's America's Cup in 1995?

2. **Name the Scotsman who won the Saga World Indoor Bowls Championship in February 1998.**

3. Who was his opponent in the final?

4. **Who was the first Briton to be named No 1 in the squash World rankings in 1998?**

5. Who did he displace in the No 1 spot in January 1998?

6. **Who were the 6ft 3ins American twins who took women's basketball by storm in 1980?**

7. Which driver won the first Grand Prix near Le Mans in 1906?

8. **What make of car was he driving?**

9. Was his average speed under 70mph or over 70mph for the 769.9 mile race?

10. **Over what period was the race contested?**

11. What was the first Irish-trained horse to win the Epsom Derby?

12. **In what year?**

13. Which team won the first Rugby League knockout trophy in 1972?

14. **Who were their opponents?**

15. What was the winning margin – 5, 10 or 15?

ANSWERS 1. New Zealand 2. **Paul Foster** 3. Mervyn King 4. **Peter Nicol** 5. Pakistani champion Jansher Khan 6. **Paula and Pam McGee** 7. Hungarian Francois Szisz 8. **Renault** 9. 73.3mph 10. **Two days** 11. Orby 12. **1907** 13. Halifax 14. **Wakefield Trinity** 15. 10 (22–11)

# Quiz 03 MIXED BAG

1. Who was given a hero's welcome by his home crowd after being expelled from the 1972 Winter Olympics in Japan?

2. **What was his 'crime'?**

3. Which county cricket side was dismissed for twelve in its first innings but drew the match?

4. **Who were they playing?**

5. In what year?

6. **What caused the draw?**

7. In 1901, Ireland beat England 10–5 at Crystal Palace. What was the sport?

8. **Who won the 1929 World Table Tennis Championship and was later to win international fame in another sport?**

9. When was the first £5,000 football transfer?

10. **Who was the player?**

11. Which clubs did the transfer involve?

12. **How many love letters did skater Katarina Witt receive after winning at the 1984 Olympics? Was it 150, 30,000 or 5,000?**

13. Which Australian swimming star broke the 100 metres butterfly record in the New Year 1998 Championships?

14. **What was his final haul of medals in that tournament?**

15. What was special about racehorses Herod, Eclipse and Matchem?

# Quiz 04 — MIXED BAG

1. Where was the first ladies' hockey club founded?

2. **In what year – 1787, 1827 or 1887?**

3. When was the first maximum snooker break televised?

4. **Who made the break?**

5. Where is Great Britain's oldest clay-pigeon shooting club?

6. **When was it founded – 1904, 1914 or 1924?**

7. Which two countries shared the two-man bobsleigh gold medal at the Winter Olympics in 1998?

8. **How many runs did both make before sharing the gold?**

9. Were their identical times for the 1,360 metres course under or over 31/2 minutes?

10. **How many British Open Squash titles did Heather Blundell (later McKay) win?**

11. Who was the first professional darts champion?

12. **In what year did he win the title?**

13. When did USA beat Britain 7–0 in the Wightman Cup without dropping a set?

14. **Who succeeded Jack Charlton as Eire's soccer manager?**

15. How many US Masters Green Jackets has Jack Nicklaus won?

ANSWERS 1. Molesey 2. 1887 3. 1982 4. Steve Davis 5. Waltham Abbey Gun Club 6. 1914 7. Canada and Italy 8. Four 9. Three mins 37.24 secs 10. Sixteen 11. Leighton Rees 12. 1978 13. June 1946 14. Mick McCarthy 15. Six

# *Quiz* 05   **MIXED BAG**

1. Who was the first gold medallist in the history of the Winter Olympics?

2. **What was the event?**

3. What was the year –1924, 1928 or 1932?

4. **Which former county cricketer was called to defrost the Stade de France pitch before the opening France–England rugby game in February 1998?**

5. For which counties did he play before setting up his firm and developing new techniques for dealing with frozen pitches?

6. **What does Adolph refer to in trampolining?**

7. Who was the first Briton to win the men's overall waterskiing title at the World Championships?

8. **In what year?**

9. Who won his sixth speedway World championship in 1979?

10. **When did he win his first World title – 1972, 1968 or 1971?**

11. What is his nationality?

12. **Who was the first woman to cox in the Boat Race?**

13. In what year?

14. **When did the Oxford crew win the Boat Race with only seven men?**

15. What happened to the eighth member of the crew?

# *Quiz* 06    MIXED BAG

1. Who won 29 Welsh Rugby caps in the early 1900s?

2. **His caps were won from three different positions. What were they?**

3. Name the greyhound unbeaten in the heats, semi-finals and finals of the English, Scottish and Welsh Derbys in 1947?

4. **Who was his owner and trainer?**

5. Who was the first Briton to win a European table tennis singles title in April 1980?

6. **What was his English ranking at the time?**

7. An Indonesian won the All-England Badminton Championship for the eighth time in 1976. Who was he?

8. **In which year of the Sixties did Jonah Barrington become World squash No 1?**

9. In that year, Barrington won the first of how many British Open Squash titles?

10. **When did the Australian Geoff Hunt win the first of his eight British Open Squash titles?**

11. Who did he beat that year?

12. **Who won the first Iditarod Dogsled Trial from Anchorage to Nome in Alaska in 1973?**

13. When did the New York Yankees win baseball's World Series for the first time in 18 years?

14. **Who did they beat to win the title?**

15. Who won the World Series the previous year?

# THE ULTIMATE SPORTS FACT AND QUIZ BOOK

# *Quiz* 07    MIXED BAG

1. Which American football player joined London Monarchs in 1996?

2. **Which American team did he leave?**

3. Which former Scottish rugby captain signed for the Scottish Claymores American football team in 1996?

4. **What success did the Claymores have in 1996?**

5. When did the British Government announce its intention to ban all tobacco advertising and sports sponsorship?

6. **Who won the first Cyclocross World Championship?**

7. In what year – 1950, 1960 or 1965?

8. **Which team won the baseball World Series in 1997 in only their fifth season?**

9. Which county did Durham defeat to win the National Indoor Bowls Tournament in 1998?

10. **What was the score in this Liberty Trophy final?**

11. How many times had Durham then won the Trophy?

12. **What year was the FA Cup Final first shown live on television?**

13. Which big horserace also enjoyed its first television coverage that year?

14. **When was the first Walker Cup played – 1912, 1922 or 1928?**

15. After whom was this golf tournament named?

**THE ULTIMATE SPORTS FACT AND QUIZ BOOK**

# Quiz 08     MIXED BAG

1. The legendary baseball player Babe Ruth played most of his career with which club?

2. **How many home runs did he hit for them in 1920, his first season?**

3. For whom did he play before joining the Yankees?

4. **What medal did Tara Lipinski win in the ladies' figure skating at the 1998 Winter Olympics?**

5. At 15 years 255 days, she became the youngest individual Winter Olympics medallist. Who was the previous youngest?

6. **What was the age difference in days – 45, 50 or 60?**

7. How long had the record stood?

8. **Lipinski's teammate took the silver medal. Name her.**

9. Which title had she taken from Lipinski only a month before?

10. **What music did Lipinski choose for her free Olympic programme?**

11. In which year did the single-seater racing car appear?

12. **Before this, why had a passenger seat been compulsory?**

13. Which team won the 1998 Budweiser Basketball League title?

14. **When did Harvey Goldsmith and Ed Simons buy that club's franchise?**

15. Who is the coach who said he would build them a championship team in three years?

ANSWERS 1. New York Yankees  2. **Fifty-four**  3. Boston Red Sox  4. **Gold**
5. Sonja Henie  6. **60 days**  7. 70 years  8. **Michelle Kwan**  9. The US
Championship  10. **Music from the film 'The Rainbow'**  11. 1927
12. **For a mechanic**  13. London Leopards  14. 1994  15. Billy Mims

# *Quiz* 09    **MIXED BAG**

1. Who was appointed youngest-ever England women's hockey captain in April 1998?

2. **Which club does she play for?**

3. In what position?

4. **How old was she when appointed?**

5. Who was the 1998 British Women's Open Squash champion?

6. **What is her nationality?**

7. When were spikes on golf shoes worn for the first time?

8. **On which horse did Ernest Piggott win the Grand National in 1912?**

9. What relation is Lester Piggott to Ernest?

10. **When did Britain win the two-man bob at the Winter Olympics?**

11. Who were the couple?

12. **Where were those Games held?**

13. Which Chinese swimmer was sent home from the 1998 World Championships?

14. **Why?**

15. What do the initials HGH stand for?

# THE ULTIMATE SPORTS FACT AND QUIZ BOOK

# *Quiz* 10      MIXED BAG

1. Which nation won the first Water Polo World Cup?

2. **When was that?**

3. Which other inaugural competition had they won?

4. **When did the Board of Education first allow sport to be part of the English school curriculum?**

5. The first golf shot to be played on the Moon was in what year?

6. **What golf club did the Apollo astronaut use in making the shot?**

7. Who in April 1998 was named as the youngest speedway rider ever to represent England?

8. **How old was he?**

9. Why was he unable to ride for England on that occasion?

10. **Who won the ice hickey gold medal at the 1998 Winter Olympics?**

11. Who were the opponents in the final?

12. **What was the final score – 3-2, 2-1 or 1-0?**

13. Which cyclist won the Tour de France, Giro d'Italia and World Championship in the same year?

14. **What year was that?**

15. Which country did he represent?

ANSWERS 1. Hungary 2. 1979 3. World Championship of 1973 4. 1906 5. 1971 6. Six iron 7. David Howe 8. 16 years 48 days 9. He had to take school exams 10. Czechoslovakia 11. Russia 12. 1–0 13. Stephen Roche 14. 1987 15. Ireland

# Quiz 11    MIXED BAG

1. Where did Britain's four-man bobsleigh team finish at the 1998 Winter Olympics?

2. **Who coached the team?**

3. Which team had he previously coached?

4. **In his 12 years with that team, how many Olympic medals did they win?**

5. How many hundredths of a second quicker did the British team need to be to take the 1998 silver instead of sharing the bronze?

6. **How many British riders before 1998 had worn the yellow jersey in the Tour de France?**

7. Who won the 1980 Grand National?

8. **What "orders" did trainer Captain Tim Forster give to his American amateur jockey before that race?**

9. Who was that winning jockey?

10. **Which British Olympic gold medallist was diagnosed as diabetic in 1998?**

11. Who retired from Moto-cross in 1998 after breaking an arm in France?

12. **How many British titles had he won?**

13. When Sandra Ortiz-Dell Valle successfully claimed that she was a victim of discrimination over her bid to become the first female basketball referee, what was her reward?

14. **When did Laura Davies become the first British winner of the US Women's Open Golf?**

15. What was her score for the 72 holes?

ANSWERS 1. Joint third with France   2. **Horst Hornlein**   3. The East German bob team   4. **Thirteen Olympic medals**   5. Six-hundredth of a second   6. **Three**   7. Ben Nevis   8. **'Keep remounting!'**   9. Charlie Fenwick   10. **Steve Redgrave**   11. Kurt Nicoll   12. **Seven**   13. $7.85 million   14. 1987

# Quiz 12 — MIXED BAG

1. How many games does the winning side need in the game of boules?

2. **Which British women's backstroke swimmer won five golds and a silver in the Commonwealth Games of 1962 and 1966?**

3. Which couple were the first in 1998 to win two Olympic golds for ice dancing?

4. **How many World titles did they hold at that time?**

5. Which country took gold in the 1998 European Karate Championships?

6. **Whose biography figures in the 1998 book entitled "Bestie: A Portrait of a Legend"?**

7. Who carried the flag for Britain at the opening ceremony of the 1998 Paralympic Winter Games?

8. **In how many Games has he competed?**

9. What is his occupation?

10. **Who in 1996 was suspended for six games and fined $20,000 for head-butting a referee in a basketball match?**

11. Which team was he playing for?

12. **Which snooker player discovered in 1997 that he is 80% colour blind?**

13. Which Englishman won the Speedway World Cup in 1980?

14. **How many TT races did Mike Hailwood win in his career?**

15. When did he retire?

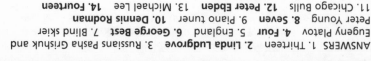
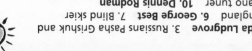

ANSWERS 1. Thirteen 2. **Linda Ludgrove** 3. Russians Pasha Grishuk and Evgeny Platov 4. **Four** 5. England 6. **George Best** 7. Blind skier Peter Young 8. **Seven** 9. Piano tuner 10. **Dennis Rodman** 11. Chicago Bulls 12. **Peter Ebden** 13. Michael Lee 14. **Fourteen** 15. After a crash at the 1974 German Grand Prix

# Quiz 13 　　MIXED BAG

1. Which rider won the 1997 Land Rover World Three-Day Eventing title?

2. **Which British rider was his nearest rival?**

3. What other major title does Tait hold?

4. **Who won the English Women's National Indoor Bowls singles title in 1998?**

5. In 1974, which racehorse won the King George VI and Queen Elizabeth Stakes for the second year running?

6. **Had this been done before?**

7. Who in 1967 became the first person since World War Two to take both British Amateur and British Open squash titles?

8. **Who won the World Amateur title the same year?**

9. Which country won the first Men's Softball Championship in 1966?

10. **Who won the first World Trampoline Championship in 1964?**

11. American Judy Wills won the first women's title for trampolining. How many years did she hold it – seven, five or two?

12. **Britain lost yachting's Admiral's Cup for the first time in 1961. Who won the trophy?**

13. When Ralph Boston leapt 8.21 metres in the long jump in 1960, whose record did he break?

14. **What was the previous record distance?**

15. What are the strokes in individual medley swimming events?

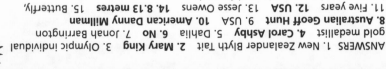

ANSWERS **1.** New Zealander Blyth Tait **2. Mary King 3.** Olympic individual gold medallist **4. Carol Ashby 5.** Dahlia **6. No 7.** Jonah Barrington **8. Australian Geoff Hunt 9.** USA **10. American Danny Millman 11.** Five years **12. USA 13.** Jesse Owens **14. 8.13 metres 15.** Butterfly, back-stroke, breast-stroke and freestyle

# *Quiz* 14     MIXED BAG

1. Which former England and British Lions Rugby star had hoped to row in the 1998 Boat Race?

2. **What happened?**

3. How old was he at the time?

4. **The Cambridge crew was the tallest and heaviest ever in 1998. What was the average height?**

5. And the average weight?

6. **Who won the race?**

7. When had Oxford last won before the 1998 race?

8. **The race was won in record time. Was it 19mins 40 secs, 19 mins 31 secs or 19 mins 19 secs?**

9. What was the previous record time?

10. **When was that recorded?**

11. By which crew?

12. **When was the first Varsity Boat Race?**

13. When did Manchester United move to Old Trafford?

14. **Who was the first King to saddle a Derby winner?**

15. When and what was the horse?

ANSWERS 1. Andy Ripley  2. He failed the final trial  3. Fifty  4. 6ft 5ins  5. 15 stone  6. Cambridge  7. 1992  8. 19min 19secs  9. 19min 45secs  10. 1984  11. Oxford  12. 1829  13. 1910  14. King Edward VII  15. Minora in 1909

# *Quiz 15*          MIXED BAG

1. Which point-to-point woman rider had her 200th winner in Cornwall on March 15, 1998?

2. **When did she ride her first winner?**

3. One other woman has achieved the same target. Who?

4. **How many men had brought home 200 point-to-point winners before Polly's achievement?**

5. Who won cycling's 1997 Tour de France?

6. **What record was Tracy Edwards and her all-woman crew hoping to break in March 1998?**

7. What happened?

8. **What was the name of the vessel?**

9. How long did Sir Peter Blake and Sir Robin Knox-Johnston take to make the journey in 1994?

10. **When was the first International Horse Show held at Olympia?**

11. Who was the first verified black player to play professional American football?

12. **When?**

13. Who did he sign for?

14. **What job was he guaranteed when he signed?**

15. Which two brothers finished first and second in the 1903 British Open Golf?

ANSWERS 1. Polly Curling  2. 1982  3. Alison Dare  4. Seven  5. German rider Jan Ollerich  6. The Jules Verne record for the fastest circumnavigation of the Globe  7. The mast broke 2,000 miles West of Cape Horn  8. Royal and Sun Alliance  9. A record 74 days  10. 1907  11. Charles W. Follis  12. 1904  13. Shelby  14. In a hardware store  15. Harry and Tom Vardon

# THE ULTIMATE SPORTS FACT AND QUIZ BOOK

# *Quiz* 16    MIXED BAG

1. Which Italian skier celebrated World Cup victory in the last slalom of the men's 1998 season?

2. **Why was the fact that it was held in the Swiss resort of Crans Montana so special?**

3. What was the margin of his win? Was it 0.14sec or 1.14sec?

4. **Hans-Petter Buraas was in second place. Which nation did he represent?**

5. How did the winner celebrate?

6. **Who were the winners of the 1998 American Super Bowl?**

7. Name the runners-up.

8. **What was the score?**

9. Who was the first winner of the cycling Tour de France?

10. **What was his day job?  Goldsmith, publisher or chimney sweep?**

11. When was the race held?

12. **Was the distance over or under 2,500 kilometres?**

13. How many days did the race last?

14. **Was his total time for the Tour under or over 100 hours?**

15. What in hours was his winning distance?

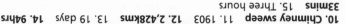

ANSWERS 1. Alberto Tomba  **2. His first medal was won there**  3. 0.14sec
**4. Norway**  5. He threw his goggles to the crowd and rolled in the snow
**6. Denver Broncos**  7. Green Bay Packers  **8. 31–24**  9. Maurice Garin
**10. Chimney sweep**  11. 1903  **12. 2,428kms**  13. 19 days  **14. 94hrs**
**33mins**  15. Three hours

# Quiz 17   MIXED BAG

1. Who was the Chinese badminton ace forced to retire with cramp when on the verge of victory in the 1997 World Finals?

2. **How did he fare in the 1998 All-England Championships?**

3. Who was his opponent in the final?

4. **How many of the five 1998 titles at the Championships went to British players?**

5. Who in the basketball Uniball Trophy Final in March 1998 broke the records for the highest individual score in a final?

6. **What was his score?**

7. Which side did he help to victory?

8. **Who were the losing side?**

9. What was the final score?

10. **Who invented the golf ball as used today?**

11. What was different about its construction?

12. **What was the inventor's profession?**

13. Which Premiership football referee is a housemaster at Harrow School?

14. **Why did he opt out of refereeing European and World Cup games in 1998?**

15. Whose autobiography was titled "The Working Man's Ballet"?

ANSWERS 1. Sun Jun   2. **He won the men's singles**   3. Malaysian Ong Ewe Hock   4. **None**   5. John Amaechi   6. **40 points**   7. Sheffield Sharks 8. **London Towers**   9. 82-79   10. **Dr Coburn Haskell**   11. He bound elastic thread round a hard core   12. **A dentist in Ohio**   13. David Elleray 14. **Pressure of work**   15. Footballer Alan Hudson

# Quiz 18    MIXED BAG

1. Name the Irishman who had won four British bowls singles titles at all levels by the time he was 24.

2. **Which titles are they?**

3. Who did he beat to win the under-25 singles final in 1998?

4. **In which sport did England celebrate a Test victory over Australia in 1998 – hockey, bowls or cricket?**

5. How many of the nine games in the three-match series did England win?

6. **Why was the series moved to an indoor arena?**

7. Who paid 317 million dollars for an American baseball team?

8. **What was that team – Toronto Blue Jays, New York Yankees or Los Angeles Dodgers?**

9. Who was the top-earning sportsman in the World in 1997?

10. **How much did he earn – £20 million, £46m or £49m?**

11. What were Tiger Woods' estimated earnings in 1997? Was the figure above or below £15 million?

12. **Who topped the UK sportsmen's earnings list in 1997?**

13. Did that person earn more or less than £8 million?

14. **Where did Alan Shearer figure on the list – second, fourth or sixth?**

15. His estimated earnings in 1997 were £2.3 million, £3.5m or £5m?

ANSWERS 1. Jeremy Henry 2. Senior and junior titles, indoor and out
3. Nicky Brett 4. Bowls 5. Eight 6. At the request of television
7. Rupert Murdoch 8. Los Angeles Dodgers 9. Basketball player
Michael Jordan 10. £46 million 11. £15.4 million 12. Naseem Hamed
13. £7.1 million 14. Fourth 15. £3.5 million

# Quiz 19     MIXED BAG

1. An Australian woman pole-vaulter set and broke her own World records four times in a month in 1998. Can you name her?

2. **What was her best in the national grand prix – 4.51 metres, 4.49 metres or 4.59 metres?**

3. Which famous Indian cricketer was hoping to represent his country at golf in the 1998 Asian Games?

4. **How many Test wickets did he take?**

5. In what year was the Grand National declared void – 1990, 1989 or 1993?

6. **Why?**

7. Which horse and jockey completed the course and thought they had won?

8. **How much money did bookmakers have to return to punters – £75million, £80m or £90m?**

9. How many European Cups did Nottingham Forest win while Brian Clough was in charge?

10. **Which Czech tennis player entered his national golf tournament in 1996 but failed to make the cut?**

11. Did he have rounds of 82 and 76 or 72 and 86?

12. **Which football star on the Premiership scene retired in 1997 to concentrate on a stage career?**

13. How old was he when he retired?

14. **Who was the youngest-ever winner of the US Masters golf tournament?**

15. How old was he?

# *Quiz* 20     MIXED BAG

1. On which English racecourse is a statue of the legendary horse Arkle?

2. **Who was the circus strongman who became World heavyweight boxing champion in 1933?**

3. What was his nationality?

4. **He was 6ft 5 3/4ins tall but what did he weigh? Was he 15st 7lbs, 18st 8lbs or 20st 6lbs?**

5. How many Classics did the famous greyhound Mick The Miller win?

6. **What did the dog's owner and breeder, Irish priest Father Martin Brophy, do with him after winning his first race at White City in 1929?**

7. What price did he fetch – 550 guineas, 700 guineas or 800 guineas?

8. **Which number on a dartboard is to the right of seven?**

9. Alpine skiing has been traced back how many years – 2,000 or 3,000 or 4,000 years?

10. **In which country have fragments of ancient skis dating back thousands of years been found?**

11. In 1984, American Bill Johnson took the Olympic downhill skiing gold at a record speed of more or less than 65mph?

12. **Who was appointed England speedway team manager in February 1998?**

13. When did he retire from full-time racing?

14. **How many international caps did he win – 92, 111 or 122?**

15. Who was the other former rider appointed to guide the Under-21 team?

# Quiz 21

## MIXED BAG

1. What disciplines are involved in the Biathlon?

2. **How many firing stations are on the 20-kilometre course?**

3. Britain's Michael Dixon has skied in five Winter Olympics biathlons. What medals has he won?

4. **When did the last London-based ice hockey team go bust?**

5. What was its name?

6. **Where was the proposed base for a new London Superleague team?**

7. Which Australian weightlifting champion and three-times Commonwealth gold medallist was banned in 1998 for two years?

8. **Why was he banned?**

9. What was his explanation?

10. **Name the venue of the 1998 Commonwealth Games?**

11. The goal area in which sport is called the 'parallelograms'?

12. **Who in 1956 was the first British swimmer for 32 years to win an Olympic gold medal?**

13. How old was she at the time?

14. **Which 100 metres final did she win: back-stroke, breast-stroke or freestyle?**

15. In what year did she win her second and third gold medals?

---

**ANSWERS 1.** Cross-country skiing and rifle shooting **2. Four 3.** None **4. 1960 5.** Wembley Lions **6. London Arena, Docklands 7.** Harvey Goodman **8. He was alleged to have an illegal level of testosterone 9.** He claimed he had taken a ginseng-based herbal remedy **10. Kuala Lumpur 11.** Gaelic football **12. Judy Grinham 13.** Seventeen **14. Back-stroke 15.** 1958

# Quiz 22 — MIXED BAG

1. How many gold medals did British women take at the British Open Judo Championships in April 1998?

2. **In those Championships, how long did it take Karina Bryant to flatten French competitor Sonia Manrin? Was it 55 secs, 14 secs or 31 secs?**

3. Why was there damage inflicted at 12 county cricket grounds in one night in January 1970?

4. **Who asked for the tour to be called off?**

5. Did the Cricket Council agree?

6. **Which nation won the first women's World Hockey Cup in 1974?**

7. In Rugby Union, when was the value of a try increased from three points to four?

8. **When did Princess Anne win two gold medals at the European Three-Day Event?**

9. In which events did she win?

10. **Name her horse.**

11. Which former Prime Minister captained the British team to win yachting's Admiral's Cup from the United States?

12. **Was that in 1971 or 1991?**

13. How old was Arnold Palmer when he won his first US Masters in 1958? Was he 19 or 28 or 32?

14. **Who in March 1998 won the Milan-San Remo cycle race for a second successive year?**

15. The seven-hour race covers how many miles – 160, 185 or 200?

ANSWERS **1.** Five **2. 14 seconds 3.** As a protest against the proposed visit of a South African team **4. Home Secretary James Callaghan 5.** Yes **6. The Netherlands 7.** 1971 **8.** 1971 **9.** Individual and team events **10. Doublet 11.** Sir Edward Heath **12. 1971 13.** Twenty-eight **14. Erik Zabel 15.** 185 miles

# THE ULTIMATE SPORTS FACT BOOK

# FACTS CONTENTS

SPORTING ASSORTMENT                          265

TENNIS                                       277

THE WORLD CUP 1930–1998                      287

CRICKET                                      317

GOLF                                         329

RUGBY                                        337

HORSE RACING                                 351

FOOTBALL – HERE, THERE AND EVERYWHERE        361

FOOTBALL – CUPS AND HICCUPS                  373

THE THINGS THEY SAID                         383

MOTOR SPORTS                                 395

ATHLETICS                                    407

BOXING                                       413

SNOOKER                                      425

ODD SPOTS                                    431

OLYMPIC GAMES                                443

# SPORTING
# ASSORTMENT

# SPORTING ASSORTMENT

After five years in retirement Helen Troke, 33-year-old mother of three, was recalled to England's 1998 badminton squad.

**Former European and Commonwealth champion Helen then aimed for the Commonwealth Games squad which was bound for Kuala Lumpur.**

George Cohen, full-back in England's 1966 World Cup team, hoped to sell his winners' medal for £80,000 to fund his old age.

**At auction in Glasgow, bids reached only £55,000. "A disappointment, but it was an unknown quantity," said the auctioneers.**

The previous record sale for a football medal was £17,600 for Ray Kennedy's 1977 European Cup winners' medal earned while he was at Liverpool.

**Colin Montgomerie was given a police escort during the 1998 US Golf Open after unpleasant abuse was repeatedly hurled at him.**

Detroit Red Wings beat The Capitals 4-1 in Washington in June 1998 to win their second consecutive National Ice Hockey League title and the Stanley Cup.

**Multi-millionaire American golfer Scott Hoch vowed that he would never play in another British Open.**

He was soon back at Royal Birkdale, however, because his new club contract said that he must play in all four Major tournaments if he qualified.

**Tom's the Best is a superdog! He won the 1998 Greyhound Derby to become the first dog to complete an English–Irish Derby double. He was also runner-up in the Scottish Derby.**

American golfer Casey Martin qualified for the US Open by holing a 25ft putt at the second extra hole at Clovernook Country Club.

**His qualification was noteworthy as he suffers from a rare circulatory disorder in his right leg, so that special permission was required for him to ride the US Open course on a golf buggy.**

When former Great Britain ice hockey skipper, Shannon Hope, decided to retire, his club Cardiff Devils, withdrew his No. 35 shirt in his honour.

# SPORTING ASSORTMENT

**Tennis star Mark Philippoussis of Australia has a tattoo of Alexander the Great on his arm.**

Henley Royal Regatta has never been so popular as in 1998, when a record entry of 552 took part.

**The overseas entry increased from 86 to 118 with Guatemala, Chile and Turkey sending crews for the first time.**

Michael Jordan led the Chicago Bulls to a sixth NBA Championship in eight years. He scored in the last seconds of play to give the Bulls an 87-86 victory over Utah Jazz.

**Jordan was named Finals MVP in all those wins. He scored Chicago's last eight points against Utah to take his tally to 45, more than half the team's total.**

Twenty-two sportsmen and women were honoured in the Queen's 1998 birthday list, among them a knighthood for World Cup 1966 hero Geoff Hurst.

**Michael Bonallack, Amateur Golf champion five times between 1961 and 1970, thought it was a hoax when he received a letter informing him of his knighthood.**

Racing trainer Michael Stoute was the third recipient of a sporting knighthood, while Linford Christie and Sally Gunnell received the OBE for services to athletics and Malcolm Henderson received one for badminton.

**Veterinary surgeon Polly Phillips, riding Coral Cove, won the Bramham International three-day event to strengthen her claim for a place in Britain's World Championship team.**

It was Polly's first three-day event victory since 1986 when she won the British Junior title.

**Rochdale-born Ed Fryatt is hardly a household name in Britain but the 27-year-old golfer, who has spent 23 years in America, finished 24th in the 1997 Open – four shots better than Nick Faldo.**

His father, Jim, scored the fastest-ever goal in Football League history – just four seconds from the whistle.

**After a career playing for Stockport, Blackburn, Oldham, Charlton and Torquay, Jim Fryatt joined the North American Soccer League and is still based in Nevada.**

# SPORTING ASSORTMENT

Seventeen-year-old Emma Mounkley, who won five gold medals in Spain in the disabled European Championships of 1997, added five more gold medals and three World records to her haul in the learning-difficulty class of the BT National Swimming Championships in Sheffield in 1998.

**She set new World records at 50 metres and 100 metres freestyle and 200 metres individual medley.**

Sergio Garcia, 18-year-old golf protege nicknamed El Niño, became the first Spaniard since Jose Maria Olazabal to hold the British Amateur and Boys Championships at the same time.

**Terry Griffiths, Dennis Taylor and Steve Davis attempted to take over as temporary Board of the World Professional Billiards and Snooker Association, claiming that they had lost confidence in the existing Board. They lost their bid for control by 38 votes to 34.**

Ice Hockey Super League's newest team, London Knights, was established in a £5 million deal with the owners of Los Angeles Kings, Anschutz Holdings, in 1998.

**Their home is the refitted Docklands Arena, and their coach the former Bracknell boss, Jim Fuyarchuk.**

England men's hockey team's hopes of glory in the 1998 World Cup ended in their defeat by Pakistan, who scored three in four minutes.

**Holland retained the title by defeating Spain 3-2 in the final.**

The return of the Open Golf Championship to Muirfield in 2002 could give Nick Faldo a chance to complete a hat-trick of Open wins on the Scottish course.

**Faldo won the first of his six Majors at Muirfield in 1987 and another there in 1992, taking another Open by one shot.**

The appearance of Scandinavian golfer Jarmo Sandelin at the Volvo PGA Championship at Wentworth wearing green, high-heeled, pointed-toed crocodile boots caused an official stir!

**He is not the only Scandinavian fashion freak in the world of golf. Jesper Parnevik favours drainpipe trousers and turned-up peak caps, and his Ryder Cup partner Ulrik Johansson cuts a dash in cloth caps worn back to front.**

# SPORTING ASSORTMENT

Two years after Rushden and Diamonds, the Conference soccer side, had paid a record non-League fee of £85,000 to Kettering for Carl Alford, he was allowed a free transfer after claiming that coach Brian Talbot made him train with the youth league side.

**American teenage ice-skaters Tara Lipinski and Michelle Kwan out-performed all others at the 1998 Winter Olympics.**

Tara at 15 became the youngest-ever gold medallist, at 60 days younger than Sonja Henie who had held the record since 1928.

**Tara is the only woman to have completed consecutive triple jumps without putting her other foot on the ice, joining Frenchman Eric Millot as the only man to execute the move in World competition.**

Scotland women's rugby scrum-half is Paula Chalmers. But did you know that her big brother is that Scot of many caps, Craig Chalmers?

**West Ham midfielder John Moncur could have a future in golf when his footballing days are over.**

Moncur, with a four-handicap, won the Philips Professional Footballers Association Classic at Marriot Meon Valley to contribute £3,000 towards a total of £50,000 raised for Great Ormond Street Hospital.

**His two brothers, Nick and Terry, are both professional golfers and all three recently qualified for the Essex Open.**

# SPORTING ASSORTMENT

Legendary American champion boxer Harry Greg died following an eye operation. During the operation it was discovered that he had fought many of his later bouts when blind in one eye.

**Tennis coach Nick Brown knows sooner than most when rain might be expected on court. His wife is TV weather expert Suzanne Charlton, daughter of Sir Bobby.**

Steve Redgrave and Matthew Pinsent are not used to coping with defeat. Their fourth place in the first round of the 1998 World Cup coxless fours was their first reverse for eight years.

**"Today we were average," said a disappointed Redgrave after teams from Romania, Germany and Poland finished ahead of them.**

Britain's cycling Prutour came to a grinding halt when 90 leading racers ended up in a parking lot!

**On the 116-mile Manchester-Blackpool stage, arrows had been removed at a roundabout and the cyclists were on their way to Nowhere before officials could call a halt.**

The few on the right course were eventually apprehended and the whole race was restarted.

**Six-year-old Robert Olsson was Britain's proudest schoolboy when his paratrooper father Sean Olsson had led the four-man bobsleigh team to bronze medal position in the Winter Olympics.**

It was the first outdoor winter medal won by Britain since 1964 and young Robert was one of the first to know. His dad phoned him from the track.

**Hockey player Karen Brown set a World record in 1998 when she won her 273rd outdoor cap for England and Great Britain.**

She was voted Woman UK Player of the Year by the Hockey Writers' Club for the third time in January 1998.

**Harvey Goodman, Australian weightlifter and triple Commonwealth gold medallist, was in line for three more golds at the Commonwealth Games in Kuala Lumpur before suffering a two-year ban.**

He recorded an illegal level of testosterone, despite his plea that a ginseng-based herbal remedy had been responsible for his downfall.

# SPORTING ASSORTMENT

Cumbria became the first club to win the Egham Trophy for a second time in defeating Rugby Thornfield 85-77 in the final of the National Mixed Bowls Inter-Club Championships.

Tommy Taylor, the Manchester United centre-forward, had scored 16 goals for England in only 19 matches before he died in the Munich air disaster.

His United teammate and captain, Roger Byrne, another victim of the crash, had played 33 times for England.

Jamie Mills, Britain's indoor bowls singles champion, retired from the outdoor game because of the unpredictable weather resulting in poor greens.

Peter Longbottom, the British cyclist who in his 20 years in competition won 44 individual and team medals and silver and bronze Commonwealth medals before retiring in 1996, was killed while riding his bike for pleasure in February 1998.

St. Louis baseball star Mak McGwire created a record for the Busch Stadium when his home run of 527ft was the longest recorded in the venue's 32 years.

Playing in their first European final for 12 years, Britain's badminton team won silver medals behind title-holders Denmark in May 1998.

Four Australians have won British Open golf titles in postwar years – Peter Thompson, Kel Nagle, Greg Norman and Ian Baker-Finch.

John Elway, American football quarter-back, had waited for 15 years for his team, Denver Broncos, to win the Super Bowl trophy.

Before the 1998 final against Green Bay Packers, 37-year-old Elway's family had voted 5-1 for him to retire.

Denver caused the biggest upset for years when they won the trophy 31-24 in San Diego, with Elway helping with the score, then still undecided about retirement.

Doug Ellis, Aston Villa chairman, has bought a new toy – a £600,000 yacht to complement his Majorca villa.

He decided there was only one name for the yacht – his own nickname 'Deadly', given to him by fans because of his habit of sacking managers.

# SPORTING ASSORTMENT

The ice rink in Sarajevo, where Torvill and Dean won a gold medal in 1984, was partly blown apart during the Bosnian war.

**The area left intact is now used as an army warehouse and at times a morgue.**

For the first time in its 99-year history, no home players were seeded in the 1998 Yonex All-England Badminton Championships in Birmingham.

**Lisa Lomas was England's leading woman table tennis player for 14 years.**

Lisa won the national crown for the fourth time in the spring of 1998, then decided to retire and start a coaching career.

**Billy Mims, coach to the London Leopards basketball team, was offered a job with the club for life after they beat the Sheffield Sharks to become champions of the Budweiser League.**

Owner Ed Simons said: "As long as Billy can shout he will coach – and I think Billy has plenty of shouting left in him."

**Thirty-three-year-old Kurt Nicoll broke his arm in a motocross practice in France and decided to retire after winning 80 races and seven British titles.**

David Howe, aged 16 and 48 days, became the youngest-ever rider at any level to represent England in the under-21 speedway team that defeated Russia 67-23 in April 1998.

**The proudest father at World Cup 1998 in France had to be Terry Owen, once a striker on Everton's books.**

His son is Michael Owen, the Liverpool and England super striker who started re-writing the record books at the tender but talented age of 18.

**Father and son made international soccer history when they played for Iceland in the same match at Tallin in the 3-0 defeat of Estonia.**

Arnor Gudjohnsen started the match and was replaced in the 62nd minute by his son Eidur.  Dad was 35, the lad 17.

**Energy-giving bananas are the new sportman's diet.  Tennis players started it, taking a quick bite or two between games.**

# SPORTING ASSORTMENT

Australian tennis commentator and former Wimbledon champion Pat Cash used to have banana muffins made for him every morning when he was a player.

**"It was my secret diet," he said, "but other players were nicking them from my bag in the locker room."**

Martina Navratilova and Ivan Lendl started the trend; now Manchester United players devour bananas and jam sandwiches before a match and Nick Faldo and Tiger Woods carry them in their golf bags.

**Bananas are the half-time snack for England's rugby union players and cricket commentator Richie Benaud finds banana sandwiches a satisfying commentary-box snack.**

# SPORTING ASSORTMENT

Paul Palmer won Britain's only medals, two bronze, at the World Swimming Championships in Perth. His successes came in the 400 metres freestyle and the 200 metres freestyle relay.

**Nigerian-born 7ft 1in basketball player Michael Olowokandi, who lives at Hendon, London, will earn £5.77 million over a period of three years.**

He moved to London when he was three with his Nigerian diplomat father and started to play basketball when he was 18.

**He went to the University of the Pacific in California and five years later, in the NBA draft where college-leavers are chosen by professional teams, he was the first choice by Los Angeles Clippers.**

"To see my name in the No. 1 spot is incredible," he said. "I really started playing properly just three years ago."

**Andy Betts, another 7ft 1in giant from Leicester, was chosen 50th overall by Charlotte Hornets.**

Alan Springell and Gary Grace became only the second team to win the All-England Bowls indoor pairs title in successive seasons by beating Simon Stevens and Ian Bond 21-13 in the 1998 final.

**The winning couple had played together for only two seasons. Gary Grace's father Ron, Alan's regular partner, went into hospital and Gary stepped in.**

Ireland won the women's Four Countries Basketball Championship in 1998 for the first time in 12 years.

**Scientists are trying to devise a plan for blood tests to be given at the 2000 Olympic Games in Sydney.**

Blood tests are considered the best deterrent in the fight against drugs in sport, but the International Olympics Committee's medical branch is not optimistic that a reliable test can be devised before the Games.

**When 500 metres speed skater Hiroyasu Shimizu won Japan's first Winter Olympics gold medal for 26 years, the Japanese Prime Minister Ryutaro Hashimoto punched the air with enthusiasm.**

He said: "As an athlete myself, I want to pay my respect unconditionally. It is a victory of his mental strength."

# SPORTING ASSORTMENT

**Chris Bartle, a 46-year-old dressage expert from Yorkshire, won the Badminton Horse Trials for Britain on Word Perfect II, but not without sending shock waves through the spectators.**

The final placing was decided in the last event, the showjumping round, after New Zealander Mark Todd on Broadcast News had had only one fence down.

**Chris Bartle had spectators gasping when he suddenly veered to his right and seemed about to take the wrong course.**

Getting Word Perfect II back on course, he went on to give Britain its first Badminton trials title since Ginny Leng in 1993 – and a first prize of £26,000.

**Squash player Peter Nicol was not born when Jonah Barrington won the British Open Championship in 1973. Twenty-five years later, he brought the title back home by defeating the holder Jansher Khan.**

Barrington, who won the title six times in the 1960s and 1970s, had a fitness routine that was said to make him the fittest man in the World.

**Apart from playing squash, Jonah had been a milkman, a greenkeeper and an artists' model.**

Jack Charlton announced his retirement from football on April 28, 1973, the same day that brother Bobby played his last game for Manchester United.

**Tracey Edwards and her all-women crew aboard the yacht Royal and Sun Alliance lost their attempt to beat the record for the fastest circumnavigation of the globe when a mast collapsed.**

After the accident 2,000 miles west of Cape Horn, the bitterly disappointed Tracey said: "It is tragic that after 43 days and 15,200 miles, all our efforts came to nothing in an instant."

**Paavo Nurmi is considered to be the greatest distance runner of the 20th Century. He collected 12 Olympic medals from 1,500 metres upwards – nine gold and three silver – and broke 20 World records.**

Johan Museeuw, the Belgian cyclist, won the Tour of Flanders World Cup classic for the third time in six years in April 1998.

**The former World champion Johan crossed the line 46 seconds ahead of Italy's Stephano Zanini.**

# SPORTING ASSORTMENT

Russian skaters Pasha Grishuk and Eugeny Platov made Olympic history when they became the first to win gold medals for ice dancing in successive Olympics.

**They danced to the music composed as a memorial to victims of the 1985 Heysel football stadium disaster.**

Barry Dancer, coach to the England hockey team, was capped 49 times for Australia and won a silver medal in the 1976 Montreal Olympics and a bronze in the 1978 World Cup.

**Basketball team Manchester Giants have the financial backing of American pharmaceutical millionaire Bill Cook and boast the largest indoor arena in Europe.**

American basketball star Shaq O'Neal said on leaving Orlando for Los Angeles: "In LA I can live my life. I'm like a big fish with other big fish in the ocean. In Orlando I was a big fish in a small, dried-up pond."

**On the tennis courts, the striking lofty American teenage girl stars Venus and Serena Williams, are all brightly coloured hair beads and dazzling smiles.**

Says the younger Serena: "Growing up as we did in the ghetto might have made us not feel pressure on the court. I'm not afraid of anybody out there." She was 16 when she said that!

**Two weeks after breaking a leg, Tina Gifford, daughter of racing trainer Josh Gifford, was competing on State Diplomat at the Canada Life Horse Trials in 1998.**

Asked about the broken leg, she said: "I can stand on the leg – the break is no problem. It is more difficult getting the bruising out." Brave, would you say?

# TENNIS

Czech Jana Novotna will be remembered for breaking down and crying on the shoulder of the Duchess of Kent after losing to Steffi Graf in the 1993 Wimbledon singles final.

In 1998, Jana won her first grasscourt final at the Direct Line Insurance Championships at Eastbourne.

She beat Spain's Arantxa Sanchez Vicario, who had taken the French Open a few weeks previously.

Arantxa Sanchez Vicario had apologised to Monica Seles after beating her in the 1998 French Open Championship.

Only 12 days earlier, Seles' father Karolj Seles, who as a coach led his daughter to the World No. 1 spot, had died of stomach cancer.

Martina Hingis was the youngest-ever winner of the Wimbledon girls' singles at the age of 13.

In 1995 she was 14 when she entered the main Wimbledon arena to face, of all people, Steffi Graf, who went on to win the title.

The following year, she won the women's doubles with Helena Sukova, endearing herself to the Centre Court crowds with her expressions of delight at every winning shot.

Twelve months later in 1997 and the crown was hers. She didn't lose a set before the final, beating the unlucky Jana Novotna.

Among her many 'firsts' in the tennis world, Martina Hingis was the youngest-ever to be named No. 1 in the World rankings.

She will not have to worry about buying a new racquet either – she is the youngest of either sex to win a million dollars in prize money.

Greg Rusedski turned down a million dollars before the French Open of 1998.

Racquet manufacturers Donnay had offered Rusedski the fortune to use their equipment, but Greg decided to stay with the Wilson-made racquet ... for which he doesn't get paid!

# TENNIS

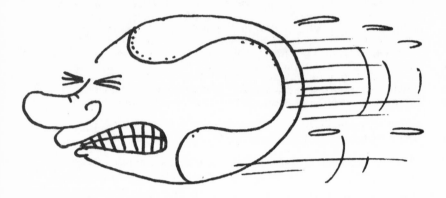

Teenage tennis protege Jennifer Capriati was an American tennis millionairess by the age of 13.

**By 15 she had the tennis world at her feet when she beat Martina Navratilova on the Centre Court at Wimbledon, but fame and fortune came too soon.**

Allegations of shoplifting and drugs were thought to have ended her tennis career at the age of 18.

**But Jennifer recovered her zest for the game and at the 1998 Wimbledon Championships she demonstrated, at the age of 22, that she retains the talent and desire to aim for the top again.**

So many teenage tennis marvels have graced the World's tennis courts. One of the most talented was Maureen Connolly in the 1950s.

**"Little Mo" was US champion in 1951 by the age of 16 and went on to take the Wimbledon singles title three years running, from 1952-54.**

So proud was her hometown of San Diego that they bought a horse, Colonel Merryboy, for her.

**While out riding in 1954 she took a bad fall, injuring her right leg, and was unable to play tennis again.**

She died of cancer in 1969 aged 34.

# TENNIS

**Britain's Christine Truman hit the tennis headlines at the age of 16.**

Although never winning the Wimbledon singles title, she was on her way to success in 1961 when she lost to Angela Mortimer after injuring her left thigh in a crashing fall.

**Australians Evonne Goolagong and Margaret Smith were still in their teens when they hit the Wimbledon heights, as were Chris Evert, Monica Seles, Andrea Jaeger and Brazilian Maria Bueno.**

In 1957, American Althea Gibson became the first black girl to win the singles championship.

**Born in South Carolina, the daughter of a share-cropper, Althea learned her sport in the ghetto where she lived.**

Tennis was not her only achievement. She was also a basketball player and a boxer.

**In 1972, Britain's Buster Mottram reached the final of the Wimbledon Junior Championship only to be beaten by a 16-year-old Swede called Bjorn Borg.**

A year later, the blond Borg was mobbed by teenage fans when he made his first Centre Court appearance, in which he lost.

Borg went on to win five successive Wimbledon singles titles.

**He showed amazing stamina and in 1977 he beat Vitas Gerulaitis in a five-set semi-final and John McEnroe in a five-set final – playing 97 games in three days.**

Billie Jean King was Queen of the World tennis courts in the 1960s and 1970s.

**She won 12 major singles titles around the World.**

At Wimbledon she won a total of 20 titles – six singles, ten doubles and four mixed doubles.

**In 1979 she won her 20th Wimbledon title, partnering Martina Navratilova to beat Betty Stove and Wendy Turnbull 5-7, 6-3, 6-2.**

She had beaten the record held by Elizabeth Ryan, who had died at Wimbledon the previous day.

# TENNIS

**Former Davis Cup captain and player Tony Pickard saw the tennis potential in 16-year-old Swede, Stefan Edberg, in 1983 and took on the job of his coach.**

They worked together for 12 years while Edberg collected two Wimbledon singles titles, together with Australian and US titles. In 1990 he held the World No. 1 title.

**Tony Pickard probably saw the same potential in Greg Rusedski when they joined forces in September 1997.**

Greg went from tenth place in the World rankings to fifth during his association with Pickard.

**The two parted company in 1998 after Greg dropped out of Wimbledon during the first round with an ankle injury.**

On the first day of the 1998 Wimbledon Championships, an 'intruder' had to be removed from the Centre Court.

**A mouse enjoyed a close-up of the match between Yevgeny Kafelnikov and Mark Philippoussis before being ushered off court to disappear near the BBC commentary box.**

The Women's Tennis Association celebrated 25 years in 1998. There were two members in 1973 to smooth the path for its members. At Wimbledon 98, there were 58, including a massage therapist for the women players.

**Athletic American sisters Venus and Serena Williams, with their beaded hair, attracted an appreciative following at Wimbledon 1998.**

Their mother followed the girls from court to court in a wheelchair, having broken an ankle in a fall down stairs.

**Frenchman Cedric Pioline, the losing finalist in the 1997 Wimbledon singles, found the 1998 circuit hard going.**

At Nottingham he was thrown out for quietly uttering an obscenity.

**He had sworn in French at Chilean umpire Pedro Bravo when a net-cord went unnoticed.**

Play was suspended until supervisor Gerry Armstrong gave his decision and Pioline was out, with Australian Scott Draper being awarded the match.

# TENNIS

**It was Gerry Armstrong who caused uproar in 1990 at the Australian Open when he defaulted John McEnroe.**

At Wimbledon, seeded No. 8, Pioline's luck ran out again and he lost 13-11 in the fifth set to Marc Rosset of Switzerland.

**With his 18th birthday still a month away, Xavier Malisse of Belgium, ranked 431st in the World, was named to play for his country in the 1998 Davis Cup quarter-final against USA.**

Steffi Graf, unexpectedly knocked out of Wimbledon 1998 by Natasha Zvereva of Belarus in the first week, had been out of the game for a year with a knee injury.

**Australian Rod Laver, known as the Rockhampton Rocket, was the first man to achieve the Grand Slam twice, winning every major title.**

He won 11 Grand Slam singles titles in the 1960s.

**In 1997, Greg Rusedski and Tim Henman finished first and second in the BBC Sports Personality of the Year awards.**

Wimbledon 1998 saw the arrival of yet another tennis fashion 'first'.

**Pam Nielson introduced the skort – shorts with a flap of material across the front.**

For Monica Seles it was a see-through dress worn over a body stocking.

**In 1911, Dorothea Lambert Chambers arrived to conquer Wimbledon in a white ankle-length dress and white blouse buttoned at the cuff and neck.**

Dorothea, daughter of a vicar, won the singles champion 6-0, 6-0 in 22 minutes.

**In the 13 times she played at Wimbledon, she won the title seven times.**

Only Wills Moody with eight titles and Martina Navratilova with nine bettered Dorothea's achievement.

**Twenty-year-old German Tommy Haas ended Andre Agassi's 1998 Wimbledon dream with a four-set win in the second round. Haas suffered a broken left ankle in 1995 and a broken right ankle in 1996.**

# TENNIS

American Bill Tilden, a failed actor who won three Wimbledon singles titles and seven US titles in the 1920s, was said to have served at 151mph.

**Frenchman Yvon Petra, winner of the first postwar Wimbledon Championship in 1946, had been so badly wounded during the war that he was in danger of losing a leg.**

He was taken prisoner-of-war and a German surgeon operated on the wound and saved the leg.

**In the late 1800s and early 1900s, brothers Reggie and Laurie Doherty dominated the men's singles of Wimbledon, winning the title nine times in ten years.**

The year they did not win, Reggie was ill and played against doctor's orders, losing to Arthur Gore 4-6, 7-5, 6-4, 6-4.

# TENNIS

**A Spanish girl camped overnight at Wimbledon 1998, queued to get a No. 1 Court ticket, had her photograph taken sitting in her seat, then immediately left to fly home without seeing a ball hit.**

In 1931, American Sidney Wood was awarded the men's singles title at Wimbledon without hitting a ball in the final.

**His fellow-American opponent Frank Shields injured an ankle in his winning semi-final game against Jean Borotra and withdrew from the final.**

When Petr Korda won his first Grand Slam singles title at the 1998 Australian Open, he climbed up to the grandstand to kiss his wife Regina and four-year-old daughter Jessica.

**Australian Norman Brookes was the first overseas Wimbledon winner in 1907.**

Britain's Fred Perry was the darling of the World's tennis courts in the 1930s.

**He was 19 before he started playing tennis but was World table tennis champion in 1928 and 1929, adapting some of these skills to the tennis court.**

He won three successive Wimbledon titles, three US championships and the French title.

**In 1964 Roy Emerson, who took the Australian, Wimbledon and US singles titles, said that the superior strength in his wrists had helped in his success.**

He had achieved this, he said, milking cows on the family farm in Queensland, and his speed around the court was developed as a schoolboy athlete.

**In 1968, tennis lost its amateur status and, on becoming open, money and sponsorship took over.**

The 1968 French Championship was the first major Open event won by Ken Rosewall of Australia.

**Rod Laver took the first men's Open singles title at Wimbledon, beating another Australian, Tony Roche.**

Billie Jean King, on winning her third successive Wimbledon singles final, was the first woman Open champion.

# TENNIS

In the same year, Tony Roche and John Newcombe beat Ken Rosewall and Fred Stolle in the longest-ever Wimbledon doubles Marathon. The result was 3-6, 8-6, 5-7 14-12, 6-3.

Wimbledon spectators were torn between the World Cup football and tennis in 1998. Not so Mandy Wainwright.

**Although captain of the Cambridge University women's football team, she concentrated on competing in the women's doubles.**

Between 1960 and 1973, Australia's Margaret Court (nee Smith) collected a staggering 67 Grand Slam titles in 92 World tournaments.

**John McEnroe once threatened to drop his shorts on Centre Court if Michael Chang won the Championship. Fortunately for everyone Mc Enroe's shorts stayed secure round his waist.**

Buster Mottram, one of Britain's leading Davis Cup players, is descended from star tennis stock.

**His parents are Tony Mottram, who played in 56 Davis Cub rubbers, and Joy Gannon, a Wightman cup player of distinction.**

# THE WORLD CUP
# 1930-1998

# THE WORLD CUP 1998

The Sixteenth World Cup in France lasted from Wednesday, June 10, to Sunday, July 12, and featured 64 matches.

**For the first time 32 nations took part in the finals, compared with 24 playing 52 matches in USA 1994.**

The tournament was a resounding triumph for the host country from start to finish, with ten superb pitches and a dream finale.

**The only black spots were the hooligans among the English and German followers in the early stages and, on the field, the feigned injuries, 'diving' and shirt-tugging which hit epidemic proportions.**

France were worthy winners in their first-ever World Cup Final after qualifying for the tenth time in their history.

**Brazil were swept aside 3-0 in their bid for a record fifth World Cup triumph.**

France's previous best performances were in 1958 and 1986, when they finished third by winning the play-offs between losing semi-finalists.

**England went out in the second round after finishing second in Group G.**

Their first match against Tunisia in Marseille raised high hopes with a stylish 2-0 win, Shearer and Scholes the scorers.

**The next match was a much sterner test, but England's luck was out as Dan Petrescu of Romania got the winning goal in the last minute.**

Moldovan put them ahead in the 47th minute but the equaliser came seven minutes from time.

**It was another dream come true for England's 18-year-old wonder lad from Liverpool, Michael Owen.**

After making his World Cup finals debut as substitute in the last five minutes with Tunisia, he again took over from Sheringham with 17 minutes to go against Romania.

**His impact was spectacular. He became England's youngest-ever World Cup scorer to make it 1-1, then hit a goalpost in another great burst.**

Sadly, Petrescu for once got the better of his Chelsea teammate Graeme Le Saux, leaving Colombia the last vital hurdle in Lens.

# THE WORLD CUP 1998

**With Romania already group winners, England needed only to draw with Colombia to progress to the second round. Colombia, with inferior goals record, had to win.**

An incentive for Colombia was that if they were to win, it would be a clean sweep for South America.

**Brazil, Argentina, Chile and Paraguay were all going through from their groups.**

A record 24.2 million people back in Britain watched the vital match on television, beating the 23.5 million for the England-Germany match in Euro 96.

**For the first time, Glenn Hoddle had David Beckham and Michael Owen, the people's choice, on from the start and they responded superbly.**

Within half an hour, Colombia were down and virtually out after goals from Anderton (20 mins) and a Beckham free-kick special (30 mins).

**Beckham's quote: "I just needed the chance to show what I can do. I was given that chance and I gave my best performance for England."**

The win had a royal touch to it, for watching in the stands were Prince Charles and his younger son Harry, who is also an Arsenal fan.

**England now faced a formidable task in the second round, their great rivals Argentina having won all their Group H games without conceding a goal.**

Only one other winner from the eight groups had a 100% record, France having totalled nine goals against Denmark, South Africa and Saudi Arabia.

**England faced Argentina with the comforting thought that they had lost only twice in ten meetings with them.**

They had clashed three times in World Cup finals, with England ahead 2-1.

**England were wearing their so-called lucky all-white strip. They wore it last in 1966 to beat Argentina on the way to World Cup victory.**

White was not right this time! One of the most nerve-tingling games in England's history ended, as it had in the past, in glorious defeat.

# THE WORLD CUP 1998

**The first half alone had enough thrills and spills for a whole series of games, with three goals in the first 16 minutes.**

Goal No. 1 went to Argentina when David Seaman pulled down skipper Simeone. Batistuta scored his fifth goal of the series.

**Goal No. 2 went to England just four minutes later when Owen was felled by Ayala on his way to an almost certain goal. Shearer scored from the spot for his second goal of the tournament.**

Goal No. 3 went to England again as Owen burst through the defence at express speed following a Beckham pass, beat two defenders and scored with a brilliant drive.

**Right on half-time, Argentina went level as Zanetti put the final touch to a well-rehearsed free kick ploy that caught the defence napping.**

With everything at stake, England were looking good when disaster struck in the 70th minute with David Beckham getting the red card.

**Beckham was brought down by Simeone and as the referee showed him the yellow card, the England man, still face down on the ground, kicked out at the Argentinian.**

The referee Kim Milton Nielsen, of Denmark, was only two yards away and instantly showed the red card to Beckham for 'retaliation'.

**It was only the second sending-off for an England player in a World Cup match. Ray Wilkins was ordered off in 1986 in Mexico.**

Here we go again – over in France facing a footballing Dunkirk with ten men against the hardest nuts in South America.

**England fought like tigers but the fates were against them. Before full time, Sol Campbell had a goal disallowed.**

Then a 'Hand of God' incident in Argentina's penalty area went unnoticed by the ref if not by the all-seeing television eye.

**The tension was almost unbearable as England incredibly survived the 30 minutes of extra time only to endure yet another penalty shoot-out!**

Sadly, England had already lost three potential penalty-takers in Beckham (sent off), Le Saux and Scholes (both substituted).

## THE WORLD CUP 1998

**The fatal shoot-out went thus: Berti 1-0, Shearer 1-1, Crespo miss, Ince miss, Veron 2-1, Merson 2-2, Gallardo 3-2, Owen 3-3, Ayala 4-3, Batty miss.**

David Batty, it was told later, had never before taken a penalty kick.

**England's exit at the second-round stage was the first time since 1958 that they had failed to reach the quarter-finals of a World Cup after qualifying.**

Don't shoot the ref, they say, but if this is any consolation, a Buenos Aires newspaper marked Mr. Nielsen nought out of ten.

**It is not said how that critic rated one Arturo Brizio Carter, the Mexican referee who 'controlled' three of the matches.**

Arturo topped the final card-call with four reds and 16 yellows.

**He was a clear winner of the reds table, but was outdone by Said Belqola of Morocco on the yellows with 17. It was also he who dished out both colours in the Final.**

Beckham was inconsolable, and returned with his head down in Concorde, then flew to the States for sympathy from his Posh Spice fiancee.

**Before he left, he issued a statement: "I have apologised to the England players and management and I want every England supporter to know how deeply sorry I am."**

# THE WORLD CUP 1998

Glenn Hoddle, almost in tears as the game ended, said: "There is so much hurt that I don't know where to start. But they can hold their heads high."

**Hoddle got "a very encouraging phone-call from the Prime Minister," saying that everyone back home was very proud of how England had conducted themselves in the tournament.**

There was also a final tribute to Michael Owen from a Spanish sports writer: "It's not the World Cup of Ronaldo, nor Del Piero, nor Ortega. It is Owen's. But the throne is left without a young king."

**Scotland's campaign had an all-too-familiar ring, promising so much then falling flat on their faces for want of a goalscorer up front.**

They notched only two goals in their three Group A matches, both by non-attackers, while Ally McCoist sat round a BBC table trying to explain their failings.

**Scotland had the awesome task of starting the tournament against the holders Brazil – and were beaten despite goals for both sides.**

They were a goal down in four minutes to a Cesar Sampaio header but John Collins from the penalty spot made it 1-1 at half-time.

**Many of the 80,000 crowd cheered on the Scots but, horror of horrors, full-back Tom Boyd scored an own-goal in the 73rd minute in his 56th match for Scotland.**

Scotland's next match with Norway was like an Old Boys' Reunion, the teams being chosen from squads that contained 19 players from the English Premiership.

**The Scots stole a point, thanks to Craig Burley's 66th minute goal to go level at 1-1, and everything hinged on their third match against Morocco.**

Scotland needed to win and Norway to lose to Brazil to earn their first-ever second-round place in eight World Cup finals.

**Said Craig Burley: "It's now in our hands and we can beat Morocco. If we do, then the big prize is there for us."**

Again, Scotland had flattered to deceive. Morocco almost unbelievably won 3-0, while Norway had people totally perplexed by beating Brazil 2-1 with goals in the 83rd and 89th minutes for a 2-1 triumph.

# THE WORLD CUP 1998

Commentator Ally McCoist bit on the bullet. But he had to say, as tactfully as McCoist every could: "I think I should have been there, but that is Craig Brown's decision and I have to live with it."

The series ended on a sour note for Burley, who was shown the red card for a late tackle on a marauding Moroccan.

Rod Stewart sang 'Flower of Scotland' before the match with Morocco, and the ever-loyal Tartan Army enjoyed themselves to the end without a single complaint from their loving French hosts.

The proud punch-line for the Scottish fans was that they were voted the best of the tournament by the International Association for Non-Violence in Sport. Joint second were Brazil and Jamaica.

Those Scots fans need to be patient souls as they consider their nation's tale of woe over eight World Cup finals. Played 23, Won 4, Drawn 7, Lost 12. Goals For 25, Against 41.

At least the Scots do not figure in the World Cup Nasties Tables of 1998. On the fouls count, Edgar Davids of Holland led the field with 21 fouls.

Number two of the Nasties was the Iranian Ali Daei, but you have to hand the crown to him because Holland played six matches on the way to the semi-finals. Ali did his in three.

The biggest casualty of the group matches was Spain, who finished third in Group D – the dreaded Group of Death – with Nigeria first, Paraguay second and Bulgaria bottom.

All the seedings otherwise won through, but spare a tear for Spain who recorded the biggest win of the groups by beating Bulgaria 6-1.

Japan and USA, a likely twosome, were the only nations without a point.

Other first-round casualties were: Morocco, Austria, Cameroon, South Africa, Saudi Arabia, Belgium, South Korea, Iran, USA, Colombia, Tunisia, Jamaica and Japan.

Of the first-time qualifiers for the finals, only Croatia won through to the second round.

The first-timers to go out included Jamaica, who went down fighting 1-3 to Croatia, beat Japan 2-1 and were swept aside predictably by the Argentinians.

# THE WORLD CUP 1998

Wimbledon's Robbie Earle got the goal against Croatia and Theodore Whitmore made a name for himself and his club Seba United with both goals against Japan.

**Argentina ran in five against the Jamaicans, with Gabriel Batistuta scoring the only hat-trick of the 1998 finals.**

First-time qualifiers South Africa performed creditably, with draws against Denmark and Saudi Arabia but losing to France 3-0.

**Jamaica's coach Rene Simoes was trying to be funny, one assumed, when he said he had banned alcohol from the hotel. "I must be strict with my players because they're mad," he added.**

One hopes Sani Toro, the Nigerian FA secretary, was not too serious when he described the team as "a bunch of money-mongers."

**He claimed the Nigerian FA had to pay the players $10,000 'incentive fee' before they would play. "We had no choice but to pay them," he said.**

Ha-Seok-ju of South Korea enjoyed brief fame. He scored against Mexico before being the first man to be sent off under the FIFA campaign over tackling from behind.

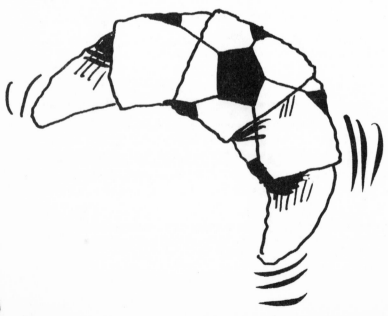

# THE WORLD CUP 1998

**Laurent Blanc, the French captain, wrote a piece of World Cup history in the second-round match with Paraguay.**

He scored the only goal, in the 24th minute of extra time – and it was a golden goal. It was the only one of the tournament.

**Brazil's odds as favourites shortened even more as they swept aside the fancied Chileans, Marcelo Salas and all, by 4-1.**

Cesar Sampaio, who scored the first goal of the finals, got two more and Ronaldo hinted at things to come with two himself.

**Salas said farewell to France with Chile's only goal.**

An earlier farewell to France was said by Tino Asprilla, the Colombian and former Newcastle striker.

**He played only 80 minutes or so of the opening game then threw a wobbly on being substituted by coach Hernan Gomez and walked out.**

He claimed he was being victimised but Gomez said: "We didn't throw him out. The decision was his."

**Germany were fortunate to head their group on goal difference over Yugoslavia, thus avoiding Holland in the second round.**

Yugoslavia were beaten 2-1 by the Dutch, whose scorers were Dennis Bergkamp and, in the 90th minute, Edgar Davids.

**The German team of 'pensioners' – the average age of their squad was 31 – as usual reached the quarter-finals.**

Their senior members with a total of 450 caps were Lothar Matthaus (37), Andreas Kopke (36), Thomas Helmer (33), Jurgen Klinsmann (33) and Thomas Hassler (32).

**The last time they failed to get to the last eight was in 1938. This was the 14th finals, either as West Germany or as a unified Germany.**

They had a few shocks against Mexico, who were leading 1-0 with a quarter of an hour to go.

**Then captain Klinsmann made it 1-1 in the 75th minute and Oliver Bierhoff got the winner four minutes from time.**

# THE WORLD CUP 1998

Romania's 'magic potion of Druid origin' was duly smeared on the team's faces, but the luck ran out when David Suker's penalty goal for Croatia pleased the bookies.

**Italy had easily qualified from their group after a tough first match against Chile ending in a fortunate 2-2 draw.**

Roberto Baggio will never forget this match and the penalty he struck home to equalise five minutes from time.

**Roberto had been haunted by his penalty miss in the 1994 Final shoot-out. It gave Brazil the World Cup.**

The Italians' second-round hero was Christian Vieri, whose first-half goal against Norway put them into the last eight.

**Italy's squad did not want for home cooking. They brought 60 Parma hams, six massive Parmesan cheeses, Italian eggs and crates of wine.**

Their 200 bottles of Chianti were supplemented after only ten minutes of their opening match against Chile.

**Vieri's goal was rewarded with 264 bottles of fine Italian wine by Italy's Wine Cities Association, one from each member.**

Christian Vieri, who was Italy's leading scorer, would also have hit a few if the French had also pitched cricket stumps.

**His Italian dad, a former football pro, and French mum went to live in Sydney and Vieri junior inevitably developed a love of cricket.**

"Cricket is great fun," he says. "It's only boring to watch for people who don't love the game." The same can of course be said for the way the Italians play their defensive brand of football!

**Norway departed with a flea in their ears from Brazil's coach Mario Zagallo, despite having beaten the champions in the group games.**

He said: "Norway just play high balls into the area. We are going to have to massage our necks before the game."

**Everyone sang Denmark's praises after the second round, apart from the Nigerians, who were four goals down before Tuani Babangida of Ajax scored a consolation goal.**

The Danes went forward for a quarter-final battle with Brazil, the pair having each recorded the biggest wins of round two, by 4-1.

# THE WORLD CUP 1998

**Danish fans back home celebrated with barbecues, and sausage sales soared by 30%, reported the manufacturers.**

Rivaldo rather than Ronaldo was the toast of Brazil as his two goals after Bebeto's first strike put paid to the gallant Danes.

**Jorgensen rocked Brazil with a second-minute goal and although Brian Laudrup of Chelsea made it 2-2, the champions held firm after Rivaldo's winner 30 minutes from time.**

Denmark's display helped to erase their most bitter 1998 memory – their 1-1 draw with South Africa when the Colombian referee went card-crazy.

**John Jairo Toro Rendon incredibly flashed seven yellows and three reds. Two of the 'reds' were substitutes and lasted only three and nine minutes. It was Mr. Rendon's only match.**

Five-goal Batistuta became a father but also a loser as Bergkamp's 90th-minute goal for Holland sent the new dad back to Argentina.

**Italy set up their usual fortress for the quarter-final with France, whose Maginot Line was equally impenetrable.**

There were no goals in 90 minutes, no golden goal this time for the French, and it was down to a breath-stopping penalty shoot-out.

**Again Italy suffered the fate that befell them in the 1994 Final. Zidane set France off to a 4-3 lead on penalties, then the Big Miss.**

This time the Italian fall guy was not Roberto Baggio but his near namesake Luigi Di Biagio, who missed and sank to his knees in tears.

**Said Luigi later: "I haven't missed a penalty all season. It hardly seems fair to lose the World Cup this way." Amen to that, said Roberto.**

Brave Roberto laid his ghost to rest by scoring with Italy's first penalty. "The 1994 penalty did pass through my mind, but I was thinking more about just levelling the score," he said.

**Germany's advancing years took toll in their needle quarter-final with Croatia, who avenged a Euro 96 bitter memory by winning 3-0.**

Croatia's mighty defender Igor Stimac of Derby County recalled the 1996 debacle, in which he was sent off.

**Igor's parting shot in Lyons was: "They beat us at Euro 96 with the help of the referee and we've been waiting for this chance for two years."**

# THE WORLD CUP 1998

The stage was thus set for two mouth-watering semi-finals, with only one of the quartet having previously won a World Cup Final.

**Holland, twice runners-up, faced four-times winners Brazil, while total newcomers Croatia faced France, whose best were two third places.**

France won a thrilling 2-1 before a crowd of 76,000 packing the magnificent new ground at Saint-Denis, the Stade de France.

**Davor Suker struck first in the 46th minute, then incredibly the French right-back Lilian Thuram scored one minute later and again with the winner 20 minutes from time.**

Thuram had never scored before for France, but the only sad note for the hosts was the sending-off of skipper Blanc for pushing Slaven Bilic. He now missed the Final.

**President Chirac went on to the pitch to declare: "This is truly the most beautiful day in French sports – France in the Final."**

Brazil's semi-final victory in Marseille was a real cliffhanger, with the 1-1 score after 90 minutes staying through extra time to a 4-2 triumph on penalties.

**Patrick Kluivert's 87th-minute header for Holland which cancelled out Ronaldo's 46th-minute goal for Brazil was just a Dutch memory.**

There was no third-place consolation either for Holland. Croatia won 2-1, Bilic was booed for 90 minutes and Suker scored to earn himself the Golden Boot award for the 1998 finals.

**Suker was top scorer with six, Vieri and Batistuta second with five each, and the trio with four each were Ronaldo, Salas and Hernandez (Mexico).**

French appeals for Laurent Blanc to be reprieved from FIFA's two-match ban failed and Frank Leboeuf came in as his deputy, with Didier Deschamps captaining the side.

**High drama preceded the Final. Ronaldo had a fit, was rushed to hospital and was back in the stadium only 40 minutes before kick-off.**

He was clearly unfit and Brazil were demoralised by two headed goals by the magnificent Zinedine Zidane.

**Arsenal's Emmanuel Petit then ran through the Brazilian defence for the coup de grâce, a third goal with almost the last kick of the Final.**

# THE WORLD CUP 1998

Brazil's captain Dunga saw his dream of two World Cup winners' medals die in the team's poorest performance in recent World Cup history.

**On the Final eve, the unloved Dunga said: "If we win I don't expect them to build a statue for me. But if we lose, they'll kill me." No news, good news?**

Four English Premiership players shared in France's triumph – Petit and Vieira (Arsenal) and Leboeuf and Desailly (Chelsea) – although the last-named was sent off for two yellow cards in the 68th minute.

**Chelsea remarkably had ten players in the 1998 finals, Manchester United nine and Arsenal and Spurs supplying eight each. Liverpool had six, Leeds and Derby five each and Blackburn four.**

Leboeuf was collecting his third major winning cup medal in a matter of months. At Chelsea he had already earned European Cup-Winners' Cup and Coca-Cola Cup medals.

**Petit also completed a memorable hat-trick of prizes. He had already collected a Premiership champions' medal to go alongside his F A Cup winners' medal with Arsenal in 1998.**

# THE WORLD CUP 1930-1998

Brazil are the only country to have appeared in every World Cup.

**The first World Cup was in 1930 in Uruguay and was won by the hosts, to add to their Olympics titles of 1924 and 1928.**

There were only 13 entries in 1930 and Uruguay triumphed by winning just four matches.

**Uruguay refused to defend their crown in 1934 in Italy, as retaliation for the poor European response to their 1930 invitation.**

Italy had to qualify for their own tournament by beating Greece 4-0. Thereafter, the host nation were in the finals automatically.

**The Italians gave Mussolini a Fascist salute – he was paying for the whole show – then beat the Czechs in extra time to win the Cup.**

Italy also won the 1938 Final in France to keep in with the dictator, who then went to war and lost his head.

**An oddity about the 1934 Final was that the captains of Italy and Czechoslovakia, Combi and Planicka, were the goalkeepers.**

England came in for the first time in 1950 by winning the Home International Championship but Scotland declined because they didn't finish top.

**In the 1950 qualifiers, Jackie Milburn got England's first World Cup hat-trick in the 4-1 win over Wales in Cardiff.**

The following month, Jack Rowley scored four World Cup goals in the 9-2 drubbing of Wales in Manchester.

**Scotland, beaten 1-0 by England, fielded a side containing only one 'foreigner' – Alex Forbes of Arsenal.**

England suffered their greatest humiliation in 1950, beaten 1-0 by USA. The scorer was Gaetjens, a Haitian.

**England's right-back that day was Alf Ramsey, who had to wait 16 years for a happier World Cup occasion.**

Brazil lost the 1950 decider to Uruguay, but the five games at their Maracana Stadium in Rio attracted an incredible 715,570 fans.

**Germany (aka West Germany) have appeared in all 14 World Cup finals for which they have been entered.**

# THE WORLD CUP 1930-1998

They did not go to Uruguay in 1930 for the inaugural tournament and FIFA told them they weren't welcome for the first post-war shindig of 1950 – also in South America.

**The Germans have played only twice in finals with South American venues and were eliminated both times at the quarter-final stage.**

Yugoslavia beat them 1-0 in Chile (1962) and Austria saw them off 3-2 in Argentina (1978) after draws against Italy and Holland in the other group quarter-final games.

**Italy have also played 14 times in the finals. They did not enter for Uruguay 1930 and failed to qualify for the 1958 finals in Sweden.**

In their 1958 three-nations group, Italy and Portugal were eliminated by surprise, surprise ... Northern Ireland!

**Northern Ireland were indeed the surprise packet of the finals, reaching the last eight before going out to France 4-0.**

They were inspired by the captaincy of Danny Blanchflower and the goalkeeping of Harry Gregg, Munich air crash survivor in February 1958.

**They were managed by their brilliant ex-captain Peter Doherty and their hero in attack was Peter McParland with five goals.**

They appeared in two other finals, Spain 1982 and Mexico 1986.

**Northern Ireland again reached the quarter-finals in 1982 and were unbeaten in four games before losing again to France by 4-1.**

Only Brazil and Italy have won the World Cup in successive tournaments.

**West Germany appeared in four of the five World Cup Finals between 1974 and 1990, winning twice.**

Brazil have come closest to emulating that period of consistency.

They made it to the Final four times in the six from 1950 to 1970 and won three of them.

**The 1998 World Cup number of finalists totalled 32 for the first time.**

The number of qualifiers for the four previous tournaments was fixed at 24.

# THE WORLD CUP 1930-1998

The number of qualifiers remained at 16 from Switzerland 1954 to Argentina 1978, a total of seven tournaments.

The increased number of qualifiers in 1998 opened the door to four countries for their first taste of the World Cup finals.

**These countries were Croatia, Jamaica, Japan and South Africa.**

A further five countries were having only their second taste of finals competition.

**These countries were Denmark, Iran, Nigeria, Saudi Arabia and Tunisia.**

Denmark's debut was in Mexico in 1986, when they threatened to storm all the way to the last stages after heading their qualifying group and first finals group.

**The Danes finished ahead of the Soviet Union, Switzerland, Eire and Norway to qualify for the finals.**

They then caused a stir by beating West Germany, Uruguay and Scotland, scoring nine goals and conceding only one.

**Uruguay scored that single goal, but the Danes hammered them 6-1, Preben Elkjaer registering a hat-trick.**

Elkjaer shared the limelight in 1986 with three other tournament hat-trick men.

**The other crack shots were Gary Lineker (England), Igor Belanov (USSR) and Emilio Butragueno (Spain).**

# THE WORLD CUP 1930-1998

The cocky Danes were taken apart surprisingly in the second round by Spain, after holding them to 1-1 for 45 minutes.

**Butragueno took his match tally to four in a 5-1 victory in which three penalty goals were recorded – and that before the days of penalty shoot-outs!**

Iran's undistinguished first appearance was in 1978, when they won their only point in a 1-1 draw with Scotland.

**That result actually deprived Scotland of their first-ever advance beyond the first-round stage in seven finals.**

Holland pipped the Scots for group runners-up spot on goal average – and then won through to the Final against Argentina.

**That's where the Dutch ran out of steam, losing 3-1 to the host country in extra time.**

Argentina's national hero was Mario Kempes, his two goals taking him into the leading-scorer spot for the tournament with six in all.

**That was the first of three Argentinian Final appearances in four successive tournaments.**

They went on to beat West Germany in the 1986 Final, then lost to the Germans four years later in Rome.

**Nigeria's debut in 1994 was dramatic. They almost shook the soccer world on meeting Italy in the second round.**

Nigeria led 1-0 until the 88th minute, when Roberto Baggio scored and followed up with a penalty winner in extra time.

**Gianfranco Zola, then with Naples, will remember that match. He came on as substitute in the 68th minute and was sent off in the 80th minute.**

The Italians rode their luck to the Final by beating Spain and Bulgaria, each match 2-1, and finally faced Brazil.

**Brazil and Italy were both bidding for a fourth trophy triumph.**

Zola wasn't in the Final, but amazingly Franco Baresi played after undergoing a cartilage operation only 24 days earlier.

**He was made captain, led from the front by taking the first penalty – and shot over the bar.**

# THE WORLD CUP 1930-1998

Ironically, Italy's star of the tournament, Roberto Baggio, took the last crucial penalty – and he too shot over the bar!

**Saudi Arabia, like Nigeria, had their brief moment of glory in the 1994 American finals.**

They were deservedly Asian champions, unbeaten in their 11 games, joining Nigeria and Greece as first-time qualifiers.

**In the group games, they beat Morocco and Belgium and led Holland at half-time before losing 1-2.**

Morocco lost 2-1 to the Saudis and finished pointless in the group, but they made history as participants in the first all-Arab World Cup finals clash.

**The 60,000 Dallas crowd fancied a surprise Arab win over Sweden in the second round, with the half-time score 1-1.**

It was not to be, as Kennet Andersson scored twice in the second half and Sweden swept to the semi-finals where they lost 0-1 to Brazil.

**This was the Swedes' finest World Cup campaign since 1958, when their dreams of glory as hosts took them all the way to the Final.**

They had beaten USSR 2-0 and West Germany 3-1 for that 1958 Final meeting with Brazil.

**Sweden's dream ended in 5-2 defeat in Stockholm, where Pele thrilled the crowd with two goals.**

Brazil's winning margin of 5-2 was in fact the largest in the history of World Cup Final games.

**Tunisia, like Iran, made their finals debut in the 1978 tournament in Argentina.**

Africa had only one finals place in those days and Tunisia earned it by heading Egypt and Nigeria in the group qualifying table.

**Although they did not progress beyond their first round group, Tunisia nearly caused a major upset.**

Having beaten Mexico 3-1 in their opening match, they faced West Germany in a crucial last group tie.

**The game ended 0-0 and the Germans survived to the quarter-finals one point ahead of the African new boys.**

# THE WORLD CUP 1930-1998

West Germany were not at their best in the 1978 finals, going out at the quarter-finals stage having won only one of their six matches.

**Only three times since the war have they failed to get beyond the quarter-finals, the two other occasions being in Chile 1962 and USA 1994. They played as a unified Germany in the States.**

In five matches in the 1994 series, for which they qualified as champions, they won three but only by one-goal margins.

**They beat Bolivia, South Korea and Belgium, drew with Spain and finally lost 2-1 to Bulgaria.**

Jurgen Klinsmann scored in the first four of those matches.

**East Germany played six games in their only finals appearance, the other side of the Berlin Wall in 1974.**

They had two tough battles with Romania to qualify, then surprisingly beat the West Germans 1-0 in their first-ever meeting.

**West Germany were the first to win 'The FIFA World Cup Trophy' in 1974, when they were hosts.**

This was a new trophy, paid for by FIFA, cast in gold, weighing eleven pounds and measuring 20 inches in height.

**The trophy was replacing the original Jules Rimet Trophy, which was won outright by Brazil on their third victory in Mexico in 1970.**

Brazil offered to supply a replacement as a goodwill gesture but FIFA said no, thank you.

**The original Jules Rimet Trophy probably has collected a few scratches and dog-bites in its well-travelled career.**

It was almost lost forever when in the so-called safe-keeping of England prior to hosting the tournament in 1966.

**The trophy was stolen from a cabinet at a Stanley Gibbons stamp exhibition at the Central Hall, Westminster, on March 20 – three panicky months before the finals were due to start.**

The plot thickened when the trophy 'lid' arrived at the FA with a ransom demand.

# THE WORLD CUP 1930-1998

**The top-selling newspaper *News of the World* then found itself involved in its biggest sports scoop in years.**

The trophy was found, wrapped in a copy of that newspaper, in the front garden of a South London house ... by a dog.

**Pickles, a black-and-white mongrel, was a star overnight and landed a film part for his efforts.**

Pickles also received a doggie medal, free dog food for a year and a place of honour at a big World Cup reception dinner.

**He was also praised by the News of the World 'for sniffing a good newspaper a mile away!"**

The trophy was to remain with England for another four years after six unbeaten matches.

**It was England's fifth successive appearance in the finals starting in 1950 and that humiliation at America's hands.**

# THE WORLD CUP 1930-1998

The winning manager, Alf Ramsey, had taken over from Walter Winterbottom in 1963.

**Ramsey said simply on being appointed: "England will win the World Cup."**

They did and he was knighted in 1967. Seven years later he was sacked as England failed to qualify for the 1974 finals.

**England scored only 11 goals in their 1966 triumph, four of them in the 4-2 win over West Germany at Wembley after extra time.**

The Queen declared the tournament open on Monday, July 11, and was there again to present the trophy to England's captain Bobby Moore, on Saturday, 30 July.

**The goalscoring hero of the Final was Geoff Hurst, who replaced the injured Jimmy Greaves in the fourth match.**

Hurst made World Cup history by scoring a hat-trick in the Final and became Sir Geoff 32 years later.

**England's team was : Banks, Cohen, Wilson, Stiles, J. Charlton, Moore, Ball, Hurst, R. Charlton, Hunt, Peters.**

Brazil started the 1966 finals hoping for a hat-trick of World Cup victories, with Pele their star.

**They started well, beating Bulgaria 2-0 with Pele scoring the first goal of the tournament.**

Then came disaster. Hungary and Portugal each beat them 3-1, and the impossible happened. Brazil were out after the first round.

**Hungary were their bogey team, having beaten them in the wretched 'Battle of Berne' in 1954.**

Brazil had then gone 13 World Cup matches without defeat until this second Hungary meeting.

**Pele missed out through injury but was back to face brutal treatment from the Portuguese and was again injured.**

He swore he would never play World Cup football again, but relented and picked up a second winners' medal in 1970.

**Disappointment for many British fans in 1966 was that Northern Ireland, Scotland and Wales all failed to qualify.**

# THE WORLD CUP 1930-1998

All three finished as runners-up in their four-team qualifying groups.

**A further disappointment was the withdrawal of 16 of the 18 nations in Group 16 of the qualifying round.**

They all pulled out in protest over FIFA's allocation of only one finals place for African and Asian teams combined.

**North Korea took their chance to join the finals by beating the other remaining country, Australia, 6-1 and 3-1.**

North Korea were making their only finals appearance and earned the admiration of northern England fans and millions of TV watchers.

**They drew with Chile then astonishingly eliminated Italy, twice champions, to reach the quarter-finals.**

Middlesbrough fans 'adopted' the little Koreans and thousands travelled to Goodison Park for the last-eight match with Portugal.

**Fifty-two thousand fans were behind North Korea as they went 3-0 in the lead against the Portuguese after 24 minutes.**

Their scorers that day will never be forgotten ... in North Korea. Pak Seung Zin, Yang Sung Kook and Li Dong Woon.

**Then the four-goal genius Eusebio restored sanity, Portugal won 5-3 and went on to a 2-1 semi-final defeat by England.**

South Korea, who are due to host the 2002 World Cup jointly with Japan, have fared better in recent World Cups.

**They automatically qualified for the 1998 finals, to add to their three consecutive finals of 1986, 1990 and 1994.**

South Korea's first World Cup finals in 1954 ended in total disaster.

**They were hit for nine by Hungary, then for seven by Turkey. The Koreans failed to score.**

They failed to progress beyond the first round in their other finals but were never disgraced.

**They managed to hold three teams to a draw in those nine games – Bulgaria, Bolivia and Spain.**

History was made in 1966 by Antonio Carbajal, the Mexican goalkeeper, when he played in his fifth successive World Cup series.

# THE ULTIMATE SPORTS FACT AND QUIZ BOOK

## THE WORLD CUP 1930-1998

**His final appearance was against Uruguay and was celebrated with a clean sheet.**

Three days earlier, more than 90,000 fans saluted him at Wembley, where he was beaten twice by goals from Bobby Charlton and Roger Hunt.

**Mexico have played in 11 World Cup finals – one more than England, Belgium, France and Spain among the 1998 qualifiers.**

They had their best series in 1986 on home ground, when they were unbeaten in five matches.

**They held West Germany to a goalless draw after extra time in the quarter-finals, only to lose 4-1 on the penalty shoot-out.**

Before being drawn to meet Brazil in 1998, Scotland had met the South Americans eight times without a win.

**Six have been lost, with two draws – 1-1 in 1966 and 0-0 in 1974.**

The 1974 match was in the World Cup, the first of three meetings in the tournament. Brazil won 4-1 in 1982 and 1-0 in 1990.

# THE WORLD CUP 1930-1998

**The one goal against Brazil in 1982 was scored by right-back David Narey, a lead they held for all of 14 minutes before the inevitable.**

Scotland had terrible luck in that for three successive finals, 1974-78-82, they failed to go through to the next round purely on goal difference.

**Incredibly, they would have created history by eliminating Brazil in 1974 had they beaten Zaire in their group match by a good margin.**

The formbook in that group was nonsensical. Yugoslavia beat Zaire 9-0, yet Scotland beat them only 2-0 then proceeded to draw with Brazil and Yugoslavia.

**The Scots were quietly fancied in the 1978 finals, having knocked out Czechoslovakia, the European champions, in the qualifiers.**

The Czechs had won the European title by beating England, Soviet Union, Holland and West Germany.

**Scotland again disappointed as Britain's only finalists, added to which Willie Johnston was sent home after failing a dope test.**

Yet surprisingly they won 3-2 against Holland, who still headed the group and went on to the Final, which Argentina won.

**Robbie Rensenbrink's penalty goal for Holland against the Scots was the 1,000th in World Cup finals.**

A record-breaker in 1982 was Norman Whiteside (Northern Ireland), who at 17 years and 41 days became the youngest player to appear in a World Cup finals stage.

**Whiteside scored for the Irish against Algeria in the 1986 finals, their third and most recent time of qualifying.**

Scotland's only point in 1986 was against Uruguay, whose player Jose Batista was sent off after 45 seconds!

**Canada made their only finals appearance in 1986. They lost all three games and failed to score, although they conceded only five goals.**

# THE WORLD CUP 1930-1998

They were not disgraced, however, thanks to the coaching of former Blackpool and England goalkeeper Tony Waiters.

**They held France to a single goal scored by Jean-Pierre Papin – and France went on to finish third.**

Australia, like Canada, qualified only once and also finished with a goals return of 5-0.  That was in 1974.

**The Aussies, however, did manage a point in a goalless draw with Chile.**

They were beaten in the two other games by East and West Germany.

**Australia came close to qualifying for the 1998 finals under the coaching of the former England player and coach, Terry Venables.**

Having won all six Oceania qualifiers for a goals record of 31-2, they then had scores of 1-1 and 2-2 against the Asian winners, Iran.

**Unfortunately, Iran went through on away goals and Australia were out without losing a single match.**

Among the other one-timers' list of World Cup finals appearances are the Dutch East Indies, now known as Indonesia.

**They have a record with a difference in that they are the only country to have played only one finals match.**

They were among only 15 teams who contested the 1938 finals in France, which were on a knockout basis throughout.

# THE WORLD CUP 1930-1998

**The Dutch East Indies were slaughtered 6-0 at Reims by Hungary, who went all the way to the Final with the holders Italy.**

Italy won again and kept the trophy for 12 years through the war years.

**The Jules Rimet Trophy remained secure in the vaults of a Roman bank, and not under Jules' bed as rumour had it.**

Greece had a brief moment of fame in 1994, their only finals appearance.

**They lost all three games without scoring, a big disappointment after their eight unbeaten qualifying matches including wins over Russia and Hungary.**

Honduras played well in their only finals, in 1982. They drew 1-1 with Spain and Northern Ireland and lost to Yugoslavia by a single goal.

**Turkey appeared once, in Switzerland in 1954, and had three crazy, memorable games.**

They lost to West Germany 4-1, beat South Korea 7-0 (three for Burhan), then lost 7-2 to the Germans in a group play-off.

**Israel will remember their one finals, 1970 in Mexico. They lost 2-0 to Uruguay but held Sweden 1-1 and Italy 0-0.**

Italy went on to beat Mexico and West Germany before losing in the Final to Brazil, who were thus winning the trophy outright.

**Brazil were proud possessors of the Jules Rimet Trophy for only 13 years.**

The trophy was stolen from the Brazilian Confederation offices and was never seen again.

**Two men were arrested but it was established that the trophy had been melted down.**

The number of entries for the 1998 World Cup was a record 171.

**The highest scoring came in the Asian qualifying section, with Iran setting a World Cup all-time record score.**

The Maldives, in their adopted 'home' ground in Damascus, were beaten 17-0 by the Iranians.

# THE WORLD CUP 1930-1998

In the same group, The Maldives were beaten twice by the same score of 12-0 by Syria.

The biggest World Cup finals win was recorded in 1982 by Hungary when they beat El Salvador 10-1.

**The first World Cup match to be played on artificial turf was in Vancouver, between Canada and USA, on September 24, 1976.**

The first World Cup finals match to be staged indoors was USA v Switzerland, in Detroit on June 18, 1994.

**The match, ending in a 1-1 draw, was watched by 73,425 spectators.**

Before the 1998 draw in Marseille on December 4, 1997, an all-star match was played between Europe and the Rest of the World.

**Counting substitutes, 30 players from different countries involved in the 1998 finals, took part.**

The first goal came in the first minute from Marius Lacatus, the veteran Romanian, but the Europeans were beaten 5-2.

**Ronaldo (Brazil) and Batistuta (Argentina) each scored twice for the Rest of the World before both were replaced in the 65th minute.**

England were represented by Paul Ince, while Scotland's Gordon Durie came on for the second half.

# THE WORLD CUP 1930-1998

**Japan, qualifying for the first time in the 1998 finals, met Macao twice in the Asian rounds.**

Macao were beaten 10-0 in March 1997 and again 10-0 in the return match three months later.

**Japan played 15 matches to qualify, winning the play-off against Iran by the 'golden goal' rule for a 3-2 margin.**

Spare a thought for Liechtenstein who, in their European group qualifiers, conceded 52 goals in losing every one of their ten games.

**Their biggest defeat was at home to Macedonia, who won 11-1 – but still failed to qualify.**

Five countries qualified from the European groups without being beaten – Germany, Italy, Norway, Romania and Spain.

**Top scorer in the qualifiers was Karim Bagheri of Iran with 18 goals. Next came Predrag Mijatovic (Yugoslavia) with 14 and Ivan Zamorano (Chile) with 12.**

England have failed to qualify only three times – in 1974, 1978 and 1994.

**On reaching the 1998 finals, England had played 105 World Cup matches.**

Forty-one of those matches were in the finals, losing 11 of them.

**Poland headed them in their qualifying group in 1974, Italy in 1978 and Norway and Holland in 1994.**

The 1978 group was the closest call, with Italy on the same points with five wins in six but with goal figures of 18-4 against England's 15-4.

**They each beat the other by 2-0 in their two matches of the 1978 qualifiers.**

Wales' only finals appearance, in 1958, was memorable – as indeed was their manner of qualifying.

**Having failed originally when headed in their group by Czechoslovakia, they were invited to meet the winners of the Afro-Asian group, Israel.**

All the other group members had withdrawn at various stages on religious grounds, so they sent for the Welsh.

# THE WORLD CUP 1930-1998

**They duly beat Israel 2-0, home and away, then excelled in the finals in Sweden by reaching the quarter-finals unbeaten in four matches.**

Grand old names John Charles, Ivor Allchurch and Terry Medwin were among their scorers on the way to meeting Brazil.

**Pele scored the only goal of the match and Brazil went on to win the Final against Sweden, whom Wales had held 0-0 in the group game.**

The Republic of Ireland had their glorious years in 1990 and 1994, the only times they have qualified for the finals.

**With Jack Charlton in charge, they reached the second-round stage both times.**

They were eliminated by Italy 1-0 in 1990, but four years later won 1-0 in a group match with the Italians, who nevertheless got to a Final shoot-out with Brazil.

**The first match of the 1998 series was played on March 10, 1996, between Dominica and Antigua.**

The result was a 3-3 draw, after which 638 more matches were scheduled in the qualifying rounds.

**Only three of the 13 contestants of the first World Cup in 1930 failed to qualify for the 1998 finals.**

The trio were all from South America – Uruguay, twice champions, Bolivia and Peru.

**The World Cup has never been won by a European country in finals outside Europe.**

Unlucky man for Scotland is Gary McAllister, who played in nine of their ten qualifying matches for France 98.

**He was the skipper in all nine matches but was forced to withdraw with a serious knee injury in February 1998.**

Australia's qualifying away match in 1997 with Iran at the Azadi Stadium, Teheran, was watched by 128,000 spectators.

**The second leg at Melbourne Cricket Ground, five days before the finals draw in Marseille, attracted 85,022 fans.**

# THE WORLD CUP 1930-1998

The previous highest gate for a soccer match in Australia was 36,200 at the Olympic Games Final in 1956.

**Any coach seeking a secure future might look beyond Saudi Arabia. At the last count, they were on their eighth coach since the 1994 finals.**

The first-ever World Cup goal was scored by Frenchman Louis Laurent against Mexico on 13 July, 1930.

**Pele is the only player to have won the World Cup three times as a player. He did so in 1958, 1962 and 1970.**

Six countries have won the World Cup on home soil – Uruguay (1930), Italy (1934), England (1966), West Germany (1974) and Argentina (1978), and now France (1998).

**France is the third country to host the World Cup twice, in 1938 and 1998. The others are Italy (1934 and 1990) and Mexico (1970 and 1986).**

# CRICKET

# CRICKET

Mark Ramprakash's batting records were second to none in the English cricket of the 1990s, although he found it hard to establish himself as a Test batsman until his late twenties.

**He first picked up a bat at the age of nine, played for Middlesex 2nd at 16 and made his first-class debut at 17.**

Ramprakash made a spectacular debut in the NatWest Trophy Final of 1988, when he was declared Man of the Match in Middlesex's victory.

**His consistent play at top level in county competitions earned him the No. 1 spot in the Whyte and Mackay batting rankings in 1995 and again in 1997, for which he received a £10,000 cheque.**

Graham Thorpe (Surrey) and Steve James (Glamorgan) were close second and third in 1997 in those highly regarded ratings, Thorpe picking up £7,000.

**James won £5,000 to which he added another £6,000 on being voted 1997 Cricketer of the Year, both by the cricket press and fellow-pros.**

It was indeed a golden year for James. He was the first player to reach 1,000 runs and helped Glamorgan to win the County Championship.

**The crowing glory of that title triumph was when he made the winning hit against Somerset at Taunton to clinch the Championship.**

James also played rugby for Cambridge University and Gloucestershire, and before joining Glamorgan he batted with Michael Atherton at Cambridge. Earlier, at under-15 level, he had been in the Wales team against England, who were captained by Atherton.

**James was England vice-captain in a close-season. A tour of Kenya and Sri Lanka and finally won his first Test cap in 1998.**

Remarkably, he made his debut at Lord's in the second Test against South Africa – as opening partner to Atherton!

**Steve James was also the top scorer in first-class cricket in England in 1996 and 1997.**

Graham Thorpe was among the prizes again when Coopers and Lybrand announced their awards at the Professional Cricketers Association dinner in London.

# CRICKET

**Thorpe got the award for the England Test Player of the Year, although only a few days later he presented a sorry sight as, crippled with a back problem, he had two ducks in the Third Test against South Africa.**

It was his 52nd Test appearance, coming exactly five years to the week since he made his debut in the 1993 Ashes series with Australia.

**Thorpe became one of the special group of English cricketers when he made a century on his debut, scoring 114 not out in the second innings of the Trent Bridge Test.**

Also among the Coopers and Lybrand awards were Shaun Pollock as the Young International Cricketer of the Year and Sachin Tendulkar as the International Player of the Year.

**Despite Thorpe's incapacity, England managed to hold South Africa to a draw in one of the most dramatic finishes in Test history.**

Old Trafford was sparsely populated on the fifth day, with England facing a humiliating innings defeat.  Incredibly they survived.

**The hero was Glamorgan's Robert Croft, who defied Allan Donald at his fastest with the new ball, aided by tail-enders Darren Gough and Angus Fraser.**

Croft batted for more than three hours for 37 to save the match on the last day in the last over with his last-wicket partner Fraser at the other end.  England, 369 behind with 11 hours 20 minutes to go, had done it!

**Croft said:  "The South Africans were chirping at me all the time with some banter and that got my Welsh blood going."**

Earlier, Gary Kirsten had scored 210 for South Africa, his highest Test innings which he described as "the worst innings I've ever played".

**It was his second double-hundred in successive first-class matches, but at 10hrs 53mins was the longest innings in 113 Anglo-South African Test matches.**

England's escape at Old Trafford brought memories of the England v West Indies match at Lord's in 1963, when last-man Colin Cowdrey, with a broken left arm in plaster, watched Gloucestershire's David Allen survive the last two balls for a draw.

# CRICKET

**Another occasion, way back in 1902, England snatched victory from the jaws of defeat by Australia at The Oval, thanks to the gritty last-wicket pair from Yorkshire, George Hirst and Wilfred Rhodes.**

England, needing 263 to win, were 48 for 5, and though the mighty smiter Gilbert Jessop hit 104, nine wickets were down with 14 runs still to get. Trust a pair of Tykes to do the trick!

**World Cup 1998 football reporters were baffled when the Italian centre-forward Christian Vieri was asked to name his sporting hero.**

An Australian cricketer called Allan Border, he said – and he meant it! Vieri had been brought up in Australia when his father Roberto went there as a Sydney football club coach.

**Vieri said: "My dad and I used to play cricket with friends in the front garden of our house. It was good business for the local glaziers because they were always coming round to fix the broken windows."**

The England and Australian women's teams now have their own Ashes to fight over, following a ceremony at Lord's in July 1998 of a signed bat being burned.

**The original idea for the Ashes came from the *Sporting Times* who, after England had been beaten in 1882 for the first time on home soil, printed a mock obituary of English cricket.**

It ended thus: "The body will be cremated and the Ashes taken to Australia."

**Whereupon, an Ashes Urn was presented by two ladies to England's captain, the Hon. Ivo Bligh, after England had beaten Australia the following winter. It was taken back to Lord's where it always remains.**

Cricket has fared better than any other sport in Lottery money awards according to figures released by the English Sports Council in July 1998.

**The game has had 428 awards – 48 more than tennis, the next 'most deserving' sport – adding up to £52 million. Although most of the awards were too small clubs, Notts received £5 million and Hampshire £7 million for ground developments.**

# CRICKET

Graeme Hick of Worcestershire and England achieved an historic milestone on May 31, 1998, when he became only the 24th player to have scored one hundred hundreds.

**It was his second century in the match at New Road, Worcester, against Sussex, and was duly celebrated on the spot in style.**

Tom Graveney, the Worcestershire president and himself the scorer of 122 centuries, strode out to the middle with a bottle of champagne and two glasses on a silver salver.

**Hick was the third Worcestershire batsman to score a century of centuries, following Graveney and Glen Turner, who celebrated his landmark by having a large gin and tonic brought out to him!**

The Zimbabwean-born Hick got the 100th century at the age of 32 years and eight days, the second youngest player to do so.

**The youngest centurion was Walter Hammond, who notched his vital ton just six days before his 32nd birthday.**

Another remarkable feature about Hick's achievement is that he did so in 574 innings, fewer than all but two of the 24 on this great list. Donald Bradman and Denis Compton alone were quicker to the target.

**Compton made his 100th after 552 innings, but nobody can ever hope to equal Bradman's record. He did it in 295 visits to the crease!**

# CRICKET

"Worcester is a very special place for me," said Hick, " and if I could have chosen anywhere to achieve this apart from a Test match, I would have chosen here – in front of the people who have been watching me for the past 13 years."

**Hick was a schoolboy protege. He actually scored a century when he was six and was still at school when he played for Zimbabwe in the 1983 World Cup, when Zimbabwe sensationally beat Australia at Trent Bridge.**

He made 405 not out for Warwickshire against Durham at Edgbaston in 1994, passing the previous highest innings in history of 499 by Hanif Mohammad of Karachi some 36 years earlier.

**Lara scored 501 not out for Warwickshire against Durham at Edgbaston in 1994, passing the previous highest innings in history of 499 by Hanif Mohammad of Karachi some 36 years ealier.**

Before Hanif's 499 marathon knock, the previous highest in history was 452 not out by Donald Bradman 29 years earlier when playing for New South Wales against Queensland.

**Bradman's incredible batting feats will surely never be surpassed. In only 80 innings spanning 52 Test matches, he had a Test average of 99.94.**

He amassed 6,996 Test runs for Australia, scoring 29 centuries. Only one Test cricketer, Sunil Gavaskar, has exceeded that figure.

**Gavaskar compiled 34 centuries playing for India in 125 Tests, having played 214 innings for a total of 10,122 runs averaging 51.12.**

A surprising name appears second to Bradman's in the list of Test match averages – that of Graeme Pollock of South Africa, whose burgeoning career at the highest level was curtailed with his country's isolation from world cricket because of apartheid.

**Pollock played only 23 Tests, in which he made seven hundreds for an average of 60.97, with a highest score of 274.**

Graeme is the brother of Peter Pollock, the former Test fast bowler and chairman of the South Africans' selectors, and is uncle of Peter's son Shaun, the red-haired all-rounder who toured England in 1998.

# CRICKET

**Shaun Pollock's fast-bowling partner was Allan Donald, who at the age of 31 became South Africa's leading wicket-taker by claiming 200 victims before touring England in 1998.**

He overtook the previous record-holder, Hugh Tayfield, the great off-spinner of the 1950s, and was on his way to a target of 250 by the end of the 1998 series in England.

**One of the most interesting players with the South African tourists was Makhaya Ntini, from the Xhosa tribe, the first black player to represent his country.**

Ntini impressed when he took over from the injured Shaun Pollock for the Third Test in Manchester. He is also a top-class athlete, having demonstrated his prowess during the winter tour of Australia when he won an invitation 400 metres race in Sydney.

**Paul Adams was the first black player to appear in a Test for South Africa. The highly promising left-arm spinner has the weirdest but most effective action which has been likened to "a frog in a blender".**

Another interesting character in the South African tour party was the veteran off-spinner Pat Symcox. At 38, when batting at No. 10 against Pakistan, he made his maiden Test century.

**The South African skipper Hansie Cronje succeeded the 1994 captain who broke the ice after apartheid had kept the two countries apart for 34 years.**

He was Kepler Wessels, who had also played Test cricket with Australia and county cricket with Sussex. He and Cronje went to the same school, Grey College in Bloemfontein.

**Cronje himself was no stranger to cricket in England. He had a season with Leicestershire and also played for Ireland in 1997.**

Another South African on familiar ground was Jacques Kallis. He made 1,000 runs for Middlesex in Championship games as their 1997 overseas player.

**Kallis made his maiden Test century against Australia in Melbourne on the 1997-98 tour and had a ton against England in the Third Test at Old Trafford to earn the Man of the Match award.**

# CRICKET

Much discussion centred in the introduction of the new 'speed gun' to measure bowling speeds which were instantly shown on a screen during the 1998 Test series.

**The top reading of 92mph for an Allan Donald delivery did nothing for the next England batsman's confidence, but caused amusement among Alan Ealham's teammates as the machine recorded an astonishing 81mph figure for one delivery by the trundler from Kent.**

England's coach David Lloyd could not resist voicing his disbelief at that figure. "He must have had a gale blowing behind him," he said.

**The machine uses military radar technology and records the speed at which the ball leaves the bowler's hand. This is what the spectator sees.**

The speed gun's designer is Henry Johnson, a scientist from South Africa. He claims that his 'gun' can plot the ball's speed at every millimetre as it approaches the batsman.

**It slows surprisingly over 22 yards stump to stump. Johnson claimed that a Donald delivery projected at 90.65mph at Atherton pitched at 81mph, which took off another 5mph to meet Atherton's bat at only 76mph.**

Speed-gun inventor Johnson made the point in favour of the 'yorker' ball. It doesn't lose speed because it doesn't pitch until it is on top of the batsman, he argues.

**Speed-gun or no speed-gun, the game goes on and perhaps this might be some way of deciding a one-day match when the weather makes a result otherwise impossible by reasonable methods.**

The last Benson and Hedges Final to be played, at Lord's in 1998, was on the brink of a crazy conclusion when the foul weather suddenly eased on the carry-over second day and normal play was possible.

**Essex having made 268 for 7 in their 50 overs, the heavens opened and the odds were on a first-ever Final 'bowl out' at the Lord's indoor nets on the Sunday afternoon.**

This would have meant five chosen players from each side bowling at an unguarded set of stumps, rather like a fairground coconut-shy with the prizes anything from the top shelf.

**Fortunately, the Lord's groundsman got the pitch fit for play in mid-afternoon, and Essex sped to a B & H Final record win.**

# CRICKET

Leicestershire, hoping to wind up the B & H in its last year in the same way that they started when they captured the first Final in 1972, were skittled out for 76 for Essex to record the biggest win in the tournament's history.

**Essex skipper Paul Prichard, playing in his only B & H match of 1998 because of a fractured shinbone, was top scorer with 92 to pick up the Gold Award as man of the match.**

It was a tough finale for Chris Balderstone, who won the first Gold Award in 1972 when Leicestershire beat Yorkshire by five wickets.

**Balderstone, one of the surviving old pros who played cricket and football for a living, was there – as the TV umpire.**

How times change!  Balderstone picked up £100 for his Gold Award while his team collected £2,500 for winning.
In 1998 Essex were presented with £43,000 for winning and Prichard got £950 for his Gold Award.

**How old is cricket?  Nobody seems to know when the game was first played but archaeologists claimed it may have had prehistoric beginnings following the discovery of what appeared to be a cricket bat on the banks of the Thames at Chelsea.**

According to carbon dating, the 'bat' originates from between 3,540BC and 3,360BC.  It is made of oak, about 2ft 6ins long and has a rounded handle.

**Wisden editor Matthew Engel's comment: "It is entirely possible that cavemen played some form of cricket.  That's probably when they started arguing with each other."**

# CRICKET

Cricket celebrated the 150th anniversary of the birth of Dr. William Gilbert Grace on Saturday, July 18, 1998, with a one-day match at Lord's involving a greater gathering of World stars than anything in the past.

**The match was also in aid of the Diana, Princess of Wales Memorial Fund and more than £1 million was raised, while some 25,000 packed the home of cricket.**

The teams were captained by Michael Atherton (MCC) and Sachin Tendulkar (Rest of the World) and among them were the likes of Glenn McGrath, Allan Donald, Wasim Akram, Ian Bishop and Javagal Srinath – and they were just the Fast Bowlers' Union representatives!

**The star performers with the bat for MCC were Shivnarine Chanderpaul (127 not out) and Mohammad Azharuddin (61), in a score of 261 for 4 from 50 overs.**

The Rest of the World team got the runs for the loss of four wickets with 6½ overs to spare, thanks to a memorable knock of 125 by Tendulkar in which four enormous sixes had the crowd ducking for cover.

**Tendulkar was accompanied by the mercurial Sri Lankan Aravinda De Silva, who scored 82 in the third-wicket stand worth 177.**

Meanwhile, MCC had collected memorabilia from all over the World for a remarkable W.G. Grace exhibition in the Lord's Museum, running from the Second Test of 1998 to the end of the cricket season.

**Items were borrowed from the National Portrait Gallery, Grace's club Gloucestershire, W.G.'s family and private collectors relating to "The Great Cricketer", as the famous Grace Gate at Lord's described him on the memorial tablet.**

The massive, bearded W.G. ruled the roost with his prodigious batting skills in the latter parts of the 19th Century and played his last Test for England at the age of 50.

**He made altogether 54,904 runs, including 126 centuries, took 2,876 wickets and caught 877.**

He made the first Test century against Australia in 1880 at the age of 32 and in his 47th year scored a thousand runs in May.

# CRICKET

**Remarkably in that year, he scored 2,346 runs for England and Gloucestershire, for which county he was captain for 29 years.**

Half a century later, the new hero of every cricketing youngster was the handsome, dashing Denis Compton, who played for Middlesex and England and also football for England and Arsenal.

**Denis was 29 when he rewrote the record books in the memorable year of 1947, along with his Middlesex 'twin' partner Bill Edrich.**

Nobody is ever likely to surpass Denis' monumental total of 3,816 first-class runs. They included a record 18 centuries.

**The record for the most centuries in a season had stood since 1925, when Jack Hobbs of Surrey and England had 16.**

Compton scored 123 centuries in a career that was curtailed by the Second World War. His death in 1997 was followed by a memorial service at Westminster Abbey, attended by famous cricketers from all over the World.

**The record for the highest number of centuries in a career is also never likely to be broken. The 197 amassed by Jack Hobbs is 27 more than his nearest rival Patsy Hendren scored for Middlesex and England and 30 more than Walter Hammond's total for Gloucestershire and England.**

Hobbs, later Sir Jack, was known as 'The Master' and seemed to go on for ever, scoring 98 of his centuries after his 40th birthday.

**Surprisingly, Hobbs' name does not figure in the first 20 of batsmen who have scored more than 3,000 runs in an English season.**

His best year was 1925 when he made 3,024 runs, whereas his famous opening partner for England, Herbert Sutcliffe of Yorkshire, topped 3,000 in a season three times.

**Sutcliffe's feat was equalled by Patsy Hendren and Wally Hammond, each of them topping the 3,000 mark in three separate seasons.**

Top of the 3,000 pile are the names of Denis Compton and Bill Edrich, both in that astonishing summer of 1947.

# CRICKET

**Compton scored 3,816 runs for the almost unbelievable average of 90.85, while Edrich's 3,539 included 12 hundreds but with a mere average of 80.43!**

Two of the stands at Lord's have been named after Compton and Edrich, though one wonders what their thoughts would have been on seeing what appeared to be an enormous 'space module' suddenly appearing in 1998 above their two stands.

**The apparition was erected as the new NatWest Media Centre, due to open for World Cup 1999, and was claimed to be the first all-aluminium building in the World.**

Critics of the England team of those years argued in favour of the money going more towards team building. In 1998, England were sixth out of nine in the World's Test rankings and fifth of the 11 countries who now play recognised one-day internationals.

**Jack Russell, England and Gloucestershire wicket-keeper, had a rare scalp for his 1,000th first-class dismissal – Mike Atherton playing for Lancashire.**

One of Russell's proud records is the hat-trick of catches he made off successive balls against Surrey at The Oval in 1986.

**He still has a lot of back-bending to do before nearing the record of Bob Taylor, whose England and Derbyshire career spanned 29 years.**

Taylor's total of wicket-keeping victims of 1,649 stands 122 above that of his nearest rival John Murray, who kept for Middlesex and England for 24 years.

**A hat-trick record of a different kind was set by Cardigan Connor in July 1998, when he took three wickets in an over for Hampshire against Essex, the first time it had happened in a NatWest Trophy match.**

That was a humiliating experience for Essex, who were the 1997 Trophy winners when they steamrollered Warwickshire by nine wickets.

# GOLF

# GOLF

Willie Park was the first winner of the British Open in 1860.

**He went on to win the tournament four times between 1860 and 1975.**

Tom Morris Snr. was the oldest winner of the Open.

**He was aged 46 years and 99 days when he won it for the fourth time in 1867.**

His son, Tom Jnr., became the youngest to win the Open the following year at the age of 17 years 5 months.

**He won four times in a row from 1868 and died from a lung infection at the tender age of 24.**

Severiano Ballesteros was 22 years 3 months when he took the Open in 1979.

**In 1973, David Russell, a 19-year-old amateur, and 71-year-old American Gene Sarazen scored a hole-in-one at the Royal Troon eighth hole within an hour of each other.**

American Bill Rogers, British Open Champion in 1981, was almost disqualified before playing a shot.

**He was held up at a level-crossing for half an hour and arrived at the Royal St. George's first tee with 30 seconds to spare.**

Three Clubs – St. Andrews, Prestwick and Musselburgh – jointly presented the prized claret jug to the Open Championship in 1872.

**During the 1936 Open at Hoylake, Alf Padgham (Sundridge Park) left his clubs in the pro's shop overnight.**

The next morning, the shop was locked and no key to be found. Alf broke in aided by a brick and went on to win the Championship.

**Sandy Lyle, the son of a golf pro, was the first competitor to represent his country at boy, youth and senior levels in the same year.**

The year was 1975 and Sandy was 17.

**Sandy Lyle turned pro after the 1977 Walker Cup and was European No. 1 in 1979 and 1980.**

Lorry driver's son Tony Jacklin became the first British golfer in 1969 to win the Open since Max Faulkner in 1951.

# GOLF

The crowd, overwhelmed by his success, sang 'For he's a jolly good fellow'.

Later that summer, Jacklin helped Britain to tie the Ryder Cup.

The following year, he won the US Open – the first Briton to do so for 50 years.

Tony played in the Ryder Cup seven times between 1967 and 1979.

When he won the US Open in 1970, he led each round from day one.

The last 25-yard putt of the tournament ended when his ball hit the back rim, jumped nine inches in the air and landed in the hole!

American Bobby Jones retained his amateur status throughout his career.

He won three British Opens and four US Opens in the 1920s.

In 1930, he was British and American amateur champion and winner of the British and American Open Championships.

After his Grand Slam achievement, he retired to become a lawyer.

He was just 28.

American Walter Hagen was the first of golf's glamour boys.

His good looks, fashionable clothes and chauffeur-driven limousine, together with his golfing prowess, made him the darling of the links.

In the 1920s, professionals were not allowed to enter the clubhouse by the front door. They were expected to use the side or back entrances.

Hagen, on his first visit to Britain, solved the problem by refusing to enter the clubhouse at all.

Playing in the 1920 British Open at Deal, he parked his car in the club driveway and ordered everything he needed to be delivered to it – including champagne.

Gene Sarazen, friend and rival of his fellow American, later said that all competitors earning big money from golf should say a prayer to Walter.

"Walter made professional golf what it is," said Sarazen.

# GOLF

**Despite his flamboyant lifestyle, Hagen was a successful golfer with a string of four British Open and two US Open victories.**

Jack Nicklaus, born in Columbus, Ohio, in 1940, burst on the American scene at the age of 22.

**Nicknamed the Golden Bear, he took over the top spot from Arnold Palmer in 1962 when he won the US Open.**

His defeat of Palmer in the play-off was unpopular with Arnie's adoring Army.

**Between 1960 and 1986, Nicklaus won four US Open titles, the British Open three times, US Masters six times and the USPGA five times.**

In the 1970s, he designed a golf course in his home state and named it Muirfield Village.

**The Scottish Muirfield course was where he won his first British Open title.**

In 1987, he was non-playing captain of the US Ryder Cup team when Tony Jacklin's British team brought off its first victory on American soil.

**The defeat was on Nicklaus's own course – Muirfield Village.**

Tom Watson, born in Kansas City in 1949, appeared on the scene in the 1970s to challenge Nicklaus for his crown.

# GOLF

**Watson won the British Open five times between 1975 and 1983, the US Masters twice (1977 and 1981) and the US Open in 1982.**

His game fell away in the 1980s and he never bettered Nicklaus's achievements.

**Ian Woosnam, the gritty Welshman, had his best year in 1991.**

He won the US Masters and was named No. 1 in the World.

**Britain's Laura Davies topped the European women's money list for the first time in 1994 and was the World's No. 1 in 1996.**

Laura liked a bet and once confessed she had gambled away £500,000.

**Nick Faldo's obsession with golf started at the age of 13, when he saw Jack Nicklaus on TV playing in the 1971 Masters.**

He persuaded his parents to let him learn at the local club, was crowned British amateur champion at 17 and turned pro at 18.

**Tiger Woods moved up the Sony World Rankings in 1996 from 510th to 75th.**

Still only 20 years old, he beat the experienced David Love III in a play-off to win the Las Vegas invitation.

**It was only his fifth professional tournament.**

On becoming a pro, he signed a £25 million contract with sportswear firm Nike.

**In 1997, Tiger won the US Masters at Augusta.**

He beat Scotland's Colin Montgomerie by a record-winning margin of 12 strokes.

**At 20 years of age, Tiger was the youngest-ever winner of the Masters green jacket.**

Bernard Gallacher, captain of the European Ryder Cup team for the first time in 1995, burst into tears when his side won at Oak Hill, New York.

**Reigning champions of the US Masters hold a dinner for fellow competitors before the tournament starts and traditionally decide on the menu.**

Tiger Woods chose for 1998 cheeseburgers, fries and milkshakes!

# GOLF

Australian Bruce Crampton never won a major tournament but was runner-up four times, taking second place to Jack Nicklaus.

On his debut as a Ryder Cup player in 1977, 20-year-old Nick Faldo partnered Peter Oosterhuis to win the foursomes and the four-ball.

**They were also successful in their singles matches yet the British team lost to the Americans 12½-7½.**

Augusta, host to the US Masters, was built on a horticultural site.

**Each hole is named after a flower or plant.**

Maurice Flitcroft of Barrow-in Furness took 121 strokes to play the 18-hole qualifying round for the 1976 British Open.

**His entry form described him as an 'unattached professional' but he had started playing only two years before.**

Seven years later, he turned up again using a false name, but having taken 63 to the ninth, he was spotted and asked to leave.

**Three brothers, Charles (captain), Reg and Ernest Whitcombe, represented Britain in the 1935 Ryder Cup at Ridgewood, New Jersey.**

America won the foursomes 3-1, the singles 6-2 and the Americans were 9-3 winners.

**Greg Norman of Australia owns a $28 million jet plane, a yacht, two Harley Davidsons, a twin-engined helicopter and several Ferraris.**

He still craves one more possession – a major US golf title.

**Golf is rated a dangerous sport by Australian Brett Ogle.**

During the Australian Open in 1990, his ball hit a tree, rebounded, struck him on the knee and caused a hairline fracture.

**Five years later at the 13th hole on February 13, his club shaft hit a tree, broke into several pieces, struck him under an eye and broke his sunglasses.**

Both tournaments were won by a little-known American, John Morse.

**Between 1956 and 1971, Arnold Palmer won 14 of his 24 play-offs – a record at that time.**

# GOLF

Mark O'Meara was the surprise winner of the 1998 US Masters, being quoted at 40-1 before play started.

**Defending champion Tiger Woods was the hot favourite at a measly 5-1.**

Before turning pro in 1971, Tom Watson gained a degree in psychology at Stamford University in the States.

**By the time he was seven, Tom was playing golf every week with his father.**

He headed the American money-winners' list five times – in 1977, 1978, 1979, 1980 and 1984.

**Raymond Floyd's first claim to fame was not as a champion golfer but as the manager of America's first topless all-girl dance band.**

Golf soon became his passion and he went on to win the US Open, US Masters and USPGA.

**In 1989, he came a most respected captain of the US team.**

New Zealander Bob Charles is one of the very few left-handed golfers.

**He is the only left-handed player to win the British Open (1963).**

Bob Charles won the New Zealand Open as an amateur at the age of 18 in 1954, but refused to give up his job as a bank clerk until he was convinced that there would be a good living in pro golf.

**Australian David Graham might have joined Charles as a left-hander.**

Graham started playing golf at 14 with a set of left-handed clubs. He used them for two years before going to work in a Melbourne golf shop and switching to right-handed clubs.

**Johnny Miller, leading money-winner on the 1974 US tour, is a Mormon and said that his religious convictions were more important to him than wealth.**

Lee Buck Trevino grew up in a poor district of Dallas and left school at 14 to work on a local driving range.

# GOLF

Golf became a passion and a way of life – although he hadn't any clubs. So he wrapped a Coca-Cola bottle in adhesive tape, competing and winning against those using conventional clubs.

Serving four years in the US Marine Corps, he increased his pay by giving golf lessons to the officers.

He left the Army in 1960 and went to El Paso as an assistant pro, practising at every opportunity on the par three course.

Trevino qualified to play in his first US Open at the age of 27.

He finished 54th but two years later he won the tournament, scoring under 70 in all four rounds.

He went on to win two British Opens, a second US Open title and the USPGA twice.

Sergio Garcia won the 1998 Amateur Championship at Muirfield at the age of 18.

Fifteen years earlier, the Amateur Championship was also won by an 18-year-old Spaniard. His name: Jose Maria Olazabal.

Lee Westwood had a round of 61 in winning the Hamburg Open in July 1998. Seven days later, the left-handed Australian Greg Chalmers fired a 61 in the English Open.

But it was not a total success story for Chalmers. Westwood went on to win that tournament as well.

That was Westwood's first victory on British soil and took him to the top of the Order of Merit table.

Finally, a date for the long-range diary. Muirfield will stage The Open in 2002 for the 15th time.

# RUGBY

# RUGBY UNION

President Nelson Mandela is a great supporter of South African rugby and he was given the ideal present on his 80th birthday on July 18, 1998.

**Playing in the Tri-Nations tournament against Australia in Perth, the Springboks challenged the Aussie boasts of being the World's No. 1 rugby team by beating them 14-13.**

South Africa's coach Nick Mallett was under no illusions about the style of the victory, even though it maintained his international 100% record. This was his tenth win in ten games in charge.

**Mallett said: "It wasn't a convincing win. We'd be fooling ourselves if we thought it was."**

The Wallabies' coach Rod Macqueen found the defeat hard to swallow after their tremendous 24-16 victory over New Zealand in Melbourne a week earlier, the first time they had beaten the All Blacks for four years.

**"We are a much better team than that," he said after the Perth flop. "We did the hard things well and the easy things badly. We can't make that many mistakes and expect to win Test matches."**

The defeat left Australia with the daunting task of winning both their away matches to secure the Tri-Nations title.

**While the Southern Hemisphere supremos of World rugby were in combat with one another, they also found time to meet and discuss the future of British and Irish tour visits – if there is indeed a future.**

The three nations decided that they would never again accept fixtures with anything except full-strength touring squads from England and the other Home Countries.

**The South African chief delegate said: "We can't keep playing under-strength Northern Hemisphere teams. Western Samoa would not be any worse than Wales and Argentina couldn't be worse than England."**

Bill Beaumont, chairman of the RFU national playing committee, had his years of World supremacy as skipper of the British Lions and was quick to reply to the SANZAR ultimatum.

**He has assured the Southern Hemisphere giants that never again would weakened teams visit them. "It does no good for the hosts or our countries," he said.**

# RUGBY UNION

Beaumont put his finger on the problem when he added: "We're in a state of dejection now, like our soccer and cricket, but I want to think that England's 1998 summer was a one-off."

**The depths of England's rugby decline were illustrated almost as he spoke. Playing in the Under-21 Five Nationals tournament in South Africa, they were demolished 41-6 by Argentina.**

That defeat in Cape Town was the fourth in the tournament and did nothing to erase the memory of England's record 93-7 defeat by the young New Zealanders earlier in the series.

**The explanation that the young England squad was weak because so many eligible candidates had to be called into the senior tour party only served to emphasise England's all-round demise.**

Among the suffering England party in South Africa was Liam Botham, son of the mighty cricketer. After starting out with West Hartlepool, he went over the Welsh border to play with Cardiff. At least he managed to kick the odd conversion with the Under-21s.

**The Welsh Rugby Union are also unhappy with the state of affairs among its leading clubs, in spite of the great boost to morale that was expected by the opening of the £120 million Millennium Stadium in Cardiff in time for the 1999 Rugby World Cup.**

The WRU chairman Glanmor Griffiths spelt it out to the big clubs when he warned that they would not be 'bailed out' if they got themselves into financial difficulties.

**"Many clubs are spending on players they simply cannot afford and they are putting their very existence in jeopardy," he said. "They must keep their own house in order and live within their budgets."**

The warning signs for Welsh rugby were sounded when Llanelli hit cash problems and were rescued by the WRU purchasing their Stradey Park headquarters for more than £1 million.

**The next club crisis was in July 1998 when Neath declared that they were facing extinction with insurmountable debts of about £600,000.**

Neath, founded in 1871 and Welsh champions in 1996, were rescued by the Welsh RU after 600 club members decided on a final SOS.

# RUGBY UNION

**The WRU secretary explained: "We are simply assuming control of the company Neath RFC and looking to ensure that rugby union continues at The Gnoll."**

One great Welsh name was on the lips of many Barbarians veterans when they got together for the 50th anniversary of their first game against a touring side, the 1948 Australians.

**The general vote was that Gareth Edwards scored the greatest goal the game has seen when playing for the Barbarians against New Zealand in 1973.**

Fittingly, the London get-together was a double celebration in that Gareth Edwards' wonder try had been scored 25 years earlier to the day.

# RUGBY UNION

One famous try so often described and also shown on a jerky black-and-white film is that by Prince Obolensky for England against New Zealand in 1936, when he wrong-footed the All Blacks to finish with a blinding sprint.

Many will recall Andy Hancock's try in the last few seconds of the 1965 England v Scotland match, when he sprinted 90 yards to deprive the Scots of victory for a 3-3 draw.

Gareth Edwards, for his part, always rated his 1972 try for Wales against Scotland as the one he most enjoyed scoring above all others.

England players in the 1995 match against South Africa at Twickenham will recall the powerful left-wing play of Chester Williams when he scored two tries.

Williams made his debut for the Springboks in 1993 against Argentina, thus becoming the first black player to represent South Africa when the international doors were re-opened in 1992 after the end of apartheid.

Williams was also a star of the Springboks' World Cup triumph of 1995. He returned from injury to run in four tries in the quarter-final against Western Samoa, helped in the semi-final defeat of France, then took part in the final victory over the All Blacks.

He didn't play again for his country, after his two-tries Twickenham triumph, from February 1996 until June 1998 after suffering cruciate ligament injuries to both knees and seriously considered retirement.

At that time, the only other non-white to have played Test rugby in Britain since apartheid was McNeil Hendricks, who made his international debut against Ireland.

Sunday, July 19, 1998, was a special day for English rugby in that the acrimonious spell of two and a half years of squabbles and crisis meetings looked to be at its end.

That day at the RFU annual meeting in Birmingham, a new management board chairman was elected to take over from Cliff Brittle, who had held office since January 1996.

The new chief, Brian Baister, was the official RFU Council candidate, supported strongly in speeches by Geoff Cooke and Graham Smith, who had both managed England sides in the past.

# RUGBY UNION

Geoff Cooke, who managed the England team which lost to Australia in the 1991 World Cup Final, is chief executive of the newly promoted Bedford club. He also criticised Fran Cotton, the old Lions manager, for supporting the deposed chairman Cliff Brittle.

**Brian Baister, 58, had served in the police force for 40 years, mostly in the Metropolitan Police before heading north and finally becoming deputy chief constable of Cheshire.**

The voting in favour of Baister as new chairman of the RFU was a clear margin in his favour. He polled 520 against Brittle's 345, with more than 100 clubs not bothering to vote.

**Fran Cotton was undecided whether to call an SGM, but Baister in the role of peacemaker said: "Fran has given a great deal to English rugby and it would be a waste if he did not throw in his lot with the game again."**

He also backed the England coach Clive Woodward after the traumatic tour of the Southern Hemisphere, saying: "Clive is the coach for the future and he has a great deal to offer England. He needs to be given the chance."

**For all its failings, the England under-strength squad that flew out to Australia in May 1998 contained several interesting selections, mainly that of Jonny Wilkinson two days after his 19th birthday. Before that, he had played as a substitute for Mike Catt at 18 years and 314 days.**

Wilkinson was England's youngest fly-half for 71 years, the previous record being held by one Henri Laird, who disappeared from the scene two years after his debut.

**Wilkinson leapt from schoolboy rugby to the highest club level in one year. As he explained: "My dad brough me up to play the game from the age of four, when I played for the under-eights. Then I was in the under-13s at ten and that was when I had the idea of playing stand-off for England."**

Spencer Brown is a member of the Royal Marines Band who was allowed time off by the Navy to play on the wing for Richmond. He was in Brisbane facing the music against Australia – without his French horn.

**Then there was Paul Sampson of Sale, the fastest wing in the Premiership – he was a former schools 100 metres champion with a best time of 10.48secs. At the age of 20, he faced the mighty Springboks in Cape Town.**

# RUGBY UNION

An international family connection of Paul Sampson is that his cousin Dean Sampson, is a Great Britain rugby league Test prop.

**England's tour was a disaster from start to finish, all seven matches being lost with a points return of only 88 against 328 conceded.**

The first match was the most humiliating of all, England losing 76-0 to Australia in Brisbane. It was the nation's heaviest defeat in 491 international matches since 1871.

**Remarkably, the Wallabies did not score their first try for 29 minutes, then followed ten more in the remaining 51 minutes.**

Over in New Zealand, the rot continued unabated. In two matches leading up to the First Test, England's best were beaten by New Zealand A (18-10) and NZ Rugby Academy (50-32).

**In the First Test at Dunedin, the All Blacks were merciless, inflicting England's second heaviest defeat in history by 64-22. Seven days later, in Auckland, the margin was 40-10. That was after a midweek pasting by NZ Maori, 62-14 at Rotorua.**

In the fourth Test match of the Southern Hemisphere tour, the punishment from South Africa was surprisingly light, England escaping with an 18-0 scoreline. England's only scoring threat was one penalty shot.

**Clive Woodward had time on the journey home to reflect on the inadequacies of his shockingly under-par squad. In four Test, England had conceded 28 tries with only four in reply.**

In the 12 Tests he had been in charge, the England coach's figures were three wins, two draws, seven defeats. And during those 12 matches, he had called on 52 players.

**His final verdict, before reporting on the tour in detail to the RFU, was: "English rugby is at is lowest ebb ever, that's the stark truth, and it won't get any better until we stop burning out our players. From now on, it's England first... we'll see just how much the England jersey means."**

There was no comfort forthcoming from the other touring British sides, particularly Wales, who suffered the heaviest thrashing of their lives against the Springboks in Pretoria.

# RUGBY UNION

**The final score was 96-13, with the South Africans running in 15 tries. The Welsh fly-half Arwel Thomas scored all his side's points.**

The last match in Pretoria was Wales' 11th meeting with South Africa, yet the closest they came to winning was back in 1970, with a 6-6 draw in Cardiff. They had Gareth Edwards and Barry John in those days.

**There was a final painful thrust from the other side of the English Channel, as France returned from an unbeaten tour of the Southern Hemisphere, which included two victories over Argentina.**

The French finished their tour with a one-off Test against Fiji, which the 1998 Five Nations champions won comfortably 34-9.

**South Africa's debut man of the year must be Stefan Terblanche. He scored four tries in his first Test outing for the Springboks, with Ireland on the receiving end by 37-13.**

Lawrence Dallaglio was asked to name his proudest rugby moment. He couldn't decide between winning the Courage League as Wasps' captain, winning the World Sevens in 1993, making his England debut and then being made captain, and playing in the Lions' series win in South Africa.

**The lowest moment was when his sister died in the Marchioness riverboat disaster on the Thames in 1989. "I have been brought up as a Roman Catholic," he said, "and my faith was one of the things that helped."**

Bristol player Steffan Jones had a moment of glory in a Sunday League cricket match in 1998. Playing for Somerset against Warwickshire, he took five wickets for one run in a single spell with the ball.

**Making his England debut in South Africa in 1998 was Dave Sims of Gloucester. His grandad Thomas Price (on his mother's side) played six times for England but it was his Welsh granny who first got him to play rugby.**

Dave dreads flying and will do anything to avoid being airborne. He once said: "I'd hold snakes, climb mountains or stroke spiders but getting in a plane frightens me to death."

**South Africa's greatest-ever player by general consent has been Francois Pienaar, who won 29 caps for the Springboks, all of them as captain. The proudest moment was receiving the World Cup from the hands of Nelson Mandela in 1995.**

# RUGBY UNION

Was the journey really necessary? The question was one that Dean Thomas, the Swansea flanker, must have asked himself after being sent off in Wales' match with Gauteng Falcons, the last opponents in their four-match tour of South Africa.

**Thomas had arrived in South Africa only 36 hours before the match as a tour replacement and was shown the red card for a high forearm smash on Falcons winger Len van Riet.**

Another Test player to be sent off on tour was Danny Grewcock, after a stamping incident during the first Test between England and New Zealand in June 1998. He was on the field for only 30 minutes.

**The only previous case of an England player being sent off in a Test match was prop Mike Burton, who in 1975 was declared guilty of fighting against Australia in Brisbane.**

Croatia can call on two former All Blacks for their World Cup matches. They are Matthew Cooper, whose maternal grandmother comes from Croatia, and Frano Botica, the ex-All Black outside-half whose name has a more familiar ring in Rugby League strongholds of northern England.

**Welsh fly-half Neil Jenkins turned down an out-of-season offer to join the European champions Bath when his club Pontypridd offered him a five-year deal said to be worth £1 million to stay with them.**

The British teams who suffered on the 1998 tours were well away from being involved in the worst-ever international hammerings. That 'distinction' belongs to the Japanese, whose national side were crushed 145-17 by New Zealand at Bloemfontein in the 1995 World Cup.

**Next on the haunted list are Portugal, who suffered to the tune of 102-11 at the hands of Wales in Lisbon in a 1994 World Cup qualifying game.**

The Barbarians were grateful for a spot of Fijian magic in May 1998 which enabled them to retain their Middlesex Sevens title at Twickenham. There were four Fijians in the Baa-Baas' line-up.

**The magician-in-chief was Paniela Quaqua, who scored eight tries in the afternoon, aided and abetted by his pal Kini Kiliraki, who kicked four conversions.**

# RUGBY LEAGUE

Rugby League underwent the most dramatic facelift in its history in 1995 when its clubs took £87 million from TV and newspaper mogul Rupert Murdoch.

**In order to satisfy Sky TV customers, the Super League was created and the game switched from its winter mudlarking to an exciting new summer programme.**

The 1998 season opened on a note of high hopes as supremo Maurice Lindsay declared: "I knew the first summer season would be one of transition, that switching from winter would be a big cultural change.

**"The political dogfighting made life difficult. The second year was one of transition. Now we are ready for the big breakthrough."**

The 1998 Super League line-up with their 'creature' nicknames was headed by Bradford Bulls, with two newcomers from the top of Division One, Hull Sharks and Huddersfield Giants.

**The nine other teams making up the Super Dozen, with their 1997 placing in brackets, were Castleford Tigers (10th), Halifax Blue Sox (7th), Leeds Rhinos (5th), London Broncos (2nd), St. Helens (3rd), Salford Reds (6th), Sheffield Eagles (8th), Wigan Warriors (4th) and Warrington Wolves (9th).**

Lindsay also said: "We have learned from the disastrous World Club Championship and come out of the depression. This will be a tremendous season."

**The future of the summer game burned even more brightly in mid-July, 1998, when a new five-year deal was struck with Murdoch and BSkyB worth £56.8 million.**

# RUGBY LEAGUE

The new TV deal, accepted by all 31 League clubs, replaced the £87 million contract that had 2½ years to run. Super League were netting £45 million spread over five years, with First and Second Division clubs getting a one-off payment of £11.8 million.

**This payment also freed the Divisions One and Two clubs to negotiate their own television deals. "The game has come to its collective common sense. It's an excellent decision," said the chairman Sir Rodney Walker.**

A further step was taken in 1998 to try to sell the Rugby League code to the nation with a series of six Super League 'on the road' games at venues where the possibility of starting RL teams had been discussed.

**The first three grounds where Super League may one day have new recruits were Gateshead, Northampton and Edinburgh.**

Returning to St. Helens for the 1998 season was Eric Hughes, who was dropped by Wigan as their coach in November 1997. Hughes was also removed as St. Helens coach in 1996, despite doing much of the background work there which resulted in the side winning the Challenge Cup twice as well as the Super League title in 1996.

**Hughes rejoined St. Helens as football operations manager and was not intended to be involved in team selection or match tactics.**

This job remained in the experienced hands of their Australian coach since January 1996, Shaun McRae, whose record before the start of the 1998 season was 48 wins, one draw and 18 defeats – an outstanding success rate of 72.37%.

**One discordant note on the Rugby League scene was struck in March 1998 when Colin Myler, chief executive of Super League Europe since its launch some 15 months earlier, resigned. He returned to his previous life in newspapers, taking over the editor's chair at the *Sunday Mirror*.**

As he left, he was quoted as saying: "I feel it's right for me to leave. Integrity and loyalty are two qualities which I believe are very important. Unfortunately, in recent times, these have been lacking in certain quarters." Think what you like on that.

**The greatest upset in the history of Challenge Cup Finals took place at Wembley in May 1998, when Sheffield Eagles against all odds completely outplayed Wigan Warriors to win by 17-8.**

# RUGBY LEAGUE

Wigan were 1-10 favourites to win – virtually unbackable – but the great hero in the opinion of Sheffield players and supporters was their quiet, bespectacled coach John Kear, a former deputy headmaster who had certainly done his homework to mastermind this triumph.

**Former Great Britain scrum-half Andy Gregory, an idol at Wigan before taking over as Salford coach, sent a good-luck fax before the match to the Eagles on behalf of the Salford players and himself. "Hope you stuff 'em!" was the simple message.**

The Eagles' defeat of Wigan was the first time a British coach had won the Challenge Cup since 1986, when John Kear's mentor Mal Reilly took Castleford to their 15-14 win over Hull KR.

**Almighty Wigan were suffering their first Wembley setback since 1984 when they lost 19-6 to Widnes. As for Sheffield, this was their first time of playing beyond the Challenge Cup quarter-finals.**

The Wigan player who was hit the hardest was Dennis Betts, who already had seven winner's medals. Coach John Monie also found it hard to bear – he had never known defeat in 25 Challenge Cup games.

**Jason Robinson, arguably the best winger in the World, was also lost for words. The Wigan wonder man had scored a try in every round leading up to Wembley. He'd had two hat-tricks and eight tries in all.**

Robinson had been voted Man of the Match for the Lance Todd Trophy two years before. He desperately wanted that award again to match the double Trophy wins by Gerry Helme (Warrington) and the Wigan pair, Andy Gregory and Martin Offiah.

**One week later, the two teams met again in the Super League. This time, Wigan were irresistible as they won 36-6 in front of the Eagles' fans.**

Wembley 1998 was also a great moment for referee Stuart Cummings, a Widnes PE teacher, who was taking his third successive Silk Cut Final to equal the record set in the 1950s by Ronnie Gelder.

**Despite the Wembley hiccup, Wigan Warriors were quoted at 8-13 to win Super League 1998 under the shrewd guidance of John Monie, their Australian coach since November 1997.**

# RUGBY LEAGUE

Their inspiring captain had a dream start in Rugby League. He made his first-team debut for Wigan at 16, became captain of the side at 18, then captain of the Great Britain side when he was only 20.

**Wigan were shocked when their chairman Mike Nolan resigned in July 1998 – he had done sterling work during the club's financial crisis – but his successor Peter Norbury, a Manchester solicitor, knew the 'business' having been acting in an advisory role for seven months.**

Wigan were already thinking of 1999 when they signed the Aussie prop forward Brett Goldspink from their rivals St. Helens, coach Monie's second signing following the purchase of another fellow countryman, the former Test stand-off Greg Florimo.

**History was written in July 1998 when the BARLA team beat Australia Aboriginals 18-16 in Sydney, thanks to a second try five minutes from time by Steve Larvin.**

BARLA had thus completed a first-ever undefeated series by a Great Britain touring side of Australia, either amateur or professional.

**Further history was made in 1998, this time much nearer to home, when two non-league clubs reached the fifth round of the Challenge Cup for the first time since records began in 1904.**

# RUGBY LEAGUE

The Cumbrian side Egremont were first to upset the applecart by knocking out Workington, then the amateurs of Ellenborough followed suit by toppling Hunslet, who finished with 11 men after Wilson and Ross were sent off for punching.

**The dreams ended in the fifth round. Sheffield Eagles ran up a record score of 84-6 against Egremont, while Ellenborough fared only minimally better. They went down 78-0 to Hull Sharks, the Great Britain star Alan Hunte crossing for five of their 14 tries.**

London Broncos were the unhappy victims of a spot of Super League history making. They were swept aside 58-6 for St. Helens' biggest win of the season and the Broncos' heaviest Super League defeat.

**New ground was broken with the announcement that all three Tests with New Zealand in the autumn of 1998 would be played at Football League venues – Huddersfield Town, Bolton Wanderers and Watford.**

Yet more history was written when Julia Lee, a 29-year-old day-nursery teacher in Leeds, was appointed referee for the 17th Varsity clash between Oxford and Cambridge.

**How old is an 'emerging' England player? Apparently there is no age limit, following Great Britain coach Andy Goodway's choice of Paul Sterling, the 33-year-old Leeds win, for the Emerging England squad to play Wales. Goodway's men won 15-12.**

# HORSE RACING

# HORSE RACING

Newmarket was declared Headquarters of the turf by Charles II and the Rowley Mile over which the 1,000 and 2,000 Guineas were run was named after the king's nickname.

**The five Classics of the season are the two Guineas races, run over one mile, the Derby and Oaks over 1½ miles, and the St. Leger contested over 1¾ miles.**

For a colt to win the Triple Crown, he must win the Derby, St. Leger and Two Thousand Guineas.

**A filly has to be successful for a Triple Crown in the Oaks, St. Leger and One Thousand Guineas – all in one season, of course.**

Gordon Richards put a remarkable record alongside his name by winning 12 consecutive winners over a period of three days.

**Having landed the last race at Nottingham on October 3, he then rode all six winners at Chepstow on October 4 and the first five at the same course the following day.**

Tony McCoy was the National Hunt jockey to follow in 1998, when he had 253 winners to break the record previously held by Peter Scudamore of 221.

**Only six fillies have ever won the Derby.  They were Eleanor (5-4 fav) in 1801, Blink Bonny (20-1) in 1857, Shotover (11-2) in 1882, Signorinetta (100-1) in 1908, Tagalie (100-8) in 1912 and Fifinella (11-2) in 1916.**

Cape Verdi, the Godolphin stables' One Thousand Guineas winner, was the filly backed to win the 1998 Derby but, although starting favourite and even with Frankie Dettori on her back, she finished ninth behind the winner, High-Rise.

**The best performance by a Derby filly since Fifinella was Nobilliary, who came second to Grundy in 1975.  Portuguese Lil did her best in 1996 but the 500-1 shot finished last.**

Mick Ryan's filly Lady Rockstar won the Brian Johnston Centre Classified Stakes at Windsor in June 1998, scoring eight straight wins in 32 days.

**Newmarket is to have a new £16 million Millennium Grandstand. The Rowley Mile Stand, built in 1875, is being knocked down and replaced with a five-storey luxury development, housing private boxes on the top floor.**

# HORSE RACING

The Rowley Mile course would be out of action in 1999, with races being run on the July Course with some alteration to race distances.

**The Cambridgeshire, for instance, was rescheduled over 1¼ miles because there is no nine-furlong start on the July Course. Trainer Gosden described the view from the Rowley Mile Stand as "watching from a railway platform."**

Trainer Martin Pipe's Ultimate Smoothie won at a Worcester night meeting in May 1998 giving him his 200th win of the season – the sixth year he had reached that landmark.

**When asked about his success, Pipe quipped: "The Ultimate Smoothie, ridden by the Ultimate Jockey (Tony McCoy), trained by the Ultimate Trainer."**

At the 1998 Cheltenham Festival, Pipe secured four wins and four places with prize money of £215,067. It was his second year running that he had saddled four Cheltenham winners.

**His Imperial Cup, County Hurdle and Scottish Champion Hurdle with Blowing Wind blew him towards his best-ever season for prize money.**

King of Kings, trained by Aidan O'Brien – no relation to Vincent – at the Ballydoyle Stables in Co. Tipperary, was flown from Ireland on the morning of the Two Thousand Guineas in 1998 and left the star of the meeting, Xaar, looking at a clean pair of heels.

**The winner had never before raced away from The Curragh. Four previous Two Thousand Guineas winners had been saddled by Vincent O'Brien, who had also trained at Ballydoyle. They were Sir Ivor, Nijinsky, Lomond and El Gran Senor.**

The Irish punters celebrated St. Patrick's Day in style in March 1998 when trainer Aidan O'Brien's prediction that Istabraq with Charlie Swan on board would win the Cheltenham Champion Hurdle became a reality.

**Three hurdles out, Istabraq stormed into the lead and won by 12 lengths, equalling the widest winning margin set by Insurance in 1932.**

Coming from the rear with Tommy Treacy in the saddle was Theatreworld, also trained by O'Brien, to take second place with I'm Supposin a length away in third.

# HORSE RACING

Owned by J.P. McManus, Istabraq was bought on the advice of the late John Durkin, a former amateur rider who intended training the horse at Newmarket. Sadly, he developed leukaemia and later died.

Shahtoush, an Aidan O'Brien trained filly, won the Vodaphone Oaks in 1998 to give the stable its second British Classic win of the season.

Mick Kinane rode a near-perfect tactical race, with Frankie Dettori on Godolphin's Bahr poised to take the race from the two-furlong mark.

What Dettori failed to see was Kinane and Shahtoush launching a challenge and the pair went on to win by three-quarters of a length.

Aidan O'Brien was under fire from the Jockey Club in June 1998 when two of his intended runners at Royal Ascot, African Skimmer and Desert Fox, failed to appear when the plane due to transport them from Ireland developed a fault.

His Derby Day plans had also been upset when his three runners – King of Kings, Second Empire and Saratoga Springs – were delayed coming from Shannon to Luton.

The stewards' inquiry said it was concerned that O'Brien was jeopardising the interests of the betting public with his travel arrangements.

The Derby, always run over 1½ miles on Epsom Downs, was founded in 1780 and named after the 12th Earl of Derby. It was always run on a Wednesday afternoon at the end of May or early June.

That was until the 1990s, when tradition was sidestepped and the race was moved to a Saturday to give more families access to the event.

The Cheltenham Gold Cup celebrated its 75th anniversary in 1998, with trainer Michael Dickinson recalling his greatest triumph.

Dickinson, watching the race for the first time in ten years, had moved to America to train at Chesapeake Bay, between New York and Washington.

In 1983, all five of his Gold Cup runners led home the rest of the field. Bregawn, the winner, was followed by Captain John, Wayward Lad, Silver Buck and Ashley House.

In 1996, Dickinson saddled Dahoss to win the Breeders' Cup Mile at Woodbine, Toronto.

# HORSE RACING

**Kieren Fallon, the 1997 champion Flat jockey, set his sights on winning for a second time in 1998 when a double for Henry Cecil on Enemy Action and Aginor at Doncaster put him on 101 wins for the season.**

Fifteen minutes before riding Master Caster to victory at Lingfield in February 1998, Kieren heard the good news that he had been awarded £70,000 in a libel action against *The Sporting Life*.

**The action was brought after the newspaper suggested in an article in May 1995 that trainers Lynda and Jack Ramsden and jockey Fallon had conspired to deceive by not trying to win the Swaffham Handicap at Newmarket with favourite Top Cees in 1995, but had won the Chester Cup three weeks later.**

The allegations were strongly denied and the jury awarded Lynda Ramsden damages of £75,000 and her husband £50,000. *The Sporting Life* was left with costs of £800,000.

# HORSE RACING

On May 12, 1998, *The Sporting Life*, the punters' bible for 139 years and 36,910 editions, closed down. There were, however, plans for an all-sports paper to be launched later in the year.

The following day, the *New Racing Post* incorporating *The Sporting Life* was born, after the *Racing Post* was leased to the Mirror Group for ten years at the cost of one penny.

**Sheik Mohammed was the former owner of the *Racing Post*. His breeding empire is the largest in the world, with more than 500 breeding mares in Newmarket, Ireland and Kentucky.**

Trainer Jack Berry celebrated his 1,500th winner at Redcar on May 12, 1998, when Red Charger won the opening novice stakes, then jockey Gary Carter went on for his hat-trick with Ansellman and Gold Mist.

**Jack Berry started in racing as a five-shillings-a-week apprentice and has earned his success both over the jumps and on the flat. His first winner was in 1969 when Camasco triumphed in a selling hurdle at Kelso.**

Willie Carson, the former champion jockey and four times Derby winner before he retired to become a BBC racing pundit, was given an honorary degree in July 1998 by his hometown University of Stirling.

**Eddy Lai, Hong Kong's champion apprentice jockey, won his first race in England when he started riding for Mark Johnston's stable.**

Riding Yavana's Pace, he won the Hong Kong Jockey Club Trophy at Sandown in July by the closest of margins from Punishment and Greek Palace.

**Lai, 25, had thought that the stalls were numbered as in Hong Kong, with low numbers nearest the inside rail. With Yavana's Pace drawn 19, he was relieved to find the opposite applies in Britain.**

Three days later Lai, after a fall at Musselburgh when he was trampled on by his mount Lady Rachel, sustained a broken collar-bone and bruised face and he decided to return home.

**Shergar, trained by Michael Stoute and owned by a syndicate headed by the Aga Khan, was the horse of 1981.**

Lightly raced as a two-year-old, he achieved just a single win and one second, but as a three-year-old he was unstoppable.

# HORSE RACING

His first race of 1981 was won by ten lengths, followed by easy success in the Chester Vase. His Derby entry with Walter Swinburn on board was considered a foregone conclusion by the punters.

At 11-10 on, he was the strongest Derby favourite for years. Even though Walter Swinburn eased up over the final furlong, Shergar galloped home by ten lengths – the biggest-ever Derby margin.

That year he also won the Irish Derby by four lengths, with commentator Peter O'Sullivan summing up: "He's only in an exercise canter." There was another win in the King George V before he was retired to stud at the end of the season.

On February 8, 1983, while standing at the Aga Khan's Ballymany Stud in Ireland, Shergar was kidnapped and £2 million ransom money was demanded.

The Aga Khan made it clear that he would not pay any ransom money. The horse was never seen again but the IRA were believed to be responsible and although the real story was never told, Shergar is thought to have broken a leg and then was killed and buried somewhere in Ireland.

Lester Piggott, who rode 4,493 winners during his career, was said to live on "thin air and cigars" to retain his riding weight.

He was only 12 when he won his first race at Haydock in 1948. He went on to win 30 British Classics, nine Derbys and was champion jockey 11 times.

Piggott had been apprenticed to his father Keith, a shrewd trainer after his riding career over the jumps.

His grandfather Ernest, rode two Grand National winners and married a sister of Mornington and Kempton Cannon, who both rode Derby winners.

He retired in 1985 after serving 12 months of a three-year jail sentence for tax evasion.

He returned to the track and won the $1 million Breeders' Cup Mile in New York on Royal Academy. He also rode another Two Thousand Guineas winner before finally hanging up his boots in 1995.

# HORSE RACING

In 1977, Churchtown Boy won the Topham Trophy over National fences two days before the National and then on the Saturday was second to Red Rum.

**Red Rum won the Grand National three times and was second twice. Retired after his 1977 success, he thrived on his fame and had public engagements, opening supermarkets and going on a round of celebrity appearances.**

Red Rum was trained at Southport by Ginger McCain and did most of his exercising on the sands. On his death, he was buried alongside the National course, the scene of his great triumphs.

**The 1998 Grand National will be remembered for the atrocious conditions, with three horses dying and only six of the 37 starters completing the race.**

# HORSE RACING

A 12-week investigation into the race suggested alterations to ensure that both horse and jockey are qualified to endure the world's toughest chase.

**In future, no horse declared at the five-day stage would be allowed to race in the days leading up to the National. Griffins Bar, one of the 1998 fatalities, had fallen at the second fence in a race two days before Saturday's National.**

The Jockey Club will have power to review and refuse entries based on previous form, and more horses with higher ratings, it was hoped, would enter.

**The investigation came to the conclusion that the three fatalities were "unfortunate accidents" but agreed to ground improvements and schooling fences, scaled down but similar to the National fences to be available at three major training centres.**

Trainer Jenny Pitman, twice a National winner with Corbiere and Royal Athlete, was not happy with the report, claiming that there were holes a foot deep in the middle of the fences in the 1998 race.

**She said she was delighted when her horse Nahthen Lad unseated his jockey. "I'm sorry I didn't have the balls to take out Nahthen Lad," she said.**

Windsor has been granted permission to scrap National Hunt racing in 1999 and to convert to Flat fixtures. Lingfield will also switch its jumping engagements to Folkestone.

**Fears that the move would jeopardise the future of National Hunt racing were dispelled by the British Horseracing Board, who said that the overall number of jumping fixtures in 1999 would increase from 525 to 527.**

Newmarket trainer David Loder, who at 34 had held a licence for just five seasons, was handed 60 two-year-olds to train for Godolphin.

**The 1996 champion trainer, Saeed Bin Suroor, is continuing to care for the older Godolphin horses.**

Loder, who in five seasons had 239 winners, then had to ask his other owners, including Chris Brasher and Andrew Lloyd Webber, to find other trainers.

# HORSE RACING

**Trainer Martin Pipe, with 208 winners during the 1997-98 National Hunt season, earned more than £1.5 million in prize money.**

The 1997-98 season was marred by the death of the popular grey One Man. He had to be put down after falling at Aintree on the day before the Grand National.

**Manchester United manager Alex Ferguson had a busy 1998 close season, keeping an eye on his two-year-old acquisition Queensland Star when not commentating on the World Cup in France.**

Queensland Star, trained by Jack Berry, was named by Alex after a ship his late father helped to build on the Clyde. His colours? Red and white, of course!

**Ferguson is in good company as an owner. Bryan Robson, Kevin Keegan and David Platt are among the number of football personalities with racehorses, while former players Mick Channon and Mick Quinn figure among the trainers.**

# FOOTBALL
# Here, There and Everywhere

# THE ULTIMATE SPORTS FACT AND QUIZ BOOK

# FOOTBALL
## Here, There and Everywhere

How's this for punishment! Fred Everiss was manager of West Bromwich Albion for 46 years, an all-time record, between 1902 and 1948.

**Fred's patience was recorded with two major honours during his command. West Brom were runaway champions in 1920 and won the FA Cup in 1931.**

Herbert Chapman was the manager with the magic touch between the two World Wars. He set the style by becoming the first club manager to win the League Championship with two different outfits.

**Chapman led Arsenal to the League title in 1931, having won the First Division in 1924 and again in 1925 with Huddersfield Town.**

Brian Clough latched on to the idea in the 1970s when he led Derby County to the Championship in 1971-72, then popped next door to Nottingham to inspire Forest to the First Division title six years later.

**Kenny Dalglish set a new fashion by becoming the first manager to win the League and Premiership Championships with different clubs.**

Liverpool won three League Championships under his guidance before he took a rest, then came back to win the Carling Premiership in 1994-95 with Blackburn Rovers.

**Dalglish had already written another page in the history books when, in 1985-86, he was the first player-manager to win the League–FA Cup double.**

He performed the feat with Liverpool, whose fans were doubly delighted that season because their deadly rivals Everton were League and Cup runners-up!

**The first man to win the League Championship with the same club, first as a player and later as manager, was George Graham.**

He played with the champions Arsenal in 1970-71 and nearly two decades later, he was their title-winning manager in 1988-89 and again in 1990-91.

**Only three clubs had hat-tricks of League Championships. They were Huddersfield Town, Arsenal and Liverpool.**

Leaders by a distance of the table of winners of the League's original First Division were Liverpool with a remarkable 18 titles.

# FOOTBALL
## Here, There and Everywhere

**Way behind come Arsenal with ten, one more than Everton and three more than Aston Villa and Manchester United. Six-timers were Sunderland.**

Until 1987, the Football League operated a system whereby the bottom team of all each season had to apply for re-election to the competition.

**'Champions' of all applicants, with an astonishing 14 times, were poor little Hartlepool United. Next came Halifax on 12, with Barrow and Southport begging for one more chance 11 times.**

There are some odd and unlikely names on that 'begging list'. For example, Merthyr Tydfil (3 times), Aberdare and Ashington (2 each) and Thames (once).

**Among the bigger names who have had to bow the knee are Norwich (4), Crystal Palace and Tranmere (3), Millwall, Oldham, QPR and Watford (2), with Charlton and Bristol Rovers one apiece.**

England have had only eight managers since 1946. They are Walter Winterbottom, Alf Ramsey, Don Revie, Ron Greenwood, Bobby Robson, Graham Taylor, Terry Venables and Glenn Hoddle.

**Sandwiched between Sir Alf and Revie as caretaker for seven games in 1974 was Joe Mercer. England lost only one of those matches.**

Winterbottom enjoyed and endured a remarkable 139 matches in charge of England over a period of 16 years. His final tally: Won 78, Drawn 33, Lost 28.

# FOOTBALL
## Here, There and Everywhere

**Terry Venables must get the vote as the most blameless of England bosses. In his short 1994-96 spell in charge, England lost only one of his 23 matches, discounting penalty shoot-outs.**

His only reverse in a 90-minute match was against Brazil, who won 3-1 at Wembley on June 11, 1995.

**Brazil won again at the next clash with England, under Hoddle's coaching regime, at the Tournoi de France on June 10, 1997. The score: Brazil 1 England 0.**

'Foreigners' won the Football Writers Association Player of the Year award four years in succession from 1995 to 1998. They were Jurgen Klinsmann (Spurs), Eric Cantona (Man. United), Gianfranco Zola (Chelsea) and Dennis Bergkamp (Arsenal).

**Before that, three Englishmen won the award in consecutive years from 1992 to 1994 – Gary Lineker (Spurs), Chris Waddle (Sheffield Wednesday) and Alan Shearer (Blackburn).**

The first winner of the FWA Player of the Year honour was Stanley Matthews in 1948. He was then with Blackpool, as he was in 1963 when he won it again.

**Liverpool scooped the award three times in succession, from 1988 to 1990, with John Barnes, Steve Nicol and Barnes again. In 1989, in association with Nicol, there was a special award to Liverpool players for their compassion to Hillsborough disaster families.**

In addition to Matthews and Barnes, the award had been won twice by Tom Finney (Preston), Danny Blanchflower (Spurs), Kenny Dalglish (Liverpool) and Gary Lineker (Everton and Spurs).

**There was a hat-trick of Bobby dazzlers on the list from 1965 to 1967 – Moore (West Ham), Collins (Leeds) and Charlton (Manchester United).**

The Professional Footballers Association also introduced their Player of the Year award in 1974, with Norman Hunter (Leeds) first on the role of honour.

**Four times in nine years during the 1980s, the players and writers settled for the same Liverpool players. They were McDermott, Dalglish, Rush and Barnes.**

# FOOTBALL
## Here, There and Everywhere

They have also agreed on the same player on three other occasions, the 'double' winners being Lineker (Everton), Clive Allen (Spurs) and Bergkamp (Arsenal).

**Two clubs shared the first Scottish League Championship in 1890-91. Rangers and Dumbarton finished level on points and drew in a play-off before honours were declared even.**

There are only five survivors of the original 11 who constituted the Scottish League. They are Celtic, Dumbarton, Hearts, Rangers and St. Mirren.

**Stirling Albion are not proud of their 1980-81 record, when they recorded the lowest goal total for a Scottish League season – a mere 18 in 39 games.**

The managerial record of Bob Paisley at Liverpool may never be surpassed in English football. Between 1974 and 1983, he took the Reds to six League Championships and won 20 trophies in all.

**Among the P.F.A. Young Player of the Year awards list is the name of Glenn Hoddle. That was won in 1980 when he was a Spurs player.**

This award has been won twice in consecutive years, first by Ryan Giggs (Manchester United) in 1992 and 1993, then by Robbie Fowler (Liverpool) in 1995 and 1996.

**Michel Platini stands alone among European Footballers of the Year, in that he is the only player to have won the award in three consecutive years – from 1983 to 1985 during his days with Juventus.**

The first recipient of the European award was Stanley Matthews in 1956, and the only Scot to have won it is Denis Law, in 1964 when he was with Manchester United.

**Along with Platini, the only other players to have been European Footballer of the Year three times are Johan Cruyff and Marco Van Basten.**

Kevin Keegan has been the most successful British player in the European list. He was twice the award winner when with SV Hamburg.

**There have been nine different winners in ten European Championships, with West Germany the only nation to have won it twice.**

# FOOTBALL
## Here, There and Everywhere

Those victories were recorded in 1972 and 1980, against the Soviet Union and Belgium, but a unified Germany were the winners in 1996.

**For the first time in the European Championship's history, the finals will have joint hosts, Belgium and Holland, in 2000.**

Michel Platini scored in every match as captain of France when they won the Championship in 1984. He set a record with nine in the series.

**Only once has a European Championship Final been decided on the penalty shoot-out. That was in Belgrade in 1976, when Czechoslovakia won it 5-3 against West Germany.**

A Football League record was set by Liverpool in 1989, when eight different players scored in the 9-0 defeat of Crystal Palace.

**They were still one behind their most remarkable scoring record in a Cup-Winners' Cup first-round match 15 years earlier.**

On that occasion, Liverpool made history with their biggest-ever win, 11-0 against the Norwegian side Stromsgodset. They had nine different scorers!

# FOOTBALL
## Here, There and Everywhere

**Scoring eight goals in a match is not an everyday event, but that feat has been achieved five times in the Scottish League over the years.**

Those eight-timers' names have a golden oldie ring about them. For the record: John Calder (Morton), Jim Dyet (King's Park), Norman Haywood (Raith Rovers), Jimmy McGrory (Celtic) and Owen McNally (Arthurlie).

**Jimmy Smith of Ayr set the British record for most League goals in a season with 66 in only 38 matches in 1927-28.**

Jimmy McGrory stands alone as the crackshot of Scottish football history. He notched 550 playing for Celtic, Clydebank and Scotland.

**The team record for the highest number of goals by a Scottish League club in one season is held by Raith Rovers, who banged in 142 in only 34 games.**

Still in Scotland to record the fastest hat-trick there, by Ian St. John during his Motherwell days. He netted three in 2½ minutes against Hibernian in 1959.

**Gerhard Muller was the goalscoring hero of Germany in the 1960s and 1970s. He hit 68 in only 62 games for West Germany and an incredible 365 in 427 games for Bayern Munich.**

Muller explained simply: "There was no secret to my goals. Every time I played I thought I would score. It was instinct."

**England had a hint of things to come when they drew 0-0 with Belgium in a World Cup warm-up match. They were beaten 4-3 on penalties.**

Bobby Moore became England's youngest captain when he skippered his country against Czechoslovakia in 1963 at the age of 22.

**Three days before the England World Cup squad was announced, Sol Campbell of Spurs became the youngest captain since Moore for the friendly with Belgium in Casablanca. He was 23 at the time.**

Sunderland finished two points higher than Charlton in the Division One final table in 1998 but missed promotion to the Premiership. They lost in a Wembley shoot-out after extra time in their play-off.

**Michael Owen scored his first international goal for England against Morocco, then said: "One goal doesn't make you an international striker. You have to keep scoring."**

# FOOTBALL
## Here, There and Everywhere

Owen was 18 years and 164 days old when he scored that goal. He beat the previous record set by Tommy Lawton, who was 19 years and six days when he scored a penalty against Wales in Cardiff in 1938.

**Owen became the youngest player for England this century – just 18 years and 59 days – when he made his debut in the 2-0 defeat against Chile at Wembley in February 1998.**

He finished his first season in the Premiership with Liverpool as joint top scorer on 18 goals with Dion Dublin (Coventry) and Chris Sutton (Blackburn).

**He was only 17 when he made his first-team debut for Liverpool, coming on as a substitute to score in a 2-1 defeat of Wimbledon.**

Andy Goram, the Scotland goalkeeper who walked out on his country's World Cup squad at a late hour, played cricket three times for Scotland in 1989.

**Around £8m was wiped off the value of Sunderland's shares the day after their play-off failure against Charlton at Wembley in May 1998.**

When David Seaman captained his country against Moldova in the qualifiers of World Cup 98, he was only the sixth England goalkeeper to do so.

**The worst soccer disaster in history occured in 1964 in Lima, Peru, when 318 people died after riots in an Olympic Games qualifying match against Argentina.**

Johan Cruyff ended his great career as manager of Barcelona for seven years. When he left in 1996, they had won the Spanish League title in four consecutive years.

**Cruyff had a memorable debut for Holland in 1966. He scored the last-minute equalising goal in a 2-2 draw with Hungary.**

Eusebio, the legendary Portugal player, has a statue in his honour at the entrance to his beloved Benfica's ground, the Estadio da Luz.

**He was only 19 when he was sent on as a substitute for Benfica against Pele and Santos of Brazil. He scored a brilliant second-half hat-trick.**

# FOOTBALL
## Here, There and Everywhere

Eusebio played with Benfica for 13 years, during which period they won the Portuguese Championship seven times. He scored 38 goals in 46 matches for Portugal.

**Diego Maradona was probably the most famous boy protege of all time. He played first time for Argentina at 16 in a friendly match against Hungary.**

Maradona played some of his greatest football with Napoli and in 1987 inspred them to an Italian League-Cup double.

**Pele also made his international debut at the age of 16, a year after his first appearance for Santos in major Brazilian football.**

His final greatest recognition came when he was appointed Brazil's Minister for Sport in 1994, the year after receiving FIFA's Gold Medal Award for his outstanding services to football.

**Glenn Hoddle said Gascoigne's smoking habit did not worry him, then added: "Ossie Ardiles was on 40 a day when Argentina won the World Cup in 1978."**

A turn-up for Scottish fans was the award of 1988 Manager of the Year to Hearts' boss Jim Jefferies, while his defender Paul Ritchie got the Young Player No. 1 vote.

**Nikolas Dabizas carved his little niche in football history when he became the first Greek to appear in an FA Cup Final when turning out for Newcastle at Wembley in 1998.**

# FOOTBALL
## Here, There and Everywhere

England's greatest win over Scotland was by 9-3 in April 1961, with five England players on the scoresheet headed by a Jimmy Greaves trio.

**That was the culmination of a five-match run in England's attack by Greaves in which he scored 11 goals.**

England piled up an incredible 32 goals in that five-match run, including another nine goals against Luxembourg in a World Cup qualifying match – and another hat-trick for Greaves.

**The England team in that 9-3 slaughter of the Scots is worth recalling: Springett, Armfield, McNeil, Robson, Swan, Flowers, Douglas, Greaves, Smith, Haynes, Charlton.**

Denmark had their surprise moment of glory in the 1992 European Championship. They got a late place when Yugoslavia were excluded and shocked everyone by beating Germany 2-0 in the Final.

**The Danes' scoring heroes were Jensen (18mins) and Vilfort (78mins), while in goal at the other end with a clean sheet was Peter Schmeichel.**

Ground-sharing was unheard of until 1985, when Charlton Athletic and Crystal Palace decided to share Palace's ground at Selhurst Park.

**Arthur Rowley was the scorer of the greatest number of goals in Football League history. His total bag was 434 when playing with West Brom, Fulham, Leicester and Shrewsbury.**

The English scoring record for the top flight is held by Jimmy Greaves, who netted 357 times during his career with Chelsea, Spurs and West Ham.

**The record among goalscorers for a player at one club was set by Dixie Dean, who hit 349 for Everton between 1925 and 1937.**

Ian Wright set a new Carling Premiership record by scoring in seven consecutive games for Arsenal in the 1993-94 season.

**The Premiership's oldest player was goalkeeper John Burridge. When he played for Manchester City in April 1995, he was 43 years 4 months and 26 days.**

David Platt, PFA Player of the Year in 1990, is England's eighth highest scorer of all time and ranks as the ace of the nation's penalty potters.

# FOOTBALL
## Here, There and Everywhere

**He was the only player to have scored in all of England's major tournament penalty shoot-outs over a six-year period.**

Platt was spot on against West Germany at Italia 90, and against Spain and Germany in Euro 96 – the last two being his final appearances for his country. That's when Glenn Hoddle took over.

**Platt played for three Italian clubs between 1991 and 1995, with £16.5 million changing hands in transfer fees. His teams were Bari, Juventus and Sampdoria.**

That was not bad going for a player who was given a free transfer from Crewe, after scoring 56 goals for them from 1985-88. He went on to win 62 England caps and captained them.

**Ray Bowden, the only survivor of the legendary Arsenal team of the mid 1930s, was the most neutral 88-year-old watching the 1998 FA Cup Final between Arsenal and Newcastle. He had played for both clubs.**

Time to savour again that wonderful Arsenal side: Wilson, Male, Hapgood, Crayston, Roberts, Copping, Hulme, Bowden, Drake, James, Bastin.

**Before the astronominal fees paid for the Brazilian stars Denilson and Ronaldo, the top foreign transfer fee for five years had been the £13 million paid by AC Milan for Torino's Gianluigi Lentini.**

Brazil have never won the Olympic soccer gold medal, but they have twice finished with silver, at Los Angeles in 1984 and Seoul in 1988.

**However, Brazil have twice had the top scorer in an Olympics. Romario had seven goals in 1988 and Bebeto six in 1996.**

Paul Durkin, FA Cup Final and World Cup referee in 1998, was a linesman in the 1980 FA Trophy Final to become Wembley's youngest-ever official at the age of 33.

**Philip Don, the former World Cup official, is the Premiership's first referees' officer, taking over at the start of the 1998-99 season. His job is to help to improve links between referees, managers and players.**

The choice of England's football managers' association as Manager of the Year for the 1997-98 season was David Jones of Southampton.

**Everton have spent more seasons in the top flight than any other club in England, despite Arsenal's unbroken run dating back to 1919.**

# FOOTBALL
## Here, There and Everywhere

Everton were founder members of the Football League in 1888 and have been out of the top division in only four seasons – 1930-31 and 1951-54. They have been champions nine times.

**Trevor Francis set some sort of record in March 1998 when he resigned from the manager's chair at Birmingham and was reinstated only 48 hours later.**

Craig Burley, the Celtic and Scotland midfielder, scooped 68% of the votes to be named Player of the Year by Scottish football writers.

**A poll of 130 European journalists voted for two Englishmen but no other British players in deciding the greatest European 'team'.**

Their choice: Yashin (USSR), Beckenbauer (West Germany), Moore (England), P. Maldini (Italy), Baresi (Italy), Cruyff (Holland), Platini (France), B. Charlton (England), Eusebio (Portugal), Puskas (Hungary), Van Basten (Holland).

**Richard Scudamore, appointed chief executive of the Football League in 1998, was once a referee in the Western League.**

His earliest football memories are of being smuggled into Bristol City's Ashton Gate ground as a six-year-old in his father's invalid carriage.

**One day, so the story goes, a disabled driver drove on to the pitch and attacked the ref. Invalid carriages were then banned – and young Richard's free trips came to an end.**

Notts County were celebrating long before their 1998 runaway promotion run. In January of that year, they became the first club to complete 4,000 matches in the Football League.

**In his farewell game, John Aldridge scored both Tranmere goals in the 2-1 win over Wolves to take his career total to 474. Before his move to Tranmere, he played for Newport, Oxford, Liverpool and Real Sociedad.**

# FOOTBALL
## Cups
## and Hiccups

# FOOTBALL
## Cups and Hiccups

It was the most discussed goal in World Cup history. Diego Maradona called it the 'Hand of God', as he flipped the ball past Peter Shilton to score for Argentina in the 1986 quarter-finals.

**The most famous goal ever for England was Geoff Hurst's extra-time goal in the 1966 World Cup Final. The ball bounced from the bar on to the line and the ref said it was a goal. Some TV pictures suggested it did not cross the line.**

England's biggest hiccup of all was the 1950 World Cup defeat by USA at Belo Horizonte in Brazil. Some papers thought 0-1 was a misprint and turned it into a 10-1 slaughter!

**The goalscorer was an unknown from Haiti and several observers thought it was not so much a header as that the ball hit his head.**

Some of the American players were so sure England would win that they stayed up half the night before the game. Their real heroes were the goalkeeper, the goalposts and the crossbar.

**England's team (whisper it!): Williams, Ramsey, Aston, Wright, Hughes, Dickinson, Finney, Mannion, Bentley, Mortensen, Mullen.**

Cup is a forbidden word around Selkirk. In December 1984, they were savaged 20-0 in a Scottish Cup match by Stirling Albion.

**That was the biggest score in so-called first-class British football in the 20th Century. Executioner-in-chief with seven goals for Stirling was Davie Thompson.**

The most widely quoted score in Cup history is 36-0. That was a few lifetimes ago, in September 1885, when John Petrie of Arbroath put 13 into the Bon Accord net.

**Cup quote of a lifetime by manager Jimmy Nicholl, after Raith Rovers' defeat of Celtic in the 1995 Scottish League Cup Final: "This would bring a tear to a glass eye."**

Preston scored six goals in a seven-minute spell during their FA Cup victory over Hyde in 1887. Preston won 26-0.

**British clubs have won the European Cup-Winners' Cup ten times, Chelsea making it double figures in 1998.**

Rangers have won the Scottish League Cup 20 times, more than twice as many as their nearest and deadliest rivals Celtic, on nine wins.

# FOOTBALL
## Cups and Hiccups

**The boot is on the other Glasgow foot when it comes to the Scottish FA Cup. Up to 1998, Celtic had won it 30 times to Rangers' 27.**

The dodgiest Cup hiccup could be said to have been perpetrated by Brazil, without kicking a ball in anger. They took away the original Jules Rimet Trophy for keeps after their third World Cup win – and had it pinched!

**On December 19, 1983, the trophy vanished from the Brazilian Confederation offices. Two men were arrested but no trophy. They said it had been melted down.**

England fared better when that same trophy disappeared a few weeks before the tournament in 1966. A clever pooch called Pickles found it in somebody's front garden.

**Ally McCoist created a Scottish League Cup record with Rangers by helping himself to nine winners' medals by 1997.**

What was the greatest club match of all? The experts plump for the European Champions Cup Final of 1960, on a mid-May day at Hampden Park, Glasgow.

**Scottish referee Jackie Mowat whistled up ten times for a goal feast between Real Madrid and Eintracht Frankfurt, the Spanish dream team winning 7-3. Ferenc Puskas scored four and Alfredo Di Stefano three.**

The Real team, in gold letters: Dominguez, Marquitos, Pachin, Vidal, Santamaria, Zarraga, Canario, Del Sol, Di Stefano, Puskas, Gento.

**That win put the seal on five consecutive Final victories since the competition's inception in 1956 by Real Madrid, with the majestic Di Stefano scoring in all five Finals.**

Benfica won the next two, in 1961 and 1962, the latter another extravaganza with Benfica winning 5-3 after a Puskas hat-trick had given Real Madrid a 3-1 interval lead.

**Real Madrid won it again in 1966, then had to wait 32 years before capturing it again as rank outsiders against Juventus. The only goal was scored by Yugoslav Predrag Mijatovic 23 minutes from time.**

Only once has the European Cup been won in a replay. That was in 1974, when Bayern Munich beat Atletico Madrid to start a hat-trick of triumphs.

# FOOTBALL
## Cups and Hiccups

**Penalty shoot-outs were the deciding factor from then onwards, and no fewer than five Finals were won and lost on spot kicks from 1984 to 1996.**

Liverpool were first to celebrate under the new system in 1984, when they beat AS Roma by four penalties to two – in Rome, too.

**Brian Clough and his Nottingham Forest merry men caused hiccups all round in 1979 and 1980 with single-goal triumphs, following two successive Final victories by Liverpool.**

With Liverpool winning the Cup for the third time, followed by Aston Villa in 1982, English club sides had conquered Europe for six years in a row.

**Manchester United's only European Cup triumph, in 1968 against Benfica at Wembley, lived long in the memories of 100,000 spectators, thanks to an extra-time thriller.**

In the first eight fantastic minutes of extra time, United scored three (Best, Kidd and Charlton) to make it 4-1 by the final whistle.

**Matt Busby's famous battlers that day: Stepney, Brennan, A. Dunne, Crerand, Foulkes, Stiles, Best, Kidd, Charlton, Sadler, Aston.**

One of the biggest hiccups of EUFA Cup Finals came in 1997, when Schalke played out of their skins in their first European final appearance of any kind.

# FOOTBALL
## Cups and Hiccups

Inter Milan, the red-hot favourites, were beaten 4-1 on penalties after the two legs had finished 1-0 in each other's favour. And the shoot-out was in Milan!

Yeovil Town caused what was probably the biggest hiccup in FA Cup history when they beat mighty Sunderland 2-1 after extra time on their famous sloping pitch at Huish.

**Incredibly, the non-Leaguers were in the fifth round against Manchester United at Maine Road. There they lost 8-0 before a crowd of 81,565.**

Yeovil's player-manager in those glory days was Alec Stock, back from World War Two in which he served as a tank commander.

**Alec became a famous League club manager and had his FA Cup moment of glory when he took Second Division Fulham to Wembley for a Final with West Ham in 1975.**

West Ham won the day 2-0 but the crowd's cheers were for Fulham's 1975 giant-killers and their two veteran heroes Bobby Moore and Alan Mullery.

**Other legendary giant-killers from the Southern League included Hereford United, whose post-war Cup exploits were rewarded with Football League status in 1972.**

During that post-war period as a non-League side, they reached the FA Cup second round 13 times, the third round three times and, unforgettably, the fourth round once – in 1972.

**After holding Newcatle to a 2-2 draw at St. James' Park, they shook the football world by beating the First Division side 2-1 after extra time at their Edgar Street ground.**

Malcolm Macdonald headed an 82nd minute goal but four minutes later John Radford equalised, then in the 12th minute of extra time Ricky George, on as a substitute, got the winner.

**Further glory followed in the fourth round, as Hereford held First Division West Ham 0-0 to force a London replay.**

The gates were locked with thousands outside as Hereford went down fighting 3-1 (Geoff Hurst got all three), and the Hammers' team lined up at the end in tribute to the non-Leaguers.

**This was West Ham's star line-up that day: Ferguson, McDowell, Lampard, Bonds, Taylor, Moore, Redknapp, Best, Hurst, Brooking, Robson.**

# FOOTBALL
## Cups and Hiccups

Tooting and Mitcham, the Isthmian League amateurs, nearly caused one of the FA Cup's greatest hiccups in 1959 when they held First Division Nottingham Forest to a 2-2 home draw – and would have won but for a hotly disputed penalty that saved Forest 13 minutes from time.

**That same Forest eleven went on to win the Final: Thomson, Whare, McDonald, Whitefoot, McKinlay, Burkitt, Dwight, Quigley, Wilson, Gray, Imlach.**

The top scorers in all FA Cup Finals since 1872 have been Blackburn Rovers in 1890, when they beat Sheffield Wednesday 6-1, and Bury in 1903, when they beat Derby County 6-0.

**Chelsea scored the fastest goal in Wembley's Cup Final history when Roberto Di Matteo scored in the 42nd second against Middlesbrough in 1997.**

That was a disastrous year for Middlesbrough. They lost that Final 2-0, were beaten in the Coca-Cola Final by Leicester in a replay, and were relegated from the Premiership.

**The World record for match receipts was a mind-blowing £4.3 million at the World Cup Final of 1990 in Rome between Argentina and West Germany.**

The first World Cup match in Uruguay in 1930 was won by France, 4-1 against Mexico on July 13, and the first-ever World Cup goal was scored by a Frenchman, Louis Laurent.

**All four Home Countries qualified for a World Cup finals for the first time in 1958, but only Northern Ireland survived the groups and were then knocked out by France.**

Northern Ireland were heralded as giant-killers in the World Cup of 1982 when they upset the hosts Spain 1-0 in a group match.

**Jimmy Delaney completed a unique treble in 1954 by winning a medal in the Irish Cup. He already had an FA Cup winners' medal with Manchester United and a Scottish FA Cup winners' medal with Celtic.**

Two players were sent off in the European Cup-Winners' Cup Final of 1998. Dan Petrescu of Chelsea got the red card in the 84th minute and Gerhard Poschner of VfB Stuttgart in the last minute.

**Many great players have never appeared in an FA Cup Final. The lost legion include George Best, John Charles, Johnny Haynes, Nobby Stiles and Martin Peters.**

# FOOTBALL
## Cups and Hiccups

The first FA Cup Final hat-trick to be scored at Wembley came from Stan Mortensen in Blackpool's 4-3 defeat of Bolton in 1953.

**Liverpool's FA Cup winning side of 1986 did not contain a single Englishman. Team: Grobbelaar, Lawrenson, Beglin, Nicol, Whelan, Hansen, Dalglish, Johnston, Rush, Molby, MacDonald.**

Four men have managed and played for an FA Cup Final team. They are Stan Seymour (Newcastle), Kenny Dalglish (Liverpool), Terry Venables (Spurs) and George Graham (Arsenal).

**Pat Rice of Arsenal is the only player to have appeared in five FA Cup Finals with the same club.**

There has never been a goalless FA Cup Final at Wembley, and there has not been a replay since 1993.

**The first FA Cup Final in 1872 was played at Kennington Oval on a pitch without a centre circle or a penalty area, and the 'crossbar' was a tape stretched between the posts.**

# FOOTBALL
## Cups and Hiccups

The 1998 UEFA Cup Final was an all-Italian affair for the fourth time in nine seasons, between Inter Milan and Lazio, the latter appearing in their first European final.

**Inter Milan, beaten finalists in 1997, won easily 3-0, with Ronaldo scoring the last goal and also being voted Man of the Match.**

Bobby Charlton was booked in the World Cup quarter-final against Argentina in 1966 – and he didn't find out until 32 years later!

**Now Sir Bobby, he always thought he had never been booked throughout his 106 games with England until in 1998 FIFA researched the match.**

That infamous match with Argentina was such a shambles that both the Charlton brothers were booked by the German referee Rudolf Kreitlein without their knowing it.

**Paul Allen was only 17 when he won an FA Cup winners' medal with West Ham in 1980.**

Dermot Reeve of cricket fame fancies himself as an auctioneer but the Somerset coach got it wrong when asking for bids for a 1966 World Cup item 'signed by the late Ken Wolstenholme'.

**The famous commentator with the immortal 1966 Final cry 'They think it's all over' hastened to assure all would-be mourners that for him it's far from over!**

Sir Alf Ramsey in reflective mood in 1995 said: "To this day my over-riding memory is the joy I brought to my team and country. I love three things in life – my wife, my country and football."

**England's most successful manager was taken ill with a stroke on the eve of the first World Cup finals games of 1998. Glenn Hoddle said: "His achievement in 1966 remains an inspiration to everybody, including me, more than 30 years later."**

England World Cup player Martin Keown's son Callum had, at the age of six, seen two matches. The first was when his dad's Arsenal team won the Championship and the second when they won the FA Cup Final.

**A hiccup never to be forgotten. . . Chris Waddle missed England's final penalty against West Germany in the World Cup semi-final.**

# FOOTBALL
## Cups and Hiccups

Scotland's 1982 World Cup campaign song was "We Have A Dream". The nightmare continued unabated in 1998 with Scotland's eighth exit from the World Cup in eight finals appearances.

**Jamaica was overcome by soccer hysteria in 1998, to such an extent that the legendary cricketer Courtney Walsh had to concede first place to footballer Deon Burton in a Sportsman of the Year vote.**

Egypt's team were welcomed passionately by President Hosni Mubarak in Cairo after they had won the 1998 African Nations' Cup for the first time in 12 years.

**The outcome was a Cup hiccup of major proportions for their rivals South Africa in the Final in Ouagadougou, the capital of Burkina Faso, with Egypt the 2-0 winners.**

Egypt's feted hero was their 60-year-old coach Mahmoud El-Gohari, who was a member of the winning Egyptian team in the same competition in 1959.

**The fall guy had to be South Africa's coach Jomo Sono, who said: "I was given no chance of reaching the final. I reached the final. I'm happy. I've done my part."**

Jomo then announced his retirement and handed over to Frenchman Philippe Troussier, who had coached Burkina Faso through the tournament. And on went Troussier to no wins out of three games in World Cup 98.

**The tournament's leading scorers were Benny McCarthy (South Africa) and Hossam Hassan (Egypt), but both fired blanks in the Final and they tied with seven goals apiece.**

The man with the money at Real Betis in Spain is their multi-millionaire president Manual Ruiz de Lopera, who aim is to put the club top of Europe.

**He immediately put his money where his mouth is by spending more than £22 million of his considerable pile from property development on the 20-year-old Brazilian Denilson.**

Mr. Moneybags Lopera then stuck in a buy-out clause which amounted to a sum of 65 billion pesetas – a mere £270 million give or take a million.

**Lopera was feeling a wee bit sick when Chelsea's Tore Andre Flo whacked in two goals in the first 13 minutes of the Cup-Winners' Cup Final first leg in Seville.**

# FOOTBALL
## Cups and Hiccups

Marcelo Salas signed for Lazio for £12 million just two days after scoring twice for Chile against England at Wembley in February 1998. But wait until after the World Cup, he said.

**Salas, captain of Chile and the South American 1997 Footballer of the Year, then agreed to say goodbye to his club River Plate and start his eight-year contract with Lazio.**

By the time Arsenal went to Wembley for the 1998 FA Cup Final, not a single Final in 25 years had there been without a club from London, Manchester or Liverpool being involved.

**The last time they were out of it was in 1973, when Sunderland and Leeds fans had to ask their way to Wembley from a bunch of disinterested Londoners.**

Just to rub in the salt, Sunderland's scorer that day in their 1-0 win was Ian Porterfield, who was later to take over as Chelsea's boss.

**Two cases of managers who were in charge of both English and Scottish FA Cup winners: Johnny Cochrane (St. Mirren and Sunderland) and Alex Ferguson (Aberdeen and Manchester United).**

Liam Brady played 72 times for Eire between 1974 and 1990 but never once was involved in the World Cup finals.

**Mark Hughes became the only player in the 20th Century to win four FA Cup winners' medals when Chelsea beat Middlesbrough in 1997.**

# THE THINGS THEY SAID

# THE THINGS THEY SAID

Roger Bannister described his feelings after breaking the four-minute mile barrier as: "I felt like an exploded light bulb with no will to live."

**On being bowled in his only Test match in 1902, enabling Australia to win by three runs, Fred Tate said: "I've a little lad at home who'll make up for that." The 'lad', Maurice Tate, became one of England's greatest bowlers.**

After Ayrton Senna died on the track at Imola, Niki Lauda described him as "the best driver who ever lived".

**"Perhaps he should take a year off," said Ian Doyle, manager of Stephen Hendry, after seeing his client lose the 1997 World Snooker Championship 18-12 to Ken Doherty, No. 7 in the World.**

After enjoying the first 'People's Day' at Wimbledon in 1991, Jimmy Connors said: "This is my kind of crowd. I wish they'd been like this the last 20 years. Where have they been?"

**Don Bradman, in praise of Garry Sobers, said: "The uncoiling of those wrists as he flicks the ball is a joy to watch because it is unique."**

Prime Minister Tony Blair on being a Newcastle United fan: "I don't see them as much as I would like these days, but I follow their progress closely enough to know they shouldn't have sold David Ginola."

**After watching his 14-year-old son Leon finishing sixth on his British 125cc Championship debut, his famous motorcycling father Ron Haslam waited as the rest left for a beer and said: "We are going to McDonald's to celebrate."**

Derby County's striker Paulo Wanchope says: "I work hard in every game but I prefer to do other things. Shooting basketball was my first love and I still like to get on court."

**When asked the reason for his amazing success as a jockey, Jonjo O'Neill said with a smile: "Because I was brilliant, you know!"**

Asked whose talent he most envied, Pat Eddery said: "Lester Piggott because he was just a genius."

# THE THINGS THEY SAID

**The Cameroon midfielder fancied by Manchester United, Marc-Vivien Foe, on suffering a fractured fibula: "In Cameroon the healers have said they could cure me in three days by burying my leg in the ground and putting fire around it.  They have also recommended massage with gorilla bones while invoking the spirits of my ancestors."**

"People will have to get used to the idea that tennis player Boris Becker belongs to the past."  So said the three-times Wimbledon singles champion on his decision not to play 1998 Wimbledon.  His name – Boris Becker.

**"I always knew that one day I would play for England, but I would be lying if I said I believed it would all happen so quickly." – Liverpool's Michael Owen after his first England goal at 18.**

On being presented with his cap by RFU President Peter Brook, England prop Phil Vickery was told: "You will never forget this day." Twelve hours later he was given a 30-day suspension.

**Football legend Bill Shankly once said: "I don't drop players.  I make changes."**

Sunderland manager Peter Reid, comforting Michael Gray after his vital missed penalty in the Division One 1998 play-off final at Wembley: "There are a million things that happen in a season that can cost you – not just a penalty with the last kick."

**Paraguayan tennis player Ramon Delgado, 21, on knocking Pete Sampras out of the 1998 French Open, waved his nation's flag and said: "It's a dream, wake me up.  I don't have the words to describe it.  I've worked all my life for this and had to go for it."**

Brian Lara, in a discussion on Don Bradman: "There are no plurals when you are talking about Bradman.  There could only be one."

**George Best: "I was signing a few books for some kids the other day.  I wondered if Gazza would be doing the same thing 25 years after the end of his career."**

Condemning FIFA's decision to ban the tackle from behind, Johan Cruyff said: "It makes things more complicated for the referee and could be a disaster for the World Cup."

# THE THINGS THEY SAID

**Not at his best when remembering names, England manager Bobby Robson greeted his captain Bryan Robson with "Good morning, Bobby." The skipper replied: "Sorry, boss, you're Bobby. I'm Bryan!"**

Advising Manchester United and Alex Ferguson to pay £10 million for Jaap Stam, Bobby Robson, who was about to join the player's old club PSV Eindhoven as manager for the 1998-99 season, said: "I knew the club would not budge on the price. Alex has done well to go for it."

**Brazilian ace Roberto Carlos thinks the present-day players are the best, but when asked to name his favourites said: "Pele, Maradona and Platini."**

Bowler Angus Fraser, discussing Brian Lara's Test record innings of 375, said: "My memories of the innings are quite magical. People tell you how good the great players were, but when you witness a great player then you realise what greatness really means."

**Alan Shearer, responding once to his critics, said: "If people see me moaning on the field, it is only because I want to win. If that's a fault, then I apologise."**

During one of the early European competitions, Liverpool let in five goals when playing Ajax. Manager Bill Shankly said: "It's no use, we cannot play against defensive teams."

**Motor racing commentator Murray Walker said: "The lead car is absolutely unique except for the car behind, which is identical."**

Lester Piggott on fellow jockeys: "It is difficult to compare the past with today but Eddery, Carson, Cauthen, Pincay, Condero, Shoemaker, Saint-Martin would have been stars at any time."

**On seeing Michael Owen sent off for a two-footed foul tackle, Pele said: "Sometimes the devil walks with the angel."**

Wicket-keeper Jack Russell, commenting on his new Zone Diet: "People would be safe in continuing to think I am eccentric. I haven't changed and I won't."

**Franz Beckenbauer, praising Ronaldo: "No, I would not have liked to play against him. He's too fast."**

# THE THINGS THEY SAID

A message on the Newcastle United tannoy: "A reminder to Barry Moat to leave at half-time. You're getting married this afternoon!"

**Angus Fraser on Brian Lara: "He's a batsman capable of taking you apart and he can make a bowler look stupid."**

Dean Headley on his legendary grandfather George Headley: "I remember he was a very small man. At the age of eleven I was probably taller than him. He bowled a couple of balls to me in the garden but that was all."

**Kevin Keegan, as manager of Newcastle giving the players the benefit of his half-time thoughts when they were losing 0-1: "If things don't improve I'm going home." Newcastle won 3-1.**

Gary Player on Arnie's Army who followed Arnold Palmer round the golf course: "If Arnold asked those people to go jump in the river, they would march straight to the river and jump."

# THE THINGS THEY SAID

**Bowler Fred Truman, when asked if he thought his total of 307 Test wickets would ever be beaten: "Aye, but whoever does it will be bloody tired!"**

Another Bill Shanklyism: "I'm only surprised that people are surprised by surprise results in football."

**Coventry manager Gordon Strachan on his outbursts from the dug-out: "I enjoy shouting and screaming. It's not abuse I'm shouting, I'm passing on information. I'm a passionate person – I care about football."**

Glenn Hoddle, relishing the thought of the World Cup: "I'm like a kid at Christmas. I can't wait to rip off the paper and get into the World Cup present."

**Commenting on his 1998 loss of form Stephen Hendry, father of a 16-month-old son: "Ten years ago snooker was my life. Now it isn't. Having a family takes away a fraction of your edge."**

Remembering the dismissal for nought of Don Bradman in his last Test by Eric Hollies, Australian batsman Arthur Morris said: "If he had bowled him today, he would have done four cartwheels and been kissed by every member of his side."

**Veteran tennis player Ilie Nastase, commenting on his idol Ken Rosewall: "I like his game so much I wanted to clap when a ball from him passed me."**

Viewing his role as captain of the West Indies, Brian Lara said: "I have been guilty of a few indiscretions as a player that would be very embarrassing if they were repeated as captain."

**Arsenal manager Arsene Wenger on the pressures of success: "You can't finish tenth in the table here. People would laugh at you."**

Boxer Chris Eubank on retirement: "Some people are just content with existing. Being in the limelight is a fantastic buzz. If I retire, I will miss that."

**Donovan Bailey, Canadian 100 metres World record holder, on retirement: "I'll be aiming to win the world title in Seville in 1999 and I think I will finish my career with the Sydney Olympics."**

Footballer Paul Merson after captaining an England side: "It was only the B side but it was my proudest moment in football."

# THE THINGS THEY SAID

**Gareth Southgate on the 'divers' in football:** "I'm sure everyone has noticed feigning has become far more prevalent. I am not being pro-England, but I do think there are times when we are a lot more honest and try to keep our feet if we get clipped on the ankles."

France World Cup star Marcel Desailly, on joining Chelsea: "I was at Milan for five years and I have won the Champions' League three times. I want to win it again and I want that to be with Chelsea."

**Frank Bruno, on winning the WBC heavyweight title:** "Thank God I won. All my dreams have come true."

Sir Tom Finney, looking at football in 1998: "When we played it was sufficient that you were playing for your country. Today it seems to be about money first and foremost."

**Graham Gooch, reflecting the state of the game when he retired as England cricket captain in 1993:** "We're not just losing Test matches, we're getting stuffed."

Greg Norman after losing the US Masters in 1996 to Nick Faldo: "I screwed up. I will win here. If I don't believe that, I might as well put my clubs away for good."

**Commenting on rumours that he was retiring, West Indies fast bowler Curtly Ambrose said:** "Only Curtly decides when Curtly retires."

Alan Hardaker, secretary of the Football League, prophesied in 1979: "If we don't watch out, football will be played on Sundays, there will be advertising on players' shirts and matches in the summer."

**Surrounded by Sir Tom Finney, John Charles, Nat Lofthouse, Sir Colin Cowdrey and Henry Cooper, TV's host of the Sporting Heroes show Dickie Davies said:** "I'm like a five-year-old in a toyshop."

John Gorman, Glenn Hoddle's No. 2, on why he thinks he got the job: "I came into training full of beans. I hated to be coached by a dour coach."

**Paul Gascoigne on not making the final 22 for the World Cup:** "It was the biggest shock I've ever had. I was furious and upset when Glenn gave me his decision. I went berserk."

Glenn Hoddle's reply to Gascoigne: "If he comes back and shows me he is willing to get fit, he could still have an international career."

# THE THINGS THEY SAID

**Boxer Chris Eubank, after being detained in hospital with a swollen and closed eye after his fight with Carl Thompson in June 1998, described his injury as "a badge of honour".**

Graeme Le Saux in supporting the appointment of Gianluca Vialli as manager of Chelsea: "I've got to know Luca and find him affable and very sensitive with amazing charisma, composure and experience. I can't see him losing any of those qualities as a manager."

**Brian Ashton, former Ireland rugby coach on returning to the England fold: "It was a mistake leaving England in the first place. England is where my heart is."**

Former manager of Nottingham Forest Brian Clough: "Very few players have the courage of my convictions."

**Lionel Pickering, chairman of Derby County, on Chelsea's decision to sack Ruud Gullit: "Sitting second in the Premiership and still in two cups – that's a brave decision to sack someone like Gullit."**

Explaining his decision to retire from rugby and Saracens, Michael Lynagh explained: "I'm just getting tired, that's all."

**Ruud Gullit commenting on TV: "You have to remember a goalkeeper is a goalkeeper because he can't play football."**

Bolton's Nat Lofthouse on his team's 4-3 defeat by Blackpool in the 1953 FA Cup Final when Stanley Matthews turned on his magic: "There were no recriminations in our dressing room. I don't think a bullet would have stopped Stan in the last 17 minutes."

**Don Bradman, after being bowled for a duck in his 80th and final Test match: "It's hard to bat with tears in your eyes."**

After watching Bjorn Borg win his fifth successive Wimbledon singles title in 1980, Ilie Nastase said: "They should sent Borg away to another planet. We play tennis – he plays something else."

**Watching her husband celebrating his third British Open triumph in 1978, Jack Nicklaus' wife Barbara pleaded: "Can you please get him to stop talking, we've a plane to catch!"**

Demon bowler Dennis Lillee of Australia, with 355 Test wickets to his name: "I don't want to do the batsman permanent injury, just to cause him concern, to hurt him a bit."

# THE THINGS THEY SAID

**After being banned by FIFA for drug abuse in 1994, Diego Maradona claimed that he had taken a cold cure, saying: "I was taking them like aspirin. Thousands of players do it, but the cost is always higher when it is Maradona."**

After surprisingly being placed only third in the 1994 Winter Games ice dance, Jayne Torvill's partner Christopher Dean said: "We like to think the audience were our judges."

**Charles Taylor, son of the owner and breeder of the remarkable racing stallion Northern Dancer, described the horse thus: "It may sound ridiculous to attribute human qualities to a horse but he was a feisty, gutsy character who knew he was number one."**

Manchester United manager Alex Ferguson on an incident in a United v Chelsea match: "You know Dennis Wise – he could start a row in an empty house."

**Comedian Jasper Carrott: "I hear that Glenn Hoddle has found God. That must have been one hell of a pass!"**

# THE THINGS THEY SAID

Italian coach Arrigo Sacchi at the start of the Euro 96 tournament: "When it is over, they will either kiss my bald pate or throw tomatoes at it."

**Nick Faldo after failing to finish in the top ten of the 1998 US Tour: "I'm going to play smart again, aim to get the ball within 20 feet of the flag and then I will trust my putter."**

David Campese after England's 76-0 rugby defeat by Australia: "I never feel sorry for the English but I was hoping this wouldn't happen – it's very unhealthy for the sport."

**Lawrie McMenemy, the first non-Irishman to manage Northern Ireland football team: "I would like to do what Jack Charlton did for the Republic. He's a good friend from the same part of England, but I'm posher and can remember names!"**

Mario Kempes, Argentina star of three World Cups, on a salary offer to manage a Singapore team: "That wouldn't keep me in tequila."

**South Africa's Jonty Rhodes in praise of England's Angus Fraser: "He's a run-miser deluxe. He admonishes himself if he concedes a run."**

Michael Schumacher, after winning the Canadian Grand Prix of 1998, said of Damon Hill: "He moved across in front of me three times. If you want to kill someone you do it in a different way."

**Damon Hill after Schumacher had incurred a penalty for putting Frentzen out of that race: "How can you take serious anything Michael says when you see what he's done on the track."**

Describing the 1998 Derby winner High-Rise, trainer Luca Cumani said: "If he was a human being, you would want him to be a friend."

**John Sillett, manager of Coventry City after they were knocked out of the FA Cup by non-League Sutton United: "It will be worse when we open the papers and find we made history the wrong way round."**

England cricket captain Alec Stewart, partnering his predecessor Mike Atherton on completing his century against South Africa at Edgbaston: "It was a crap shot!"

**Athlete Roger Black on being asked whether he is the greatest 400 metres runner ever born: "I don't think so. I'm very, very good but Michael Johnson is outstanding."**

# THE THINGS THEY SAID

Arantxa Sanchez Vicario, on winning the 1998 French Open, brought tears to the eyes of her final opponent Monica Seles with: "One has to win, one has to lose, that is the game. I congratulate you because you are a great champion."

**After being sent to prison on a rape charge in 1992, former World heavyweight champion Mike Tyson was described by a reform school supervisor as "a tulip among the weeds".**

Norman Whiteside, who at 17 was the youngest-ever World Cup footballer, warned Michael Owen how precarious a football career can be: "When injury left me on the scrapheap at the age of 26, I would wake in the mornings and cry my eyes out."

**Cricketer Nasser Hussain's advice on winning matches: "We have to get a bit of nastiness into our game."**

Bill Foulkes, survivor of the Manchester United air crash at Munich: "What is so wonderful about this current United side is that you can see a similar sort of togetherness. Like us, so many of them have grown up together."

**Gary Neville, 1998 player with Manchester United: "It means a lot to me that I grew up with all the tradition of this club. We owe everything to those lads and Sir Matt Busby as a club."**

Mick Cleary, Daily Telegraph rugby writer, on England's chance of success in 1998: "England have never won a Test in Australia, never mind with a side so raw and inexperienced that they ought to be sponsored by Farley's Rusks."

**Lee Westwood, after using his golf club to hit out at a bush, was ticked off by his 90-year-old grandmother: "She told me it wasn't the bush's fault I played a bad shot. She was right – I won't be hitting any more bushes."**

Joy for Olivier Peslier, French rider of the 1998 Derby winner: "He goes very fast, my 'orse. He gallop, fast gallop. I think we might win. Then, we win. We win! C'est superbe! Alleluia!"

**Birmingham City managing director Karren Brady, on her disagreement with manager Trevor Francis: "If he is trying to turn it into a me-versus-him situation, there'll be only one winner. Me!"**

Tony Jacklin, former Ryder Cup winning captain, on playing in 1998 Seniors matches: "It's a hard game when you're pushed into playing whether you want to or not. You could say I've been happier."

# THE THINGS THEY SAID

**Formula One driver Martin Brundle, discussing racetrack safety: "Would you fancy being a mechanic in a busy pit lane or a marshal with cars hurtling past at 190mph? No – inside the cockpit suits me better."**

Hubert Green, on coming third at the 1977 Open behind Tom Watson and Jack Nicklaus: "Two gods of golf played their own game. I won the tournament for the mortals."

**Newcastle Kenny Dalglish on the behaviour of Stevenage in their 1998 FA Cup ties: "They were a credit to the town of Stevenage on the pitch, but off it they left a lot to be desired."**

Stevenage manager Paul Fairclough on the replay with Newcastle: "When we got back to 2-1 there was always a chance. When I looked at their bench I could see fear."

**Dave Whelan, millionaire owner of Wigan in rugby league's Super League: "Murdoch put his money in because he wanted to control the game. That's not worked and I believe the game can survive without him."**

On being appointed captain of Britain's team of amateurs for the 1999 Walker Cup, Peter McEvoy pleaded: "Let's hope there are some players left."

**Venus Williams on the arguments she has with her sister Serena on their tennis travels: "We argue over stupid things, like the colour of someone's hair, and we just had an argument about who was in the semi-finals of the French Open. We keep score of the arguments and I think I won the first set 6-2."**

Terry Venables on returning in charge of Crystal Palace in 1998: "This was my first club as a manager and maybe it will be my last."

**Portugal's champion Marathon runner Antonio Pinto says he finds wine relaxing: "When I broke my 10,000 metres record, I drank two bottles to celebrate."**

# MOTOR SPORTS

# MOTORCYCLING

The Isle of Man TT racing has claimed 170 victims on its winding course.

**The course consists of 37.73 miles of public roads.**

There are no mass starts in the Isle of Man. Competitors leave at intervals and race against the clock.

**Joey Dunlop, a veteran of the Isle of Man course, celebrated his 23rd TT win in 1998 by taking the 250cc Lightweight race.**

Only a month before he was in hospital with a broken collar-bone, cracked pelvis and injuries to his wrist, hand and ankle, and had lost part of a finger.

**Dunlop, a 46-year-old publican, won in pouring rain 44secs in front of Bob Jackson.**

Italian Giacomo Agostini, who dominated the scene in the 1960s and 1970s, won 122 Grands Prix, taking 54 on his 350cc and 68 on his 500cc machines.

**Agostini rode an MV Agusta for most of his career, changing to Yamaha in 1974.**

Honda celebrated a century of TT victories when Jim Moodie, riding a Fireblade, won the production TT with Nigel Davies on a Kawasaki in second place.

**Mike Hailwood won his first championship race, in the 125cc Ulster Grand Prix, in 1959 on a Ducati.**

Riding in four different classes, he battled with his big rival Agostini.

**After winning 75 motorcycling Grands Prix, Mike Hailwood started a full-time career in motor racing in 1967, having competed in both sports for several years.**

His career in Formula One lasted from 1963-74. His best performance was in 1972 in a Surtees-Ford TS9B.

**He finished second in the Italian Grand Prix at Monsa.**

He was also second in the Race of Champions at Brands Hatch.

**A Nurburgring crash in 1974 ended his career on four wheels after he sustained ankle and foot injuries.**

The lure of motorbikes returned in 1978 and Hailwood was back in the Isle of Man for the TT.

# MOTORCYCLING

**In 1978 he won the Formula One production TT on a Ducati.**

The following year on a Suzuki 500, he won the Senior 500cc TT.

**That year the World Championship was decided on the one TT race, and Hailwood was declared the champion.**

At the end of his career on two wheels, he had won 14 TT races.

**John Surtees won seven World motorcycle titles before making a career on the motor-racing circuit.**

World motorcycle trial champion Dougie Lampkin started the defence of his title in 1998 on a new Beta machine built for him at the Italian factory.

**The 23-year-old Yorkshire champion is the son of multiple World champion Martin.**

Trial biking is a tough sport taking competitors through woods, streams and over rocks.

**A new marking system, devised for the 1998 season, and tough opposition from Japanese and Spanish riders has brought additional pressure to the sport.**

Britain's Barry Sheene broke almost every bone in his body at Daytona in 1975.

**Sliding along the Daytona tarmac at 180mph left Sheene with crushed bones, needing metal plates and screws to hold him together.**

He was never expected to ride again, but Barry had been brought up in a family obsessed by motorbikes and was soon back in action.

**Not only did he return to the sport, he won the World Championship two years running.**

With his amiable manner, good looks and shoulder-length hair, he was a sporting pin-up of the 1970s.

**Now, Scott Smart, nephew of Sheene and 1997 British 250cc champion, is trying to emulate his uncle Barry.**

Scott survived a 100mph crash in training which left him with gravel burns and bad bruising but nothing broken.

**Twenty-two-year-old Scott was testing 500cc bikes in Jerez, Spain, when the accident happened.**

# MOTORCYCLING

Six-times motocross champion Kurt Nicoll was not so lucky after his crash in France, where he was testing.

**His smashed arm needed a plate and ten screws to mend the bone and Nicoll decided to retire.**

Spaniard Alex Criville dedicated his 500cc win in Jerez in May 1998 to his father, who had died of cancer earlier in the year.

**Taking the lead 12 laps from home, he kept 500cc World champion Mick Doohan and 250cc World champion Max Biaggi at bay to win by half a second.**

Four-times 250cc World champion Max Biaggi of Italy made a sensational start in his first season in the 500cc class.

**Biaggi started from pole position in the Japanese Grand Prix at Suzuka.**

Riding his ERV Kanemoto-prepared Marlboro Honda, he took the lead on the third lap.

**He completed the full 21 laps without being challenged to become the first rider for 25 years to win first time out on the 500cc circuit after leaving the 250cc.**

The late Jarno Saarinen was the last man to do this 25 years ago in the French Grand Prix.

**Australian Mick Doohan, defending 500cc champion, had a poor start, quitting the race six laps from the finish when his engine seized.**

In a Transatlantic meeting at Brands Hatch over Easter 1980, a new young American sensation hit the headlines.

**The 18-year-old Freddy Spencer helped to crush the British team who had Mike Hailwood as their manager.**

Young Leon Haslam, son of the great champion Ron Haslam, is competing against Marco Melandri.

**Marco became the youngest Grand Prix winner in June 1998, finishing first in the 125cc race at the Dutch Grand Prix at Assen.**

Marco was fourth, despite a first-lap slide, and Leon was a praiseworthy 17th on his Grand Prix debut.

# MOTOR-RACING

Nineteen-ninety-seven was Jacques Villeneuve's year. He won the FIA World Drivers' Championship in a ding-dong battle with Michael Schumacher.

**They went in to the final stage in Spain in October with Schumacher one point ahead.**

Third place was enough for Villeneuve to take the title, while Schumacher's attempt to block him left him out of the race.

**Thirty years earlier, Jack Brabham, a Sydney greengrocer's son, won the World Championship at the wheel of his own Brabham car – the last driver to do so.**

Between 1959 and 1966, 'Black Jack' Brabham – later to become Sir Jack – won three World Championships.

**Austrian Jochen Rindt, who was killed practising for the Italian Grand Prix at Monza in 1970, was the only driver to be awarded the World Championship posthumously.**

Graham Hill, father of Damon, another of the charismatic drivers of the 1960s and 1970s, won two World Championships yet he was 24 before he even learned to drive.

**His successes in five Monaco Grands Prix included 1965, when he was forced down an escape route, pushed his car back on track and still went on to win.**

He returned in 1975 to concentrate on team management but was tragically killed a few months later, together with five team members, when his light aircraft crashed near Elstree airfield.

**Damon Hill had some near misses before taking the World title in 1996. He was third in 1993, second in 1994 and 1995.**

Despite his World Championship, he was sacked by Williams after his 1996 success, drove for Arrows in 1997 and Jordan in 1998.

**Monaco, with its 78 laps of high-speed driving through winding streets, could leave unlucky drivers going for a swim.**

It happened to Albert Ascari in 1955 when his Lancia D50 crashed through the harbour wall and Ascari had to be dragged from the sea.

**Ascari was tragically killed the week after that sea rescue when the Italian was testing a Ferrari sports car at Monza.**

# MOTOR-RACING

His father Antonio died in the 1925 French Grand Prix. Both were 36 and both died on the 26th of the month following a lucky escape.

**In 1961 Stirling Moss, driving an under-powered, four-cylinder Lotus 18, defeated the Ferraris to win his second successive Monaco Grand Prix.**

Phil Hill, who finished third for Ferrari, described his chase with Moss as "like a carthorse chasing a greyhound round somebody's living-room"!

**Stirling Moss won 16 Grands Prix during his career and was runner-up four times in the World Championship but never won it.**

Colin McRae won the Corsica Rally in May 1998 for the second year running, giving him top place in the world table.

**Seventy-three-year-old Ken Tyrrell sold his Grand Prix team for £20 million to British American Racing in 1998.**

He intended to stay in charge at Tyrrell for one more year, but disagreements with the new owners led him to retire, together with his son Bob.

**He came into Formula One in 1968 and, with his backing, Jackie Stewart won three World Championships driving Tyrrell cars in 1969, 1971 and 1973.**

After a crash in the Belgian Grand Prix in 1966 when he was trapped in his fuel-soaked car, Stewart started his campaign for greater safety measures.

**At Spa he was rescued by fellow drivers Graham Bill and Bob Bondurant and never again drove without a screwdriver taped to the steering wheel to assist in its removal if necessary.**

Jackie Stewart was the first Grand Prix driver to wear a seat belt.

**The princess Royal opened the Stewart Racing team's £5 million research, design and production centre at Milton Keynes in June 1998.**

Jackie still found time to send a message of encouragement to McLaren driver and fellow Scot, David Coulthard.

**Stewart hoped his own team would be strong enough to challenge the McLaren team in another two years.**

Jim Clark, another hero of the 1960s, was the son of a Scottish farmer.

# MOTOR-RACING

**He won 25 of the 72 Grands Prix in which he competed and was World champion in 1963 and 1965.**

Grand Prix racing was not his only love – he was British Touring Car champion with a Lotus Cortina.

**He is the only driver to have won both Formula One and BTTC titles. His 1965 win in the Indianapolis 500 proved his ability to win at all levels.**

In 1968, after winning the South African Grand Prix, he returned to Europe and entered Formula One events in Spain and Germany.

**He retired in the Barcelona race and went on to Hockenheim, where a blown tyre is thought to have caused him to hit a tree. He was killed instantly.**

China were expected on the Formula One motor-racing calendar in 1999.

**The Zhuhai circuit, 20 miles from Hong Kong, was completed in 1996.**

With Grand Prix commercial agreements all signed, the Zhuhai track were awaiting the F1 all-clear following two international sports car races successfully undertaken during the first half of 1998.

**McLaren's supremacy again showed when the team's junior driver, German Nick Heidfeld, snatched the Formula 3000 Championship round the streets of Monte Carlo in May 1998.**

# MOTOR-RACING

Danish driver Jason Watt had a four-second lead when he crashed at Casino Square with nine laps to go, leaving Heidfeld to cruise home.

**Alister McRae won the 1998 Scottish International Rally for the second year in succession, with co-driver David Senior in a VW Golf GTI.**

Alister is the brother of Colin McRae, the 1995 World Rally champion.

**Alain Menu, driving for the Williams-Renault team, took the 1997 Auto Trader BTCC after three years as runner-up.**

Eleven wins secured the title for Menu with six races still to go.

**Nigel Mansell, the 1992 F1 World champion, returned to the track for the first time in 4½ years at Donington Park in June 1998.**

His last visit to Donington in 1993 had come to a quick end when his touring car crashed at Old Hairpin.

**Mansell was unconscious as he was cut from the car.**

Driving for the Ford Mondeo team in a BTCC race in June 1998, he qualified for the sprint race but, when lying eighth, he crashed into the Coppice barriers at 100mph.

**This time he was uninjured and mechanics took two hours to repair the car in time for the feature race.**

He started in 19th position but crept through the field to contest third place with his former Grand Prix rival, Derek Warwick.

**He was finally awarded fifth place after being penalised for overtaking under yellow flags.**

Alan Gow, chief executive of BTCC, said: "Nigel gives value for money – he still has fire in his belly."

**Ford were reputed to be paying £600,000 for Mansell's services.**

He was the first driver to win the F1 Championship and the American Indy 500 Championship in successive years – 1992 and 1993.

# MOTOR-RACING

**After winning his F1 Championship, he had walked out of the Williams team following a dispute with Frank Williams and joined the Newman-Haas Indy Car Team.**

The 1976 Formula One Championship was a nailbiting affair involving Niki Lauda and James Hunt.

**Halfway through the season, the reigning World champion Lauda was 45 points in the lead, then Hunt won the French Grand Prix while his rival retired from the race.**

Hunt was then first in the British Grand Prix but lost the victory because his car had been repaired after a first-lap collision.

**Hunt won the German Grand Prix after Lauda's car hit a kerb, engulfing him in flames.  Lauda suffered terrible burns, scarring him for life.**

Six weeks later, he was back behind the wheel and still hoping to retain the championship.

**Hunt won two races in North America and when the last race of the season – the Japanese Grand Prix – came round, Lauda was two points ahead.**

In pouring rain and visibility down to 100 yards, Hunt took the lead.

**Driving behind him in clouds of spray, Lauda decided to retire.  Hunt needed a fourth place to clinch the title.**

Then the rain ceased and Hunt's wet-weather tyres were now a liability on a drying track.  He was forced into a pit stop for new tyres.

**He emerged in fifth place, but two drivers ahead of him were also forced to make pit stops and he finished third – World champion by just one point ahead of Lauda!**

Lauda was champion again in 1977 and both men announced their retirement in 1979.

**Lauda was tempted back in 1982 and won his third World title in 1984.**

For British fans there was good news about Goodwood.  The Sussex circuit, once one of the premier tracks, was due to re-open late in 1998.

# MOTOR-RACING

**Damon Hill, at 37, was 18 years older than Minardi's Esteban Tuero, the youngest driver on the grid, in 1998 but he didn't let it worry him.**

Damon could replay that his father Graham and Nigel Mansell were both 39 when they won the World Championship.

**Tony Brooks, runner-up in the 1959 World Championship, had this to say of the present F1 regime: "It is like climbing Everest with a safety net – take out the element of danger and it changes everything."**

The success of the 1998 McLaren MP4-13 car is the brainchild of Adrian Newey, chief designer to Williams until the end of 1997.

**Under his supervision, the car was put together in less than six months.**

During Newey's time at Williams, the cars won five manufacturers' and four drivers' titles.

**Now, drivers David Coulthard and Mika Hakkinen are reaping the benefit of Newey's know-all.**

Juan Manual Fangio, the Argentinian driver who started his racing career in 1938, won five World Championships during his 19 years in the sport.

**He died aged 84 in 1995, the year that Michael Schumacher won his second World title and signed a £30 million two-year contract with Ferrari.**

In 1958, four British drivers had won all but one of the ten Grands Prix.

**Stirling Moss in his Vanwall and Mike Hawthorn in a Ferrari were both eyeing the title as they started the final race in Casablanca.**

Stirling, still seeking his first Championship win, had 32 points at the start to Hawthorn's 40.

**He needed a win and the fastest lap to take the title, providing Hawthorn finished no higher than fourth.**

It was not to be. Moss won by a minute and made the fastest lap, but Hawthorn snatched the title by one point.

# MOTOR-RACING

**He was the first Briton to become World Champion, even though Moss had won five Grands Prix and Hawthorn only one that year.**

Hawthorn announced his retirement, prompted by the death of his friend and teammate Peter Collins at Nurburgring.

**Three months later, Hawthorn was killed when his Jaguar skidded on a wet road and hit a tree.**

New Zealander Denny Hulme won the 1967 drivers' championship with 41-year-old Jack Brabham in second place.

**But the hero of the season was Jim Clark and his amazing performance in the Italian Grand Prix.**

He was leading on the 13th lap when he took a pit stop to change a wheel.

**Rejoining the race a minute later, he was a lap behind the leaders and in 15th place with only one car behind him.**

Twelve laps later and after some magnificent driving, Clark had pulled back the lap.

**With seven laps to go, he overtook the leader Brabham and looked sure to win.**

Came the last lap and his Lotus was fading with fuel problems. Brabham and John Surtees both overtook him, laving him in third place.

**New regulations for Formula One cars introduced for the 1998 season included three 14mm-wide grooves on the front tyres and four on the rear, 2.5mm deep.**

In addition, drivers had to be able to remove the steering wheel, get out and replace the steering wheel within ten seconds.

**Tyres cost £400 each and Goodyear provided 1,650 of them at the 1998 Melbourne Grand Prix.**

Johnny Herbert, partnering Jean Alesi in the Swiss-based Sauber Petronas team, was due to end his two-year contract at the finish of the 1998 season.

**The moment he will always treasure is his 1995 win at Silverstone in a Benetton Renault.**

# MOTOR-RACING

The Union Jacks and champagne that greeted a British victory in the British Grand Prix is something he strives to repeat.

**Frank Williams welcomed the appointment of former Grand Prix driver Gerhard Berger as BMW's new motorsport director in July 1998.**

The Williams team will link up with BMW in 2000 and Frank Williams hopes Berger's influence will help the team back to winning ways.

**Gerhard Berger, who left Formula One racing at the end of 1997, had ten victories from 210 races.**

In his successful days in F1, Berger had a reputation as a brilliant driver and also a practical joker.

**He once threw a briefcase belonging to Ayrton Senna out of a helicopter.**

On another occasion, he was accused of leaving a large number of frogs in his partner's bedroom.

**Tom Walkinshaw and Piers Portman announced in July 1998 a collaboration of their Arrows Formula One and Portman British Formula Three teams to help young drivers' to progress to F1.**

The 1994 San Marino Grand Prix at Imola was a sad affair with two drivers killed, ending the sport's 12 years without a fatality.

**Austria's Roland Ratzenberger, in his first F1 season, was killed at Villeneuve Corner during a qualifying lap, and Ayrton Senna met his death on the day of the race.**

Senna, driving for Williams, was battling with Michael Schumacher, who had won the season's first two F1 races.

**Accelerating to 180mph at the Tamburello curve, Senna was leading when he lost control and hit a concrete wall on the seventh lap. He was declared dead four hours later.**

After the tragedies, both the Villeneuve and Tamburello were adapted and made safer.

**Senna, 34 when he died, had won three F1 World Championships.**

When he was buried in Sao Paulo, a million Brazilians lined the streets and the Brazilian Air Force drew a heart and a huge S in the sky.

# ATHLETICS

# ATHLETICS

Morocco was banned by the IAAF from hosting future events after the Israel team was refused visas to take part in the World Cross-Country Championships in Marrakesh in 1998.

**Marion Jones, America's new superwoman athlete, declared at 22 that she planned to better the feats of Florence Griffith-Joyner's feats of the 1980s but without the flamboyance.**

Flo-Jo set her records in glamorous style – long fingernails accentuated with brightly coloured nail polish, designer bodysuits and immaculate make-up.

**Jones, a former North Carolina basketball star, set her sights on winning five gold medals – 100 and 200 metres, long jump and both relays – something never achieved by a woman athlete.**

One world-class athlete could become a multi-millionaire before the turn of the century, thanks to the IAAF's Golden League scheme.

**From meetings in Oslo, Rome, Monte Carlo, Zurich, Brussels and Berlin, with the final Grand Prix in Moscow, athletes are competing for the biggest prize-money ever.**

At the end of the series, any athlete who can remain unbeaten at a single event in the seven Golden League meetings receives £800,000 on top of the individual prizes awarded at each meeting.

**Britain's Mark Richardson became only the second runner to beat American Michael Johnson over one lap of 400 metres in Oslo in July 1998 in the Bislett Games.**

Richardson beat Johnson in a time of 44.37secs, a personal best and just one-hundredth of a second outside the British record running in lane one, the most difficult of the course.

**In second spot was Britain's Iwan Thomas in 44.50secs, pushing Johnson into third place. The American, not a good loser, did not shake hands with the Brits but spent the evening alone, contemplating his defeat in the corner of a bar.**

Jonathan Edwards, World triple-jump record holder, found his form again in Oslo in 1998 with a jump of 18.01 metres, his best for three years and not far behind his World record of 18.29 metres.

**The Oslo jump by Edwards was the fourth longest of all time, pushing Denis Kapustin, the Russian, into second place.**

# ATHLETICS

In June 1998, Britain's athletes showed the World that they were a formidable combination when the men's team retained the European Cup in St. Petersburgh, collecting 111 points.

**Before the closing event, the 4 x 400 metres relay, Germany stood in first place but the relay team, led by Roger Black in his final year, with Jamie Baulch, Iwan Thomas and Mark Richardson, knew they had to finish two places ahead of the Germans.**

The British team earned their eight winners' points, pushing Germany into fifth place and retaining the Cup. Richardson celebrated by using the baton as a cigar in Marx Brothers style.

**Mark Richardson had every reason to celebrate, having already won the 400 metres in 45.81secs, to join winning teammates Jonathan Edwards (triple jump), Colin Jackson (110 metres hurdles) and Doug Walker (200 metres).**

Paula Radcliffe, taking over as women's captain from Sally Gunnell, put in a tremendous performance to win the 5,000 metres and then came a close second in the 1,500 metres behind the Russian, Komyagina.

# ATHLETICS

A third place in the 4 x 400 metres relay put the women's team in fifth spot, with Russia in the top placing.

Captain Roger Black, double Olympic silver medallist, revealed that as an 11-year-old he had been banned from representing his school at athletics because of a heart defect.

He has had yearly check-ups ever since and admits that he has suffered chest pains throughout his successful career. He has helped Mark Richardson in his training for two years.

British shot putter Guy Marshall, after being banned in 1995 following a positive drugs test, won his appeal to return to the sport in July 1998.

The International Amateur Athletics Federation voted in 1997 to halve doping bans to two years.

Marshall commented: "I am grateful for the chance to resume my career. To any youngster tempted to take drugs, my message is 'Don't'."

Middle-distance runner Kelly Holmes underwent surgery for an Achilles tendon injury in 1998 and stayed awake throughout the operation.

She was anaesthetised from the waist down while scar tissue was removed, but kept her wits about her in case surgeons needed her permission to extend the operation.

Britain's former World 5,000 metres record holder David Moorcroft and the former 400 metres hurdles Commonwealth champion Alan Pascoe, are aiming to put British athletics back on track after the liquidation of the British Athletic Federation with debts of £500,000 in 1997.

Looking for fresh sponsorship to spotlight athletics, they signed a three-year £300,000 deal with Nivea in June 1998, while the daily running costs of £4,000 were reduced by cutting staff from 40 to 30.

Britain's top 140 athletes have their coaching, travel and medical bills supported by money from the National Lottery, amounting to £2.5 million in 1998.

Two British pole-vaulters, Nick Buckfield and Janine Whitlock – both aged 24 – raised their UK records by the same margin and on the same night in May 1998, but they were at different meetings thousands of miles apart.

# ATHLETICS

**Nick Buckfield, competing in Khania, Crete, improved his UK record from 5.75 metres to 5.80, while Whitlock in Cottbus, Germany, recorded her 25th national record with a clearance of 4.30 metres.**

Haile Gebrselassie, the Ethiopian, took five seconds off the World 10,000 metres record in Holland in June 1998, then later improved his time with a run of 26mins 22.75secs.

**It was his 13th World record time and his fourth record-breaking run in Holland's Fanny Blankers-Koen Stadium, roared on by a 15,000 capacity crowd.**

Gebrselassie became only the third man to have held the 10,000 metres World record three times, joining the legendary Emil Zatopek and Ron Clarke. He ran the last mile in just over four minutes and devoured the last lap in 58 seconds.

**Nawal El Moutawakel, the first Muslim woman to win an Olympic gold medal and a member of the IAAF Council, helped to organise the first athletics meeting in Qatar in the Arabian Gulf in which women were allowed to take part.**

Competing women athletes were warned that bare midriffs or skimpy leotards would not be allowed – modesty was the order of the day. Mikaela Ingberg, winner of the javelin event, wore a scarf, baggy T-shirt and knee-length shorts.

**Asked whether American sprinter Marion Jones' ambition to be the first to capture five gold medals at the 2000 Olympics was a serious possibility, the all-time great Carl Lewis said: "If she can stay clear of problems and master the long jump, she has every chance."**

Former Yorkshire chef and restaurant owner Keith Anderson, who took up jogging in 1988 to lose weight, qualified to represent England in the Marathon at the 1998 Commonwealth Games in Kuala Lumpur.

**At the age of 30 he was an overweight smoker who joined his wife Gill on a sponsored slim. Now he is a full-time athlete clocking up 140 miles a week.**

Former 1,500 metres World record holder Seb Coe says: "Athletics is for everybody. You can be fat or thin, tall or short, and there is something for you whether it is putting the shot or sprinting 100 metres."

# ATHLETICS

**Seven-year-old Eilish, daughter of Liz McColgan and husband Peter, a former Irish international 3,000 metres steeplechaser, has inherited some of her parents' talents. She has already won her school's mini-Marathon.**

When Tegla Loroupe, the tiny Kenyan runner, recorded the fastest Marathon time for a woman in Rotterdam in April 1998, she collected a bonus of £94,000 for breaking the record.

**Ingrid Kristiansen's previous Marathon record, set in London 13 years before, was bettered by 19secs as Tegla jumped through the tape in 2hrs 20mins 47secs.**

To achieve the records, both women had been paced by male runners. Bernard Boiyo and Jacob Losian, Kenyan teammates, stayed with Loroupe throughout the race encouraging her to speed up and protecting her from the wind.

**The first Women's World Games in Paris in 1922 attracted only six nations and the first-ever five events for women were included in the 1928 Olympic Games.**

Britain's young athletes are issuing warnings to their seniors with some outstanding performances. Fifteen-year-old Mark Lewis-Francis, a pupil at George Salter High School in West Bromwich, shattered the under-17 indoor record for 60 metres three times in February 1996.

**Carl Myerscough, a 23 stone, 6ft 10ins Millfield School boy, broke his own British junior shot-putt record with 19.24 metres at the British Under-20 Championships in July 1998.**

Junior discus champion and European junior champion Emeka Udechuku twice broke his own record at the meeting with throws of 60.72 metres and 60.97 metres.

**Christian Malcolm, a 19-year-old from Cardiff who is the 200 metres European junior champion, won both the 100 and 200 metres and brought this comment from 1980 Olympic sprint champion Allan Wells: "This boy could be phenomenal."**

In 1966, Roberta Gibb was the first woman to run in the Boston Marathon and finished in the unofficial time of 3hrs 21mins 40secs. This was considered quite remarkable, although Ingrid Kristiansen won the London Marathon some 30 years later with an hour to spare on that time.

# BOXING

# BOXING

The Romans reputedly arrived in Britain to start a fist fight or two, but James Figg is acknowledged as the first heavyweight champ in 1719.

**He was already an expert swordsman when he added to his teaching repertoire 'the noble art' for the benefit of the young bloods of the land, which he popularised by setting up fairground booths.**

The sport developed until, in 1838, it was put on a firmer footing by the introduction of the 'London Prize Ring Rules'.

**The Marquis of Queensberry Rules some 30 years later ultimately pointed the way to rounds of three minutes each, with one minute rest, and to the first World heavyweight contest using gloves.**

This contest, in New Orleans on September 7, 1892, was between the World bareknuckle champion John L. Sullivan against the bank clerk from California, James J. Corbett. They wore five-ounce gloves.

**Sullivan, known as 'The Boston Strong Boy', had a weight advantage of 37lbs over the 12½-stone Corbett, but the champion's lack of fitness told when he was knocked out in the 21st round.**

'Gentleman Jim' Corbett reigned until March 17, 1897, when the Cornishman Bob Fitzsimmons flattened him in the 14th round at Carson City, Nevada.

**Fitzsimmons was an unlikely-looking World heavyweight champion. He was 34, weighed one pound under 12 stone, and was under 6ft tall.**

Fitz's coup de grace was a lightning left blow to the pit of the stomach which forever more became known as the solar-plexus punch.

**The glamorous Corbett tried a comeback but was twice knocked out by James J. Jeffries, Fitz's conqueror, and finally decided on a stage career.**

Corbett was the first great scientific boxer of the Queensberry era, and the sporting world mourned his death from cancer at the age of 66 at his Long Island home.

**Although claimed as the first British heavyweight winner of the World title, Fitz was only nine when his family moved to New Zealand.**

# BOXING

The first cries of 'We wuz robbed!" may have been heard when Bob Fitzsimmons fought Tom Sharkey in San Francisco in December 1896.

**Sharkey was knocked out by a blow delivered above the belt in the eighty round, but incredibly Fitz was disqualified for a 'low blow'.**

The referee who gave that decision was Wyatt Earp, whose greater fame was earned outside the ring as a marshal out in the Wild West.

**Joe Louis, known as the 'Brown Bomber', built up a reputation as a first-round knockout specialist. He had ten of them in his career of 60 pro fights.**

Louis' most famous one-round slaughter took place in June 1938 in New York against Max Schmeling, the German. It was Joe's fourth defence of his World heavyweight crown.

**Louis had been beaten in 12 rounds in his pre-championship days by Schmeling. Two years later, he gained sweet revenge in 2mins 4secs of savage punching.**

Louis defended his title 25 times between 1937 and 1948 before he retired as undefeated champion. Five of his title fights ended in the first round.

**He was persuaded back to the ring in 1950 for title fights with Ezzard Charles and Rocky Marciano but was past his prime and lost both.**

Louis was in need of dollars, however, and tried his hand at wrestling in 1956 but was persuaded to give it up by his doctor who discovered he had a heart condition.

**Joe Louis was the first black heavyweight champion since Jack Johnson became champion in 1908 and is still rated by many boxing experts as the greatest heavyweight of all time.**

Other experts advance the claims of Rocky Marciano, who held the title and retired undefeated with a record of 49 wins in 49 fights. Only five of his opponents went the full distance against him.

**Marciano died in an air crash at the age of 46.**

Jack Dempsey was another of the legendary heavyweight champions, although his beginnings were something of a mystery.

**He was a mixture of Irish, Scottish and American, and in his early fighting career at the start of World War I was known as Kid Blackie.**

# BOXING

Later he was known as the Manassa Mauler, a tigerish fighter who as World title contender could not master the jinx of Gene Tunney.

**Tunney twice outpointed him in title fights and was, in fact, beaten only once in 77 contests – by Harry Greb, whom he later defeated.**

Both Tunney and Dempsey had creditable World War II records, both were commissioned officers – Tunney with the US Navy and Dempsey with the US Coast Guard.

**Dempsey's fighting record was bizarre. In 1926, on a February day, during an exhibition in Memphis in his World Championship heyday, he took on six opponents in succession, flattening four of them in the first round.**

Although beaten in a title bout by Harry Greb, he later met him four times, winning twice with the other two no-decision.

**Before the days of fat ex-champions coming back in their Forties for any of five different World titles, four heavyweights won World title fights at the age of 37.**

This quartet of 'ancient warriors' were Bob Fitzsimmons, Jack Johnson, Jess Willard and Jersey Joe Walcott.

**Before Mike Tyson came on the scene, the youngest holder of the World heavyweight title was Floyd Patterson, who was only 21 when he beat Archie Moore for the vacant crown.**

Marciano gave up the title after defending it six times, the last one against 'ancient' Archie Moore, who was really only a light-heavyweight and in fact held the World title in that division.

**Marciano's penultimate fight was against an Englishman, Don Cockell, in San Francisco. Cockell bravely stood up to the champion's heaviest punches before the referee intervened in the ninth round.**

Wales has produced many great boxers but none stands higher in the nation's ring history than Jimmy Wilde, a tiny man of most unlikely appearance.

**Wilde's phenomenal punching power belied his waif-life appearance. He fought as a flyweight and won the World title, although never at any time did he weigh more than 7st 10lb – four pounds below the weight limit.**

# BOXING

Known as 'The Ghost with the Hammer in his Hand', Wilde won the majority of his fights inside the distance, largely due to his fearsome punching which he had developed in the booths.

**There was a story told by Welsh old-timers that he once knocked out 19 booth challengers in 3½ hours, then rested for 30 minutes before polishing off four more unwise volunteers in 45 minutes.**

Many professional judges placed him as pound for pound the greatest-ever fighter. This lovely little man spent his later years as correspondent for the *News of The World*, although there were times when he could barely see above the ring apron.

**The Welsh also idolised in the early 1900s the Cardiff-born featherweight Jim Driscoll, renowned for his classical upright stance coupled with the immaculate straight left.**

They loved Driscoll's style in the States, and he laid claim to the vacant World featherweight title by clearly beating the great Abe Attell in a 'no-decision' ten-rounder.

**Driscoll also won a Lonsdale Belt outright as British featherweight champion, served in the Army throughout World War One, and died at the age of 44 from pneumonia.**

Another great featherweight stylist beloved of Welsh fans half a century later was Merthyr Tydfil's Howard Winstone, who won two Lonsdale Belts and retired as undefeated British champion after seven title bouts.

# BOXING

**Winstone challenged World champion Vincente Saldivar, the Mexican southpaw, three times for his title but failed bravely each time.**

Those bouts were in London, Cardiff and Mexico City. The first two ended on points over 15 rounds, the third went 12 before Winstone retired, whereupon the Mexican announced his ring retirement.

**Winstone's great ambition was realised when he beat Mitsunori Seki in London, but the WBA would not recognise the Welshman as champion.**

Fate decreed that Winstone would not hold his World crown for long, and he was well past his best when he lost to the Cuban Jose Legra at Porthcawl in 1968. He never fought again.

**Ironically, Legra's only defeat in 83 fights over five years had been a points defeat by Winstone in 1965.**

The Welsh also had their fair share of heavyweight heroes. Jack Petersen, Tommy Farr, Johnny Williams and Joe Erskine all held the British and Commonwealth titles.

**Added to that quartet of the same era is the name of Dick Richardson, who won four European heavyweight championship bouts.**

A famous Swede deprived Richardson of his title. Ingemar Johansson won by a knockout in nine rounds then retired the following year.

**Johansson held the World title for one year when he beat Floyd Patterson in June 1959.**

The pair met again in 1960 and 1961 for the title. Patterson won both contests. All three fights between the pair lasted only 14 rounds.

**Not much value for money in Patterson's next two World title fights either, as the widely detested Sonny Liston twice knocked him out.**

Those two meetings, in Chicago and Las Vegas, both ended in the first round. The total action for both fights was 4mins 16secs!

**That was the signal for the arrival of Cassius Clay, considered by many to be the greatest of all time – and certainly by the man himself. He never suffered from modesty and immediately labelled himself 'The Greatest'.**

# BOXING

Clay stopped Liston, whom he had taunted as the 'Ugly Bear', in six rounds in Miami and promptly declared that his name in future would be Muhammad Ali.

**The fight game was never the same again. Ali's name was constantly in the headlines for the next 16 years as the result of his antics in and out of the ring.**

When his book 'The Greatest – My Own Story' was published, Ali said: "This book is so great, so good – it's hard to be humble."

**Yet he was still Clay and was almost toppled before he reached his perch one memorable day in June 1963 in London.**

British champion Henry Cooper put him down in the fourth round with his famous left hook – his fans dubbed it 'Enery's 'Ammer – but the bell came to his rescue.

**It was then that one of Clay's gloves was seen to be split and the extended interval before the fifth round was sufficient for the American to recover his equilibrium.**

His shrewd manager Angelo Dundee was quoted some time later in a Philadephia newspaper on the incident. He said: "There was a rip in the glove. All I did was make the rip a little bigger."

**Then Dundee explained: "They're hunting round for gloves and I'm buying my man time. The way he recuperates, all we need is a couple of minutes."**

Clay cut loose in the fifth round and the fight was stopped with Cooper suffering from facial cuts.

**The next time they met was on May 21, 1966, again in London, with Ali's World title at stake. This time it was at Highbury, home of Arsenal Football Club, before a 46,000 crowd.**

Henry put up a tremendous show before the contest was stopped in the sixth round, with the challenger bleeding badly from a cut eye.

**It was the first time a World heavyweight title fight had taken place in Britain since Tommy Burns defended his title in London in February 1908.**

Cooper's title tilt was promoted by Harry Levene, and less than three months later rival promoter Jack Solomons put on Ali v Brian London at great expense at Earls Court.

**London, a former British and Empire champion, performed feebly and was counted out in the third round.**

# BOXING

Ali also disposed of two other British challengers – Joe Bugner on points over 15 rounds in Kuala Lumpur and Richard Dunn on a fifth-round stoppage in Munich.

**The career of The Greatest virtually ended on October, 1980, in Las Vegas. Ali had foolishly taken on Larry Holmes, a good champion, at the age of 38.**

Ali was clearly a spent force and Holmes repeatedly stepped back instead of inflicting any more punishment before Ali's corner retired him at the end of the tenth round.

**The final humiliation came in Nassau when Trevor Burbick beat him on points in a 'nothing match'.**

Mike Tyson then ruled the heavyweight roost as the youngest-ever champion, beating all-comers including Frank Bruno, whom he stopped in five rounds in Las Vegas in February 1989.

**Tyson in 1990 suffered a shock defeat in ten rounds by James 'Buster' Douglas, followed by a spell in prison after a rape charge.**

There followed confusion in which World titles were claimed under WBC, WBA and IBF rulings.

**Britain's Lennox Lewis and Frank Bruno both in turn held the WBC title, but Bruno's tenure ended when Tyson demolished him in three rounds.**

The 'alphabets' farce wasn't restricted to the top weight. The heavily boosted 'Judgement Day' fight in 1993 in Manchester was a clash of WBO and WBC super-middleweight champions.

**That contest between Chris Eubank (WBO) and Nigel Benn (WBC) added further to the dilemma. The verdict was a draw.**

Steve Collins was the first to beat Chris Eubank, capturing the WBO super-middleweight crown in the process. In their return match, Steve Collins was again the winner on a split decision.

**Collins also beat Nigel Benn twice and retired undefeated as WBO World champion. He became trainer of Scott Welch, former British heavyweight champion.**

# BOXING

Chris Eubank still retains his taste for top-level challenges and he indulged in an epic World title battle at 12 stone against Joe Calzaghe.

**Calzaghe won, whereupon Eubank tackled the WBO cruiserweight champion, Carl Thompson, in April 1998 over 12 rounds in Manchester.**

Eubank suffered severe punishment and a fractured eye socket and had to stay in hospital for two nights to recover.

**It was Eubank's fourth defeat in 51 fights, but he refused to retire and had another losing contest with Thompson, this time on a ninth-round stoppage.**

Joe Bugner, at the age of 48, finally won the World title he had sought vainly for 29 years in July 1998 in the strangest of big fight venues.

**He beat James 'Bonecrusher' Smith, both having been refused licences by the British Boxing Board of Control, in a World Boxing Federation heavyweight bout on Australia's Gold Coast.**

# BOXING

Smith, a mere 45, was forced to retire at the end of the first round with a dislocated shoulder.

**Bugner, a Hungarian refugee who settled in Bedford before moving Down Under and becoming a naturalised Australian, then talked of defending his title against ancient ex-champions Larry Holmes and George Foreman.**

Bugner once held British, European and Commonwealth titles, and is now on record as the oldest World champion, once held by the light-heavyweight Archie Moore of 48 years and 59 days (if that's all he was, some may ask).

**Bugner twice went the distance with Muhammad Ali and once with Joe Frazier. "This is my final hurrah," he said.**

Bugner summed up his career thus: "I retired at the age of 25. Then I made a comeback at 27. I retired again in 1977 and made a comeback in 1980. I retired in 1982 and made another comeback in 1987. I also retired in 1987. Then I made a comeback in 1995."

**One ex-British champion heavyweight who will not be making his comeback is Gary Mason. He lost only once in 36 fights – to Lennox Lewis – and retired from boxing with a detached retina.**

Ronnie Davies, who was Eubank's trainer before a split in 1997, claims a record of 21 World title fights with the British boxer.

**Nigel Benn has two super-middleweight cousins, Paul and Michael Bowen, who are managed by Benn's old guide Peter De Freitas, who predicts both will win titles in the year 2000.**

When the younger Michael was injured, Paul stepped in at short notice to defeat the experienced Eddie Knights in three rounds.

**Prince Naseem Hamed has a couple of top-drawer VIP fans in USA. They are George Foreman and the President himself, Bill Clinton.**

The President, on meeting the HBO chief Seth Abraham who shows all Hamed's fights in the States, said: "I like watching your fights, especially the Prince. He's pretty cool. When is he back in the States?"

**And Foreman... : "Hamed is a one-off. He is just the breath of fresh air boxing needs. I'm a big fan. I hope he comes back to America soon."**

# BOXING

Hamed thrilled Americans in December 1997 at Madison Square Garden when he was put down three times by Kevin Kelley but rallied to save his WBO featherweight title with a fifth-round stoppage.

**Hamed won his WBO title in 1995 when he beat the Welshman, Steve Robinson.**

When he made his tenth defence of his WBO title, Hamed showed he had learned from his Kelley experience as he kept his head before finally beating Wilfredo Vazquez, the 37-year-old Puerto Rican, in seven rounds.

**Terry Dunstan delivered a lightning smacker on St. Valentine's Day 1998 to win the vacant European cruiserweight title.**

His victim was Alexander Gurov, whom he demolished with a right to the jaw at the Elephant and Castle Leisure Centre in only 20 seconds – and that included the count!

**When the BBB of C sanctioned an IBO World title bout in England in March 1998, they became the sixth body to be recognised. The others are the WBA, WBC, IBF, WBO and WBU. Any more for any more?**

The search is on for the oddest name in boxing since Fidel Castro Smith hung up his gloves. That was his real name, and though he changed to Slugger O'Toole, he soon reverted to FCS again.

**The Bloxwich featherweight Elvis Parsley looked a likely successor to FCS – until the sudden arrival in Britain of the Tasmanian cruiserweight Chris P. Bacon.**

Hogan 'Kid' Bassey was the first Nigerian boxer to win a World title in 1957, although fighting for France at the time.

**He lost his featherweight crown two years later to the American Davey Moore. Bassey was awarded an MBE in 1958. He died in January 1998 aged 65.**

Spencer Oliver had a miraculous escape from death after being admitted to hospital with a brain clot following his tenth-round defeat by Ukranian Sergei Devakov.

**Oliver, who was defending his European super-bantamweight title at the Royal Albert Hall, underwent a three-hour operation. He came off the danger list after three days and, a fortnight later, was up and about and all smiles.**

# BOXING

Londoner Oliver was named Young Boxer of the Year at the age of 22. He won a silver medal at the 1994 Commonwealth Games and had won all his 14 pro fights before the near-fatal bout with Devakov.

**Not so lucky were Bradley Stone, who died from brain damage after a super-bantamweight title fight in 1994, and Scotland's James Murray, who died from a brain haemorrhage after a British bantamweight title fight in 1995.**

The new American menace on the heavyweight scene is Michael Grant, aged 25, 6ft 7in and 18st 3lb – and he says "not an ounce of fat and still growing."

**At the last count, Grant had won his first 29 pro fights, all but nine of them inside the distance.**

Floyd Patterson was unperturbed when he was once told that he had been knocked down more times than any other heavyweight champion.

**His smiling reply: "I always say that if I hold the record for going down, I must also hold it for getting up. Ain't that right?"**

# SNOOKER

# SNOOKER

Louis XI of France was said to have had a billiards table and Mary, Queen of Scots, was not pleased when her 'table de billiard' was removed by her captors.

**Australian Walter Lindrum, born in 1898 in Kalgoorlie, was king of the billiards players before Joe Davis appeared on the scene. Walter made his first 100 break at the age of seven, a 500 break at 14 and, a year later, beat the reigning champion – his older brother – to take the title.**

On a visit to England in 1931, he was invited to Buckingham Palace by King George V before winning the World Championship in 1933 and 1934.

**Joe Davis of Whitwell, near Chesterfield, was England's top billiards player and held the World title from 1928-32. But Joe realised that people were bored with billiards, each game lasting a week with two sessions a day.**

Snooker, he argued, with relatively short frames and easier handicapping, would be a better gambling game and would be more popular with the public.

**Using the cue he bought as a boy for 7s 6d, Joe won the first World Snooker Championship in 1927 with a prize of £6 10s. He held the title until 1946 when he beat Horace Lindrum, nephew of Walter, 78-67.**

Joe retired undefeated but had seen his prophecy come true, with 1,200 spectators packing Westminster Hall twice a day for a fortnight. His younger brother, Fred Davis, took over from him.

**As chairman of the Professional Billiard Players Association, Joe still controlled snooker and any young amateur planning to turn pro needed Joe's approval.**

When television showed an interest in the sport in the 1950s, it was Joe they negotiated with and Joe was featured in the exhibition matches shown on screen.

**Joe lived to see his beloved snooker given full TV coverage in 1978, agreeing with brother Fred who said: "The public are getting the feel of what it is like playing under pressure hour after hour for days on end." Joe died after collapsing during the 1978 World Championships**

# SNOOKER

By the 1970s, household names such as Ray Reardon, who was six times World Champion, Eddie Charlton, John Spencer, Cliff Thorburn, Perry Mans, Dennis Taylor and Terry Griffiths were coming to the TV screens.

**But one man caught the public eye more than any other – a slight Irishman with a cheeky grin who could be an angel playing the game he loved and, at times, a devil away from the table. He was the one-and-only Alex Higgins.**

Brought up in Belfast, Alex says he spent more time in the local snooker hall, The Jampot, than at school, using his sixpence dinner money to play.

**Alex left school at 15 and decided he wanted to leave Ireland and, thanks to missing his school dinners, he weighed just seven stone. He loved horses and decided to be a jockey.**

With a new overcoat and a few bare necessities, he arrived in England and got a job as a stable boy at Eddie Reavey's Berkshire stables.

**It was not to be. After starving himself in Belfast, the three meals a day supplied at the stables were his downfall. His weight went up to ten stone, too heavy for the horses, and he was on his way to the London snooker halls and set his sights on improving his game.**

Working shifts in a paper mill to finance his snooker, he returned to Belfast to join the YMCA snooker team. He travelled to Bolton with them in 1969 for the Players No. 6 Trophy Championship, which he won almost single-handed. He was on his way.

**Alex was 22 when he won the World Championship at his first attempt in 1972, beating John Spencer 37-31 in the final. Alex 'Hurricane' Higgins, the People's Champion, was in business.**

That was the last year in which the World Championship was played over a season. From 1973, it was reduced to a two-week tournament.

**Bad publicity and fines for misdemeanours followed his Championship win and Alex had to wait ten years for his second World title when he beat Ray Reardon 18-15.**

Steve Davis, tall, calm and totally unflappable, the total opposite of Alex Higgins, was the snooker face of the 1980s. He won his first World Championship in 1981, defeating Doug Mountjoy 18-12 at The Crucible, Sheffield. His prize was £20,000. When Alex won the title in 1972, his prize was £480.

# SNOOKER

**Steve Davis was the first player to make a maximum break on television and took six World titles and six UK titles under the management and guidance of Barry Hearn.**

Billiard balls were made from ivory until 1926, when a satisfactory composition ball was accepted by both amateur and pro players.

**Alf Gover, the Surrey and England cricketer, entered the World Amateur Billiards Championship in 1935 won by Horace Coles of England.  Sir Arthur Conan Doyle also entered in the early days of the competition.**

In the quarter-finals of the 1973 World Snooker Championship in Manchester, Alex Higgins was playing Fred Davis.  Heavy rain leaked through the roof on to Fred's glasses and then on the table.  Covers were put on the table and play suspended while the roof was repaired.

**Higgins finally won 16-14 but was beaten in the semi-finals 23-9 by Eddie Charlton, having lost his cue and unable to settle with a replacement.**

Fred Davis, ten times World snooker champion, was the oldest World champion in any sport when, at the age of 66, he won the World Billiards Championship in 1980.

**He died in 1998 at the age of 84.  Despite recovering from two heart attacks and with arthritis in his left leg, Fred was still playing into the 1990s.**

John Parrott, World and UK snooker champion in 1991, said on reaching the age of 34 in May 1998:  "There's no way I've got five or six more seasons left in me."

**Welshman Terry Griffiths was an insurance agent in July 1978.  Eight months later he was the World champion at his first attempt, beating Dennis Taylor 24-16 in the final.**

The Crucible Theatre was packed and 9.8 million television viewers saw the virtually unknown Welsh amateur champion win enough money to give him financial security.

**Terry, who came from Llanelli, was so in demand after the final that he travelled 17,000 miles in the 12 weeks following the championship.**

He also had two compulsory weeks at home when he caught chickenpox and was faced with problems he had never even thought of before – like income tax.  "I've never had enough money to worry about it before," he said.

# SNOOKER

**His local bakery made Terry a cake in the shape of a snooker table, with green icing for the baize and brown marzipan moulded for the wood surround.**

Ever-optimistic Jimmy White dreams of winning the World Championship. The popular Londoner has reached the final six times since his first visit to The Crucible in 1981.

**In 1984 he lost to Steve Davis 18-16 in the final. He was close again in 1990 when he met the man who had idolised him, Stephen Hendry, losing 18-12. It was the start of Hendry's domination of the 1990s.**

The 1991 final brought defeat for White by John Parrott 18-11, when he praised his opponent: "Parrott played like a God."

**Another final battle in 1992 with arch-rival Hendry again went against Jimmy, this time 18-14 with Hendry winning ten frames in a row.**

The 1993 final, again with Hendry who won 18-5, was followed in 1994 by one of the best finals ever staged at The Crucible, with White needing the black in the last frame to take the title at last. He missed and Hendry was the champion 18-17. "I'm absolutely gutted," said White.

**Steve Davis, at 40, was the oldest competitor in the 1998 World Championship. He hopes still to appear at the Championships when he reaches 50.**

# SNOOKER

Scotsman John Higgins'; victory in his first Embassy World Championship in 1998 brought a sequence of broken records.

**His 18-12 victory over the 1997 champion, Irishman Ken Doherty, ended in tears of joy as his parents and girlfriend Denise congratulated him.**

In the 26th frame he broke Stephen Hendry's record of 12 tournament centuries set at The Crucible in 1995.

**In the 20th frame, his 130 secured a new record of five breaks of 130 or more in a single tournament.**

His break of 143 meant that he shared the highest-break prize with Jimmy White, who had made a similar break against Darren Morgan in the second round.

**By winning, Higgins became the third youngest holder of the title at the age of 22, just 13 days before his 23rd birthday. Stephen Hendry was then the youngest at 21 and Alex Higgins was 22.**

John Higgins' win meant that he took over the No. 1 spot from Stephen Hendry, collected £220,000 in prize money and took his winnings to £1.3 million since turning professional in 1992.

**Jimmy White may not have won the tournament but he defeated Hendry 10-4 in the first round to "put a few ghosts to bed". Hendry had beaten him in four previous finals.**

Cliff Thorburn's great year was 1980, when he beat Alex Higgins 18-16 to become the first Canadian to win the World Championship.

**Stephen Hendry's entry into the record books started in 1986 when, at the age of 17, he took the Scottish professional title and held it for two years.**

He dominated the game between 1990 and 1996, winning 65 major titles from 86 finals, including six World Championships in 1990 and 1992-1996.

**At the Thailand Masters in Bangkok in March 1998, Stephen's luck changed and a 9-6 win over John Parrott won him a prize of £50,000. It put him one ahead of Steve Davis' record of 28 ranking-event wins.**

# ODD SPOTS
# The weird and wacky side of sport

# ODD SPOTS
## The weird and wacky side of sport

When underground heating was being installed at the Germany club Borussia Dortmund, a 1,000lb World War Two bomb was discovered buried just below the halfway line. Bomb disposal men defused it.

**At 1998 Royal Ascot, a tracksuited gambler minus topper and trappings visited bookies William Hill, took £5,000 from a green carrier-bag, put it all on Frankie Dettori's winning mount Bahr – and had time to collect his £8,625 winnings before being shown the exit.**

A Romanian fan, watching his team play Colombia, murdered his wife when she switched off the TV. He went to a bar to watch the rest of the match but was arrested before the game ended. Romania won 1-0.

**Superstitious Hatem Trabelsi, 20-year-old Tunisian right-back, shaves his head the night before each match. He believes it brings him luck.**

Commentator John Motson, faced with pictures of three bald heads, guessed Dion Dublin and Gianluca Vialli correctly, but the third left him stumped. It was baby Motty himself!

**Playing in a 1987 cricket match between a Trainers' XI and a West Indian team, jockey Walter Swinburn took the wickets of Sir Garry Sobers, Seymour Nurse, Peter Lashley and Wes Hall's son. Man-of-the-Match Walter led Michael Stoute's Newmarket team to an eight-run victory.**

Maria de las Nieves Garcia, a 21-year-old Mexican lightweight boxer, withdrew from a fight in New York when found to be pregnant.

**Dan Petrescu, Romanian and Chelsea footballer, loves life at Stamford Bridge so much that he has named his baby daughter Beatrice Chelsea.**

Pompey fan John Portsmouth Football Club Westwood – that's his name – takes two large bass drums along to matches, a move supported by the club who pay half the cost.

**Mexican striker Cuauhtemoc Blanco introduced a new move to football during the 1998 World Cup. The Blanco Bounce involves trapping the ball between his ankles and bouncing past defenders.**

Trying his hand at fishing for the first time during the Madeira Island Open Golf in June 1998, golfer Grey Owen hooked a 300lb blue marlin within minutes of taking the rod. "My previous knowledge of fish was in a goldfish bowl or with chips for supper," he said.

# ODD SPOTS
## The weird and wacky side of sport

**Hoping to pickpocket a couple of tickets for the Scotland-Norway World Cup match from a well-dressed fan, two Scottish supporters recognised their 'victim' as Bryan Robson and left smartly with his autograph.**

Actor Warren Mitchell was at odds with his TV character Alf Garnett when it came to football loyalty. Alf, always an 'Ammers fan, would have been upset if he knew that Warren supported Spurs.

**Paul Adams, South Africa's left-arm spin bowler, has an action described by some as like 'a frog in a blender' or 'a man removing a hub cap from a moving car'.**

Under-10 footballers Mickleover Lightning Blue Sox and Chellaston Boys B tied 1-1 after extra time, calling for a penalty shoot-out. After 56 failed attempts, the ref moved the penalty spot two yards nearer goal. The Lightning Blue Sox were winners of their longest day.

**Dr. Dafydd Rhys Williams took a Welsh cap belonging to rugby legend Gareth Edwards with him on a space mission from the Kennedy Space Center in Florida in April 1998.**

Batting for England on St. David's Day in Guyana during a Test match against West Indies, Robert Croft tucked a daffodil in his pad strap to show his Welsh pride and scored 26 valuable runs.

**At the same match, play was delayed while a shovel was found to remove an unwanted present left by a stray dog.**

A Romanian football club sold a midfielder for 500kg of pork worth £1,750 to pay players' wages.

**Butcher Lee Howard sold blue-and-white sausages at £2 per pound to raise money for the fighting fund to bring Brighton and Hove Albion back to the town.**

After being substituted 60 minutes after making his debut for Wigan, former Hearts and Juventus defender Pasquale Bruno decided to retire from football and open an Italian restaurant.

**In February 1998, WBO heavyweight champion Herbie Hide changed his training camp from London to Norwich to be with his two new German shepherd guard dogs. They joined his twelve rottweilers.**

Three of Kirsty Hay's five-strong women's curling team have the Olympic rings tattooed on their bottoms.

# ODD SPOTS
## The weird and wacky side of sport

**After seeing teammate Juninho break a leg playing for Atletico Madrid in a previous game, Italian Christian Vieri scored twice then pulled up his shirt to reveal Juninho's No. 7 shirt under his own. "The goals are for him," he said.**

Breaking the 2,000 metres record in February 1998, Ethiopian Haile Gebrselassie picked up a purse of £15,000 and claimed that running to the loud music of his chosen record, 'Scatman' by Scatman, helped him to achieve his right rhythm.

**A pre-World Cup course for English supporters visiting France and organised by Wolverhampton Wanderers FC and Bilston Community College, was titled 'Ici, mon fils, sur mon tete' – meaning "Here, my son, on my head".**

Luca Vialli's first match as Chelsea player-manager started with a glass of champagne in the dressing room. "I wanted to have a toast to wish good luck to the players," he said. Chelsea won.

**Whenever Curtly Ambrose takes yet another Test wicket, his mother marches into the street in his hometown of Swetes, Antigua, and rings a bell.**

# ODD SPOTS
## The weird and wacky side of sport

England goalkeeper David Seaman wears a new pair of gloves each time he plays. "It drives me crazy thinking what would happen if the ball hit a tiny scuff mark and went in," he says.

**England wicket-keeper Jack Russell wore the same cap, gloves and wicket-keeping pads for 15 years.**

Within three days of the opening of the 1998 French Open tennis, Chilean Marcelo Rios was awarded a trophy, the Prix Citron, for the third time. It is awarded by the Parisian press for the player said to be 'the most unamenable'.

**Martina Hingis, top Swiss Miss of tennis, sees Rios in better light. "He's nice to me. I don't think he's the monster everybody thinks he is," she says.**

As a schoolboy at Ampleforth, Lawrence Dallaglio was an all-round sportsman with sufficient interest in cricket to take jobs as a waiter at Lord's and The Oval – before rugby became his main attraction.

**Referee Melvin Sylvester awarded himself a red card when a player pushed him and he retaliated with a slap. He was far from happy when the FA banned him for six weeks and fined him £20 – a more severe punishment than the offending player received.**

Iranian footballers took their minds off a forthcoming England game by attending a three-hour religious ceremony the previous evening, weeping as they mourned the death of a 7th Century Shiite Moslem saint.

**Parents were banned from caddying for their daughters after two fathers came to blows on the last green of the 1962 Girls' Golf Championship at Alnworth.**

Mohamed Al Fayed's plans for the redevelopment of Fulham's Craven Cottage ground were brought to a temporary halt when conservationists found foxes living in a bomb shelter under the terraces.

**The Romanian World Cup team were presented with a 'magic' potion made with holy water, basil, olive oil and honey. "Put it on your faces and make the sign of the cross three times," they were told, "and anoint the goal net too to stop the opposition scoring"**

David Beckham likes to wear a new pair of boots for every game. Boots with the leather stretched never make a good contact, he claims.

# ODD SPOTS
## The weird and wacky side of sport

Three Barnsley MPs took out an early-day motion in Parliament in February 1998, criticising the failure of the referee to give Barnsley a penalty in their midweek match with Manchester United, bringing their FA Cup dreams to nothing.

In 1997 when Irishman Ken Doherty became World snooker champion, beating Stephen Hendry, not a single crime was reported to Dublin Police while the final match was played.

**Prisoners in Dublin's Mountjoy Jail watched Doherty's triumph after threatening a revolt if they were not allowed to see the game.**

Yukie Ochida, a 95-year-old Japanese grandmother, entered for the 1998 World Veterans' Table Tennis Championship women's doubles with her 'young' partner, Kaoru Uto, a sprightly 83.

**Paraguay's World Cup goalkeeper, Jose Chilavert, had scored 27 goals for his club, Velez Sarsfield, before arriving in France.**

South African cricket umpire Cyril Mitchley was a professional footballer with Sheffield United for a year. Cricket fan and former manager Dave Bassett sent Cyril one of his proudest possessions – a Blades club tie.

**Animal lovers queued to phone Portsmouth FC after some wit ran an advertisement for "approximately five acres of grazing land for sale, currently housing eleven donkeys". The club's phone number was given.**

A Stenhousemuir v Clydebank game was held up for eight minutes in the 1997-98 season while a hacksaw was found to free a Clydebank fan who had handcuffed himself to the home goalpost.

**In March 1935, England played against a Football League team at West Bromwich with two referees controlling the game, each in charge of one half of the pitch. The result was a 2-2 draw.**

Columnist Brian Oliver, commenting in The *Daily Telegraph* on the introduction to Indian cricket of K.N. Ananthapadmanabhan, wonders how scoreboard operators would cope with K.N. Ananthapadmanabhan c Kaluwitharana b Wijegunawardene.

**Football fans at Sunderland's Stadium of Light have been entertained to some pre-match culture including dancers performing Prokofiev's 'Dance of the Knights', Durham Choir School, an orchestra and excerpts from opera.**

# ODD SPOTS
## The weird and wacky side of sport

Paul Crabb, an Ilfracome cricketer, chased a ball that cleared the boundary and continued down a steep hill. He retrieved the ball but brought it back to the ground by bus.

**Referee Roger Furnandiz accidentally hit Swindon striker Iffy Onuora in the face with his elbow and caused a compressed fracture of the cheekbone in a match against Charlton. Swindon lost 0-1.**

Pele knows a good thing when he sees it. Asked who was his favourite Manchester United player, he replied" "Michael Owen." No comment from Liverpool fans!

**Vicente Rodriguez Guillen, 16-year-old Spanish whizz-kid, has signed a £140,000 contract with his local second division side Levante. His transfer fee has been set at £130 million – after playing one game with Spain's youth team.**

One theory is that Paul Gascoigne was not included in the World Cup final squad because he is a Gemini. There were no Geminis in the England 1966 winning squad and none was chosen by Glenn Hoddle in 1998.

# ODD SPOTS
## The weird and wacky side of sport

A new race was introduced to World sport in February 1998 – running up the Empire State Building in New York. Australian Terry Purcell won the men's race up 86 flights and 1,575 stairs in 10mins 49secs. American Cindy Moll took 14mins 17secs to win for the women.

Golfer Todd Obuchowski, playing at Haydenville, Massachusetts, hit his tee shot beyond the green, saw it bounce on to the road, hit a passing car and rebound into the hole. It cost him £100 to repair the damaged car.

**New York Yankees' pitcher, David Wells, paid $30,000 for a faded blue cap said to have belonged to the legendary Babe Ruth, then wore his expensive purchase in a game.**

Portsmouth FC faced an outstanding £800 bill for mince pies ordered by Terry Venables and given away to supporters at Christmas 1996.

**During the England v Romania World Cup match, British Telecom said there were 16 million fewer telephone calls than usual. After the match, there was a surge of electricity as 450,000 kettles were switched on.**

Wimbledon tennis spectators in 1998 devoured 12 tons of salmon, 24 tons of strawberries, 200,000 sandwiches, 22,000 pizza slices, 30,000 servings of fish and chips, 150,000 buns and 135,000 ice-creams.

**Wimbledon residents can earn up to £10,000 during the tennis fortnight by renting their homes to tennis stars who prefer not to stay in hotels.**

An Argentinian goalkeeper, Hugo Orlando Gatti, once took a broom during play and swept the penalty area. He was also known to borrow a chair and sit down when play was in the other half.

**A Romanian gypsy fortune-teller, Andromeda, has told the World Cup team what they were in a previous life. She told Constantin Galca he was a Japanese geisha girl in 425 AD and skipper Gheorghe Hagi was an Eskimo woman with five children.**

A yellow-and-green flag the size of half a football pitch and signed by supporters wishing their side good luck was received by the Brazilian World Cup squad.

**Third Division club Scarborough invited supporters with a few pounds to spare to pay £25 a week for a year to help pay players' wages. In return they would receive 5% of any transfer fees.**

# ODD SPOTS
## The weird and wacky side of sport

Scottish World Cup supporters at the Jaggy Thistle pub in Blackpool were told their flag measuring 175ft by 90ft was too heavy to be flown to their favourites in France. The star customer of the pub watching the games on TV was Andy Goram, the goalkeeper who walked out from the Scottish squad days before they left for France.

**You may wonder why the people of County Mayo should cheer Argentina's 5-0 victory over Jamaica in France. An Irish ancestor, William Brown, emigrated to Buenos Aires at the age of nine and later founded the Argentine Navy.**

Durham's Australian cricket skipper David Boon urged his team to get fit for the start of the new season. Boon reputedly once consumed 51 cans of Fosters lager on a flight from Australia to England to break the record held by his former teammate, wicket-keeper Rodney Marsh.

**British No. 1 and No. 2 tennis players, Greg Rusedski and Tim Henman, share the same birthday – September 6.**

Playing in the 1998 Volvo PGA Championship, Sandy Lyle hit a ball into a man's pocket. On retrieving the ball, Sandy joked: "I'm not really a pickpocket!"

**West Indian fast bowler Nixon McLean was named after the American President. McLean's father himself took the names Truman McArthur and called his other children Regan, Kissinger and Golda Meir.**

Carlos Valderrama, Colombia's World Cup star with the eye-catching hair style, had to meet a £70,000 tax bill, unsettled since his playing days with Montpellier in 1988-91, before returning to France.

**Cricketer Michael Atherton has a lady admirer who sends cakes to him and calls herself 'Your No. 1 Suffolk Fan and Crazy Cake Lady'.**

A Hampshire League cricket match was declared void when, at a drinks interval, one fielder complained because he didn't get a drink. There were twelve men on one side!

**Arsenal and England goalkeeper David Seaman never watches a replay of a match in which he has made a mistake. He disappears to the kitchen to make a coffee.**

During her victory over Gabriela Sabatini in the 1991 Wimbledon final, a fan called to Steffi Graf: "Marry me, Steffi." And the imperturbable Steffi checked her serve to reply: "Are you rich?"

# ODD SPOTS
## The weird and wacky side of sport

Before the Scotland-Brazil match in the 1998 World Cup, a vicar was heard on Scottish radio to ask God: "Make it Brazil 1 Scotland 2." Somebody up there got it wrong – the score was Brazil 2 Scotland 1.

Joe Johnson, former World snooker champion, used to sing with a pop group called 'Made in Japan'.

Des Lynam, Alan Hansen and David Ginola, the BBC World Cup team of pundits, were criticised by the British Guild of Tie Makers as 'slovenly' for wearing open-necked shirts. They repented and wore ties the following day.

Fashion experts voted Argentina as the best-dressed 1998 World Cup team on the field. Brazil and Italy were named runners-up, with England and Scotland in the middle places.

England striker Les Ferdinand was faced with a bizarre situation when playing for Besiktas in Turkey in 1989. Before a match, a lamb was slaughtered and the blood was daubed on players' boots and foreheads.

When Third Division Scarborough asked the 91 other League clubs for a shirt to help with their fund raising, all responded when the commercial manager Russ Green toured round with his Reliant Robin to collect – except Mohamed Al Fayed's Fulham. They offered four match tickets instead.

Fareham Town's football stand was favoured by seagulls and pigeons, so spectators were offered umbrellas to protect themselves from unwanted droppings.

Asked by Italian Prime Minister Romano Prodi why he was not playing Vieri, Roberto Baggio and Del Piero together, team coach Cesare Maldini replied sharply: "I understand the Prime Minister is keen on cycling."

Phil Vickery, England and Gloucester front-row rugby star, is 6ft 3ins and weighs 19st. With a Chinese war cry 'I'll fight you to the finish' tattooed in Chinese on his left arm and the flag of St. George and a bulldog on his right arm, he is a formidable opponent!

Alex Ferguson, manager of Manchester United, left Govan High School in Glasgow at 15 to become an apprentice toolmaker. He has been given honorary degrees from five universities.

# ODD SPOTS
## The weird and wacky side of sport

**Barry Fry, manager of Peterborough United, advises Biggleswade Town manager Dave Northfield to urinate in all four corners of the pitch when they move to a new ground previously used by travellers. "It will remove the gypsy curse," says Fry.**

When Arbroath won a Scottish Cup tie 36-0 against Bon Accord, the Arbroath goalkeeper Jim Milne was so bored with nothing to do that he sheltered from the rain under a spectator's umbrella and lit his pipe.

**Readers may have thought that England were about to win a cricket Test in the West Indies when a local newspaper headlined: 'England on brink of Test victory'. Alas, it was referring to a triangular dominoes tournament between England, Guyana and USA.**

Eleven-a-side football was said to have originated in the 1850s at English public schools – the teams made up with ten boys to a dormitory and a teacher in goal.

**Shropshire cricket groundsman Brian Lucan found that his false teeth had been crushed by his own roller.**

# ODD SPOTS
## The weird and wacky side of sport

Elephant polo, popular in the Indian continent, is played with 12ft polo sticks and each player needs a man to drive the elephant, who will only take commands from a familiar voice.

**Australian motor-cyclist Kirk McCarthy was unable to join the Castrol Honda team in June 1998 after a cow trod on his hand and broke the top of his thumb.**

Gavin Roebuck, wicket-keeper for Darfield in the Barnsley Sunday League, suffered a broken elbow when teammates surrounded him to offer congratulations for a match-winning stumping.

**When Frank Sibley was offered an assistant manager's job at Fulham, he was chauffeuring film stars from hotels to film sets in France.**

Suspicions of skullduggery were roused in 1979-80 in what was then Yugoslavia when some odd scorelines were recorded in football matches, culminating in a 134-1 result from a match between Split and Zagreb.

**Blood-testing procedures in Sri Lanka were changed after a technician, distracted by cricket on television, told a male patient: "You're pregnant!"**

Valentino Rossi, Italian 125cc motor-cycling champion in 1997, arrived at a meeting at Donington Park dressed as Robin Hood with bow and arrows at hand.

**After the World Cup Final in Rome in 1990, thieves stole the reinforced centre spot from the pitch.**

# OLYMPIC GAMES

# OLYMPICS
# The Ancient Games

The first Games are thought to have taken place in Greece in 776 BC.

**There was only one event – astade. This was a sprint over 19.27 metres.**

The coveted prize was a wreath of wild olive leaves.

**No women were allowed to compete and were banned as spectators.**

Any female sneaking into the stadium, if discovered, faced death by being hurled over a cliff.

**It was decreed that the Games would take place every four years.**

The Games lasted just a single day.

**By 708 BC more events were included – pentathlon, discus, javelin and wrestling.**

Competition duration was extended to three days by 632 BC.

**Chariot racing and pankration – a savage mixture of boxing and wrestling – became crowd pleasers.**

Trumpet blowing was added to the repertoire and approved by the 20,000 plus crowds.

**An early hero was Pharos of Pellene, the first triple gold medallist, at the Games of 512 BC.**

From 164-152 BC, Leonidas of Rhodes won three events at successive Games to take the equivalent of 12 gold medals.

**Competitors dressed simply in the early days, but nude racing was encouraged by 720 BC.**

The original, uncomplicated idea behind the Games gradually changed and bribery and corruption crept in.

**The decline in principles seemed to set in under the influence of the Romans.**

In AD 67, Emperor Nero accepted the crown for the chariot race even though he failed to complete the course. He was the only entrant!

# OLYMPICS
## The Ancient Games

**Because so much glory was bestowed on the birthplace of champions, judges were offered bribes and the Games lost their appeal.**

In AD 393, the Games ended by decree of Roman Emperor Theodosium I.

**Olympia, the site that had seen so many sporting heroes, was deserted and ravaged by flood and earthquakes.**

During the 17th and 18th Centuries, memories of the Ancient Games were recalled.

**Poems recalling the finest aspects of the early Games rekindled thoughts of its noblest principles.**

During the 17th Century the Cotswold Olympic Games were started.

**Then, in 1850, Dr. William Penny Brookes introduced the Much Wenlock Olympic Society.**

In Germany Johann Guts Muths, the originator of modern gymnastics, put forward his thoughts on re-introducing the Olympic ideal.

**The French started archaelogical work on the original Olympia.**

In 1859 Major Evangelis Zappas presented a Pan-Hellenic sports festival in Greece. The event was greeted with great enthusiasm.

**Pierre de Fredi, Baron de Coubertin, was finally instrumental in reviving the Games.**

He put forward his ideas in a lecture at the Paris Sorbonne in 1892.

**In June 1894 a decision was finally made to introduce a sports competition based on the principles of Ancient Greece.**

# THE MODERN OLYMPICS
## Athens 1896

The International Olympic Committee was formed, with Baron de Coubertin as secretary-general and Demetrius Vikelas of Greece as president.

**Baron de Coubertin had hoped that the first of the Modern Olympics would take place in France in 1900.**

Other members were impatient and wanted an earlier start.

**Plans went ahead and Athens was chosen as the 1896 venue.**

A wealthy Greek businessman, Georges Averoff, donated one million drachma for the rebuilding of the Panathean Stadium in Athens (first built in 330 BC).

**The Games were opened by the Greek king, George I.**

It was the 75th anniversary of Greek independence from Turkish rule.

**Forty thousand packed the stadium, with many more watching from the surrounding hills.**

Fourteen countries sent 211 competitors to Athens to take part.

**Greece had 23 competitors and gained the most medals overall – 10 gold, 19 silver and 18 bronze.**

Britain, also with 23 entrants, went home with three golds, three silver and one bronze.

**USA, with 22 taking part, mainly college students, travelled by ship to France and by train to Athens.**

The Americans returned home with 11 gold medals.

**Americans John and Sumner Paine became the first brothers to win Olympic gold medals.**

John's gold came in military pistol and Sumner's in free pistol shooting.

**John Boland, an Irishman who happened to be on holiday in Greece when the Games started, entered for the tennis event.**

He won a gold medal in the singles and also in the doubles with a German partner.

# THE MODERN OLYMPICS
## Athens 1896

On the suggestion of a Frenchman, Michel Breal, the Marathon was introduced to the Games.

It was based on the legend of Pheidippides, a courier who ran about 22 miles from Marathon to Athens bearing news of a Greek victory in battle over the Persians in 490 BC.

**Legend has it that on delivering the news with "Rejoice! We conquer", he collapsed and died.**

To the delight of the crowd the Marathon was won by Spyros Louis, a Greek shepherd.

**To the further delight of all he was escorted into the stadium by Crown Prince Constantine of Greece and his brother, Prince George.**

No women were allowed to compete.

**The most successful competitor was a German gymnast, Hermann Weingärtner.**

He finished with three gold medals, two silver and a third place.

**Another German competitor, Carl Schuhmann, won three medals in the gymnastic events and also took the gold in wrestling.**

Georgios Orphanidis, a 36-year-old Greek competing in the free rifle event, was the oldest gold medallist.

**Hungarian swimmer Alfred Hajos, just 18, was the youngest with gold medals in the 100 metres and 200 metres freestyle.**

A member of the Greek gymnastic team was said to be only 11 years old, but this was never confirmed.

**The sportsmanship of the Greek spectators was applauded around the world.**

# OLYMPIC GAMES
## France 1900

Greece had hoped to be given exclusive rights to organise all the Olympic Games.

**It was not to be. France was awarded the 1900 Games to run alongside the World Exhibition.**

A total of 1,225 competitors from 26 countries converged on Paris.

**After the outstanding success in Athens four years earlier, hopes were high.**

There was disappointment for both organisers and competitors.

**The crowds did not materialise and the organisation left something to be desired.**

The shortage of spectators was perhaps fortunate as the discus champion of 1896 threw his 4lb disc among them!

**He did this three times in all but, as luck would have it, there were no casualties.**

Women were allowed to compete for the first time.

**Nineteen women entered but they were restricted to the lesser sports.**

The major athletics classes were strictly no-go areas for them.

**Two Frenchwomen were the first to appear in an Olympic competition. They played croquet!**

Great Britain's Charlotte Cooper won the tennis title.

**Charlotte was loudly acclaimed as she was already Wimbledon champion.**

Athletes were unhappy with the facilities and uneven surfaces on the turf in the Bois de Boulogne in Paris, where the track and field events were held, caused much consternation.

# OLYMPIC GAMES
## France 1900

**Most of the Americans competing were again college students.  Few had ever run on grass, particularly uneven grass surfaces.**

Even so, Frank Jarvis from Princeton and John Walter Tewksbury of Pennsylvania both equalled world records.

**It was decided that for the first time Sunday events should be held, much to the consternation of some of the Americans.**

Many of the Americans were church-goers and Sunday competition was banned.

**Myer Prinstein, world long jump record holder, was in silver medal position at the end of Saturday's qualifying rounds.**

Because he was under the wing of the University of Syracuse, a strict Methodist institution, he was unable to compete in Sunday's final.

**The eventual winner of the long jump was a fellow American, Alvin Kraenzlein.**

Kraenzlein then went on to a final haul of four individual gold medals.

**Ray Ewry, another American competing in the 'standing jump' event, gained three gold medals.**

Yet another American, Irving Baxter, led the field in the regular high jump and the pole vault.

**Baxter is also remembered as the first American athlete with American Indian ancestors to win Olympic gold.**

In the same year Norman Pritchard, representing India, became the first Asian to win Olympic medals.

**Pritchard later became an actor and appeared in several Hollywood silent films.**

In the coxed pairs rowing final a young French boy was persuaded at the last moment to cox the Dutch boat.

**The team won the gold medal – but the boy disappeared without collecting his medal or giving his name!**

# OLYMPIC GAMES
## USA 1904

After the disappointing attendance for the 1900 Games, it was hoped that an American venue would present the 1904 Olympics with a high profile.

**President Roosevelt chose St. Louis to present the Games.**

Unfortunately travelling to middle America proved too far a prospect for many European nations.

**The consequence was that only 13 countries took part, with a total of 687 competitors.**

Eighty five percent of the competitors were from the United States.

**Of the 99 gold medals awarded, 80 went to America.**

Some events turned into purely American inter-college competitions.

**The cycling contests attracted no overseas participants and there were suggestions that professional riders had entered.**

To add to the farcical situation, no heats were run for the 400 metres track event.

**All 13 runners went straight into the final.**

Britain were represented by just two athletes and both won medals.

**Thomas Kiely, an Irishman representing Britain, won the ten-event competition, later to become the decathlon.**

Another Irishman, John Daly, was the silver medallist in the 2,500 metres steeplechase.

**Myer Prinstein, who had missed the opportunity of going for gold in the 1900 long jump because of his religious objection to competing on a Sunday, was finally rewarded.**

This time the long jump gold medal was his.

**Following his long jump win, Myer Prinstein completed a golden double by winning the hop, step and jump.**

Prinstein, representing the Greater New York Irish A.A., was also placed fifth in the 60 metres and the 400 metres finals.

**Etienne Desmarteau, a French-Canadian policeman from Montreal, was among the few non-Americans to win medals.**

# OLYMPIC GAMES
# USA 1904

He won the 56lb weight throw.

**Under the 1904 Olympic rules a false start carried a one-yard handicap.**

Archie Hahn, the only one of four contestants not handicapped, had an easy win in the 200 metres final.

**He also completed a treble gold by winning the 100 metres and the 60 metres dash.**

Joseph Stadler, silver medallist in the standing high jump, and George Poage, third in the 200 and 400 metres hurdles, made history as the first two black Americans to win Olympic medals.

**Probably the first real Olympic scandal happened in the Marathon, when American Fred Lorz was first out of the stadium and first back in.**

Spectators were amazed to see him finishing fresh as a daisy and certainly not out of breath.

**Lorz admitted later that after leaving the stadium, he suffered cramp and accepted a lift in a car. When the car broke down, he resumed his run.**

He was banned for life but was competing again within a year.

**The Marathon gold medal went to a British-born American, Thomas Hicks, who finished the race in a daze.**

He had been given strychnine and brandy as a stimulant by a friend!

**A Zulu named Lentauw, running for South Africa, came in 11th and had the honour of being the first black African distance runner to compete in an Olympics.**

# ATHENS GAMES
## Greece 1906

Greek disappointment at not being allowed to stage every Olympics Games was assuaged somewhat when it was agreed that a four-yearly event, interspersed with the main Games, should be held in Athens.

**Despite the enthusiasm shown by the host country, 1906 was the only time such an event took place.**

From April 22 – May 2, 826 competitors from 20 countries gathered in Greece. The numbers included six women.

**A leading medal winner was Raymond Ewry of USA, who won gold in the standing long jump and the standing triple jump.**

Ewry was a remarkable athlete. As a child he was confined to a wheelchair, a victim of polio, and was not expected to walk again.

**He forced himself to exercise and developed incredibly strong leg muscles, which made him unbeatable in anything involving a standing start.**

Between 1900 and 1908 he won ten gold medals.

**Unfortunately his fame was short-lived, for all the events in which he scored gold were eliminated from the Olympic programme.**

He was also the amateur champion for the backward standing long jump with a record 9ft 3ins.

**The year 1906 was the first that America sent an official team rather than athletes travelling as individuals or in college teams.**

Fernand Gonder of France won the pole vault – the only non-American to win the gold in the event between 1896 and 1968.

**Paul Pilgrim, a member of the New York Athletic Club, was the unexpected winner of the 400 metres.**

He was not a chosen member of the official team but, having paid his own way to Athens, he was allowed to compete.

**The following day he took another gold in the 800 metres, a feat unequalled until 1976.**

His glory was also his swansong. He never again won a major race.

**Greece was set on repeating the 1896 Marathon win.**

# ATHENS GAMES
## Greece 1906

As the date approached the excitement grew and local merchants, hoping to encourage a Greek success, made expansive offers to potential winners.

**Providing the winner came from Greece, a statue of Hermes was offered.**

Not to be outdone, one shopkeeper came forward with the offer of a free loaf of bread daily for a year.

**Others came up with freebies that included free shaves for life, three cups of coffee a day for a year and Sunday lunch for six for a year.**

All these offers were void if the winner was not a Greek.

**Billy Sherring, a Canadian railwayman, badly wanted to win the Marathon and saved hard.**

Even with $75 donated by his local athletics club, he hadn't enough for the trip to Greece.

**In desperation he put the 75 dollars on a horse called Cicely. It won at 6-1 and Billy was on his way.**

He arrived quietly two months early to complete his training while working as a railway porter.

**When a trial run was organised by the Greek runners, Billy was delighted for he knew that his best time was 20 minutes faster than the winner.**

George Blake, an Australian, and William Frank, a New Yorker, shared the lead for 15 miles, whereupon Billy joined Frank for a further three miles.

**Billy then turned to the American, said goodbye and tore off to build up such a lead that he walked part of the way to victory.**

Billy Sherring was 135 lbs when he left Canada; at the start of the race he was down to 112 lbs; on completion he had lost another 14 lbs.

**He did not qualify for the free offers but he was presented with a three-foot statue of Athena with a lamb, while back home, the city of Hamilton honoured him with a gift of 5,000 dollars and Toronto chipped in with 400 dollars.**

# OLYMPIC GAMES
## England 1908

The 1908 Olympic Games should have been held in Rome, but the Italians withdrew two years earlier because of financial problems.

**Britain agreed to stage the Games and a 68,000 capacity stadium was built at Shepherds Bush at a cost of £40,000.**

The new stadium incorporated an athletics track, a banked 600-yard concrete cycle track and a 100-metre swimming pool.

**Tennis was staged at Wimbledon, rowing on the Thames starting at Henley, while the Isle of Wight put on a fine show for the yachting events.**

A new sport, motorboating, took place in Southampton Water but it had a short life as an Olympic event.

**A total of 21 sports was organised, including ice-skating for the first time.**

British amateur featherweight boxing champion Richard Gunn came out of retirement at 37 to win gold and promptly retired again.

**Gunn still holds the record as the oldest boxer to win Olympic gold.**

John Douglas, an Essex and England cricketer, won the gold medal at middleweight. With Christian name initials of JWHT he became known as 'Johnny Won't Hit Today' Douglas.

**His glory was short-lived. The silver medallist, Australian 'Snowy' Baker, knocked out Douglas a few days later in a re-match.**

Baker, an all-rounder, used to compete in 29 different sports. In the 1920s he starred in silent films and later in Hollywood taught swimming, riding and fencing to Douglas Fairbanks.

**Although the Games had been fairly well organised there was some rancour between British and American teams after the US flag bearer refused to dip the flag as he passed Queen Alexandra.**

Disagreements came to a head in the 400 metres final in which three Americans and one Briton lined up.

**The Americans were accused of impeding Lieut. Wyndham Halswelle, the British runner, and a re-run was ordered for the following day.**

# OLYMPIC GAMES
## England 1908

The Americans refused and Halswelle became the only man in Games history to win a gold medal in a walkover.

**John Taylor, one of the Americans involved in the 400 metres dispute, was a member of the successful relay medley team and became the first black American to win a gold medal.**

As in previous Games the Marathon proved a controversial spectacle.

**Princess Mary, anxious for her children to see the start from their nursery window at Windsor, requested that a further 385 yards be added to the usual 26 miles.**

The 1908 Marathon thus became 26 miles 385 yards. Later, as from the 1924 Games, this became the accepted distance.

**It was a hot and humid day as the 56 runners lined up in Windsor Castle gardens.**

British runners, anxious to please the huge crowds, started at a brisk pace. By the halfway mark they were exhausted and overtaken.

**Dorando Pietri, a slightly built Italian, and South Africa's Charles Hefferon led with the Americans in close pursuit.**

Two miles from the finish Hefferon led the Italian by three minutes and accepted a premature victory glass of champagne.

**Poor Charlie then became dizzy and Dorando, closely followed by three Americans, took the lead with a mile to go.**

Dorando was first to appear in the stadium, but he was totally exhausted and ran in the wrong direction.

**Back on the right track he fell, got to his feet, staggered on and fell again and again. Within yards of the tape he fell for a fifth time.**

Officials thought he was dying and helped him across the line, closely followed by John Hayes, a 22-year-old American.

**The Italian's triumph was short-lived. Hayes, protesting that Dorando had been assisted across the line, was declared the winner.**

Dorando's superhuman effort was rewarded when Queen Alexandra presented him with a gold cup and Dorando and Hayes later made fortunes by turning pro and running Marathons around the world.

# OLYMPIC GAMES
## Sweden 1912

The 1912 Olympic Games, staged in Stockholm, introduced new technology in the form of timekeepers and electronic timing devices.

**Boxing was eliminated from the Games as the Swedes refused to accept the sport.**

At the suggestion of Baron de Coubertin, the number of events was limited to 14 with 2,547 competitors taking part from 28 countries.

**Two new events, the pentathlon and the decathlon, were introduced and both were won by Jim Thorpe, son of an Irish father and part French, part American Indian mother.**

Thorpe had been chosen to represent America after gaining recognition in 11 different sports and winning the 1912 inter-collegiate championships for ballroom dancing.

**Kind Gustav V of Sweden, on presenting Thorpe with his gold medals, said: "Sir, you are the greatest athlete in the world."**

The young athlete is said to have replied: "Thanks, King."

**On his return to the States, Thorpe was honoured with a ticker-tape parade down Broadway but the glory faded a few months later.**

It was revealed that Thorpe had been paid 25 dollars weekly to play in a North Carolina baseball minor league in 1909.

**Despite his plea of innocence, declaring that as an Indian schoolboy he failed to realise he was doing wrong, his name was removed from all records and his gold medals were returned.**

Silver medallists Hugo Wieslander (Sweden) in the decathlon and Ferdinand Bie (Norway) in the pentathlon both refused Thorpe's gold medals.

**Seventy years after the 1912 Games, Thorpe was forgiven and the IOC returned his gold medals to his family.**

The first of the 'Flying Finns' emerged during the 1912 Olympics.

**Johan Kolehmainen, a Finnish vegetarian bricklayer, won the 10,000 metres, followed two days later by taking the gold at 5,000 metres, then picked up a third gold in the 12,000 metres cross-country.**

In nine days he ran a total of 41 kilometres, winning six races.

# OLYMPIC GAMES
## Sweden 1912

**On becoming a triple gold medallist he had only one regret – as a Finn he had to compete under the Russian flag.**

Football was given a high profile for the first time and a crowd of 25,000 saw Great Britain beat Denmark 4-2 in the final.

**Vilhelm and Eric Carlberg of Sweden were the first twins to win gold medals, both in the shooting events.**

Sweden's Oskar Swahn won gold in the running-deer shooting event. At 64 he was, and still is, the oldest Olympic gold medallist of all.

**He continued to represent Sweden in the event into his 70s.**

In the six-metre yachting class the French winners were three brothers crewing 'Mac Miche' – another Olympic first.

**Swimming highlighted the talents of a member of the Hawaiian royal family, Duke Paoa Kahanamoku. He won the gold medal in the 100 metres freestyle.**

He competed in three more Games before becoming a film star.

**Britain did well in Stockholm winning 10 gold, 15 silver and 16 bronze and finishing third in the overall table.**

During the Ancient Games wars were halted to allow athletes to reach the stadium and compete. Such niceties were not observed in 1916 and the Berlin Games were cancelled.

# OLYMPIC GAMES
## Belgium 1920

Belgium was awarded the honour of staging the 1920 Olympic Games in recognition of all the misery the country had endured between 1914 and 1918.

**It was a struggle to arrange the Games in Antwerp so soon after the end of the war.**

Heavy rain held up work on the running track in the new stadium which had seating for 30.000.

**Enemies from the war – Austria, Bulgaria, Germany, Hungary and Turkey – were not invited to compete.**

Despite this, 2,668 competitors from 29 countries converged on Antwerp from April to September.

**Competitors stayed in school buildings – not to the Americans' liking.**

A new Olympic flag, designed by Baron de Coubertin, was revealed.

**The design was based on a Greek artefact with five interlaced coloured rings.**

The red, blue, yellow, black and green rings, together with a white background, symbolised friendship between nations, with all national flags having one of their colours included.

**Argentina, Brazil and New Zealand – previously part of the Australasia team – all took part for the first time.**

Finland competed under its own flag after gaining independence from Russia in 1917.

**Britain again produced a double gold medal star in Albert Hill, a 31-year-old railway guard, who had spent four years fighting for his country.**

Hill won five races in five days, winning the 800 metres by two metres and then the 1,500 metres.

**In the 1,500 event he was shadowed by team-mate Philip Baker, the silver medallist, who ran alongside Albert for part of the final lap 'to protect him from attack'.**

Baker later added his wife's maiden name and became Philip Noel-Baker, a popular MP and Nobel Prize winner.

**Johan 'Hannes' Kolehmainen, triple gold medal winner in 1912, returned to win another gold for Finland in the Marathon.**

# OLYMPIC GAMES
## Belgium 1920

A fellow Finnish athlete, Paavo Nurmi, made his Olympic debut and took gold in the 10,000 metres and the cross-country.

**It was the start of a brilliant career on the track that would bring him nine gold medals.**

Nurmi had hoped for a third gold in the 5,000 metres but was beaten into second place by his French rival Joseph Guillemot.

**Guillemot was only 5ft 3ins tall and was said to have his heart on the wrong side of his chest.  He also smoked a packet of cigarettes a day.**

Charley Paddock, a Texan, was a great favourite with the crowds.

**About 12ft from the finishing line, he would fling up his arms and take an enormous leap to the tape.**

Four Americans, including Charley, qualified for the 100 metres final.  He ended the race with a flying leap to win by a foot.

**The other Americans finished second, fourth and sixth, while Harry Edwards of Great Britain won the bronze medal.**

Like many athletes, Charles was superstitious.  On the way to the start he would knock on wood. Then, just before the off, he would put his hands over the starting line, withdrawing them at the call 'get set'.

**American bricklayer John B. Kelly won two gold medals – in the single sculls and with his cousin in the double sculls.**

In the same year his application to row at Henley was refused. Officials said that a bricklayer would have an unfair advantage over gentlemen!

**Later John Kelly became a millionaire and his son rowed and won at Henley in 1947.**

His daughter was Grace Kelly, who became a famous film star and married Prince Rainier of Monaco.

# OLYMPIC GAMES
## Belgium 1920

**Women were taking a greater part in the Olympics and, in 1920, there were 77 entries.**

Aileen Riggin, a 14-year-old diver from USA, was the youngest gold medallist of the 1920 Games.

**Ethelda Bleibtrey, also of the American women's team, won three gold medals – the 100 and 400 metres freestyle and the 4 x 100 metres freestyle relay.**

In six days she swam in five races of the three events and each time broke her own world record.

**In 1919 Ethelda had been charged with swimming nude and arrested under American decency laws. In fact she had taken off her stockings before swimming!**

The men's events were also dominated by an American, Norman Ross, who helped himself to three gold medals.

**He finished first in the 400 metres and 1,500 metres, and swam in the winning 4 x 200 metres freestyle relay.**

Ross also figured in the 100 metres freestyle final which ended in confusion and controversy.

**The royal Hawaiian Duke Paoa Kahanamoku repeated his 1912 Games success, setting a new record.**

Australian William Herlad claimed that Norman Ross had impeded him and a re-swim was ordered, with Ross disqualified.

**The dashing Duke confirmed his gold medal place at the second effort, Herlad coming fourth.**

Daniel Carroll won a gold medal with the American team in the rugby final when they beat France 8-0.

**The same Mr. Carroll had won gold 12 years earlier with the victorious Australian team.**

He thus became the first man to win gold for two countries, having emigrated to the States.

**Tennis was increasing in popularity and among the Olympic entrants was Suzanne Lenglen, the Frenchwoman who had won all three Wimbledon titles that year.**

She was again the star, taking the gold medal after beating Dorothy Holman of Great Britain 6-3, 6-0.

# OLYMPIC GAMES
## France 1924

France got a second bite of the cherry when Paris was chosen to host the 1924 Olympic Games.

**De Coubertin was determined to erase the memory of the poorly organised Paris Games of 1900.**

The Winter Games were held for the first time as a separate meeting at Chamonix in France, with 16 countries sending 258 competitors.

**Charles Jewtraw of USA was awarded the first ever Winter Games gold medal on January 20, 1924, by winning the 500 metres speed skating event.**

Norway and Finland dominated the Winter Games, each country winning four gold medals.

**Britain entered a team and ended with three medals – a silver in the four-man bobsleigh and bronze in the women's figure skating and the ice hockey.**

William Dettart Hubbard was the first black American to win an individual gold medal, taking the long jump with 7.44 metres.

**A team-mate, Robert LeGendre, was left out of the long jump event, but in the pentathlon he broke the world record with a leap of 7.76 metres.**

The Finns again dominated the track events, with Paavo Nurmi capturing five gold medals.

**He won the 1,500 and 5,000 metres, the cross-country team and individual events, followed by the 3,000 metres team race.**

The remarkable Nurmi, having won the 1,500 metres with ease, paused only to collect his sweater and stopwatch on the way to the dressing room for a rest before lining up less than an hour later for the 5,000 metres final.

**He then ran a brilliant tactical race to beat fellow Finn Vilho Ritola by two yards.**

There was intense rivalry between these two and Nurmi was far from pleased when Ritola was invited to contest the 10,000 metres, which he won.

**Returning home, Nurmi set up a new world record for the 10,000 metres.**

# OLYMPIC GAMES
## France 1924

A statue of Nurmi was erected outside the Helsinki stadium to commemorate his remarkable achievements in 1924.

**Harold Abrahams and Eric Liddell, whose story was told in the film 'Chariots of Fire', did Britain proud in the 100 metres and 400 metres.**

Abrahams was the first European to win an Olympic sprint title and gave full credit to his coach, Sam Mussabini.

**Sam had told him to think only of the pistol and tape: "When you hear one run like hell until you break the other." He did.**

New Zealander Arthur Porritt won the bronze in the 100 metres and until Abrahams' death in 1978 the two men and their wives met for dinner at 7pm every July 7 – the time and date of their historic sprint.

**Eric Liddell, the son of a missionary, was a promising rugby player but gave it up to concentrate on running.**

He entered for four events but withdrew from the 100 metres and the relay because they were being run on a Sunday.

**Running on the sabbath was contrary to his beliefs but he went on to win bronze in the 200 metres.**

He set off like a man inspired in the 400 metres, but onlookers feared he could not keep up the pace. Incredibly he lengthened his stride in the second half to win by more than five metres.

**Liddell joined his father in China the following year to help with his missionary work. He died in a Japanese internment camp in 1945.**

Nick Winter, a 29-year-old fireman, was the first Australian to compete in a field event and won the triple jump.

**The event was barely known in Australia, but Winter enjoyed trying odd events. Backward cycling and tug-o'-war were two of his hobbies.**

Johnny Weissmuller, some years later to find fame and fortune as the film Tarzan, came to the Olympics at 20 and was already the 100 metres swimming world record holder.

**He started the 100 metres final with the defending champion Duke Paoa Kahanamoku on one side and his brother Sam Kahanamoku on the other.**

# OLYMPIC GAMES
## France 1924

Weissmuller won easily, followed by Duke and Sam for a hat-trick of American medals.

**The same day Johnny won another gold medal in the 4 x 200 metres relay and a bronze in the water polo.**

Johnny Weissmuller continued to thrill the crowds by winning gold in the 400 metres freestyle.

**The spectators also loved Tarzan's comedy diving act which he put on after his serious swimming events.**

An American team of teenage girls swept the board in the women's swimming, despite the restrictions imposed by the US Olympic Committee.

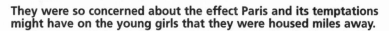

**They were so concerned about the effect Paris and its temptations might have on the young girls that they were housed miles away.**

The boxing finals ended in uproar with Britain's Harry Mallin at the centre of things.

**In the quarter-finals of the middleweight division the 32-year-old London policeman met Frenchman Roger Brousse.**

At the end of the contest Mallin pointed out to the Belgian referee bite marks on his chest. The referee ignored him and awarded the fight to Brousse.

**Ringside observers were convinced that the verdict should have gone to Mallin and a Swedish member of the International Boxing Association demanded an inquiry.**

The appeal ruled that Mallin had been bitten, but unintentionally. Brousse was disqualified and burst into tears and his fans demonstrated noisily for the rest of the event.

**The final between Mallin and British team-mate Jack Elliott brought more noisy protest from the French when they entered the ring.**

Mallin won on points and justice was done.

# OLYMPIC GAMES
# Holland 1928

After three unsuccessful bids to stage the Games, Holland was finally chosen as the 1928 host.

**A 40,000 capacity stadium was built on reclaimed land in Amsterdam and 3,014 competitors from 46 countries arrived in the capital.**

So impressive was the stadium that the architect, Jan Wils, was awarded a prize in the Olympic architecture competition.

**For the first time women competitors, totalling 290, were allowed to take part in five track and field events, despite considerable opposition.**

The events were 100 and 800 metres, 4 x 100 metres relay, high jump and discus.

**When several runners showed distress and exhaustion at the end of the 800 metres, anti-feminists called for a total ban from further Games.**

As a result the women's 800 metres was discontinued and 36 years elapsed before women were allowed to compete over more than half a lap of the track.

**The Olympic flame continued to burn throughout the Games for the first time.**

Another first was the release of pigeons, denoting peace, at the opening ceremony.

**A third innovation was the erection of a large results board.**

Germany returned to the scene for the first time since 1912 with a formidable team.

**The first track and field gold medal awarded to a woman went to Lina Radke of Germany in the 800 metres.**

Her world record time of 2min 16.2sec was unbeaten for 16 years.

**Elizabeth Robinson, a 16-year-old schoolgirl from Illinois, USA, won the 100 metres and equalled the world record of 12.2sec.**

She had become a competitive sprinter after a teacher saw her running for a bus and encouraged her into the sport.

**Elizabeth Robinson's gold medal resulted incredibly on only her fourth competitive appearance.**

# OLYMPIC GAMES
## Holland 1928

The teenager also collected a silver medal with the American 4 x 100 relay team.

**Fanny Rosenfeld, a chocolate factory worker from Toronto, was proof that women were not too weak to compete on the track.**

Fanny was second to Robinson in the 100 metres, a gold medallist in the Canadian 4 x 100 metres relay team and was fifth in the 800 metres.

**Japan's Kinue Hitomi, silver medallist in the 800 metres, was a world record holder in the 200 metres and long jump but was unable to display her talents in 1928 as these were not Olympic events.**

Two years later at the Women's World Games she won one gold, one silver and two bronzes. She died the following year of tuberculosis, aged 23.

**Canadian Ethel Catherwood, an 18-year-old known as 'The Saskatoon Lily', won the high jump with ease, clearing 5ft 2½ins.**

Returning home to a heroine's welcome, she was awarded a $3,000 trust fund to continue her piano studies.

**A world record discus throw of 129ft 11¾ins earned gold for Polan's Halina Konopacka.**

The Finns again dominated the men's track events.

**Harry Larva won the 1,500 metres, so emulating fellow Finn Paavo Nurmi's 1924 triumph, and set a new Olympic record of 3min 53.2sec.**

The Finnish team of Nurmi and Vilho Ritola headed the 5,000 metres field, the gold going to Ritola and the silver to Nurmi.

**The roles were reversed in the 10,000 metres – Nurmi gold, Ritola silver.**

The remarkable Nurmi then earned another silver in the 3,000 metres hurdles, his fifth distance race in a week.

# OLYMPIC GAMES
## Holland 1928

It was Nurmi's final Olympic run.  He had won nine gold medals overall.

Nurmi's colleague Vilho Ritola also retired with a total of five gold medals and three silvers.

**Britain's athletes finished well down the Amsterdam medals table with three gold, ten silver and seven bronze.**

David Burghley – or to give him his proper title, Lord David George Brownlow Cecil Burghley, heir to the Marquess of Exeter – was a popular medal winner.

**He set an Olympic record for the 400 metres hurdles of 53.4secs to take the gold medal.**

To improve his technique he put matchboxes on the hurdles and practised knocking them off with his leading foot but without touching the hurdles.

**Lord Burghley was president of both the British and International AAA and a member of the International Olympic Committee for 45 years.**

Britain's Douglas Lowe retained his 800 metres title with an Olympic record time of 1min 51.8sec.

**Irishman Patrick O'Callaghan took the gold in the hammer throw just 13 months after his first competition.**

Percy Williams, a 20-year-old slightly-built Canadian, won both 100 and 200 metres, beating British entries into the silver medal positions.

**He looked no match in the 100 metres for 6ft 2in John 'Jack' London, but he took the lead from the start and kept it to the tape.**

In the 200 metres final, his eighth race in four days, Williams raced neck and neck with Walter Rangeley, a Lancashire lad, to win by a yard.

**Mikio Oda of Japan became the first Asian gold medallist with a winning triple jump of 15.21 metres.**

Dhyan Chand, a 22-year-old Army captain, led India to its first Olympic hockey gold medal.

**So powerful was the Indian team that not a single goal was conceded throughout the tournament.**

# OLYMPIC GAMES
## Holland 1928

India defeated Holland 3-0 in the final.

**Johnny Weissmuller ended his Olympic career with two more gold medals.**

He set a new Olympic record of 58.6sec in the 100 metres freestyle swim, despite almost blacking out after swallowing water.

**He collected his second gold in the American 4 x 200 metres freestyle relay.**

Weissmuller had intended to defend his titles in the 1932 Games but Hollywood beckoned and Tarzan took over.

**Another American star, Buster Crabbe, made an appearance in 1928, winning a bronze in the 1,500 metres freestyle and a gold in the 4 x 200 metres freestyle relay.**

Crabbe was spotted by Hollywood and starred as Tarzan, Buck Rogers and Flash Gordon.

**Eighteen-year-old German swimmer Hildegard Schroder won gold in the 200 metres breaststroke but couldn't get out of the pool at the end of the race.**

The straps on her swimsuit had broken and she had to stay submerged until a repair job could be done!

**The Winter Olympics were held at St. Moritz in Switzerland with 464 participants from 25 countries.**

A 15-year-old Norwegian skater, Sonja Henie, who had finished last in 1924, became the darling of the 1928 Games.

**Her interpretation of 'The Dying Swan' put skating on a new plane and earned her a gold medal.  Some years later Hollywood called.**

For the only time in history, the bobsleigh event was contested by five-man teams.

**America took the bobs gold, with William Fiske at 16 the youngest ever Olympic driver.**

Thomas Doe jnr., also American, was the youngest medallist of them all, winning a silver in the bob at the age of 15.

**Poor weather conditions led to the cancellation of some events, but Norway led the medals final table with six golds.**

**THE ULTIMATE SPORTS FACT AND QUIZ BOOK**

# OLYMPIC GAMES
## USA 1932

Doubts were cast on the choice of Los Angeles as the venue for the 1932 Olympics.

**The cost of competitors travelling to California and the depression hitting most of the world left the organisers in a dismal state.**

However, despite numbers being down on 1928 – 1,408 competitors from 37 countries – America made a bold effort to achieve success.

**A first ever Olympic village was built for male competitors comprising 550 small houses.**

Cowboys rode the perimeter fences to restrain intruders.

**No women were allowed in the compound, which meant that the Finnish team lost the services of their female cook.**

The women competitors, totalling 127, were given rooms in an hotel.

**There was strict prohibition in the States at the time but concessions were made for the French and Italian teams to bring in wine for their own consumption.**

Another first in Los Angeles was the introduction of a photo-finish camera.

**The triple-tiered victory rostrum appeared for the first time and the raising of national flags and playing of national anthems at the medal presentation proved popular and permanent.**

The Los Angeles Coliseum had been enlarged to hold 101,000, with a track specially prepared with a crushed peat surface.

**The swimming stadium could seat 10,000 in comfort and a similar number of seats were in the Olympic auditorium for boxing and wrestling events.**

Despite the arduous travelling, it was generally agreed that the perfect weather and well conceived facilities made it worthwhile.

**Housing, transport and food charges were subsidised by the organising committee and a new three cent postage stamp depicting a runner helped with the cost.**

Paavo Nurmi, the legendary Finn, was banned from competing in the Marathon because he was said to have accepted large expenses on a German tour, thus making him a professional.

# OLYMPIC GAMES
## USA 1932

The rest of the Games went off fairly smoothly, apart from an incident in the 5,000 metres.

The Finnish athlete, Lauri Lehtinen, twice blocked Ralph Hill, the American, deliberately in the eyes of the home crowd.

**Loud booing was quelled by the announcer, Bill Henry. "Remember, please, these people are our guests," he said – and the booing ceased.**

A typist from Illinois, Mildred 'Babe' Didriksen, was to her disgust allowed to enter only three events – 80 metres hurdles, javelin and high jump.

**The three-event rule barred her from the shot putt, long jump, discus and baseball throw, in all of which she also excelled.**

She won the javelin with an Olympic record throw of 143ft 4ins. It would have gone farther, she said, but the javelin slipped from her hand!

**Her second gold medal came in the 80 metres hurdles, in which she beat American teammate Evelyne Hall by two inches.**

A third gold in the high jump was in her grasp, having tied with Jean Shiley (USA) at 5ft 4¼ins in a jump-off.

**Judges gave the gold to Shiley because Babe's western-roll technique meant that 'her head cleared the bar before her body.'**

Babe was barred from competing as an amateur because a photo of her and an interview were used by an advertiser, so she turned to vaudeville and later golf.

**Using her married name, Babe Zaharias was voted the world's best woman golfer and the greatest female athlete. She died of cancer at 45.**

Stanislawa Walasiewicz won the women's 100 metres for Poland in a joint world record time with Canada's Hilda Strike of 11.9secs.

**Stanislawa had been brought up in America with the name Stella Walsh. She was the first woman to record 11secs for the 100 yards.**

Out of work in the depression and with no hope of anything, she took a job with the Polish consulate.

**She decided at the last minute not to sign her American naturalisation papers and offered to run for Poland.**

# OLYMPIC GAMES
## USA 1932

A single run over a 400 metres hurdles course in March 1932 convinced Bob Tisdall that with hard work he could make the Irish Olympic team.

**He had three months to go before the All-Ireland Championships.**

He resigned his job, moved into a converted railway carriage in a Sussex field with his wife and trained – but he had no hurdles.

**In June he won the event in the Irish Championships and was chosen for the Olympics.**

Weakened by a difficult two-week journey to America, he regained his energy by spending 15 hours a day in bed, then fought his way to the finals.

**There he faced Lord Burghley and Morgan Taylor, former gold medallists, and American Glenn Hardin, the world record holder.**

Taking an early lead, he was five yards ahead when he struck the last hurdle and stumbled towards the tape.

**Tisdall was there first in a world best time of 51.7secs for the 400 metres course, but the time was disallowed because the rules at that time stipulated that if a hurdle fell it had not been cleared.**

He kept the gold medal but second-placed Hardin was credited with the world record in a slower time.

**In the 3,000 metres steeplechase, Thomas Evenson of Britain gained a silver medal because an official failed to change the lap counter and everyone ran one extra.**

Evenson moved from third to second in that extra last lap.

**India retained the hockey gold by beating Japan 11-1 and USA by a record breaking 24-1.**

The 400 metres freestyle swimming final was a nail-biter. The American Buster Crabbe and Frenchman Jean Taris were neck and neck 25 metres from the finish.

**People were rushing to the poolside to see the drama as Crabbe touched inches ahead of Taris.**

# OLYMPIC GAMES
## Germany 1936

The award of the 1936 Olympics had been made to Germany in 1931, before the rise of Adolf Hitler.

**With the world watching, Hitler grasped the opportunity and put his propaganda machine on full alert.**

Some countries, including America, were in favour of boycotting the Games but Avery Brundage, president of the US Olympic Committee, felt they should go ahead.

**A new 100,000 seat arena was built and competitors were housed in a speedily erected village.**

Three thousand runners relayed the torch from Greece to Berlin.

**Ironically, Spyros Louis, the Greek shepherd who had won the 1896 Marathon, entered the arena for the opening ceremony and, wearing national dress, presented Hitler with an olive branch.**

As Hitler opened the Games a 16½ ton bell chimed and thousands of pigeons were released.

**The German team were formidable – 406 strong and well prepared. As they marched into the stadium the Hindenberg airship flew overhead.**

Some teams gave the Nazi salute but, to the irritation of the Germans, Britain and America offered the usual 'eyes right'.

**Ten black American athletes, led by Jesse Owens, dampened Hitler's intention of proving Aryan superiority.**

Jesse Owens' track record was well known for he had the previous year broken five world records and equalled a sixth – all in the space of 45 minutes at the Big Ten Championships in Michigan.

**Before the Games were over Owens had won four gold medals.**

The team of ten – termed 'Black Auxiliaries' by Hitler's propaganda machine – won between them a total of seven gold, three silver and three bronze medals.

**The first gold went to Cornelius Johnson in the high jump.  He cleared the bar at 6ft 8ins, an Olympic record.**

He jumped still wearing a sweatshirt until the bar reached 6ft 6¾ins.

**David Albritton and Delos Thurber, also Americans, took silver and bronze to complete a clean sweep in the high jump.**

# OLYMPIC GAMES
## Germany 1936

Jesse Owens, whose grandparents had been slaves, won the
100 metres in 10.3secs, with fellow American Ralph Metcalfe in
silver position.

**Owens won the 200 metres with an Olympic record time of 20.7secs,
finishing four yards ahead of team-mate Matthew 'Mack' Robinson.**

Americans Archie Williams and James LuValle were first and third in
the 400 metres, separated by Arthur Godfrey Brown of Britain in the
silver spot.

**In fact Brown was within inches of gold when Williams pipped him
on the tape.**

There was another silver for the Brown family the next day when
Arthur's sister Audrey ran in the women's 4 x 100 metres relay.

**Arthur then added gold to the family fortunes in Britain's
4 x 400 metres relay winning team.**

John Woodruff, a 21-year-old from Pennsylvania, won another gold
medal for USA by unusual tactics in the 800 metres.

**Totally boxed in after 300 metres he slowed to a walk to let the
others move ahead.  He then switched to the outside
and attacked the field with his ten-foot stride to win by
two yards.**

Another gold for the Americans came in the 100 metres hurdles
when Forest 'Spec' Towns beat Britain's Donald Finley into second
place.

**Towns, from Georgia, had learned his trade jumping over a
broomstick held by his parents.**

The 4 x 100 metres men's relay was won by the Americans, but the
victory proved a great embarrassment.

**Although the team had been settled weeks before, two Jewish
members, Glickman and Stoller, were dropped and replaced by
Owens and Metcalfe.**

Fifty years later Glickman returned to the stadium and said that he
thought the decision had been made so that Hitler would not be
humiliated.

# OLYMPIC GAMES
## Germany 1936

**The laid-back British quartet of Frederick Wolf, Godfrey Rampling, William Roberts and Arthur Godfrey Brown confounded the athletics world by beating the Americans to the gold in the 4 x 400 metres relay.**

Wolf was eight metres behind after the first leg, but Rampling fought back for a two-metre lead and Roberts and Brown finished it off.

**Harold Whitlock, a 32-year-old motor mechanic, did Britain proud in the 50,000 metres walk. Despite sickness in the early stages, he kept going to finish well ahead of the field.**

The Marathon brought joy and sorrow for the victor, Korean Sohn Kee-Chung. His country was occuped by Japan at the time and, to compete, he had to run for the Japanese team.

**Sohn spoke later of the humiliation of hearing the Japanese anthem and seeing the Japanese flag raised as he received his gold medal.**

Ernest Harper, a 34-year-old British runner, took the silver medal.

**Finland again dominated the long distance track events, with gold and silver in the 5,000 metres and a clean sweep in the 10,000 metres.**

The three-day event equestrian course proved unusually difficult, but the Germans had an advantage in that they had been practising for 18 months on an identical course.

**The Germans took the gold, with Britain's team fighting for bronze.**

Richard Fanshawe was thrown from his horse, chased it for 2½ miles, remounted and – despite accumulating 8,754 penalty points – clinched the third position.

**Peter Scott, son of the explorer, won a bronze in the single-handed Olympia class yachting.**

Dorothy Odam took the silver medal for Britain in the high jump.

**The German in fourth place, Herman Dora Ratjen, admitted many years later that she was really a he and had been made to pose as a female by the Nazi Youth Movement.**

The Indians retained the hockey gold by beating Germany 8-1 in the final.

# OLYMPIC GAMES
## England 1948

The Games were back in Britain after a 40-year gap and two World Wars.

**Food and clothes were still rationed and war-damaged buildings were under repair.**

There was criticism from some quarters that the Games were a waste of time and money so soon after six years of war.

**The Games, which were opened on July 29 by King George VI, were said to have cost less than £600,000 – a fleabite compared with the millions spent in later years.**

Under the direction of Lord Burghley, president of the British Olympic Association and himself an Olympic gold medallist, the Games were voted a success under difficult circumstances.

**Army and RAF camps housed male competitors and the women lived in colleges.**

A new cinder running track was laid at Wembley Stadium.

**Germany and Japan were not invited to take part.**

A total of 4,099 competitors representing 59 countries converged on London.

**The weather was typically British, with the first half of the Games contested in warm sunshine and, for the remainder, it rained.**

The United States topped the medals table with 38 gold, 27 silver and 19 bronze.

**Heroine of the Games was 30-year-old Francina 'Fanny' Blankers-Koen, a mother of two from Holland.**

She won four gold medals in the 100 and 200 metres, 80 metres hurdles and 4 x 100 relay.

**Britain's Maureen Gardner, a 19-year-old ballet dancer, was unlucky not to have won the gold in the 80 metres hurdles.**

It was neck and neck with Fanny at the tape and when the band struck up with 'God Save The King', it was thought that Maureen had won.

**Fanny Blankers-Koen had won the hurdles event by a whisker but both she and Maureen were given the Olympic record time of 11.2secs.**

# OLYMPIC GAMES
## England 1948

The band had played the English national anthem to herald the arrival of the Royal Family.

**Although world record holder for the high jump and long jump, Mrs. Blankers-Koen had decided to concentrate on the track events.**

Dorothy Tyler (Great Britain) and Alice Coachman (USA) tied at 5ft 6ins after a jump-off in the high jump.

**Both were credited with the Olympic record.**

Tyler had to be satisfied with silver because she needed a second attempt to clear the bar.

**Coachman became the first black woman to win an Olympic gold medal.**

France's Micheline Ostermeyer, an accomplished pianist, took gold medals in the shot putt and discus and bronze in the high jump.

**The same hands that threw the discus and shot had, three months earlier, gained her the highest honours at the Paris Conservatory of Music.**

The men's 100 metres was won by Harrison 'Bones' Dillard, who as a schoolboy had been given his first pair of running shoes by the great Jesse Owens.

**Between May 1947 and June 1948 he notched up 82 consecutive victories.**

Arthur Wint, a 6ft 4½in Jamaican who had served with the RAF during the war, won the 400 metres and took a silver in the 800 metres.

**Wint, the son of a minister, remained in England after the war and studied medicine at the University of London.**

He was said to have a stride measuring 10ft.

**Emil Zatopek, a Czech army lieutenant, took the 10,000 metres gold in the Olympic record time of 29min 59.6sec and the 5,000 metres silver.**

The Marathon, not unusually, ended dramatically in the stadium.

# OLYMPIC GAMES
## England 1948

Etienna Gailly, a 25-year-old Belgian, Deifo Cabrera a 29-year-old Argentinian fireman, and 38-year-old Welsh nurse Tom Richards were fighting for the lead as they approached the stadium.

The Belgian was first to appear but seemed totally exhausted.

Hardly able to push one foot in front of the other, he was pursued into the stadium by his two rivals.

First Cabrera and then Richards overtook Gailly with 60 yards to go.

Cabrera ran on to win the gold with Richards in silver position.

The plucky Gailly finally reached his goal and took a well deserved bronze.

American schoolboy Bob Mathias, only 17, took the decathlon gold medal after a nailbiting finish.

The weather was fine for the start of the second day of the event at 10am.

By the afternoon the weather had deteriorated and events were running late with Mathias in third place.

Throwing the discus, his best event, he achieved a throw of about 145 feet, but the marker had been knocked over.

A half hour search in mud in half light ended with the judges crediting him with 144 feet.

By the time he had completed the 1,500 metres it was 10.35pm, but he had won the gold medal – the youngest ever in Olympic history.

Britain had to settle for silver in the hockey final with India, who brought their own hoard of eggs because of rationing in the UK.

Britain finished with three golds, 14 silvers and six bronzes.

# OLYMPIC GAMES
## Finland 1952

The 1952 Games, hosted by Finland, included a strong team of athletes from the Soviet Union, competing for the first time.

**Fears that American and Soviet competitors might not be compatible were unfounded, with all nations embracing the Olympic spirit.**

The Soviets were given permission to set up their own 'village' away from the other competitors.

**At the opening ceremony the name of the runner bringing the flame on its final lap had not been disclosed.**

When the 55-year-old Finn, Paavo Nurmi, winner of nine long distance medals in the 1920s, appeared with the torch, the stadium erupted.

**Cheers turned to amazement when, having lit the flame, he handed the torch to Hannes Kolehmainen, a gold medal winner from 1912.**

Emil Zatopek, the Czech runner, was king of the Games, winning three long distance gold medals.

**His facial expression always gave the impression that he was near to collapse, his head lolling from side to side.**

He once explained that he did not have the talent to 'run and smile at the same time'!

**Having won the 10,000 metres and shattering his own Olympic record time with 29min 17sec, he went on to the 5,000 metres and another gold medal in Olympic record time.**

Zatopek liked to chat with fellow competitors during his races and was known to have offered advice to them before setting off.

**Never having run a Marathon he decided to follow the man he felt to be the most likely winner – Britain's Jim Peters.**

Peters set off at a cracking pace, with Zatopek and Sweden's Gustav Jansson in contention.

**After 15 kilometres they came alongside Peters and ran together for some time.**

Zatopek, in chatty mood, turned to Peters and asked if he thought the pace was right.

# OLYMPIC GAMES
## Finland 1952

**Jim Peters, secretly exhausted after his initial effort in the Marathon, told Zatopek he thought the pace was too slow.**

With that the Czech sped away with Jansson in pursuit and left Peters trailing.

**Zatopek, unused to taking refreshment during a race, saw his rival Jansson take a piece of lemon at a feeding station.**

He said afterwards that if this made Jansson run well, he would take two slices of lemon at the next station.

**Jansson tired, Peters dropped out with cramp and Zatopek entered the stadium well in front.**

The Jamaican relay team had carried him on a lap of honour before the silver medallist, Argentina's Reinaldo Gomo, hit the tape.

**The Games became a family affair for Zatopek with his wife Dana also winning a gold medal in the javelin.**

Fourteen years later, Zatopek presented his 10,000 metres medal to Australian runner Ron Clarke, world record holder at the distance, who failed in his attempt to win gold.

**Horace Ashenfelter, an American FBI agent, was the unlikely gold medal winner of the 3,000 metres steeplechase.**

His previous times had not been impressive but at the water jump he left Russian Vladimir Kazantsev well behind.

**His training method – jumping over park benches at night – paid off with gold and a world record.**

After winning the 4 x 400 metres relay in world record time and pushing America into second place, the Jamaicans celebrated with the Duke of Edinburgh.

**They all drank out of their only container – a toothbrush mug!**

# OLYMPIC GAMES
## Finland 1952

The pole vault brought a duel between two American team-mates, the Rev. Bob Richards, a Californian theology professor, and Donald Laz.

**Both needed two attempts at 14ft 9ins, both missed after two vaults at 14ft 11ins and officials puzzled over the medals distribution.**

The Rev. Bob solved the problem by clearing 14ft 11ins at his third attempt to take the gold.

**Bob Mathias retained his gold for America in the decathlon after a hiccup in the javelin event.**

His Stanford University coach, Jack Weiershauser, persuaded a group of supporters to chant: "Oh Bob, hey you, don't forget to follow through."

**Mathias took the advice and his next throw was a winning 194ft 3ins.**

Viktor Chukarin, a Ukrainian in the Soviet team, won four gold medals and two silver in the gymnastics, having spent two years in a wartime concentration camp.

**Australian Marjorie Jackson won the 200 and 400 metres and was welcomed back to her home town with a 250lb cake.**

Britain did not have its best Olympics, winning only one gold, two silver and eight bronze.

**In the final event of the Games, the team showjumping, Col. Harry Llewellyn completed a faultless round on Foxhunter to win Britain's only gold.**

Sheila Lerwill won a silver medal in the high jump with 5ft 5ins, which was 2¾ins below her world record leap.

**Germany, back for the first time since World War II, left without gold but won seven silver and 17 bronze.**

The Soviet Union, in its first ever Games, finished second in the medals list with 22 gold, 30 silver and 19 bronze.

**America topped the table again with 40 gold, 19 silver and 17 bronze.**

In the Winter Games in Norway Jeanette Altwegg won gold in the ladies' figure skating for Britain.

# OLYMPIC GAMES
## Australia 1956

The 1956 Games were awarded to Australia – the first time the southern hemisphere had been honoured.

**It proved to be a controversial choice and the strict Australian animal quarantine laws gave the IOC a few headaches.**

Becase of this the Games had to be split between two venues.

**The equestrian events – apart from the cross-country section of the three day eventing – were transferred to Stockholm.**

In Melbourne, there were further problems when six countries decided to boycott the Games.

**Egypt, Iraq and Lebanon refused to send teams as a protest to the Israeli takeover of the Suez Canal.**

Holland, Spain and Switzerland boycotted the Games because of the invasion of Hungary by the Soviet Union.

**Switzerland later decided to take part, but there was insufficient time for their full team to reach Australia.**

China also withdrew when Taiwan sent its own team.

**Any hopes that calm would prevail once the Games, opened by the Duke of Edinburgh, got under way were soon quashed.**

The water polo semi-final between Hungary and the Soviet Union was stopped by the referee with the Hungarians leading 4-0.

**He reported that the game had deteriorated into 'an underwater boxing match'.**

Hungary were awarded the game and went on to win the gold medal.

**In 1952 Roger Bannister had broken the four minute mile and, before the Melbourne Olympics, nine other athletes had done likewise.**

All ten were present when the 1,500 metres was run in Melbourne.

**Six four-minute milers – John Landy, Britain's Brian Hewson, Laszio Tabori, Ron Delaney, Gunnar Nielsen and Istvan Rozsavolgyi – were out on the track for the start of the 1,500 metres.**

Roger Bannister, Chris Chataway, Derek Ibbotson and Jim Bailey were watching from the stand.

# OLYMPIC GAMES
## Australia 1956

**Before the race Australia's John Landy told Delaney, the youngest competitor, that he had a good chance of winning.**

With only 300 yards to go, Delaney was boxed in.  Nielsen, just ahead of the Irishman, knew he couldn't win himself and made way for Ron.

**Delaney worked his way through the field, increasing his speed with every stride to win by six yards.**

Delaney fell to his knees, head in hands, and third placed Landy rushed to his side thinking he was ill.

**The Irishman was far from ill.  He was on his knees – praying – having won Ireland's first gold medal since 1932.**

The 3,000 metres steeplechase brought joy and sadness to Britain's Chris Brasher.

**Ernst Larsen (Norway) and Sandor Rozsnyol (Hungary) approached the fourth hurdle from home when Brasher took his chance and pushed between them.**

He sprinted to a 15-yard victory but was disqualified for interfering with Larsen, whereupon both men said that the pushing had not affected the result.

**So the gold medal to Brasher was restored, with Rozsnyol taking the silver and Larsen the bronze.**

Britain's Gordon Pirie and Volodymyr Kuts, bitter rivals in the 5,000 and 10,000 metres, did their best to out-fox one another.

**Kuts emerged the winner each time.  In the 5,000 metres Pirie got the silver and team-mate Derek Ibbotson the bronze.**

The 10,000 metres saw Pirie out-manoeuvred by the crafty Kuts, who went on to win the gold, leaving Piries struggling in eighth place.

**America again almost swept the board on the track.**

Bobby Joe Morrow, a 6ft 1½in carrot and cotton farmer from Texas, won three gold medals.

**His successes came in the 100 and 200 metres and the 4 x 100 metres relay.**

Morrow, a deeply religious man, claimed he needed 11 hours sleep a night to keep up his strength.

# OLYMPIC GAMES
## Australia 1956

**His success depended on being totally relaxed, he said, so that he "could feel the jaw muscles wiggle."**

Three times in the Olympics, France's Alain Mimoun had finished second behind the great Zatopek in the 10,000 metres.

**Consolation came for him in the Marathon, with a gold for Mimoun and Zatopek in sixth place.**

Mimoun waited for his old friend to finish 4½ minutes after him when Zatopek saluted and embraced him. "That was better than the medal," said the Frenchman.

**Eighteen-year-old Elizabeth Cuthbert gave Australians something to cheer about when she won three gold medals.**

The shy, unassuming Elizabeth took the 100 and 200 metres gold and was a member of the successful 4 x 100 metres relay team.

**Britain's three-day event team of Francis Weldon, Laurence Rook and Albert Hill took the gold medal.**

In the team jumping Wilfred White, Pat Smythe and Peter Robeson took home the bronze behind the German and Italian teams.

**Dick McTaggart won a gold medal for Britain in the lightweight boxing and was also awarded the Val Barker Cup, having been judged the best stylist at the Games. Londoner Terry Spinks won the flyweight title.**

India again dominated the hockey, winning their sixth successive gold medal.

**Britain finished with six gold medals but the Soviet Union, with 37 golds overall, topped the medals list pushing America, with 32 golds, into second place.**

The Games ended with competitors entering the stadium en masse instead of organised groups. The idea was put forward by John Wing, an Australian-born Chinese boy.

# OLYMPIC GAMES
## Italy 1960

In AD393, the Roman Emperor Theodosius banned the Olympic Games.

**In 1960, Rome celebrated hosting the Games in Theodosius' home town.**

A new 100,000 seater stadium was built, but full use was also made of ancient Roman sites.

**Gymnasts performed in the Baths of Caracalla and the Basilica di Massenzio was home to the wrestlers.**

Live television pictures were beamed round the world for the first time.

**Drug tests were introduced after the death of Knud Jenson, a Danish cyclist.**

Excessive heat was at first blamed when Jenson collapsed during the time trials, crashing to the ground and fracturing his skull.

**Later the drug Ronicol was detected.**

Wilma Rudolph, a 20-year-old from Tennessee, was the star of the Games winning three gold medals.

**She was the 20th of 22 children and weighed only 4½lbs at birth.**

Wilma had been struck down by polio, losing the use of her left leg and having to wear a brace.

**Each day her brothers and sisters rubbed the leg and, as her condition improved, she wore a special shoe and played basketball.**

At the age of 11 she threw away the shoe and by the age of 16 and standing 5ft 11ins, she qualified for the US Olympic team.

**In 1956 she won a bronze in the relay but 1960 saw her winning the 100 and 200 metres and the 4 x 100 metres relay.**

Britain's Dorothy Hyman took the silver in the 100 metres and bronze in the 200 metres.

**Tamara Press and her sister Iryna of the Soviet Union between them won two gold medals and a silver.**

# OLYMPIC GAMES
## Italy 1960

Iryna won the 100 metres hurdles with Carol Quinton of Great Britain in silver position, and Tamara won the shot putt and a silver in the discus.

**The women's 800 metres was contested for the first time since 1928 and was won by Lyudmyla Shevtsova of the Soviet Union in world record time.**

The Marathon was run at night for the first time on a course lined by Italian soldiers holding torches.

**Rhadi Ben Abdesselem, a fancied Moroccan runner and a barefooted Ethiopian soldier Abebe Bikila, unknown and unfancied, set off shoulder to shoulder.**

One mile from the finish Abebe drew away from Rhadi to win by 200 yards.

**Abebe had been a private in Emperor Haile Selassie's Imperial Guard when he left. He was promoted to sergeant on his return.**

Peter Snell of New Zealand was the unexpected gold medallist in the 800 metres, setting a new Olympic record.

**Exhausted at the end he asked Roger Moens, who had been expected to win: "Who won?" Moens told him: "You did!"**

Fellow New Zealander Murray Halberg won the 5,000 metres with unusual tactics.

**Instead of waiting until the last lap to make a final burst, he went ahead with three laps to go.**

By the start of the last lap and with a 25-yard lead he was exhausted, but somehow kept going and won by eight yards.

**Halberg was a courageous man. As a 17-year-old he was left with a paralysed and withered arm after a rugby tackle. He had to learn how to run and walk again.**

Herb Elliott, an Australian who trained on a diet of raw and natural foods, not only won the 1,500 metres but set a world record that stood for seven years.

**Elliott never looked behind during the race and had no idea that he was leading the field by 20 yards.**

After winning the 1,500 metres, Herb Elliott's main concern was to protect his kangaroo-hide trackshoes from potential thieves.

# OLYMPIC GAMES
## Italy 1960

**Elliott retired at the age of 22 after winning 44 consecutive races at 1,500 metres.**

Asked why he retired at his peak he said that once he was satisfied that his spirit could dominate his body, he saw no point in continuing.

**The United States had won the gold medal in every 4 x 100 metres relay since 1920 and were anxious to make it nine straight wins.**

They finished first just ahead of a strong German team but disaster struck when they were disqualified.

**Ray Norton, in his determination to get a good start to the second leg, had overstepped the passing zone by three yards.**

The American disqualification meant that Britain gained a bronze medal.

**Britain shone in the 50,000 metres walk with Don Thompson taking the gold.**

Having failed to finish the distance in 1956 Don decided on a red-hot training course.

**For several nights each week he took steaming kettles and heaters into his bathroom, sealed the door and windows and exercised in the oppressive 100°F heat.**

An 18-year-old teenager took the gold in the light-heavyweight boxing final. His name? Cassius Clay.

**Anita Lonsbrough, a 19-year-old clerk from Huddersfield, won the 200 metres breaststroke setting a new world record time.**

Australian Dawn Fraser retained the gold in the 100 metres freestyle but was later shunned by her fellow competitors for refusal to swim in the 4 x 100 metres relay qualifying heat.

**India reached the final of the men's hockey for the seventh successive Games but were beaten to the gold by Pakistan.**

The Soviet Union again headed the medals table with 43 gold, followed by the United States with 34.

# OLYMPIC GAMES
## Italy 1964

Tokyo celebrated being chosen to host the first Games in Asia by spending US$3 billion on facilities.

**Ninety-three countries sent 5,140 competitors.**

The Games were opened by Emperor Hirohito.

**The Olympic flame was carried into the stadium by a runner who had been born in Hiroshima the day the atom bomb was dropped.**

The Olympic flag was flown from a pole measuring 15.21 metres, the triple jump distance that gave Mikio Oda Japan's first gold medal in 1928.

**Mary Rand and Lynn Davies presented Britain with a golden long jump double.**

Davies, a PE teacher from Wales, only just qualified for the final at his last attempt.

**It was wet, cold and windy for the men's long jump final – Welsh weather.**

Igor Ter-Ovanesyan, the Russian, took the lead in the first round and the American Ralph Boston took over in the second.

**At the start of the fifth round Lynn was in third place.**

The wind dropped momentarily as he set off to make the longest jump of his career, 26ft 5¾ ins.

**The other two could not match Lynn's jump and the gold medal was his.**

He said afterwards: "The Welsh gods must have been looking down on Tokyo that day."

**Mary Rand, jumping into a strong wind, registered a distance of 6.76 metres in the final round.**

She had broken the world record and became the first British woman to win a track and field gold medal.

**A few days after her gold medal in the long jump, Mary Rand won a silver in the pentathlon and bronze in the 4 x 100 metres relay.**

Ann Packer of Great Britain had almost decided to go shopping instead of running in the 800 metres final, believing she had no hope.

# OLYMPIC GAMES
## Italy 1964

**With 70 yards to go she went into overdrive and won by five yards in the Olympic record time of 2 min 01.1sec, to the delight of her fiance Robbie Brightwell after his disappointing fourth in the 400 metres.**

With Packer also winning a silver in the 400 metres she and room-mate Mary Rand really had cause for celebration.

**Ikuko Yoda, competing in her home town, was favourite to win the 100 metres hurdles and went through her usual pre-race routine.**

This involved sucking a lemon, sweeping her lane to the first hurdle and dabbing cream behind her ears. Alas she finished in fifth place.

**The women's 4 x 100 metres relay was won by Poland with USA and Britain in silver and bronze positions.**

The world record time credited to the Poles was later rescinded when one of their team failed to pass a sex test.

**Tamara Press of the Soviet Union again took gold in the shot putt to add to her discus gold. When sex tests were introduced in international competitions she disappeared from the athletics scene.**

Her sister Iryna took the gold in the pentathlon, beating Mary Rand into second place.

**Elvira Ozolina, Soviet javelin thrower, was so disgusted by her poor fifth place performance that she shaved her head.**

Mihaela Penes, a 17-year-old schoolgirl from Bucharest, won the gold with a throw of 198ft 7in – 19ft farther than Elvira's.

**American Al Oerter completed a trio of gold medals in the discus despite wearing a neck harness to protect a chronic disc injury and with a torn cartilage in his lower ribs.**

# OLYMPIC GAMES
## Italy 1964

After his final throw he doubled up in pain as he set an Olympic record of 61 metres.

**Britain's Paul Nihill was beaten into second place in the 50,000 metres walk by Italian Abdon Parnich.**

Ken Matthews, a Sutton Coldfield electrician, who had collapsed and failed to finish the 20,000 metres walk in 1960, felt he could win if his wife could make the trip with him.

**Friends and workmates raised £742 to send Sheila to Tokyo and Ken rewarded them with a gold medal.**

Australian Ron Clarke seemed a certainty to take the 10,000 metres gold approaching the home stretch.

**But American Billy Mills, part Sioux Indian, who had been pushed aside by Clarke earlier in the race, came with a lightning final sprint.**

He finished three yards ahead of Tunisian Mohamed Gammoudi, with Clarke collecting the bronze.

**As Billy crossed the line Japanese officials, looking on in total amazement, asked him: "Who are you?"**

Abebe Bikila, the barefooted Marathon gold medallist of 1960, donned socks and shoes in Tokyo but a recent appendix operation had put his stamina in doubt.

**Nevertheless, he entered the stadium first to the cheers of 75,000 people and won in the fastest ever Olympic time. Britain's Basil Heatley took the silver.**

When Bikila climbed the rostrum the Japanese didn't know the Ethiopian national anthem and played the Japanese anthem instead.

**Kokichi Tsuburaya, the Japanese bronze medallist, was ordered not to see his fiancee but to resume strict training for the 1968 Marathon.**

Three years later, after a series of injuries, he realised he had no chance of gaining a Marathon gold and took his own life.

**USA headed the medals list with 36 gold, 26 silver and 28 bronze. The Soviet Union finished second and Britain tenth with four golds.**

# OLYMPIC GAMES
# Mexico 1968

Controversy surrounded the choice of Mexico City for the 1968 Games.

**Pundits forecast exhaustion and even death for athletes in the thin atmosphere 2,240 metres above sea level.**

Forty countries threatened not to compete when South Africa was re-admitted.

**As a result the IOC reversed its decision and South Africa was banned once more.**

Riots at the University of Mexico shortly before the opening of the Games were suppressed, resulting in dozens of deaths and hundreds of injured.

**Rumblings of discontent from black American athletes led to further feelings of unease.**

However, the Games were opened by President Gustavo Diaz Ordaz, with 5,530 competitors from 112 countries – a record number.

**Enriqueta Basilio, a Mexican hurdler, became the first woman to light the Olympic flame.**

The rarefied atmosphere led to some outstanding results in the short distance events.

**Most remarkable was the long jump performance of Bob Beamon, a 6ft 3ins, 22-year-old New Yorker.**

Two of his three jumps in the qualifying round had been fouls. In the final he stood at the start of the runway repeating to himself: "Don't foul!"

**He sprinted down the runway, hit the board perfectly and took off like a rocket. He hit the sand so hard that he bounced out of the pit.**

The reigning champion, still waiting to jump, could not believe the distance Beamon had jumped.

**Officials set out to measure the distance but their optical measuring stick was too short.**

An ordinary steel tape was produced and showed 29ft 2½ ins, beating the world record of 27ft 4¾ins.

# OLYMPIC GAMES
## Mexico 1968

**Bob Beamon had broken the 28ft and 29ft barriers with his long jump, the record remaining until 1992. Lynn Davies finished ninth.**

An American team then smashed the 4 x 100 metres relay record in 2min 56.16secs, a time which was unbeaten for 20 years.

**Tommie Smith and John Carlos, gold and bronze medallists in the 200 metres, raised a furore at the awards ceremony.**

Both climbed the rostrum barefooted with black-gloved right hands.

**As the national anthem sounded both bowed their heads and raised gloved hands in a Black Power salute.**

Both were suspended and made to leave the Olympic village.

**The men's high jump caused more sensation when American Dick Fosbury introduced a new style of jumping, to be known later as the 'Fosbury Flop'.**

Instead of clearing the bar scissors fashion, he went over head first with his back to the bar.

**He took the gold medal with a new Olympic record jump of 7ft 4¼ins and started a revolution in the sport.**

David Hemery, the British hurdler, made all the running in the 400 metres hurdles.

**He led from the third hurdle to win by eight yards in a world record time of 48.12secs.**

Team-mate John Sherwood took the bronze to set up a family celebration.

**His wife Sheila had won the silver in the long jump the day before.**

Hemery was presented with his gold medal by David Burghley, who had won the same event at the 1928 Games in Amsterdam.

**Boyd Gittins, an American hurdler, was unfortunate not to be competing.**

Gittins had been eliminated from the US Olympic trials when a contact lens was dislodged as a pigeon dropping hit him in the eye.

**He requalified but a leg injury then ended his ambition to compete.**

The end of the 20,000 metres walk led to pandemonium in the stadium.

# OLYMPIC GAMES
## Mexico 1968

**Volodymyr Holubrychy entered the stadium first followed by his Soviet colleague Nikolai Smaga.**

Then, to thunderous applause, Jose Pedraza Zuniga, a 31-year-old Mexican soldier, bustled into the stadium.

**With 200 yards to go he passed Smaga and set off to catch the leader but failed to land the gold by three yards.**

The thin atmosphere took its toll in the long distance events, but Kenyan, Tunisian and Ethiopian runners came into their own.

**Kip Keino, an uncoached Kenyan tribesman, entered the 1,500 metres, 5,000 metres and 10,000 metres.**

In his first race – the 10,000 metres – Kip, who was suffering from a gall bladder infection, collapsed with two laps to go.

**Four days later he was running the 5,000 metres and winning a silver medal, losing to Tunisia's Mohamed Gammoudi by four feet.**

On the day of the 1,500 metres Kip was up against Jim Ryun, the American who was unbeaten at the distance for three years.

**On the way to the stadium Kip was held up in traffic so he ran the last mile.**

The race started and he took over the lead after 400 metres, going off at a cracking pace – too fast, many thought.

**Kip did not run out of steam as many expected and despite Ryun's late kick the race was won by 20 yards – the biggest margin in Olympic history.**

Back home in Kenya his wife gave birth to their third daughter and named her Milka Olympia Chelagat.

**The 10,000 metres was won by Kenyan Naftali Temu, with Ethiopian Mamo Wolde in silver position and Mohamed Gammoudi, Tunisian winner of the 5,000 metres, in bronze.**

Australia's Ron Clarke, record holder at the distance, was the only competitor not from a high altitude country to finish.

**His sixth place run had left him exhausted and after crossing the line he collapsed and was unconscious for ten minutes.**

Favourite for the women's 400 metres race was Britain's Lillian Board, a 19-year-old with enormous talent.

# OLYMPIC GAMES
## Mexico 1968

**Colette Besson, a little-known French girl, overtook Lillian just before the finishing line to win by two feet.**

Lillian did not get her revenge for the defeat. Tragically, she died from cancer shortly after her 22nd birthday.

**Irena Kirszenstein, a Polish Jew, had competed in five Olympics when she won the 200 metres to make her tally seven medals from five different events.**

The 100 metres hurdles brought gold and silver success to Australians Maureen Caird and Pamela Kilborn.

**Bronze medallist Chi Cheng from Taiwan became the first Asian woman to win a field and track medal in 40 years.**

Mark Spitz, American wonder swimmer who had won five gold medals at the Pan American Games in 1967, forecast that he would take six golds in Mexico City.

**His prediction misfired – he won gold in the 100 and 200 metres relays, silver in the 100 metres butterfly and bronze in the 100 metres freestyle – but his best was still to come at the next Olympics.**

Chris Finnegan, a 24-year-old bricklayer, won the middleweight boxing gold for Britain but did have a problem.

**Officials wanted a urine sample but he could not oblige. He drank pints of water and beer but it was not until 1.40am, with officials still tagging along, that he had success.**

# OLYMPIC GAMES
## Germany 1972

Germany, anxious to impress after the Nazi Games of 1936, lavished £3 million on facilities.

**All venues, apart from sailing, were reached in an area of one square mile in Munich.**

However, on the eleventh day, all dreams of gold medals and superhuman efforts were forgotten.

**Eight Arab terrorists climbed a fence into the Olympic village, gunned down two Israeli athletes and took nine others hostage.**

After negotiations the terrorists were allowed to leave by helicopter, with the hostages, and land at a nearby airport.

**A gun battle followed. The nine hostages, a German policeman and five terrorists died.**

The Games were suspended for 24 hours and a memorial service for the victims was held in the stadium.

**What was left of the Israeli team went home, together with some athletes from Holland and Norway, and the Games resumed in sombre mood.**

The first week saw some incredible feats in the swimming pool, with Olympic records beaten daily.

**Mark Spitz, the American, stormed through the swimming events, breaking records in every event to win seven gold medals.**

He won four individual titles, the 100 and 200 metres freestyle and butterfly, and three golds in the relay events.

**In each of the events world records were broken.**

In the 200 metres breaststoke Britain's David Wilkie brought home a silver medal, a welcome consolation prize.

**Shane Gould, a 15-year-old Australian schoolgirl, dominated the women's swimming events with three gold medals, a silver and a bronze.**

In the 100 metres freestyle Shane lost her first freestyle race in two years when two Californian schoolgirls beat her into third place.

# OLYMPIC GAMES
## Germany 1972

**Shane's freestyle defeat delighted the Americans, who had been wearing T-shirts with 'All that glitters is not Gould' across the front.**

One year after the Olympics, Shane found her gruelling training schedule too much and she announced her retirement at the tender age of 16.

**One the track the Flying Finns were back – this time in the shape of Pekka Vasala and Laase Viren.**

Viren, a policeman from the Arctic Circle, dashed the hopes of Dave Bedford of Britain in the 10,000 metres.

**Viren was invincible, leaving behind Bedford and all contenders. He was tireless, setting a world record of 27mins 38.4secs. Bedford trailed in sixth.**

Viren repeated his superiority in the 5,000 metres, leaving Tunisia's 1968 champion Mohamed Gammoudi with silver and Britain's Ian Stewart the bronze.

**In the 1,500 metres Vasala was something of an unknown quantity and was nicknamed Mr. Unpredictable by his Finnish supporters.**

Kip Keino, Kenya's defending champion, and America's Jim Ryun had been favourites until a fall in the fourth heat ended Ryun's hope of gold and his career.

**Vasala shadowed Keino all the way until the home stretch then made his move and swept to victory by three metres. Britain's Brendan Foster was fifth.**

In the 100 metres Americans Eddie Hart, Rey Robinson and Robert Taylor were expected to line up in the final with Ukrainian Valery Borzov.

**The quarter-finals were due to start at 7pm, or so the Americans thought.**

When they actually began at 4.15pm they were at a bus stop waiting for the stadium coach and idly watching the Games on a TV monitor.

**Robinson asked if they were showing a re-run of the first round. When told it was live he realised it was the heat he was supposed to be running in.**

A dash to the stadium by car just enabled Taylor to join his heat but the other two had been eliminated.

# OLYMPIC GAMES
## Germany 1972

**The blond, blue-eyed Borzov took the lead after 30 metres in the final and finished, arms raised, with Taylor in second place.**

Valery Borzov also won the 200 metres to become the first non-American to win the Olympic sprint double.

**Dave Wottle, an American from Ohio who always ran in a battered golf cap, was on honeymoon in Munich when he lined up for the 800 metres.**

The final was a battle between Wottle and the favourite, Yevhen Arzhanov. The Ukranian slipped as he approached the tape and had to settle for silver behind Wottle.

**Mary Peters, a 33-year-old secretary from Belfast, was trying for a pentathlon gold for the third time. In 1964 she was fourth, in 1968 ninth.**

At the end of the first day Mary had achieved personal bests in the 100 metres hurdles and high jump to lead Germany's Heide Rosendahl by 301 points, but with two of her worst events to come.

**Both then had personal bests in the 200 metres and long jump with Rosendahl soaring to 22ft 5ins, one centimetre short of her world record.**

The shot-putting proved decisive for Mary. It was her speciality as she had competed in the individual shot for ten years.

**When the nailbiting result was worked out Mary, with a world record total of 4,801 points, had won the gold medal by ten points.**

Had she run the 200 metres one second slower she would have lost.

**Renate Stecher of Germany dominated the women's sprints, taking gold in the 100 and 200 metres.**

She was the first woman to win the sprint double since Fanny Blankers-Koen in 1948. Stecher won 90 sprint races in a row between August 1970 and June 1974.

**The star of 1972 was gymnast Olga Korbut, a 4ft 11ins Russian girl. With an infectious grin, win or lose, she infatuated the crowds.**

She won three gold medals and although she was not the Games' all-round champion, she was the best in the eyes of the public.

# OLYMPIC GAMES
## Canada 1976

Chaos and confusion reigned before the opening of the 1976 Games in Montreal.

**So much money – estimated at $800 million – had been spent on the project that the taxpayers were far from happy.**

Then, days before Queen Elizabeth opened the Games, 20 African and Third World countries withdrew.

**The boycott was because New Zealand, whose All Blacks rugby team had toured South Africa, refused to withdraw its athletes from Montreal.**

Consequently some athletes, particularly the middle distance runners, would never get a chance to shine in the Olympics.

**The torch was carried into the stadium by two 15-year-olds – English-Canadian Sandra Henderson and French-Canadian Stephane Prefontaine.**

The pair married some years later.

**Olga Korbut, the darling of Munich, was overshadowed by a 14-year-old Romanian, gymnast Nadia Comaneci, who scored maximum points in the gymnasium.**

She ended the Games with three golds, a silver and a bronze.

**Olga had to be content with a team gold and a silver.**

Japan won the team gold in the men's gymnastics for a fifth time, partly thanks to a competitor who went through routines with a broken leg.

**Shun Fujimoto suffered the injury completing his floor exercises. Because of the intense rivalry of the Japanese and Soviet teams he kept quiet about his injury.**

He completed his side horse routine and gave an almost perfect performance on the rings. However, on landing he dislocated his knee above the broken leg.

**He was forced to accept medical attention and described the pain thus: "My whole blood was boiling at my stomach."**

Hasely Crawford, a 6ft 2¼in Trinidadian, won the 100 metres to become his country's first Olympic champion.

# OLYMPIC GAMES
## Canada 1976

**So popular was Crawford's win that when he returned home, his face was on two postage stamps, six calypso songs were written about him, an aeroplane was named after him and he was honoured by his country with the Trinity Cross.**

Jamaican Donald Quarrie had been trying for an Olympic medal since 1968 but had been dogged by injuries.

**Quarrie took the silver medal in the 100 metres, a close second to Crawford and in front of the 1972 winner Valery Borzov of Russia.**

Quarrie made no doubt about it in the 200 metres, winning by two feet. A statue was erected in his honour in his home town of Kingston.

**Alberto Juantorena, a 6ft 2in Cuban, was the first man from a non-English speaking country to win both 400 and 800 metres.**

When the Games ended he had run in nine races and had lost 11 pounds.

**With Filbert Bayi from Tanzania and Kenyan Mike Bolt not competing because of the African boycott, New Zealander John Walker's winning time in the 1,500 metres was the slowest in 20 years.**

Lasse Viren, the Flying Finn, repeated his 5,000 and 10,000 metres victories of 1972. Britain's Brendan Foster won the 10,000 bronze.

**Viren completed the 10,000 metres in 27min 40.38sec. The slowest competitor, Olmeus Charles from Haiti, took 42.00.11.**

It was not unusual for Haitians to finish last. Dictator 'Baby Doc' seldom sent the best to the Olympics, and it was his friends and trusted soldiers who were rewarded with trips to Montreal.

**One year before the Montreal Olympics, French hurdler Guy Drut predicted he would win the 110 metres event in 13.28secs.**

He did – to the last one hundredth of a second!

**John Aki-Bua was unable to defend his 400 metres hurdles title because of the African boycott so Ed Moses of USA had little to fear.**

# OLYMPIC GAMES
## Canada 1976

The 20-year-old Moses, an engineering and physics student, had taken up the sport only four months before the Games but set up a world record of 47.63secs.

**In the 20,000 metres walk Danie Bautista Rocha won Mexico's track and field gold. He was so dehydrated at the finish that he drank ten tins of soft drinks before he could satisfy the drug test.**

The modern pentathlon was devised by Pierre de Coubertin, founder of the Modern Olympics, and was based on the idea of a soldier delivering a message.

**Setting off on an unfamiliar horse he dismounts to fight a duel with swords. He escapes but has to shoot his way out with pistols. He then swims a river and runs the last 4,000 metres through woods to deliver his message.**

The Soviets were favourites to win the team pentathlon but met with serious trouble in the fencing bouts.

**The epee of Borys Onyshchenko, a Soviet Army major, was seen to light up without touching an opponent.**

An investigation found that the major's weapon had been wired so that he could register a hit at any time.

**Disqualification followed and Onyshchenko was sent home, never to be seen again outside Russia.**

But his name lived on in the sport... as Borys Dis-Onyshchenko.

**As a result of the disqualification Britain won the gold medal thanks to Adrian Park, Danny Nightingale and Jim Fox.**

The Americans again dominated the men's swimming events, taking 12 of the 13 gold medals on offer.

**Britain's David Wilkie prevented a clean sweep by setting a world record in the 200 metres breaststroke, leaving the Americans in silver and bronze positions.**

# OLYMPIC GAMES
## Soviet Union 1980

In December 1979 the Soviet Union invaded Afghanistan. American President Jimmy Carter called for a boycott of the 1980 Games in Moscow.

**USA, Canada, Japan and West Germany, together with many smaller nationals, decided to support the boycott.**

Great Britain supported the call to boycott the Games but left it to individual athletes to decide whether or not to compete.

**Facilities were good in the 103,000 capacity Lenin Stadium but the Soviet crowds were far from sportsmanlike, booing foreign competitors and particularly those from the Eastern bloc.**

Britain finished an honourable ninth in the medals table with five gold, seven silver and nine bronze. The Soviets topped the list with 80 gold, 69 silver and 46 bronze.

**Sebastian Coe and Steve Ovett, rivals for the 800 and 1,500 metres titles, had avoided clashing since the 1978 European Championships.**

Coe had been favourite for the 800 gold and Ovett for the 1,500.

**In fact Coe ran a bad 800 metres race and Ovett took the gold with Coe three metres behind in silver position.**

After the event Coe said he had run the worst race of his life but vowed to win the 1,500 metres.

**Ovett lined up as favourite for the 1,500 metres, having won 42 consecutive races at the distance.**

Coe had struggled through his first-round heat and suffered from criticism of his poor showing at 800 metres.

**Jurgen Straub of East Germany took an early lead but Coe, conscious of his 800 metres errors, stayed close until 200 metres from home.**

Coe then 'kicked' to pass Straub in the home straight to beat the Germany by four metres, Ovett taking the bronze.

**Before the men's 100 metres heats, Poland's Marian Woronin boasted he would win the gold in 10.10secs.**

Defending champion Hasely Crawford of Trinidad and Cuban Silvio Leonard were equally confident.

# OLYMPIC GAMES
## Soviet Union 1980

**Little attention had been paid to 100 metres contestant Allan Wells, son of a Scottish blacksmith, who had started his career as a long jumper – until he won his heat, that was.**

Wells and Leonard were neck and neck in the final, but seven metres from the tape Wells lunged forward with his shoulders and chested the tape inches ahead of the Cuban.

**Wells was Britain's first 100 metres gold medallist since Harold Abrahams in 1924. He then took the silver in the 200 metres.**

In 1976 Britain's Daley Thompson finished 18th in the decathlon. In Moscow he was unstoppable.

**His greatest rival, West Germany's Guido Kratschmer, did not compete because of the boycott and Daley took the gold in style.**

Even the unfriendly Soviet spectators cheered his victory.

**Perhaps the happiest gold medallist of the Games was swimmer Duncan Goodhew of Great Britain.**

Duncan became bald at the age of ten after falling from a tree and was also dyslexic. He suffered derision throughout his schooldays.

**He decided to become an Olympic champion and, in Moscow in 1980, his dream came true when he won the 100 metres breaststroke.**

He also helped the British team to win bronze in the 4 x 100 metres medley relay.

**Ethiopia's Miruts Yifter had been trying for ten years to win a gold medal at 5,000 metres.**

In 1971 in the US-Africa Games he thought he had won before discovering he had miscounted the laps and had run one short.

**In 1972 he won an Olympic bronze in the 10,000 metres but missed the start of the 5,000 metres when he was directed to the wrong check-in gate.**

In 1976 Ethiopia boycotted the Games but in 1980 Yifter won at last, taking gold not only in the 5,000 metres but also in the 10,000.

**The bronze went to Kaario Nyambui of Lapland, one of 23 children. He pushed Ireland's Eamonn Coghlan into fourth place.**

# OLYMPIC GAMES
## Soviet Union 1980

Victor Markin, a 23-year-old Siberian medical student, was the surprise winner of the 400 metres.

**His time of 44.60secs was the fastest for two years and 0.73secs faster than his previous best.**

Victor said afterwards: "I don't know my own limits. I finished as in a dream."

**East German Waldermar Cierpinski retained his Marathon title – two days before his 30th birthday.**

He was only the second man to win the Marathon in consecutive Olympics. Abebe Bikila of Ethiopia was first in 1960 and 1964.

**In the 20,000 metres walk, officials decided to watch especially closely for illegal walking techniques after pictures taken in 1976 showed competitors with both feet off the ground.**

Seven competitors had been disqualified when Italy's Maurizio Damilano, an outsider, came home to win the gold.

**His twin brother Giorgio finished 11th and Thipsamay Chanthaphone of Laos was last, half-an-hour after all the others, to celebrate his 19th birthday.**

Bronislaw Malinowski, son of a Polish father and Scottish mother, had been fourth in the 3,000 metres steeplechase in 1972 and a silver medallist in 1976.

**Moscow 1980 brought him the gold medal he had dreamed of winning. A year later at the age of 30, he was killed in a car crash.**

In the women's javelin, the virtually unknown Cuban Maria Colon took the gold with her first throw of 224ft 5ins, an Olympic record.

**She was the first Cuban woman to win an Olympic gold and the first non-white athlete of either sex to win an Olympic throwing event.**

Britain's Tessa Sanderson failed to qualify for the final.

**Russian gymnast Aleksandr Dityatin was the first person to win eight medals at a single Olympics. He was awarded three golds, four silver and a bronze.**

Earlier in the year, Robin Cousins had taken the gold for Britain in the men's free skating at the Winter Olympics.

# OLYMPIC GAMES
## USA 1984

The 1984 Games opened in Los Angeles in July without any Soviet involvement.

**USSR had decided on a tit-for-tat boycott after USA refused to take part in the 1980 Games in Moscow.**

The Russians declared their intentions on the day that the Olympic flame arrived in the States.

**The boycott resulted in fewer competitors in some sports but 140 countries – more than ever before – took part.**

Financing for the Games came from private sponsorship for the first time, TV rights alone amounting to $287 million.

**Gina Hemphill, granddaughter of the legendary Jesse Owens, carried the Olympic torch into the stadium.**

President Ronald Reagan declared the Games open, setting the stage for a three-hour, Hollywood-style extravaganza with marching bands and 85 pianos.

**Controversy raged after the women's 3,000 metres final when America's darling athlete Mary Decker claimed that she had been tripped and pushed off the track by Zola Budd.**

Shy, slight, five foot Zola had been brought up on a farm in South Africa where she had broken Decker's 5,000 metres record by six seconds.

**Unable to compete at Olympic level because of South Africa's apartheid attitude, she applied for British citizenship, claiming that her paternal grandfather was British.**

On March 24, 1984, Zola and her parents arrived to live in Guildford, Surrey, and within two weeks her citizenship was confirmed.

**She was included in the British team and the much-hyped meeting with Decker was due to take place in the 3,000 metres.**

When the final arrived, Zola – running barefoot as always – saw Decker take an early lead but kept in close touch.

**Decker, Budd, Romanian Maricica Puica and Britain's Wendy Sly pulled ahead of the field.**

Coming out of a turn Budd took the lead on the outside edge of lane one. Decker was on the inside of the lane.

# OLYMPIC GAMES
## Soviet Union 1980

At about 1,700 metres Decker's running spikes caught Budd's heel, knocking her momentarily off balance.

A few strides on and there was another bump. Budd, regaining her balance, stuck out her left leg and Decker tripped over her right leg.

**Decker's spikes struck Budd's bare heel. The American lost her balance and fell, writhing in agony and weeping.**

Budd, still in the lead, looked back to see Decker on the ground, then slowed to a jog and finally finished seventh.

**Puica took the gold, Wendy Sly the silver – there was nothing for Decker or Budd.**

Decker blamed Budd for the fall but when the initial cry had died down, it was generally felt that both athletes had made mistakes.

**Decker did not run again in 1984 but the following year she was undefeated.**

Budd won the world cross-country championship in 1985 and 1986 but in 1988 the British Amateur Athletics Board, on the recommendation of the IAAF, suspended her from international athletics.

**She had, they said, attended – but not taken part – a cross-country meeting in South Africa. She returned there emotionally drained and her Olympic dreams shattered.**

To end the sad story it must be said that, as a young athlete in South Africa, Zola had kept a poster of her heroine by her bed. It was Mary Decker!

**Not all was doom and gloom in Los Angeles where a shy young man called Carl Lewis equalled Jesse Owens' feat of winning four golds.**

The first came in the 100 metres which Lewis won by eight feet, the largest margin in Olympic history.

**As a 15-year-old, Lewis had grown 2½ins in one month and had to use crutches until his body could adjust to his height.**

He went on to win the 200 metres in a new Olympic record time then helped the USA team to win the 4 x 100 metres relay.

**His fourth gold came in the long jump with a first leap of 28ft ¼in. Leading up to the Olympics Carl Lewis had had 36 straight wins.**

# OLYMPIC GAMES
## Soviet Union 1980

Daley Thompson was back to defend his decathlon title. This time German world record holder Jurgen Hingsen was there to make life difficult for him.

**Daley took it all in his stride, winning the gold medal and equalling the world record.**

Tessa Sanderson brought more good news for Britain when she took gold in the javelin.

**Tessa created an Olympic record of 228ft 2ins with her first throw.**

She was the first British athlete to win a throwing event and team-mate Fatima Whitbread came in with the bronze.

**Steve Ovett and Sebastian Coe were back to battle it out in the 800 and 1,500 metres.**

Coe again took the silver in the 800 metres, Ovett trailing in seventh.

**Ovett was clearly unwell and twice collapsed in the tunnel leading from the track with bronchitis.**

They both lined up again for the 1,500 metres together with British compatriot Steve Cram.

**Seb Coe again rose to the occasion, becoming the first man to retain the 1,500 metres title in successive Olympics.**

Cram brought further joy to the British camp by taking the silver, but sadly Ovett was again overcome with chest pain and pulled out.

**Said Aquita of Morocco took the 5,000 metres gold medal in style, sprinting ahead with half a lap to go and waving to the crowds.**

King Hassan II of Morocco was so impressed that he gave Aquita a villa in Casablanca and the Rabat-to-Casablanca express train was named after him.

**Britain's Charlie Spedding and Ireland's John Treacy had home TV watchers out of their seats as they led in the Marathon.**

The dreams of gold were broken, however, when Carlos Lopes of Portugal cruised ahead of the pair and proved unstoppable despite a last lap of 67 seconds by the Irishman.

# OLYMPIC GAMES
## Soviet Union 1980

**John Treacy consoled himself with a silver medal and Spedding, who had won the London Marathon, picked up the bronze.**

Malcolm Cooper was on target for Britain with a gold in the small-bore shooting event.

**Steve Redgrave of Britain won his first rowing gold medal in the four-oar with cox.**

Redgrave's team-mates were Martin Cross, Richard Budgett, Andrew Holmes and Adrian Ellison

**British swimmer Sarah Hardcastle earned a silver medal behind the 18-year-old American Tiffany Cohen, who swam the world's fastest women's 400 metres since 1978.**

Three days later Sarah won a bronze in the 800 metres freestyle. Tiffany was again the gold medal winner.

**David Ottley of Britain raised hopes when he took a surprise lead in the javelin with a throw of 281ft 3ins.**

With the Soviets out because of the boycott, gold was in sight until Arto Harkonen of Finland produced a fourth round throw of 284ft 8ins and Ottley was left in silver position.

**Ed Moses, America's gold medallist in the 400 metres hurdles in 1976, was favourite for the 1984 gold.**

Moses had already broken the 48secs barrier for the event 27 times.

**He didn't disappoint the home crowds as he went to the front from the start and stayed there.**

Second place went to fellow American Danny Harris, an 18-year-old who had run his first 400 metres hurdle race only a few months earlier.

**China entered a team for the first time and went home with 15 gold medals.**

At the Winter Games, Torvill and Dean of Britain took their first gold medal in the ice dance.

**Performing to Ravel's Bolero, they were awarded nine sixes – the first time such marks had been given.**

# OLYMPIC GAMES
## South Korea 1988

Doubts had been raised at the choice of Seoul in South Korea for the 1988 Games, but facilities were good and everything went fairly smoothly.

**North Korea wanted to stage half the events but despite several being offered they decided to boycott the Games completely.**

Albania, Cuba, Ethiopia, Madagascar, Nicaragua and the Seychelles followed suit, leaving 160 competing countries.

**Roh Tae-Woo, President of Korea, opened proceedings and the torch was carried part of the way round the track by Sohn Kee-Chung, the 76-year-old who had won the 1936 Marathon.**

At the time, Korea was occupied by Japan and he had been forced to run under the Japanese flag.

**Tennis was reintroduced for the first time since 1924 and Germany's Steffi Graf took the gold.**

Sergei Bubka, a Ukranian, had already set nine world records before taking gold in the pole vault.

**As a child his parents would never have imagined him winning gold medals. At three he ran away from home and at four he almost drowned when he fell into a barrel of salted cabbage. Later he could have died when he fell from a tree. His braces caught on a branch and saved him!**

The men's 100 metres was expected to be a battle between America's Carl Lewis and Canada's Ben Johnson – rivals since their first meeting at the American Junior Championships in 1980.

**Before Seoul, Johnson had developed a unique start, almost leaping out of the blocks, and had beaten Lewis in their previous few clashes.**

# OLYMPIC GAMES
## South Korea 1988

Johnson's over-developed muscles and yellow-tinged eyes brought him the nickname 'Benoid' but he always said "drugs would never pass into my body".

**When the final got under way Lewis was in lane three and Johnson in lane six. Britain's Linford Christie was between the two.**

Johnson again leapt from his blocks at the pistol and was well in the lead for the entire 100 metres.

**Lewis had to accept the silver and Christie the bronze.**

Johnson appeared on Canadian TV and finally went for a drug test. It took 1½ hours and several beers before he could provide a sample.

**He then had a sauna, ate half a cream cake, dined in an Italian restaurant and went to a disco. That was Saturday night.**

His unnamed urine sample went to the Doping Control Centre where traces of steroids were found.

**The diagnosed sample was identified as Johnson's and by Tuesday morning he had been asked to give back his gold medal.**

Johnson denied taking steroids and his coach claimed that he had been given a spiked drink.

**Later, testifying before a Canadian commission, his coach and doctor admitted that Johnson had taken steroids for seven years but never within 28 days of competition so that he would be clear before tests.**

He was said to have had an injection 26 days before the 100 metres final of a compound used to fatten cattle.

**Belatedly, the gold medal went to Lewis and the silver to Christie.**

In 1987 Lewis's father had died and at the funeral he put the gold medal won in Los Angeles in his father's hand, saying: "I want you to have this. I will win another."

**Britain's Adrian Moorhouse, having finished fourth in the 100 metres breaststroke in Los Angeles, came out in fighting mood to win the gold.**

As a 12-year-old he had seen David Wilkie winning a gold on television and decided: "I want one of those." It took him 12 years but he did it in the end.

# OLYMPIC GAMES
## South Korea 1988

**The outstanding woman athlete of the Games was America's Florence Griffith-Joyner, affectionately known as 'Flojo'.**

She was a colourful character with long, painted nails and a selection of equally colourful running suits.

**She was the seventh of eleven children from Los Angeles.**

On one occasion she was asked to leave a shopping centre when she appeared with a pet boa-constrictor wound round her neck.

**Flojo won three golds and a silver in the 100 and 200 metres, the 4 x 100 and 4 x 400 metres relays.**

Her sister-in-law, Jackie Joyner-Kersee, took gold in the heptathlon and the long jump.

**After all the bad feeling between Mary Decker and Zola Budd in 1984, Decker returned to try again in the 3,000 metres but came nowhere.**

Olha Bryzhina of the Ukraine set an Olympic record in winning the 400 metres. Her husband Viktor also won gold in the 4 x 100 metres relay.

**Lined up for the women's 800 metres were two East German girls with much in common. Sigrun Wodars and Christine Wachtel were both 23 and 5ft 5¼in tall.**

Both were trained by Walter Gladrow at the same club and both had a liking for chocolate, ice-cream and champagne.

**In 1988 Wodars won the gold and Wachtel the silver although Wachtel had taken first place in seven of their eight meetings before the Olympics.**

Fatima Whitbread took the silver medal for Britain in the javelin despite a trapped nerve in her throwing shoulder, foot and hamstring problems, an abscess, mouth infection and a bout of glandular fever before the Games.

**Britain's Liz McColgan lost her chance of gold on the last lap of the 10,000 metres.**

Russian Olga Bondarenko burst past Liz, running the last 200 metres in 31.2secs.

# OLYMPIC GAMES
## Spain 1992

The choice of Barcelona for the 1992 Games was good, with no boycotts and 9,364 competitors from 169 countries taking part in Spain.

**Spanish competitors excelled, taking 13 gold medals. Until 1992 their total had been just four golds.**

Television coverage was greater than ever with NCB paying a record $401 million dollars for American rights.

**Britain's captain Linford Christie, at 32, became the oldest sprinter by four years to win the 100 metres gold.**

Carl Lewis, suffering from a virus, had failed to qualify in the US Olympic trials and Leroy Burrell, who had beaten Lewis ten times in three years, was expected to be Christie's big rival.

**A false start seemed to upset Burrell and it was Frank Fredericks of Namibia who took the silver and became the first black African to win a medal at 100 metres.**

Sally Gunnell, captain of the British women's team, took the gold in the 400 metres hurdles and then helped to win the bronze in the 4 x 400 metres relay.

**Steve Redgrave, with new partner Matthew Pinsett, won his third successive gold for Britain in the coxless pairs, leading all the way.**

Chris Boardman of Great Britain, riding a streamlined superbike weighing less than 20lbs, won gold in the 400 metres cycling pursuit.

**He twice broke the world record in the heats and lapped world champion Jens Lehmann of Germany in the final.**

It was Britain's first cycling gold medal since 1920.

**The 4 x 100 metres relay gold was won by America for the 15th time. Carl Lewis, brought into the team when Mark Witherspoon dropped out with Achilles tendon problems, won his eighth gold medal.**

Britain took the bronze medal and Kris Akabusi, a member of the team, then added another bronze in the 400 metres hurdles.

**Carl Lewis, spurning all suggestions that he was 'over the top', took his third consecutive gold in the long jump with a leap of 28ft 5½ins.**

# OLYMPIC GAMES
## Spain 1992

The men's shot putt was sensational in that all three medal winners had served suspensions for taking illegal drugs.

**Michael Stulce (USA), who took the gold, was suspended for two years in 1990. James Doehring (USA), in silver position, had a 14-month suspension imposed also in 1990, and bronze medallist Vyacheslav Lykho of Russia had served a three-month ban.**

When Hwang Young-cho won the Marathon in hot, humid conditions, he collapsed and was taken out on a stretcher.

**After recovering he attended the medal ceremony and then went to telephone his mother.**

There was no reply – his mother had spent the day in the temple praying for him.

**When Russia's Valentina Yegorova qualified to run in the women's Marathon at the Olympics everybody in her village of Iziderkino, a small farming community, wanted to see the event.**

There was a snag. Nobody in the village owned a television set.

**All 1,500 inhabitants gave as much as they could and bought a 30-year-old black-and-white telly.**

On the night of the race the set was placed in the open doorway of Valentina's home and the whole community gathered outside to watch.

**They were not disappointed. Valentina battled her way through the field in a temperature of 84°F and won by 40 metres from Japan's Yuko Arimori.**

It was after midnight before the TV set was switched off, when the village had seen Valentina receive the gold medal.

**The women's 100 metres hurdles was expected to be a straight duel between Gail Devers of America and Lyudmila Narozhilenko of Russia.**

The Russian strained a hamstring and pulled out and the American hit the final hurdle, losing her balance and the race.

**Voula Patoulidou, a young Greek athlete, who was amazed to find herself as a final qualifier, was declared the gold medal winner.**

She thought that she might have gained the bronze position and had to watch the replay before she believed she had won.

# OLYMPIC GAMES
## Spain 1992

**She was the first Greek woman to qualify for a track final and the first of either sex to win a track and field event since 1912.**

The men's high jump results were disappointing despite the high quality field.

**The winning jump of 7ft 8ins by Cuban Javier Sotomayor was the lowest since the 1976 Games.**

So poor was the jumping that the last 20 attempts to clear the bar were failures.

**Tim Forsythe, an 18-year-old Australian, took the bronze medal. Four years earlier, watching the Olympics on television, he found the high jump boring and offered to cut the lawn rather than watch.**

With 30 world records to his name, the Ukranian pole vaulter Sergei Bubka was favourite to retain his gold medal place.

# OLYMPIC GAMES
## Spain 1992

**He repeated the tactics that gave him the gold in Seoul by not entering the competition until the bar reached 18ft 8¼ins.**

His luck ran out and he failed.  His pupil, Igor Trandenkov, won the silver and 21-year-old Russian Maksim Tarasov took the gold by clearing 19ft 0¼in at his first vault.

**Bubka blamed his failure on swirling winds, nervousness and "unbelievably bad biorhythms"!**

Within a month of his Olympic flop Bubka had set two new world records.

**Britain's Tessa Sanderson again qualified for the javelin final but failed to get a medal, finishing fourth with a throw of 208ft 7ins.**

Jackie Joyner-Kersee again took the gold medal in the heptathlon, leading from the first event and amassing 7,044 points.

**She had been christened Jacqueline after Jackie Kennedy because her grandmother predicted that some time "this girl will be First Lady of something".**

Britain's Steve Backley took the bronze in the javelin with a throw of 273ft 7ins but Jan Zelezny of Czechoslovakia, with a first throw of 294ft 2ins, set a new Olympic record.

**Ireland had never won an Olympic gold medal for boxing but in Barcelona two Irishmen reached finals.  Belfast bantamweight Wayne McCullough lost his final to 21-year-old Cuban Joel Casamayor.**

Services welterweight Michael Carruth of Dublin, a triplet in a family of ten children, won gold and was immediately promoted from corporal to sergeant.  Local Dublin pubs dropped the price of Guinness to 4p a pint in his honour.

# OLYMPIC GAMES
# USA 1996

Atlanta was the controversial venue for the 1996 Games and was certainly not a happy choice for British competitors.

**Great Britain's share of the medals was bitterly disappointing, with just one gold, eight silver and six bronze.**

The transport facilities in Atlanta, taking competitors between the various venues, was strongly criticised for its unreliability.

**American television was accused of being 'uninterested' unless their own competitors were taking part.**

A bomb exploded in a park in the city to add to the chaos.

**A total of 842 medals were awarded, with America taking the lion's share of 101.**

USA's superiority was illustrated by their winning of 44 gold medal events. They also won 32 silver and 25 bronze.

**Russia with 26 gold medals was the nearest rival to USA. Their total medal haul was 63.**

China jumped to fourth place in the golds table with 16, only four fewer than third-placed Germany.

**Britain's Roger Black deservedly won a silver in the 400 metres, which was won inevitably by Michael Johnson (USA).**

Carl Lewis, no longer a sprinter in his prime, proved his everlasting athleticism by winning the long jump for the fourth time.

**Jonathan Edwards, Britain's triple jumper, met with disappointment following his successes in the World and European Games.**

His hopes faded with a series of foul jumps and he had to be content with second place.

**However, after receiving his silver medal, he then warmly congratulated his American conqueror Kenny Harrison with genuine Olympic grace.**

Linford Christie, defending his title in the 100 metres, was sensationally disqualified from the final after being blamed for two false starts.

**Christie disputed his dismissal with the starter and officials before accepting the decision, then ran a circuit of the track waving to booing spectators.**

# OLYMPIC GAMES
## USA 1996

He claimed later that the boos were not for him but were aimed at the judges' decision.

**Despite the uproar Canadian Donovan Bailey kept his cool and won in a world record time of 9.94secs.**

Controversy again reigned in the women's 100 metres final.

**A photo-finish was thought to show Jamaica's Merlene Ottey to be the winner in a close finish.**

The judges' verdict favoured Gail Devers of USA with a time of 10.94secs.

**The surprising winner of the Marathon was an 'unknown' black runner from South Africa, Josia Thugwane.  His time: 2 hrs 12mins 36secs.**

The swimming results brought a few raised eyebrows among Americans with Hungary being accused of 'inventing' venues and qualifying times to increase the size of its swimming team.

**The Hungarians still managed three swimming golds – two in the men's events and one for women.**

The major talking point concerned Michelle Smith, the Irish woman who dominated the swimming events with three gold medals in the 200 and 400 metres individual medley and the 400 metres freestyle.

**Swimming consolation for the Americans came in the relays, with their lads and lasses winning all six of them.**

Britain's solitary gold was won by oarsmen Steven Redgrave and Matthew Pinsett in the coxless pairs.

**It was Redgrave's fourth Olympic gold in this event.**

He immediately announced his retirement, saying: "If anyone sees me near a boat again they can shoot me".

**Within months he was back with the 2000 Games on his mind!**

# QUIZ SCORE SHEETS

# QUIZ SCORE SHEETS

# QUIZ SCORE SHEETS

# QUIZ SCORE SHEETS